# ROUTLEDGE LIBRARY EDITIONS: LITERARY THEORY

Volume 19

# THE TAMING OF THE TEXT

# THE TAMING OF THE TEXT

Explorations in Language, Literature and Culture

Edited by
WILLIE VAN PEER

Routledge
Taylor & Francis Group

LONDON AND NEW YORK

First published in 1988 by Routledge

This edition first published in 2017
by Routledge
2 Park Square, Milton Park, Abingdon, Oxon OX14 4RN

and by Routledge
711 Third Avenue, New York, NY 10017

*Routledge is an imprint of the Taylor & Francis Group, an informa business*

*British Library Cataloguing in Publication Data*
A catalogue record for this book is available from the British Library

ISBN: 978-1-138-69377-7 (Set)
ISBN: 978-1-315-52921-9 (Set) (ebk)
ISBN: 978-1-138-68337-2 (Volume 19) (hbk)
ISBN: 978-1-138-68338-9 (Volume 19) (pbk)
ISBN: 978-1-315-54452-6 (Volume 19) (ebk)

# THE TAMING OF THE TEXT

EXPLORATIONS IN LANGUAGE, LITERATURE AND CULTURE

EDITOR
*Willie Van Peer*

ROUTLEDGE
London and New York

First published in 1988 by Routledge
11 New Fetter Lane, London EC4P 4EE

Published in the USA by Routledge
in association with Routledge, Chapman and Hall Inc.
29 West 35th Street, New York, NY 10001

Set in Optima and Palatino
by Witwell Ltd, Southport
and printed in Great Britain
by T. J. Press (Padstow) Ltd
Padstow, Cornwall.

British Library Cataloguing in Publication Data
The Taming of the text : explorations in
   language, literature and culture.
   1. Literature. Linguistic aspects
   I. Peer, Willie van
   801'.4

Library of Congress Cataloging in Publication Data
The Taming of the text.

   Bibliography: p.
   Includes Index.
   1. Discourse analysis, Literary.   I. Peer, Willie
van.
P302.5.T36   1988       808'.0141       88-6748

ISBN 0-415-01309-7

# CONTENTS

# PREFACE

As it is a pleasant duty to acknowledge help, I would first of all like to thank the contributors for their generous and patient cooperation throughout the whole project of preparing the present volume. A sabbatical term from my own university and a fellowship from Clare Hall, Cambridge, have greatly facilitated the final stages of its preparation. Thanks are also due to Andrew Kennedy, for his invaluable comments on the introductory chapter.

Since the 'taming of texts' is essentially an experiment in social learning, I wish to express the hope that readers may *enjoy* the results of this joint enterprise. This is perhaps singularly important, as

> No profit grows where is no pleasure ta'en.
> (*The Taming of the Shrew*, I. i. 39)

W. Van Peer

# ACKNOWLEDGMENTS

For permission to reproduce material from works in copyright the author and publisher make grateful acknowledgment as follows:

'Conventions of representation: where discourse and ideology meet', by Mary Louise Pratt is reprinted by permission of Georgetown University Press: *Contemporary Perceptions of Language: Interdisciplinary Dimensions*, Heidi Byrnes, Editor; passages from 'In zwei Sprachen leben', edited by I. Ackermann, 1983, are reprinted by permission of Deutscher Taschenbuch Verlag, Munich; material from *Gastarbeiterkinder aus der Türkei*, edited by H. Birkenfeld, 1982, is reprinted by permission of C. H. Beck Verlag, Munich; 'Send No Money' is reprinted by permission of Faber and Faber Ltd from *The Whitsun Weddings* by Philip Larkin; material from 'High Windows' is reprinted by permission of Faber and Faber Ltd, and Farrar Straus and Giroux Inc., New York, from *High Windows* by Philip Larkin copyright © 1974; quotation from 'Poetry of Departures' is reprinted from *The Less Deceived*, by permission of The Marvell Press, England; material from 'Questions from a Worker who reads' is reprinted by permission of Methuen London from *Poems 1913–1956* by Bertolt Brecht, trans. Michael Hamburger; 'Dichtung und Wahrheit', 'Them & Uz' and 'The Ballad of Babelabour' are from Tony Harrison's *Selected Poems*, 1984, Penguin Books Ltd, and are reproduced by kind permission of the author; material from *The Dialogic Imagination: Four Essays*, by M. M. Bakhtin, edited by Michael

Holquist, translated by Caryl Emerson and Michael Holquist, Copyright © 1981 by the University of Texas Press; 'Poetic discourse: a sample exercise', by John Sinclair is reprinted by permission of Murdoch University, Murdoch, Australia; 'Krishna', first published in *Westerley*, is reproduced by kind permission of the author Edwin Thumboo; 'Stopping By Woods On A Snowy Evening', from *The Poetry of Robert Frost*, edited by Edward Connery Latham, is reproduced by permission of Jonathan Cape Ltd and of Holt Rinehart & Winston Inc., New York, on behalf of the Estate of Robert Frost; 'The reader's need for conventions: When is a mushroom not a mushroom?', by Irene Fairley, is reprinted by permission of *Style* magazine in which it was previously published; 'Mushrooms', Copyright © 1961 by Sylvia Plath, is reprinted from *The Colossus and Other Poems*, by Sylvia Plath, by permission of Alfred A. Knopf Inc., and © 1967, Ted Hughes, published by Faber and Faber Ltd, by permission of Olwyn Hughes; 'Whatever Happened' is reprinted from *The Less Deceived*, by Philip Larkin, by permission of The Marvell Press, England.

Every reasonable effort has been made by the author and publisher to contact the copyright holders mentioned above. Where this has not been successful, credit has been given, and it is hoped that any omissions can be corrected in a future edition.

# INTRODUCTION

Reading (literary) texts does not normally pose serious problems in daily life. Normally we know quite well how to deal with them. Most people, in watching a play, reading a novel, or listening to a poem, will hardly wonder at the nature of the event they are involved in. Unproblematic as such everyday forms of handling literary texts may be, they are not so from a theoretical point of view. For one thing, they do not guarantee a full understanding of the works under consideration. In fact the form and function of these texts make them into complex cultural phenomena, the understanding of which requires a long process of experience, producing knowledge about their structure and meaning as well as intuitive concepts and general expectations as to what such texts are and mean. As a result of this (literary) texts have become an object of study from the earliest times onwards. In our time their academic study is undertaken from a number of different vantage points. Generally, these may be divided into either linguistic or literary approaches. Although there has always been a keen sense of linguistic detail in literary studies, from Aristotle onwards, and although linguists have often displayed an attentive responsiveness to literature, the marriage between the two disciplines has not been a very stable one. While structuralism reigned, it seemed to flourish, especially in the works of eminent scholars such as Roman Jakobson, Jan Mukařovský or Claude Lévi-Strauss. The type of linguistic analysis undertaken by them generally appealed to both linguists and literary scholars.

This began to change, however, during the 1960s, when other more formal types of linguistic theory became fashionable. Subsequently, the relationship between linguistics and literature grew much colder, and it has not really been a very close one since. Sometimes happy moments are recorded, especially in the field of stylistics, which genuinely tries to combine both approaches to the study of literary texts. By and large, however, the situation may be characterized as one of mutual mistrust, sometimes of contempt. For instance, literary scholars frown upon linguists and their methods because of their formalism and their stubborn rationality. They feel that somehow the real 'literary' nature of the works studied is not done justice to, and they therefore prefer to exclude linguistics (and linguists) from their field of study altogether. Since literature also deals with emotions and with the irrational side of human existence, they feel that little help is to be expected from an all-too-narrowly-defined rational approach. The linguists, on the other hand, find fault with the looseness of terms and methods adopted by literary scholars, their superficial linguistic knowledge and their lack of system, as a result of which they also question the validity of conclusions arrived at in literary scholarship. They also feel that literary language *is* amenable to linguistic analysis.

Now it may be observed that whenever both disciplines keep within the narrow confines of their own field, no perceptible tension arises. As soon as they interact, however, all sorts of frictions may emerge. One may approach this dispute in a variety of ways. The one which has been tried hardest is that of *persuasion* of the other side. While interesting and sophisticated arguments have resulted from such efforts, the arguments have not been very successful at the job they were meant to do, i.e. to bring about a reconciliation, preferably even a cooperation, of linguistics and literary studies. Alternatively, while this state of affairs continues, one may also raise the question of *why* there is a quarrel in the first place. The results of such an enquiry may reveal underlying forces which bring about the processes of misunderstanding and antagonism. Perhaps one of the best ways to do this is to understand the quarrel in terms of different *definitions* of the field of study itself, involving different concepts of validity and different standards on how to proceed in its development. At the same time, the tenacity with which the conflict continues reveals a fundamental indeterminacy in *each* of the disciplines concerned.

First of all, as a symptom of such indeterminacy, one may notice that the old pretences of linguists have worn off. When generative grammar emerged as a potential tool, linguists hardly doubted the merit of their contribution to the field of literary scholarship. For a moment it seemed as if a good number of intricate old problems were going to be solved in an efficient and elegant manner. I think it is fair to say that few linguists still hold such grand pretences. The generative approach soon found itself confronted with qualitatively new problems not foreseen in the earlier stages, which called for continuous repair work, involving so much energy that no attention could be spared to literary matters. Perhaps more important still, a number of other approaches were developed, such as psycholinguistics, socio-linguistics, pragmatics, text linguistics, discourse analysis and ethnography of communication, all of which promised a much closer link with the 'social' aspects of language than generative grammar had ever been able to offer. Trying to cope with all these changes was hard enough in itself, let alone their integration with literary studies. Thus the proliferation of methods and theories within linguistics and the failure of its most powerful model to fulfil its earlier promises has led to internal uncertainty, the perception of which has stimulated literary scholars to go their own way instead of waiting for the linguists to sort out their problems.

Literary studies, however, face their own difficulties too. Their internal cohesion, for instance, is not really very strong either: one finds semiotic studies next to hermeneutics, accompanied by psychoanalysis and historical approaches of various kinds; deconstruction next to structuralism, Marxism next to feminism, and so on. The consensus over what constitutes the right theoretical conceptualization and the most appropriate methods must be deemed very low indeed. Instead literary studies swim with the tide (which is largely driven by extra-literary forces), changing its aims and methodology according to the fashion of the day. And if no great illusions have been shattered in this field it is only because no hopes of integrating these various strands have been raised and no grand promises of solving the ever-present problems have been made. Again the fragmentation of the field into various methods (being partially incompatible) and the inability to come up with generalizable insights and a coherent and systematic framework has produced a relative degree of uncertainty, and this in turn has strongly eroded the old splendour of literary studies. On close investigation, a number of the so-called 'literary' approaches are even imports from neighbouring fields, such as history, psychology, sociology, philosophy, even linguistics, raising the problem of what constitutes literary studies in its own right.

Thus the past decades have witnessed a growing number of changes in linguistics and literary studies. These have made things less uniform, less coherent and less clear from an overall theoretical point of view, thus introducing uncertainty into their practice. Uncertainty is hard to live with, however, also for scholars: some kind of self-assertion is needed. In a situation in which opposing claims to the definition of study exist, certainty may be gained by discrediting the definition of your opponents. Thus the uncertainty of both linguistic and literary approaches, resulting from internal forces in their respective fields, is projected outwards on to the other competing field, in order to gain back some kind of confidence through a mechanism of dissension. (If we are not that good at our job, we are certainly better than our neighbours.) It is this self-deception that has haunted both linguistic and literary approaches for some decades and which, seen from a distance, is perhaps only a defence mechanism hiding the epistemological unsteadiness that lurks beneath the surface.

It may be just as well, therefore, to analyse somewhat further the fundamental deficiencies revealed by both disciplines. One limitation lies in their *object* of analysis. To start with linguistics, the study of language has largely been confined to issues at the level of word and sentence, with little or no attention given to *supra-sentential* structure and meaning. But literature does not consist of words and sentences, but of texts. Although texts are made up of words and sentences, they also have their own specific structural qualities and their own potential for meaning which cannot be accounted for solely in terms of units at a lower level of organization. As a consequence, most linguistic approaches miss a fundamental ingredient of literature, its *textuality*. This danger is obviously avoided in literary approaches since these deal quite explicitly with texts and their meaning, albeit sometimes at the expense of other linguistic aspects. However, there is reason for concern here too. Literary approaches by and large take the textuality of their study-object for granted, without much reflection on what exactly texts *are*. And although linguists may hardly have faced the nature of textuality, it is unmistakably the case that texts are largely *linguistic* structures. Thus the escape from linguistics is impossible, while linguistics cannot yet offer the necessary concepts and methods for study. A paradox.

Furthermore, in the same way that linguistics has been confined to the boundary of the sentence, literary studies have largely been limited to the study of individual texts, thereby impeding any progress in our knowledge of *supra-textual* phenomena. Admittedly, some efforts in this direction have been made, for instance in the study and comparison of authors, or of schools and traditions. Generally, however, this has not led to a coherent theoretical insight into the functional differentiation of literary types. What has been gained is a large body of data on individual texts and on some of their interrelationships. What is lacking is a good understanding of how these operate generally. This demands both a unified and a diversified theoretical approach at once: *unified* in the sense that all texts must somehow function in the same or similar way (that is why they are all 'texts'); *diversified* because different texts do different things to people – a satire is not a eulogy, and an epigram is not an epic.

The limitations to sentence and to text, typical of the linguistic and the literary approach, indeed calls for such a unified yet diversified perspective. It calls firstly for a *theoretical* perspective: how to understand textuality and its functioning in society; what institutional constraints operate over it and what forms are generally available for realizing certain of these functions; what general questions are to be framed and how to answer them. As may be appreciated, theory in this stage will be but the *beginning* of raising questions; the formulation of answers is not to be expected overnight. Yet, for all the difficulties involved, the issue of theory can no longer be avoided.

Secondly, the situation calls for a *typological* differentiation. The problem of how literature is distinct from other text types, for instance, is still largely unsolved. The fact that some non-literary texts display 'literary' characteristics poses complex problems. Yet this does not logically entail that the very concept of literature has thereby become empty. Most people can quite easily tell the difference between a romance and a recipe. Comparisons of literary and non-literary texts make us consider the similarities and (apparent) differences, as well as their distinctive features with greater scrutiny and caution. But literature is not a monolithic concept in itself either. Instead it is composed of different genres (narrative, drama, poetry), each of which itself consists of various sub-genres (folk-tale, epic, novel, short story...) and further subdivisions which at all levels may combine into amalgamated forms. What is needed, then, is a range of different text types, literary and non-literary, to be analysed from a theoretical perspective. Needless to say, such an approach will have to face the basic issue of textuality and its social functioning, and will have to try to overcome the traditional limits imposed by the linguist's concentration on sign and sentence, and the literary student's virtually exclusive attention to individual texts or authors.

The limitation to sentence and text, and its consequences for the theoretical and typological study of literature, as outlined in the previous paragraphs, is only one shortcoming of these approaches. A second one lies in their often unidimensional view of the communication process itself. A simple face-to-face interaction, in which a speaker communicates a message to an addressee is taken as a *model* for written forms of (literary) discourse, without much reflection on how adequate such a model might be. Looked at in detail, however, all sorts of problems arise from this analogy. First of all, it presupposes some direct relationship between thought and language, so that the words uttered by the speaker are only the verbal wrapping of the ideas that make up the 'message'. It is obvious that the application of such a concept runs into serious problems when applied to complex cultural phenomena, such as literary texts. Secondly, the assumption that there is a direct relationship between speaker (author) and addressee (reader) is simply to be refuted on empirical grounds. It is typical for written texts to be communicated across time and space, regardless of the intention of writer and reader. Thirdly, the model assumes a uniformity and substantiality of its components that may be highly idealized and therefore shows little correspondence to the situation in reality. Is the author really only one 'voice'? Certainly in the novel various voices are heard, not only of characters but also of narrators. Who are we then to associate with the author's voice? Often this may be unproblematic, but that does not dispose of the tricky cases. Irony and satire illustrate the point, as does Shakespeare's theatre; the debates surrounding the interpretations of his plays demonstrate that the application of a simple communicative model, even when modified or enriched (for instance in contemporary semiotics), must be largely misconceived. That the readership of literary texts is similarly multifarious is so evident that it need not be demonstrated here. But the same is true of the 'message', i.e. the text itself. Its uniformity is certainly a chimera in narrative and drama. There a multitude of styles, registers and dialects may be heard. In poetry, as well, the situation may not be so simple: conflicting norms and conventions may put the poet under the obligation to meet contradictory demands, resulting in choices that still bear the traces of the stylistic conflicts the author was involved in.

In this sense the title of the present volume already presents an ambiguity: the text may be either the subject or the object of the 'taming'. As various contributions show, texts may also function as instruments of conservative or repressive ideologies. What these studies do, then, is open up such conventions and expose these practices, while simultaneously demonstrating the texts' potential for creating *new* modes of experience. Studying texts from such a perspective reveals all sorts of taming. It is with the description and analysis of these processes, their origins and their outcomes, at different levels, and relating to different domains, that the present collection of studies is concerned.

In sum, then, the *model* of textual communication that is often taken for granted must be viewed with suspicion, if not replaced by more realistic ones. Again, such a model may need subtle adaptations for various text types. In order to refine our knowledge in this respect, then, a concentration on *methods* to study the texts can hardly be avoided. The traditional linguistic model, be it of a Jakobsonian or Chomskyan type, will not do. Nor will more recent cognitive or semiotic models as long as they take the basic 'sender-message-receiver' picture as their underlying model. But the literary approach, concentrating on the historical author and his personality, or on interpreting the text as a 'message' the author wished us to share in, similarly falls into the trap of oversimplifying the real nature of literary discourse. The methods for avoiding such traps are perhaps few at the moment, and one might do well to be reasonably eclectic on this side. Traditional linguistic and literary methods should be combined (and not felt to be at odds) with more recent developments in text-linguistics, pragmatics, discourse analysis and reception theory. Admittedly, these are but young twigs growing on an old tree; yet their contribution may be of high importance for the vitality of the tree as a whole.

A third area in which linguistics and literary studies show deficiencies is that of *interpretation*. A text may be relatively well understood (in spite of serious problems remaining here too) at the level of words and sentences. But how the meanings of words and sentences 'add up' when they occur in a text as a whole is less well known. The problem here is perhaps not so much a theoretical one conception, as one bearing on the relative width of freedom that is allowed (or not). Applying a gross simplification to the issue one may distinguish between the two basic ingredients which are at play in constructing an interpretation. As a first, and evident, element there is the text as a linguistic manifestation. It is a material, yet also symbolic, sign, made up according to rules and principles of the language which it uses. Hence its *form* must in some way or other be indicative of its sense. However, as has become clear enough over the past decades, linguistic form is not the sole determining factor in interpretation. Equally important is the *context* in which such form occurs. Whether the utterance 'Nice place here' is to be interpreted as an expression of admiration or as an ironical statement expressing criticism is mainly to be determined on the basis of the concrete situation in which the utterance occurs. That does not mean that the linguistic form of such an utterance is irrelevant to its interpretation, only that it is not the exhaustive determinant of meaning. In other words, linguistic form presents itself in the act of interpretation as a necessary, not as a sufficient, condition. Alternatively, since no utterance can be interpreted 'neutrally', contextual information likewise constrains the number of potential interpretations and hence must be seen as a necessary (and similarly not sufficient) condition. Thus two necessary conditions, neither of which is sufficient by itself, operate over the act of interpretation.

It is with respect to this *double* condition (i.e. of form and of context) that linguistic and literary analysis show (opposite) deficiencies. Linguistic analysis has an in-built tendency to *over*estimate the importance of linguistic form, and to *under*estimate the influence of context (except in some areas, such as pragmatics and discourse analysis). Literary studies, on the other hand, tend to the opposite, i.e. to *under*estimate the importance of form and to *over*estimate the contribution of contextual information (except in some areas, such as stylistics and poetics). It is not difficult to see how an overemphasis on either of the necessary ingredients may easily lead to one-sided or ill-founded interpretations. Not surprisingly, the quarrel between linguistics and literary studies has often led to reproaches that the other side does not pay enough attention to either form or context. Thus the criticism of text-immanent interpretations must be said to be a valid one. Conversely, a critique of interpretation unconstrained by considerations of linguistic form is equally justified.

As an example of this, attention may be drawn to a frequently addressed issue in literary studies, i.e. that of *character*. Both in narrative and dramatic genres (to a much lesser extent in poetry) the issue of character is an important one. However, the very concept of character is itself susceptible to historical change. More important still is that the category of character is, for its very formation, dependent on linguistic forms. Character, it can hardly be denied, is what readers infer from words, sentences, paragraphs and textual composition depicting, describing or suggesting actions, thoughts, utterances or feelings of a protagonist. Thus the linguistic organization of the text will predetermine to a certain degree the kind of 'picture' one may compose of a protagonist. Therefore the particular *forms* by which this is achieved need to be studied in detail. It appears that at present there is hardly a theoretical framework providing for this necessity. There is not even a general theory of something as 'straightforward' as speech presentation. The same goes without saying, but presumably with still greater force, for the presentation of thoughts and feelings. In short, then, although character seems to be an important literary category of investigation, its investigation, as dependent on specific linguistic forms (albeit transformed into conventional literary devices), demands close scrutiny of the way in which such forms contribute to an interpretation.

On the other hand, numerous examples may be cited in which contextual information is crucial to the process of interpreting the text. The use of classical mythology, for instance, needs background information in order to allow for an interpretation to be constructed at all. Similarly, since conventions of interpersonal relations change over time, older historical texts will need information on these changes in order to be correctly interpreted. Changes in the meanings of words over time present another case in point. The same goes for literary forms themselves and for aesthetic expectations, as well as for sociopolitical ideas w hich are often at the heart of literary discourse. Similarly, biblical and intertextual references withstand an interpretation on the basis of form alone. And imagery is often only interpretable with reference to general cultural knowledge.

In short then, the relative weight of linguistic form, *vis-à-vis* non-linguistic elements in the interpretative act needs to be studied with care. Although it is easy to see how any overemphasis on one at the expense of the other must be regarded as theoretically ill-founded and methodologically unsound, the problem remains how to determine the relative weight of both aspects in practice. As a first step in this direction, individual cases in which the interplay between both forces is well-documented can be subjected to a detailed analysis.

What has been pointed out so far leads to some conclusions which may be summarized as follows.

1  Whatever the present state of linguistics as a discipline, the linguistic nature of (literary) texts is inescapable. Neglecting this nature gives rise to an unwarranted lack of descriptive adequacy.
2  Whatever the present state of literary studies as a discipline, the literary nature of some texts is an inescapable object of study and presents an enrichment to linguistics. Neglect of this research area produces an unnecessary poverty of linguistic knowledge and theory.
3  The multiplicity of theoretical and methodological perspectives in both linguistics and literary studies does not allow a strict separation of their fields when it comes to the study of literature; instead their interaction may be beneficial in trying to remedy their mutual deficiencies.
4  The deficiencies are largely of a theoretical nature; hence an effort should be made to come to terms with such theoretical issues as textuality in its unity and typological diversity.
5  The prevailing models of literary communication and the methods used to study them are open to critical debate and refinement.
6  The intricate relationship between linguistic form and interpretation is in need of clarification and should be further studied from a theoretical and methodological perspective.

These conclusions are taken up and further developed in the contributions to this volume. Accordingly, it is subdivided into three sections, corresponding to the major problem areas that have been outlined above.

The volume opens with the theoretical study of texts and their typological diversity, under the title 'Type and theory'. Different types of text (landscape descriptions, ballads, newspaper headlines and columns, and drama) are investigated; the kind of linguistic material in each of these is similarly varied; description, dialogue, speech, propaganda and personal names. The contributions, moreover, are based on different theoretical perspectives; sociolinguistics, pragmatics, stylistics, discourse analysis and literary studies. Together they form a picture of literary and non-literary texts (and their relationship) that is dynamic rather than static.

The second part, 'Models and methods', deals with the general issue of literary communication. The mechanistic model of communication is replaced by a multidimensional model, in which the text as a product is seen as the outcome of a complex linguistic decision-making process which is embedded within the socio-political and historical context in which it originates. Thus a precise reading of a text is only possible on the basis of a view of 'writing' which does take these processes, and their inherent conflicts, into account.

The third part of the volume takes up the complicated issue of 'Form and interpretation'. Textual forms confront the reader (and the scholar) with problems of ambiguity and multivalency of meaning, the understanding of which poses considerable problems, not only in linguistic terms but also in general psychological and sociological terms. Meaning in texts is not 'given' in any direct sense, but results in a complex way from the cultural environment in which its quality is reconstructed; this meaning, however, is not completely unstable, since the text itself, in its formal aspects, must appeal to general knowledge, minimally stable over time, in order still to function in the culture at large.

The parts themselves do not, of course, provide water-tight compartments. Any consideration of the nature of literary communication, for instance, will inevitably face questions of theory and method alike. Similarly, the analysis of models will involve aspects of form and of type, as well as (again) theory and method. Instead, the parts simply provide useful ways of looking at the problems under consideration from different perspectives, while by themselves representing some internal coherence. It is hoped, however, that the reader may establish cross-links between the various papers and sections while reading. The principal aim of this book is to improve the understanding of textual communication in a cultural perspective, from a variety of angles which complement each other. It is taken as a presupposition that, in view of the complexity and multi-dimensionality of the object of study, this complementarity has become a necessity.

# PART I

## Type and theory

---

Evermore cross'd and cross'd,
                    nothing but cross'd

(*The Taming of the Shrew*, IV. v. 10)

# 1

# Conventions of representation

Where discourse and ideology meet

*Mary Louise Pratt*

*The production and consumption of text and discourse serves particular purposes. Apart from aesthetic ones, which are studied in poetics and stylistics, texts also represent social values and traditions and relate to ideological positions. These originate in extra-textual structures of reality and society. Literary as well as non-literary texts encode these values and their inherent contradictions.*

    *By looking at what at first sight presents itself as a 'neutral' event, i.e. landscape descriptions (in texts), Mary Louise Pratt reveals how such descriptions function socially, especially as manifestations of domination. The landscapes described in both literary and non-literary texts since the seventeenth century emanate from a conventionalized discourse in which the landscape is viewed first and foremost as a commodity. Hence its description needs not so much a neutral rendering of facts, but rather an 'enrichment' in terms of value. A careful textual analysis reveals what linguistic means authors employ in arriving at such a codification of value. In particular the aestheticization of the landscape (in comparing it to a painting), the creation of semantic density (by over-modification and nominalization) and the rendering of a relationship of dominance between the seer and the seen (through the use of metaphors) are given special prominence. Such conventions of representation as revealed by the analysis are not static, though. Their very existence creates the potential for their being contradicted and eroded. As a comparison with other texts reveals, the conventionalized discourse of domination in landscape description is prone to both variation and undermining. In this respect, textual analysis may contribute to a better understanding of the process of historical evolution of text types and the power by which they function in society. Such understanding is a prerequisite for a general theory of literature.*

Consider the following passage, the opening paragraphs of Defoe's *Robinson Crusoe*, first published in 1719.

> I was born in the year 1632, in the city of York, of a good family, tho' not of that country, my father being a foreigner of Bremen, who settled first at Hull. He got a good estate by merchandise, and leaving off his trade lived afterward at York, from whence he married my mother, whose relations were named Robinson, a very good name in that country, and from whom I was called Robinson Kreutznaer; but by the usual corruption of words in England, we are now called, nay, we call ourselves and write our name, Crusoe, and so my companions always called me.
>
> I had two elder brothers, one of them was lieutenant collonel to an English regiment of foot in Flanders, formerly commanded by the famous Coll. Lockhart, and was killed at the battle near Dunkirk against the Spaniards. What became of my second brother I never knew any more than my father or mother did know what was become of me.
>
> Being the third son of the family, and not bred to any trade, my head began to be filled very early with rambling thoughts. My father, who was very ancient, had given me a competent share of learning, as far as house-education and a country free-school generally goes, and designed me for the law; but I would be satisfied with nothing but going to sea, and my inclination to this led me so strongly against the will, nay, the commands of my father, and against all the entreaties and perswasions of my mother and other friends, that there seemed to be something fatal in that propension of nature tending directly to the life of misery that was to befal me.[1]

This text deploys a set of conventions of representation readily recognizable to any reader of eighteenth-century novels or the picaresque tradition. There is the opening statement of pedigree, and even some outright arbitrariness in the acquisition of one's name. There is the early emergence of wander-lust in the redundant middle child, the abandonment of family and community against all entreaties, and the life of supposed misery and misfortune which results. Many of these same conventions are used in the following passage as well. This text is the opening of Richard Lemon Lander's book *Records of Captain Clapperton's Last Expedition to Africa*, published in 1830.

> Many allusions to my earlier history occurring in the following pages, it may not, perhaps, be deemed impertinent on my part, if I should attempt to give a short and hasty sketch of my life, devoted as it has been to perpetual wanderings and chequered by a thousand misfortunes.
>
> My family is as ancient, I dare say, as that of any upon the face of the earth, although, notwithstanding the profoundest research, I have been unable to trace its descent, with genealogical accuracy and precision, to a more remote era than the period of my grandfather's nonage; the history of all my ancestors previous to him being either mixed with fable, or involved in doubt and uncertainty...
>
> I am the fourth of six children, and was born at Truro, in Cornwall, in 1804, on the very day on which Colonel Lemon was elected Member of Parliament for the Borough. Owing to this striking coincidence, singular as it may seem, my father, who was fond of sounding appelations, at the simple suggestion of the doctor who attended the family, added Lemon to my baptismal name of Richard: an example of the trivial means by which people are oftentimes accommodated with an extra name. As nothing remarkable occurred for the first five or six years after I came into the world, I shall pass them over in silence, simply observing that when yet in infancy, whilst I was in the act of gazing one morning at something attached to the ceiling of my father's stable, a piece of iron, having a sharpened edge, fell and entered my forehead; which accident was of so serious a nature that I was ill for several weeks, and narrowly escaped with life.
>
> My rambling inclinations began to display themselves in early youth. I was never easy a great while together in one place, and used to be delighted to play truant and stroll from town to town, from village to village whenever I could steal an opportunity.[2]

Here again, we find the comic lack of pedigree, the arbitrariness of name, the reference to a life of misery resulting from the passion-driven individualism of the wanderer. Lander here invokes another commonplace of eighteenth-century narrative, that of the child-hood accident, made most memorable for us by Tristram Shandy's excruciating encounter with a window sash. The childhood accident is a comic device whose function is, among other things, to overexplain, or to overdetermine, the eccentricities and the immoderacies of the protagonist's character in adulthood.

The point I want to examine in these texts is the very obvious one that they use many of the same conventions of representation – one might even say they are instances of the same discourse – though one is from a fictional novel and the other from a nonfictional travel account. Now we might want to account for these similarities by saying that Richard Lander is 'novelizing' his travel account, that he is borrowing or imitating, or redeploying the novelistic discourse exemplified by the *Robinson Crusoe* passage. At the same time, however, we would probably also want to say that Defoe is borrowing or imitating or redeploying in his novel the discourse of nonfictional autobiography. We are left with what looks like a chicken and egg problem. Are the conventions of representation which these texts share primarily novelistic or primarily autobiographical? Are they primarily associated with fiction or with nonfiction? The answer I'd like to consider is that they are not primarily one or the other. They exist as conventions of representation relatively independent of both genre distinctions and the fiction–nonfiction distinction. They can – and indeed should – be studied across those categories.

The next four passages quoted here exemplify another case of the kind of convention of representation I am talking about, and again the examples come from novels as well as nonfictional travel accounts. These four passages are all versions of what I have called the 'woe-is-me' scene. Here, after a peak experience, whether of triumph or defeat, the speaker-protagonist pauses in solitude to assess his or her situation. There follows an enumeration of misfortunes and woes, then a plunge into the pits of despair, from which the protagonist is rescued by some new hopeful thought, often religious in character. This self-generated consolation mobilizes the protagonist again physically, and the narrative action proceeds. Again, I think most novel readers will find this device a familiar one. The four examples here include:

1  Sir James Bruce the night after discovering what he believed
   to be the source of the Nile (1770);
2  Robinson Crusoe after completing his first house (1719);
3  Mungo Park in Africa having been robbed of all his
   possessions by Moorish bandits (1802); and
4  Samuel Richardson's Pamela having failed in a nocturnal
   attempt to escape from a country house where she is being
   held (1740).

There is no need to work through these examples individually here
– the conventions are clear. Some of the common surface linguistic
features of the 'woe-is-me' scene are indicated in these quotations
by my italics, notably the introductory time phrase that suspends
the narrative sequence, the enumeration of troubles and woes, and
the *but*-clause that introduces the ray of hope.

1  *The night of the 4th*, that very night of my arrival, melancholy
   reflections upon my present state, the doubtfulness of my
   return in safety, were I permitted to make the attempt, and
   the fears that even this would be refused, according to the
   rule observed in Abyssinia with all travellers who have once
   entered the kingdom; the consciousness of the pain that I
   was then occasioning to many worthy individuals, expecting
   daily that information concerning my situation which it was
   not in my power to give them; some other thoughts,
   perhaps, still nearer to the heart than those, crowded upon
   my mind, and forbad all approach of sleep. . .
      I went to the door of my tent; everything was still; the
   Nile at whose head I stood, was not capable either to
   promote or to interrupt my slumbers, *but* the coolness and
   serenity of the night braced my nerves, and chased away
   those phantoms that, while in bed, had oppressed and
   tormented me.
      It was true, that numerous dangers, hardships, and
   sorrows, had beset me through this half of my excursion; *but*
   it was still as true that *another Guide*, more powerful than my
   own courage, health or understanding, if any of these can be
   called man's own, had uniformly protected me in all that
   tedious half; I found my confidence not abated, that still the
   same Guide was able to conduct me to my now wished for
   home.[3]
2  *Having now fixed my habitation*, I found it absolutely necessary to
   provide a place to make a fire in, and fewel to burn; and what

I did for that, as also how I enlarged my cave, and what
conveniences I made, I shall give a full account of it in its
place. But I must first give some little account of my self, and
of my thoughts about living, which it may well be supposed
were not a few.

I had a dismal prospect of my condition, for as I was not
cast away upon that island without being driven, as is said,
by a violent storm, quite out of the course of our intended
voyage, and a great way, viz. some hundreds of leagues out
of the ordinary course of the trade of mankind, I had great
reason to consider it as a determination of Heaven, that in
this desolate place and in this desolate manner I should end
my life; the tears would run plentifully down my face when I
made these reflections, and sometimes I would expostulate
with my self, why Providence should thus compleately ruine
its creatures, and render them so absolutely miserable,
without help abandoned, so entirely depressed, that it could
hardly be rational to be thankful for such a life.

*But* something always returned swift upon me to check
these thoughts, and to reprove me.[4]

3   *After they were gone* I sat for some time looking around me with
amazement and terror. Whichever way I turned, nothing
appeared but danger and difficulty. I saw myself in the midst
of a vast wilderness, in the depths of the rainy season, naked
and alone; surrounded by savage animals, and men still more
savage. I was five hundred miles from the nearest European
settlement. All these circumstances crowded at once on my
recollection, and I confess that my spirits began to fail me...
*The influence of religion, however,* aided and supported me. I
reflected that no human prudence or foresight could possibly
have averted my present sufferings. I was indeed a stranger
in a strange land, *yet* I was still under the protecting eye of
that Providence who has condescended to call himself the
stranger's friend.[5]

4   ... *and so when I came to the pond side,* I sat myself down on the
sloping bank, and began to ponder my wretched condition;
and thus I reasoned with myself.

Pause here a little, Pamela, on what thou art about, before
thou takest the dreadful leap; and consider whether there be
no way yet left, no hope, if not to escape from this wicked
house, yet from the mischiefs threatened thee in it.

I then considered; and after I had cast about in my mind

everything that could make me hope, and saw no probability;
a wicked woman, devoid of all compassion! A horrid helper,
just arrived in this dreadful Colbrans! An angry and
resenting master, who now hated me, and threatened the
most afflicting evils!...

I was once rising, so indulgent was I to this sad way of
thinking, to throw myself in: *but* again, my bruises made me
slow; and I thought, What art thou about to do, wretched
Pamela? How knowest thou, though the prospect be all dark
to thy short-sighted eye, *what God may do for thee*, even when
all human means fail?[6]

Again, the claim I would make is that we should resist the impulse
to view the 'woe-is-me' scence as primarily associated with the
novel or with fiction, and see it rather as unmarked with respect to
fictionality or genre.

Within poetics, formal narrative analysis has for a long time been
making generalizations at the level I am talking about. That is, it
has long been agreed that 'narrative' and 'story' as formal
constructs are not specific to literature nor to fiction, but are highly
generalized discourse structures that operate even outside verbal
representation. This same highly generalized perspective can be
extended beyond rudimentary narrative-sequencing to other
aspects of discourse structure and content. Such an undertaking,
however, requires going beyond the tendency in at least some
sectors of linguistics, to treat representative or assertive discourse
primarily in terms of the presence or absence of truth claims. This
has been a limitation, for instance, in speech act theory, where the
analysis of representative speech acts scarcely gets beyond simply
defining nonfictional representatives by the presence of a truth
claim, and defining fictional negatively by the suspension of such
claims. Clearly, there is a great deal more to say about the ways
people represent the world to themselves linguistically. Poetics has
as a rule had more to say about fictional utterances, but its
treatment of nonfictional linguistic representations has been
impoverished. There seems to be a tendency in poetics to assume
that conventions found to be operating in literature must by
definition be literary conventions, that is, conventions primarily
associated with literature and constitutive of 'literariness'. This
judgment usually means in turn that such conventions are taken to
be primarily associated with fictionality, and are studied primarily
from an aesthetic viewpoint. Their historical, social and ideological
dimensions are not explored, though these dimensions are as

germane to the study of discourse as aesthetics. Indeed, an understanding of the social, historical and ideological dimensions of discourse can contribute a great deal to the interests of aesthetics. There is much to be gained, then, from an analysis of linguistic representation which decentres the question of truth versus falsehood, fiction versus nonfiction, literary genre versus nonliterary genre, and focuses instead on generalized strategies of representation. At Stanford my colleague Rina Benmayor and I have been examining such strategies in novels and nonfictional travel accounts, such as those I have been citing here. These two genres provide extremely fruitful terrain in which to examine shared conventions of representation. From at least the sixteenth century on, the two have completely interpenetrated and mutually determined each other. This is a fact that gets obscured by a literary theory centred on fiction and committed to a radical distinction between fictional and nonfictional representation.

Using some further examples from these two genres, I propose in the rest of this paper to exemplify a kind of stylistic analysis that:

1  works across the fiction-nonfiction line; and
2  deals simultaneously with aesthetic, social and ideological dimensions of discourse.

The case I have chosen to focus on is landscape description in the context of colonial and neocolonial relationships. What I want to illustrate is how landscape descriptions, in some cases, embody aesthetically and ideologically a kind of 'discourse of empire', while in others the representation is designed to undermine or replace such a discourse. Landscape description has, of course, long been recognized as an exceedingly fruitful case for studying the interaction of aesthetics and ideology. This interaction is particularly conspicuous in the context I am dealing with here.

I begin with a convention that I like to call the 'monarch-of-all-I-survey' scene, in which a speaker-protagonist stands up on a high place of some kind and describes the panorama below, producing a simultaneously verbal and visual 'picture in words'. This device is a commonplace of European romanticism in particular, and is found widely in nineteenth-century poetry and narrative alike. In travel accounts, the monarch-of-all-I-survey scene is typically used by Victorian explorers to render moments of discovery of geographically important phenomena such as lakes, river sources, islands, and so on. Here, for example, is Sir Richard Burton's rendering in 1860 of his discovery of Lake Tanganyika in Central Africa (emphasis mine).

Nothing, in sooth, could be more picturesque than this first view of the Tanganyika Lake, as it lay in the lap of the mountains, basking in the gorgeous tropical sunshine. Below and beyond a short foreground of rugged and precipitous hill-fold, down which the foot-path zigzags painfully, a narrow strip of *emerald green*, never sere and marvellously fertile, shelves towards a ribbon of glistening yellow sand, here bordered by sedgy rushes, there cleanly and clearly cut by the breaking wavelets. Further in front stretch the waters, an expanse of the lightest and softest blue, in breadth varying from thirty to thirty-five miles, and sprinkled by the crisp east-wind with tiny crescents of *snowy foam*. The background in front is a high and broken wall of *steel-coloured* mountain, here flecked and capped with *pearly mist*, there standing pencilled against the azure air; its yawning chasms, marked by a deeper *plum-colour*, fall towards dwarf hills of mound-like proportions, which apparently dip their feet in the wave. To the south, and opposite the long, low point, behind which the Malagarazi River discharges the red loam suspended in its violent stream, lie the bluff headlands and capes of Uguhha, and, as the eye dilates, it falls upon a cluster of outlying islets, speckling a sea-horizon. Villages, cultivated lands, the frequent canoes of the fishermen on the waters, and on a nearer approach the murmurs of the waves breaking upon the shore, give a something of variety, of movement, of life to the landscape, which, like all the fairest prospects in these regions, wants but a little of the neatness and finish of Art, – mosques and kiosks, palaces and villas, gardens and orchards – contrasting with the profuse lavishness and magnificence of nature, and diversifying the unbroken coup d'oeil of excessive vegetation to rival if not to excel, the most admired scenery of the classic regions ... Truly it was a revel for soul and sight! Forgetting toils, dangers, and the doubtfulness of return, I felt willing to endure double what I had endured; and all the party seemed to join with me in joy.[7]

A stylistic analysis of this passage requires, among other things, identifying the convention of representation being invoked, specifying which aspects of the discourse are determined by it and which are not, and establishing what sort of meaning-making task the convention is being called upon to accomplish in the particular context in which it has been invoked. In Burton's case, and in nineteenth-century discovery narrative in general, the monarch-of-all-I-survey scene is invoked to render momentously meaningful the act of discovery, itself practically a nonevent. The 'discovery' of Lake Tanganyika, for example, involved going to the region and asking the natives if they knew of any big lakes in the vicinity, then paying them to take the explorers there, whereupon the explorers 'discovered' what the natives had already told them. We are all familiar with the contradictions that the term 'discovery' holds in this context. In Burton's situation, the contradictions are particularly acute, since he has been so ill he has had to be carried to the site, again by native assistants, while his companion John Speke, though able to walk, has been blinded by fever and is therefore unable properly to discover anything. The discovery itself consists of what in our culture counts as a purely passive experience, that of seeing something. At this point in history there is, for example, no taking of possession for England or for God, no sacking of cities, no bringing home of spoils. At most, an English name might be given. In short, the explorer's achievement can exist almost exclusively through language – a name on a map or a tree trunk, a report to the Royal Geographic Society, a lecture, a travel book.

In the Burton passage one can identify at least three conventional means by which Burton creates qualitative and quantitative value for his achievement. First, the landscape is aestheticized. The sight is seen as a painting and the description is ordered in terms of background, foreground, symmetries between foam-flecked water and mist-flecked hills, and so forth. Notice that the aesthetic pleasure of the sight is here declared to constitute singlehandedly the value and significance of the journey – he would do it twice over for the same thrill. Second, density of meaning in the passage is sought. The landscape is represented as extremely rich in material and semantic substance. This density is achieved especially through the huge number of adjectival modifiers. Scarcely a noun in the text is unmodified. Notice too that many of the modifiers are derived from nouns (such as *sedgy, capped, mound-like*), and thus add density by introducing whole new material referents into the discourse. Of particular interest in this respect are nominal colour expressions: *emerald green, snowy foam, steel-coloured mountains, pearly mist, plum-colour*. Unlike plain colour adjectives, these terms introduce new material referents into the landscape, referents which all, from steel to snow, tie the landscape explicitly to the speaker's (and the reader's) home culture, infiltrating it with 'a little bit of England'.

Thirdly, a relation of dominance is predicted in the passage between the seer and the seen. This relation is expressed most clearly by the metaphor of the painting. If the scene is a painting, then Burton is both the viewer-critic there to appreciate it, and the verbal painter who produces it for us. The scene, in other words, is produced by and for Burton. From the painting analogy it also follows that what Burton sees is all there is, and that the landscape was intended to be seen from precisely where Burton has emerged upon it. Thus the whole scene is deictically ordered with reference to his vantage point. The viewer-painting relation also implies that Burton has the power if not to own, then at least to judge this scene. And it is quite revealing that his judgment is that what is lacking here is more Art, where Art is defined, surprisingly, as the presence of mosques and kiosks, palaces, gardens, and so forth. Art, that is, is equated with a Mediterranean concept of civilization, and the conclusion is that the villages and cultivations already present in the scene are not enough aesthetically. This depiction of the 'civilizing mission' as an aesthetic project is an old and familiar strategy in Western imperialism. It is a way of interpreting the Other as not only available for, but actually in need of intervention from, the outside. (We will be looking shortly at some contemporary versions of this strategy.)

The point I want to stress here is that in this example, and in any other, of the monarch-of-all-I-survey scene, the conventional aestheticization of the landscape simultaneously articulates a particular social meaning, an ideology. In Burton's discourse, on the one hand the aesthetic impact of the landscape is made to constitute the social value of his discovery, and on the other hand a judgment of aesthetic deficiency is used to articulate a relation of dominance of the (civilized) West over (barbarous) Africa. This same set of connections operates in almost reverse fashion in the following description, produced by Burton's partner and rival, John Speke. Accompanying Burton on the expedition, Speke became convinced he knew where the coveted source of the Nile was located. Upon their return to England, Speke immediately mounted a second expedition to return to Africa to prove himself right and the sceptical Burton wrong. With his new partner, Grant, Speke arrived at the lake he was looking for – the Victoria N'yanza – but was prevented by a number of circumstances from trekking all the way around it to prove absolutely his hypothesis, which ultimately did turn out to be correct. Many readers will be familiar with the deadly polemic which ensued back in England between Burton and Speke, and which resulted in Speke's apparent suicide. What is of

interest here is the way in which Speke's retrospective description
of his discovery translates his disappointment as an explorer into
aesthetic disappointment at the landscape (emphasis mine).

> We were well rewarded; for the 'stones' as the Waganda call the
> falls, was by far the *most interesting sight* I had seen in Africa.
> Everybody ran to see them at once, though the march had been
> long and fatiguing, and *even* my sketchbook was called into play.
> *Though beautiful*, the scene was *not exactly what I had expected*; for the
> broad surface of the lake was shut out from view by a spur of
> hill, and the falls, about 12 feet deep, and 400 to 500 feet broad,
> were broken by rocks. *Still* it was a sight that attracted one to it
> for hours – the roar of the waters, the thousands of passenger-
> fish ... hippopotami and crocodiles lying sleepily on the water,
> the ferry at work above the falls, and cattle driven down to
> drink at the margin of the lake – made all in all, with the *pretty
> nature* of the country – small hills, grassy-tipped, with trees in
> the folds, and gardens on the lower slopes – as *interesting* a
> picture as one could wish to see.
>   The expedition had now performed its functions. I saw that
> old father Nile without any doubt rises in the Victoria N'yanza,
> and as I foretold, that lake is the great source of the holy river
> which cradled the first expounder of our religious belief. I
> mourned, however, when I thought of how much I had lost by
> the delays in the journey which had *deprived me of the pleasure of
> going to look* at the north-east corner.[8]

Here again we see the language of aesthetics being used to encode –
and mystify – the significance of the event. Speke's disappointment
is expressed as the loss of a personal aesthetic pleasure rather than
the loss of a social triumph or a piece of geographical knowledge.
Likewise, the sight/site he does get to see is evaluated in purely
aesthetic terms, and found acceptable but wanting. It is surely not a
coincidence that the particular aesthetic defects the frustrated
Speke finds are first a barrier to the visibility of the lake, and,
second, an interruption of the forward movement of the falls.

In twentieth-century travel accounts, the monarch-of-all-I-
survey scene is repeated all the time, but now from the balconies of
hotels, where again we find our cultural mediators perched,
assigning significance and value to what they see. Here are two
typical examples, the first by the Italian novelist Alberto Moravia,
writing about a trip to Africa in 1972, and the second by the
American Paul Theroux, also a novelist, writing about a train

journey through Latin America.

> From the balcony of my room I had a panoramic view over
> Accra, capital of Ghana. Beneath a sky of hazy blue, filled with
> mists and ragged yellow and grey clouds, the town looked like a
> huge pan of thick, dark cabbage soup in which numerous pieces
> of white pasta were on the boil. The cabbages were the tropical
> trees with rich, trailing, heavy foliage of dark green speckled
> with black shadows; the pieces of pasta the brand-new
> buildings of reinforced concrete, numbers of which were now
> rising all over the town.[9]

> Guatemala City, an extremely horizontal place, is like a city on
> its back. Its ugliness, which is a threatened look (the low
> morose houses have earthquake cracks in their facades; the
> buildings wince at you with bright lines) is ugliest on those
> streets where, just past the last toppling house, a blue volcano's
> cone bulges. I could see the volcanoes from the window of my
> hotel room. I was on the third floor, which was also the top
> floor. They were tall volcanoes and looked capable of spewing
> lava. Their beauty was undeniable; but it was the beauty of
> witches. The rumbles from their fires had heaved this city
> down.[10]

The contrast between these grotesque and joyless cityscapes and
the gorgeous, sparkling panorama depicted by Richard Burton
could hardly be greater. And yet, upon inspection, it becomes clear
that the three strategies operating in Burton's discourse –
aestheticization, density of meaning and dominance of seer over
seen – are also at work here. The difference is that they are being
invoked at a different historical moment to make a very different
sort of meaning. A different, historically later, ideology is being
expressed. Density of meaning was created in Burton's discourse
through the plentiful use of adjectival modifiers and a general
proliferation of concrete, material referents introduced either
literally or as metaphors. The Theroux and Moravia texts clearly
share these properties. In Burton, the speaker positioned himself in
a relation of dominance over the landscape and the Other,
particularly through the extended metaphor of the painting. Like
Burton, both Moravia and Theroux situate themselves in the
position of judge over what they see. Despite the fact that they are
on unfamiliar terrain, like Burton they both claim complete
authority for their vision: what they see is all there is. No sense of

limitation on their knowledge or authority is suggested. And perhaps less explicitly than in Burton, relations of dominance and possession are articulated through metaphors.

For Theroux, Guatemala is a city on its back, in a position of submission or defeat before him, and with a threatened look. Moravia sees Accra as a plate of soup, that is, a dish Ghana has prepared – pasta and all – for him to eat. Aestheticization we also have in these texts, except that where Burton found beauty, symmetry, order and the sublime, Theroux and Moravia find the precise aesthetic opposites: ugliness (ragged clouds, morose houses), incongruity (the beauty of witches, bits of pasta in the cabbage soup), disorder and triviality. It is striking that in both descriptions, the landscape is represented as violating the conventions on colours so central to landscape description: Moravia sees yellow clouds, Theroux a blue volcano. And as with Burton's description, the aesthetic vision expresses and at the same time mystifies a social and political vision. On reading beauty, order and grandeur in his landscape, Burton makes it a worthy prize for the explorer and his country. His is the heady optimism of incipient empire. Moravia and Theroux, on the other hand, are voicing the era of neocolonial dependency, when historical reality, and most conspicuously the reality of Third World cities, has long since belied the myth of the civilizing mission. For them, the meaning to be produced, the task to be accomplished, is a negative one of rejection, dissociation and dismissal. It is a quite different but historically related strategy for authenticating the self through the mediation of the Other.

As with Burton's concept of 'discovery', this strategy too has its contradictions. It is impossible for Westerners to dissociate themselves fully from the manifestations of Western intervention and exploitation, whether in the form of concrete skyscrapers or crumbling slums. Perhaps this contradiction explains why both writers express a fear of violence on the part of the landscapes they are describing. Theroux is threatened by the volcanoes, which could bring down the city, including the hotel in which he is perched. Moravia sees the Western-style buildings, including the one he is standing in, as on the boil in a pot of otherwise African soup, like the cartoon missionaries in the cannibals' pot. The absence of such paranoia in Burton and Speke is striking by contrast.

The Theroux and Moravia texts exemplify a discourse of negation and devaluation which has become in the late twentieth century the predominant strategy constituting the West's consciousness of the Other. No longer a cornucopia of resources inviting the artful hand of development, the Other is represented negatively as a conglomeration either of incongruities and asymmetries or of absences and scarcities. One thing that stays constant, however, is the relation of dominance embodied in the monarch-of-all-I-survey convention.

Conventions can, of course, be undermined and changed. Consider, for instance, what is done with the monarch-of-all-I-survey convention in the following passage from an account of another trip to Ghana, by Afro-American novelist Richard Wright.

> I wanted to push on and look more, but the sun was too much. I spent the afternoon fretting; I was impatient to see more of this Africa. My bungalow was clean, quiet, mosquito-proof, but it had not been for that I'd come to Africa. Already my mind was casting about for other accommodations. I stood on my balcony and saw clouds of black buzzards circling slowly in the hazy blue sky. In the distance I caught a glimpse of the cloudy, grayish Atlantic.[11]

On the one hand, Wright produces what is a very reduced instance of the conventional scene. He gives us a 'glimpse' of a landscape which does have the negative connotations found in Moravia and Theroux. At the same time, however, Wright explicitly documents his discomfort with the vantage point of the balcony, from which, he feels, one can see almost nothing. He acknowledges, in other words, the limitations on his perception and on his position. To see, he says, one must be walking in the streets, not immobilized above the scene. At one and the same time, then, we find Wright reproducing the dominant discourse and undermining its authority.

The modern ideology of negation I have been discussing takes a somewhat different form in descriptions of rural landscape, and the contrasts are instructive. In the following two descriptions of rural landscape, again from Theroux and Moravia, what is found is not ugliness (as in the cityscapes), but scarcity of any kind of meaning, a kind of aesthetic and semantic underdevelopment which both writers connect with the prehistoric. First Theroux, who by now is in Patagonia:

> The landscape had a prehistoric look, the sort that forms a painted backdrop for a dinosaur skeleton in a museum: simple

terrible hills and gullies; thorn bushes and rocks; and everything smoothed by the wind and looking as if a great flood had denuded it, washed it of all its particular features. Still the wind worked on it, kept the trees from growing, blew the soil west, uncovered more rock, and even uprooted those ugly bushes.

The people in the train did not look out the window, except at the stations and only then to buy grapes or bread. One of the beauties of train travel is that you know where you are by looking out the window. No signboards are necessary. A hill, a river, a meadow – the landmarks tell you how far you have come. But this place had no landmarks, or rather it was all landmarks, one indistinguishable from the other – thousands of hills and dry riverbeds, and a billion bushes, all the same. I dozed and woke: hours passed; the scenery at the window did not alter. And the stations were interchangeable – a shed, a concrete platform, staring men, boys with baskets, the dogs, the battered pickup trucks.

I looked for guanacos. I had nothing better to do. There were no guanacos.[12]

Then Moravia, generalizing on the African landscape.

Thus a journey to Africa, when it is not a mere full excursion from one to another of those big hotels that the inhabitants of the Western world have strewn across the Black Continent, is a veritable dive into prehistory.

But what *is* this prehistory that so fascinates Europeans? First of all, it should be said, it is the actual conformation of the African landscape. The chief characteristic of this landscape is not diversity, as in Europe, but rather its terrifying monotony. The face of Africa bears a greater resemblance to that of an infant, with few barely indicated features, than to that of a man, upon which life has imprinted innumerable significant lines; in other words, it bears a greater resemblance to the face of the earth in prehistoric times, when there were no seasons and humanity had not yet made its appearance, than to the face of the earth as it is today, with the innumerable changes brought about both by time and man. This monotony, furthermore, displays two truly prehistoric aspects: reiteration, that is, repetition of a single theme or motif to the point of obsession, to the point of terror; and shapelessness, that is, the complete lack of limitation, of the finite, of pattern and form, in fact.[13]

Again, the contrast with Burton's description could hardly be more pronounced. But this time the contrast is not between positive and negative aesthetic judgments, but between density and scarcity of meaning. One need hardly comment on the ideological significance of representing parts of the world as having no history and therefore in need of being given one by us. What is of interest here is the association of the prehistoric with absence of differentiation. One of the most conspicuous hallmarks of high-technology, industrialized societies, especially capitalist ones, is precisely the endless creation of differentiations, specializations, subdivisions. In a rather different way, then, these two texts say, as Burton did, that what is needed is more of 'us'. And again, in both texts we find that no limitations on the speakers' interpretive authority are suggested, despite the fact that they are in a completely alien environment. What they see is all there is. Here the authority of the home culture is incorporated in the form of generalized assertions, such as Theroux's statement that 'one of the beauties of train travel is that you know where you are by looking out the window'. Here a statement that obviously could have meaning only with reference to a specific cultural and material context is asserted as a context-free norm from which the Other is then seen to deviate. Semantically, the natives of Patagonia are failing to travel correctly on their own trains, and Patagonia itself is failing to provide the right kind of landscape for the train to go through.

Again, the point to be stressed is that it is not necessary to claim this kind of interpretive authority. The following text by Albert Camus illustrates one writer's effort to work against both the rural commonplace (landscape as undifferentiated and ahistoric) and the urban commonplace (cityscape as ugly and trivial), and against the overall authoritative stance of this discourse. The excerpt is from Camus' story 'The Adulterous Woman', about a French-Algerian woman making a trip into the interior on a sales trip with her husband. The trip turns into an existential crisis for her. Here we have her at an oasis in the desert, standing at the top of the southernmost French fort, looking out over the Sahara. It is an obvious invocation of the monarch-of-all-I-survey convention. Notice in this passage the way the stereotypical prehistoric, lifeless landscape is successively postulated, then rejected or qualified. Notice, too, the severe limitations postulated on the completeness and reliability of the outsider's perceptions – what she sees is very far indeed from being all that is there.

From east to west, in fact, her gaze swept slowly, without

encountering a single obstacle, along a perfect curve. Beneath her, the blue-and-white terraces of the Arab town overlapped one another, splattered with the dark red spots of peppers drying in the sun. Not a soul could be seen, but from the inner courts, together with the aroma of roasting coffee, there rose laughing voices or incomprehensible stamping of feet. Farther off, the palm grove, divided into uneven squares by clay walls, rustled its upper foliage in a wind that could not be felt up on the terrace. Still farther off, and all the way to the horizon extended the ocher-and-gray realm of stones, in which no life was visible. At some distance from the oasis, however, near the wadi that bordered the palm grove on the west could be seen broad black tents. All around them a flock of motionless dromedaries, tiny at that distance, formed against the gray ground the black signs of a strange handwriting, the meaning of which had to be deciphered. Above the desert, the silence was as vast as the space.[14]

No sooner is the perfect undifferentiated curve of the horizon postulated than the eye shifts to the multicoloured irregular shapes of the terraces and the uneven squares of the palm groves. Everywhere there are signs of things going on that the observer can perceive only partially. The undifferentiated landscape is invoked a second time ('the ocher-and-gray realm of stones'), and again immediately complicated by the presence of the tents and dromedaries. And again, the protagonist's authority is limited – she cannot decipher the handwriting which is nevertheless in need of decipherment. In short, what is produced here is a drastic qualification of the monarch-of-all-I-survey scene. What is not produced here, or anywhere else in Camus' work, is a new or more acceptable vantage point. In the final passage I propose to discuss, again from Richard Wright, we do see an attempt to establish a different, non-dominating position from which he, like Camus, produces a discourse that rejects the roles of interpretive authority and judge in favour of representing the very experience of one's own ignorance, disorientation and limitation. It is no accident that Wright here portrays himself at night, when you know that what you perceive is not all that is there.

Night comes suddenly, like wet black velvet. The air, charged with too much oxygen, drugs the blood. The scream of some wild birds cuts through the dark and stops abruptly, leaving a suspenseful void. A foul smell rises from somewhere. A distant drumming is heard and dies, as though ashamed of itself. An inexplicable gust of wind flutters the window curtain, making it billow and then fall limp. A bird chirps sleepily in the listless night. Fragments of African voices sound in the darkness and fade. The flame of my candle burns straight up, burns minutes on end without a single flicker or tremor. The sound of a lorry whose motor is whining as it strains to climb the steep hill brings back to me the world I know.[15]

Wright is representing an experience of incomprehension and self-dissolution that does not give rise to terror or madness, but rather to a serene receptivity and intense sensuality. Notice how the fragmentation and abruptness of impressions are counteracted by a strong, continuous rhythm. As impressions flow in and out, the subject's consciousness – here symbolically represented as *my candle* (the *my* is significant, since there is no *I* previously in the passage) burns peacefully in the heart of the unknown, without a tremor of fear – a steadiness that seems to surprise Wright himself. In this context the arriving lorry does not have its usual meaning of the nick-of-time rescuer. Wright feels no need to move at all – he stays exactly where he is. The lorry does not bring him back to the known world, it brings that world back to him.

The foregoing discussion will doubtless have communicated a set of ideological commitments of my own – a criticism of discourses that implicitly or explicitly dehumanize, trivialize and devalue other realities in the name of Western superiority, and an appreciation of discourses that do not do these things and instead acknowledge the limitations on the West's ability to make sense of other peoples and places (especially those it seeks to hold in subjugation). Some may wish to argue that such commitments have no place in academic investigations, or in linguistics, but I think they are wrong. To begin with, that argument is obviously as ideologically committed as my own. More generally, any discourse has ideological dimensions – values – just as it has aesthetic and sociological ones. Poetics and sociolinguistics are equipping us with a stylistics that can deal with these latter two dimensions. Ultimately, we will need a stylistics that can deal with the first one too.

# NOTES

1  Daniel Defoe, *The Life and Adventures of Robinson Crusoe*, Harmondsworth, Penguin, 1965, p. 27.

2  Richard Lander, *Records of Captain Clapperton's Last Expedition to Africa*, London, Henry Colburn & Richard Bentley, 1830, pp. 1–3.

3  James Bruce, *Travels to Discover the Source of the Nile*, edited by C. F. Beckingham, Edinburgh University Press, 1964, p. 163.

4  Daniel Defoe, *op. cit.*, p. 80.

5  Mungo Park, *Travels in the Interior of Africa*, Edinburgh, Adam & Charles Black, 1878, p. 225.

6  Samuel Richardson, *Pamela*, London, J. M. Dent & Sons, 1914, Vol. I, pp. 150–1.

7  Reprinted from *The Lake Regions of Central Africa*, by Richard Burton. Copyright 1961, by permission of the publisher, Horizon Press, New York.

8  John Speke, *Journal of the Discovery of the Source of the Nile*, London, Blackwood & Sons, 1863, pp. 466–7.

9  Alberto Moravia, *Which Tribe Do You Belong To?*, trans. Angus Davidson, New York, Farrar, Straus & Giroux, 1972, p. 1.

10  Paul Theroux, *The Old Patagonian Express*, Boston, Houghton Mifflin, 1978, p. 123.

11  Richard Wright, *Black Power*, New York, Harper, 1954, p. 154

12  Paul Theroux, *op. cit.*, p. 397.

13  Alberto Moravia, *op. cit.*, p. 8.

14  Albert Camus, 'The Adulterous Woman', in *Exile and the Kingdom*, trans. Justin O'Brien, New York, Vintage Books, 1957, pp. 22–3.

15  Richard Wright, *op. cit.*, p. 263.

# 2

# A pragmatic approach to ballad dialogue

*Dick Leith*

*The discourse conventions, as described and analysed by Mary Louise Pratt in the previous chapter, are not the exclusive realm of landscape descriptions, nor of written literature. They are also at the heart of oral culture. However, specific problems of description and analysis are posed by orally transmitted (and performed) genres of literature. These problems are further multiplied when such oral texts, by virtue of their being recorded in writing and because of their literary or social interest, enter into the canon of established literary works. One of the problems caused by such a transfer from the spoken to the written mode is that the original discourse must be rendered indirectly, i.e. again through the use of language. Hence its representation must needs remain incomplete, as a result of which the interpretation of the speech acts concerned becomes more complicated.*

*In the following chapter Dick Leith tackles some of the problems involved in such an analysis. By looking closely at the structure and functioning of dialogue in traditional ballads, it becomes clear that its occurrence is motivated by more fundamental forces than a mere evocation of conversational tone or a matter-of-fact presentation of the protagonists' words. In particular, dialogue acts as an engine which drives the plot of the ballad forwards. Furthermore, it appears that the dramatis personae in the ballads are, in a sense, shaped by the words they utter rather than shaping their utterances themselves. The dialogue also often acquires a formulaic quality, contributing to a more impersonal style in the ballads. These characteristics add to the particular aesthetic appeal that ballads still have for modern readers. As Leith's analysis shows, it is possible – with the help of theoretical insights derived from pragmatics and discourse analysis – to reveal those elements that generate such an appeal.*

In common with other so-called traditional genres such as folk-tales and folk-songs, the ballad tends to have been neglected by practitioners of the modern discipline of stylistics. One reason for this is that stylisticians, influenced by the Formalist preoccupation with the notion of poetic language, have accordingly concentrated on those kinds of texts – usually modern poems, short stories or extracts from prose fiction – which as *printed* literature are felt to be fixed in form and of sufficient brevity and complexity for detailed linguistic analysis. Another reason is that 'traditional' material – which, by contrast, is often characterized by its extreme fluidity of form – has been widely felt to be the preserve of folklorists who have their own special interests and approaches. Thus, while folkloristic analysis has not entirely lacked a linguistic perspective it has rarely, unlike stylistics, been pursued within the context of modern linguistic theory.[1]

In this chapter I shall be looking at one aspect of ballad language, namely dialogue, from the perspective of that branch of modern linguistics known as pragmatics (for a definition see below). For illustration I have chosen a sample of one of the most famous ballad repertoires, that of Anna Brown (the famous 'Mrs Brown of Falkland' in Fife, Scotland, who died in 1810), whose ballads, so highly esteemed by the famous nineteenth-century ballad scholar F. J. Child, have recently been intensively and illuminatingly analysed by David Buchan.[2] Like Buchan, I have tried to analyse particular ballad versions as meaningful structures, even as (loosely speaking) performances in their own right. Ballads – like many other orally-performed genres – make extensive use of dialogue, but no-one to my knowledge has yet made a systematic study of this feature.[3] There are a number of scattered comments in the literature, but these appear to be based on a kind of idealized ballad with properties abstracted from an unspecified corpus rather than on a particular repertoire. Gerould (1974), for example, maintains that the texture of ballad dialogue is determined by ballad action:

'nothing matters except the action,' and often what has just been *said* is followed by the deed itself, a pattern which affords the audience 'a satisfaction in the kind of emphasis obtained by first proposing something in words and immediately getting it accomplished in deed'.[4] Ballad dialogue is felt to be direct, decisive and clear; tentative or speculative speech belongs not to the ballad of 'tradition' but of 'literacy'.[5] For Bronson (1959) the parallelism of melody and stanza 'leads to simple confrontations of agreement and disagreement, to the obvious balance of repetitional statement in formulaic reply'. Moreover, while everyone knows that question-and-answer sequences abound in ballads, the character of these according to Bronson is rigidly delimited. Questions not only tend to be asked in threes, and answered 'in a straightforward manner', but there is also no room in ballads for complex verbal games: 'People ask questions in ballads in order to learn what they do not know, or in the case of the riddling ballads – because they believe the persons questioned do not know and cannot answer' (see Bronson, 1969a). While it is one purpose of this article to test the validity of these remarks, I want to suggest that pragmatics can take us a great deal further by helping to highlight crucial relationships between dialogue, character and plot.[6] These in turn raise further issues of genre and aesthetics, and the nature of the Brown repertoire itself, which will be discussed in the conclusion to this article.

## 2.1 The ballad sample: general considerations

From Anna Brown's corpus of thirty-three ballad-stories I have chosen eleven. Their titles and Child numbers are: 'Gil Brenton' (5A), 'Young Bicham' (53A), 'Fair Annie' (62E), 'Child Waters' (63B), 'Lady Maisry' (65A), 'The Lass of Roch Royal' (76D), 'The Gay Goshawk' (96A), 'Johnie Scot' (99A), 'Willie O Douglas Dale' (101A), 'Bonny Baby Livingstone' (222A) and 'The Kitchie Boy' (252C). (For ease of reference they will be referred to, in addition to their Child numbering, as GB, YB, FA, CW, LM, LRR, GG, JS, WODD, BBL and KB respectively.) Morphologically all ballads in the sample are similar, in that an amatory relationship between the leading male protagonist (H) and the female (S) is threatened by a third force (T)[7] which may be realized in different ways. At the outset a love-contract between *S* and *H* (verbal or physical, resulting in pregnancy) is either presented (as, for example, in KB (252C), WODD (101A) and YB (53A)), or revealed (as in CW (63B) and LM (65A)). There follows a change in spatial setting; either *H* undertakes a journey with *S* (as in GB (5A), CW (63B) and WODD (101A); in FA (62E) *H* journeys with *T*) or the lovers are separated, so that either *H* or *S* must travel to be reunited with the other (as in YB (53A), LM (65A), BBL (222A), GG (96A), LRR (76D), KB (252C), JS (99A)). *S* is subsequently tested: this may take the form of seizure, either imprisonment or abduction by a member of her family (LM (65A), JS (99a)), or an outsider (BBL (222A)); or the test may consist of a series of trials and humiliations perpetrated on *S* by *H* himself, with varying degrees of deliberation (GB (5A), FA (62E), CW (63B), YB (53A)), or by someone acting on *H*'s behalf (LRR (76D)). All the ballads end with the lovers united or re-united, either in marriage (explicitly mentioned, or implied), as in YB (53A), WODD (101A), CW (63B), BBL (222A), GG (96A), JS (99A), KB (252C), GB (5A) and FA (62E), or in mutual death (again, this can be implied rather than expressed), as in LRR (76D) and LM (65A). This rather abstract summary of the structure of the ballads is fleshed out in section 2.3 below.[8]

In the transcriptions (following the presentation of Buchan (1972b)) of Anna Brown's ballads, dialogue stanzas are usually clearly marked with quotation marks. Only occasionally, however, are they 'tagged' with the names of the particular speaking voice, as in CW (63B):7: '"Ohon, alas!" said the lady,/"This water's oer deep for me."' Examples of reported speech, such as 'Said he was bound to ride' (CW (63B):2), are relatively rare. Usually a whole dialogue stanza is allotted to one speaker at a time but sometimes a dialogue stanza is split between two speakers (as in JS (99A):33) and there are a few examples of a single line of dialogue (often without quotation marks) occurring in what I shall call narrated stanzas (as in CW (63B):5). Grammatically, dialogue stanzas contain declarative, interrogative and imperative sentences, while narrated stanzas generally have only the first; both modal and negative constructions are common in dialogue, rare elsewhere.[9]

Although no ballad in the sample is purely dialogue, it is clear that in every one dialogue plays a central role.[10] In every ballad at least half the stanzas are dialogue, and in some cases (GB (5A), GG (96A)) the proportion is about three-quarters. If we filter out the narrated stanzas of each ballad and view them as story-versions in their own right, they appear rather similar to what Labov (1972) has called unevaluated narratives; we sense that the heart, even the *raison d'etre*, of the story is missing. As Buchan (1972a, p. 83) says, at the core of the ballad is the emotional interaction of a limited number of characters; and it is this interaction that is usually expressed through dialogue. But dialogue can also tell us the story itself, as in the attempted rescue sequence in 'Lady Maisry', so that it is arguable that in many cases the narrated stanzas function only to fill out certain kinds of narrative detail, providing 'orientating' information about the initial situation, introducing characters and bridging sharp shifts in time and space. Orientations are often highly economical, while formulaic, 'floating' stanzas are often used to mark shifts between scenes.

## 2.2 The pragmatics of ballad dialogue

Pragmatics - broadly speaking, the study of the communicative aspects of language in use - offers a useful set of perspectives for the study of dialogue representation. One such perspective, based on the sociological tradition of conversation analysis, focuses on the *sequencing* of utterances and on the ways in which different speakers take turns in conversation. According to both Goffman and Coulthard, a fundamental unit of conversation is the *adjacency pair*, such as questions and answers, offers and acceptances (or rejections), greetings followed by greeting, etc.[11] Such pairs can be further analysed in terms of *preferred* versus *dispreferred* sequences; if I ask you a question, I expect to get an answer, and you expect that I am wanting one. This is the preferred sequence. If, on the other hand, you ignore my question or say something that I consider is no answer, there is a dispreferred or unexpected sequence. To refuse either a request or an offer/invitation, to disagree with an assessment and to admit rather than deny the attribution of blame is to use the dispreferred second part of an adjacency pair.

On the face of it, adjacency-pair sequences of this kind seem singularly characteristic of ballad dialogue in the sample. It is so often that we find a stanza allotted to a question followed by one that answers it, or a command followed by its implementation. This helps to give ballad dialogue a flavour of ritual, an impression reinforced by the tendency to allocate to each speaker one whole stanza, so that we hear the second unit of the adjacency pair sung to the same tune as the first. This also has the effect of dragging out the pace of the exchange to a slow-motion speed, contributing to the 'lingering' aspect of the general 'leaping and lingering' narrative technique commonly ascribed to the ballad.

The question of whether we find preferred or dispreferred sequences in ballad dialogue cannot be posed, however, without reference to the issue of narrative structure. Dialogue is so bound up with the action, as Gerould (1974) suggests, that the response to any utterance has clear consequences for the narrative. Thus, if the warning in stanza 1 of 'Child Waters' – '"I warn ye all, ye gay ladies,/That wear scarlet an brown,/That ye dinna leave your father's house,/To follow young men frae town"' – were to be heeded, there would be no narrative; in ballads, like fairy tales, interdictions are there to be violated (see Propp 1968, pp. 26–7 and *passim*). Interdiction and violation actually constitute *paired* functions; cf. the notion of adjacency-pair discussed above. Thus the utterance in stanza 2 explicitly and immediately rejects the warning. Similarly, in 'Fair Annie' the lord requests that his bridal preparations be made and his new bride welcomed; in stanza 2 his addressee agrees to meet the request. It is only then, in the next two stanzas of alternating dialogue, that we learn the identity of the answerer; it is the lord's mistress, no longer a maiden, who must none the less 'gang like maiden fair' and attend the new bride. Thus, by complying with his request, she abets the sequence of events that lead to her humiliation. Other sequences play a less crucial role in the narrative. In 'Young Bicham', Shusy Pye's question in stanza 12 – '"Is this Young Bicham's gates?" says she,/"Or is that noble prince within?"' – is answered in the affirmative, but a negative answer (or even, perhaps, no answer at all) would still have yielded a narrative, similar, say, to 'The Lass of Roch Royal'. In general dialogue is so closely tied to action that where an utterance is not matched with an immediate *verbal* response it is often echoed by a narrated stanza: Anny of Roch Royal's 'O wha will shoe my fu fair foot?' in stanza 1 is paired with 'Her father shoed her fu fair foot' in stanza 3. Such sequences are termed *causative repetition* by Pettitt.[12] Finally, it sometimes occurs that an utterance is answered by neither speech nor action; in 'Lady Maisry' we assume, correctly as it turns out, that the action implied in stanza 17 by the words of Lady Maisry's brother:

> 'O whare is a' my merry young men,
> Whom I gi meat and fee,
> To pu the thistle and the thorn,
> To burn this vile whore wi?'

is immediately acted upon. When such utterances occur in the very last stanza of a ballad, the impulse to interpret their force similarly is even stronger; we assume that Lord William really will revenge Maisry and then commit suicide, and that despite what protests the mother of Young Bicham's new bride may make, her daughter *will* be abandoned on her wedding day in favour of the faithful and ill-used Shusy Pye.

Occasionally a sequence may pose interesting problems of interpretation and evaluation. In the same ballad-version, Shusy's request at stanza 9 that Bicham return and marry her after seven years is not answered. Can we assume from this that he could be half-hearted about the love-contract, or that he actually had no intention of honouring it? Does he agree to the contract in the first place only because it affords an escape from a horrible imprisonment and torture (described in some detail in three narrated opening stanzas)? To pose questions like these is of course to raise the issue of motivation, and this goes beyond the tendency of much traditional ballad criticism to assume that ballad characters lack psychological complexity and that their attributes and motives are straightforward and unambiguous. I shall be examining the relationship between dialogue and character in section 2.4 below.

Another perspective from pragmatics helps to illuminate what we have so far described rather loosely as questions, requests, commands, and such-like. What exactly constitutes each of these? Austin's theory of speech-acts, later developed and refined by such scholars as Searle and Hancher, alerts us to the importance of distinguishing between the grammatical and semantic *form* of an utterance, and its *illocutionary force*.[13] For the three basic grammatical patterns, usually termed declarative, interrogative and imperative, can be made to perform a very large number of different speech acts - threats, warnings, promises, bets, vows, as well as questions, commands, etc. Some examples from ballad dialogue should make this clear. Both 'Fair Annie' and 'The Lass of Roch Royal' have interrogatives in their opening stanzas:

> 'O wha will bake my bridal bread,
> And brew my bridal ale?
> Wha will welcome my bright bride,
> That I bring  oer the dale?'
>
> (FA,62E)

> 'O wha will shoe my fu fair foot?
> An wha will glove my han?
> An wha will lace my middle gimp
> Wi the new made London ban?'
>
> (LRR,76D)

From what follows in the case of each ballad, however, it is clear that whereas in FA (62E) the stanza functions as a request, the illocutionary force of the LRR (76D) stanza is, as Buchan says, a plaint; Anny is lamenting her condition, so a response is not necessarily expected. Elsewhere, the illocutionary force of an interrogative may be an invitation, as in KB (252C):28 ('Says, "Will ye leave your bonny ship/And come wi me this day to dine?"') or a command, as in the stanza from LM (65A) quoted on page 40. Other interrogatives are more clearly rhetorical, as when Johnie Scot's imprisoned sweetheart asks '"How can I come to my true-love/Except I had wings to flee?"', and in YB (53A):20 the male is confronted by his lover with a question that challenges him to confirm its assumption: '"O hae you tane a bonny bride?/An hae you quite forsaken me?"' We recognize its illocutionary force and so does Bicham – he immediately renounces his new bride, promises her a 'double dowry' and vows to marry Shusy.

Speech-act theory, in effect, is based on the notion that all utterances can be interpreted as examples of *actions*, intended by human subjects, which need language in order to be realized. Particularly good examples of such utterances are those speech-acts called *commissives* and *directives*; these are essentially contractual acts of speaking which 'work to control in language what the speaker will do (commissives) or what the hearer will do (directives)' (Hancher, 1979, p. 3). An example of the former is a promise, which, if sincerely intended and duly kept, will produce some change in the world or, as Austin puts it, have a *perlocutionary effect*; an example of a directive is a command, which, if carried out, can be described as having a similar effect. Thus, taking once again stanza 17 of LM (65A), it is interrogative in form, directive (a command) in illocutionary force – Maisry's brother clearly has the power to command his 'merry young men' – and its perlocutionary effect is clear, as we soon learn.

From everything that has been said so far it should surprise no-one that most dialogue stanzas in the sample are commissives and directives. Only very rarely, however, do they announce themselves as such by means of a verb *naming* the speech act, as in the explicit use of *vow* (a commissive) in BBL (222A:29): '"For I vow I'll neither eat nor sleep/Till I get my love again."' We usually have to infer the illocutionary force of a vow, as in the magnificent final two stanzas of 'Lady Maisry', the last of which is:

> 'An I'll gar burn for you, Maisry,
> The chief of a' your kin;

An the last bonfire that I come to,
Mysel I will cast in.'

Another kind of speech-act we might expect to find in such an action-oriented genre is the *declaration*. A declaration (not to be confused with the grammatical term declarative) is the example, *par excellence*, of language-as-action, in that something in the world is immediately and irrevocably changed simply as a result of certain words being uttered. The effect, then, of a policeman *arresting* you, a monarch *knighting* you, a clergyman *christening* you can be described as illocutionary, in that your circumstances are altered by the words themselves rather than by an action which may (or may not) be carried out as a result of those words (they therefore have a binding force stronger than, say, commissives like promises, which may or may not be kept). Declarations, however, are rare in the ballad sample, although the explanation is not hard to find; they are rooted in a highly specific and elaborate institutional framework such as law or religion, and are therefore a rather specialized kind of speech-act. The nuncupative (orally declared) testament, to which Bold draws attention (see note 13), seems a likely candidate for inclusion within this group of speech-acts, but there are no examples in the sample; the nearest we get to one is the *undertaking* to dispose of goods or wealth in a certain way, as when the father of Willie's sweetheart in 'The Kitchie Boy' says (stanza 37) '"So a' my gowd is yours to claim"'.

There is a sense, however, in which such undertakings could be said to have the force of declarations simply by virtue of the fact that they occur in final position within the ballad. Unlike the events of real life, which form a complicated and often bewildering continuum of actions, inaction, intention and indecision, the actions in the ballad, like those of drama and of other forms of verbal art, are clearly circumscribed by a definite beginning and end. Not only does this give the actions and speech-acts within the ballads a clear profile but the clear sequences of commissives and directives accustom us to expect that ballad protagonists mean what they say, recognize and respond to the illocutionary force of utterances, and, in a more general sense, subscribe to the view of language we have been describing above – that language itself is a form of action, that what you say has immediate consequences for other people.

To some extent, however, the picture painted above is misleading. Once we look in detail at individual versions we find these impressions have less validity. Tentativeness and speculation in ballad speech, as discussed above, are not what we might expect to find; neither, we might think, would we expect ballad protagonists to try to justify what they say, or to correct another's misunderstanding of a situation. Yet examples of each occur across the sample. In WODD (101A:19) Dame Oliphant's

> 'O had I a bunch o yon red roddins,
> That grows in yonder wood,
> But an a drink o water clear,
> I think it woud do me good.'

seems tentative, a cross between a plaint (common in ballads) and a mildly-worded request. In KB (252C), stanzas 18–24 are couched in conditionals and modal verbs as Willie resists the Spanish lady's temptings by speculating about what would happen if he married her. Stanza 21 is characteristic:

> 'O ladie, shoud I your proffer take,
> You'd soon yoursell have cause to rue,
> For the man that his first love forsakes
> Would to a second neer prove true.'

The second half of the stanza is also interesting in that it appeals to a kind of proverbial wisdom; similarly 'gnomic' is brother John's justification of his advice to Glenlion that he forget about the unwilling Bonny Baby Livingstone:

> 'Commend me to the lass that's kind,
> Tho na so gently born;
> And, gin her heart I coudna gain,
> To take her hand I'd scorn.'
>
> (Stanza 12)

And there is a 'rationalizing' feel to his explanation to Glenlion in stanza 37 that the latter has mistaken the sound of the rescuing Johny's bridle for that of the marrying priest:

> 'O brother, this is not the priest;
> I fear he'll come oer late;
> For armed men with shining brands
> Stand at the castle-yate.'

It is interesting to speculate here that Bertrand Bronson, one of the most stimulating commentators on ballad dialogue, would probably have doubted that these stanzas were 'good traditional ballad style' because they were too 'reasonably argumentative' (Bronson, 1969a, p. 11).

The same scholar's views on ballad questions noted above could also be challenged. Bearing in mind the distinction between interrogative form and illocutionary question, we need to be aware also of the difference between what linguists call polar questions (inviting a straightforward 'yes' or 'no') and wh-questions (beginning with such words as 'where', 'why', 'how', etc.). What looks like a simple polar question, for instance, can sometimes turn out to be rather more subtle. In stanza 5 of 'Child Waters' Lord John, safely mounted, asks Burd Ellen as they approach the river: '"Lady, can ye wide?"' (wade). Is he asking the question to elicit information? Or does it have a challenging force: if you *must* go with me, you'll have to wade this river? And how sincere is her answer, how much bravado? '"O I learnt it i my father's house/An I learnt it for my weal/Wenneer I came to a wan water/To swim like ony eel."' Another example, this time involving a wh-question, concerns the question posed by Love Gregor's mother to Anny as the latter shivers outside the castle: '"What taiken can ye gie that ever/I kept your company?"' (stanza 13; here, of course, the mother is happy to let Anny think it is her lover who is asking the question). Once again, is the question seriously asking for evidence, or is the mother simply testing Anny, perhaps merely to prolong the latter's agony? Similar issues are raised by the questions asked of Gil Brenton by his mother who, as in LRR (76D), acts as a kind of intermediary between *H* and *S*. The mother asks Gil Brenton what he has done with certain tokens, after learning that his new wife had been seduced in the past by a man offering her the self-same tokens. Surely the mother then at least suspects that her son has just wedded a girl he has already lain with?

It is not only question-and-answer sequences that suggest a level of subtlety and complexity greater than that allowed by Bronson. Is Love Gregor's mother telling the truth when she reports to him what has happened?

> 'O there was a woman stood at the door,
> Wi a bairn intill her arms,
> But I woud na lat her within the bowr,
> For fear she had done you harm.'
>
> (LRR, 76D:24)

And what is the illocutionary force of Lord John's words as he and Burd Ellen approach his castle?

> 'O my dogs sal eat the good white bread,
> An ye sal eat the bran;
> Then will ye sigh, an say, alas!
> That ever I was a man!'
>
> (stanza 15; cf. note 12)

Is this a threat, a warning, or a prediction? Is he testing her, or trying to put her off? Later in the same ballad a highly complex dialogue interchange occurs. Lord John's mother compares his 'bonny boy' to a pregnant woman – is she being ironical? He scoffs at the suggestion and, in order to 'prove' that Burd Ellen is a boy, he orders her, in front of his mother, to go out and feed his horse (to which Ellen instantly agrees). The three stanzas run consecutively (25-7):

> 'Sometimes his cheek is rosy red,
> An sometimes deadly wan;
> He's liker a woman big wi bairn,
> Than a young lord's serving man.'
>
> 'O it makes me laugh, my mother dear,
> Sic words to hear fra thee;
> He is a squire's ae dearest son,
> That for love has followed me.'
>
> 'Rise up, rise up, my bonny boy,
> Gi my horse corn an hay:'
> 'O that I will, my master dear,
> As quickly as I may.'

Faced with such an elaborate pretence on the part of all three protagonists it is *our* turn, as the audience, to start asking questions: How much does each suspect, or know? What, precisely, is the motivation of each protagonist?

## 2.3 Ballad dialogue and plot

In discussing the sphere of action or event in any kind of narrative it is useful to make a distinction between a level of analysis related to *story*, and one related to *discourse*. Story refers to the chronological sequence of events as we are able to reconstruct it from its presentation in discourse – the picture of events which is actually presented to the audience. Discourse, then, includes the category of *plot*; the way the event-sequence is handled in the discourse by means of such techniques as flashback, flashforward and ellipsis (the actual omission of an event that we infer happened at the level of story). Discourse also includes another range of choices; whether to summarize a sequence of events or present them as a series of scenes, in which the characters interact through dialogue (as in drama). Discourse also includes the complex issue of *point of view*; whether or not the narrating voice is felt to be omniscient, say, or intrusive, or virtually effaced (see Chatman, 1978).

Ballad plots tend to be single-stranded, to use Olrik's (1972) term, and the complex relationships between story-time and discourse-time characteristic of some other types of narrative do not arise. The event-sequence in the plot can also be said to match that of the story, as in the narrative of personal experience analysed by Labov; flashbacks and flashforwards are rare. Discourse-time, however, has some highly distinctive characteristics; events which we feel would have taken hours, days or years are ruthlessly compressed in favour of concentrating on one or two crucial *scenes*, which, as we noted above, tend to be drawn out in ritual exchanges of direct speech. Thus, we have a combination of ellipsis, in which discourse-time is radically faster than story-time, and stretch, where the reverse is the case. This 'leaping and lingering' technique, moreover, is narrated with the utmost detachment and impersonality, according to ballad scholars, who tend to compare the traditional ballad favourably with the broadside and street ballad of print.[14]

As is well-known, balladry tends to truncate the earlier sections of the plot and to focus on the later ones – the 'conflict-laden scene' that belongs to either Act IV or V (see Würzbach, 1983). In such scenes we find one or two protagonists *in extremis*: the shivering lass of Roch Royal, baby in arms, pleading with the 'fa'se mither' at Gregor's castle door; the defiant Lady Maisry taunting her brother as Lord William arrives, too late, to save her from the flames.[15] The impetus towards the creation of such a scene is so strong, of course, that some ballads dispense with everything else, as we find in the wholly dialogic ballads 'Edward' and 'Lord Randal'. In these cases the ballad-maker must find ways of letting the dialogue *reveal* the antecedent events.

For the ballads under discussion we have already established some key story-elements, albeit at a highly abstract level. Obligatory story-elements are CONTRACT, JOURNEY, TEST and REUNION; ballad-discourse concentrates on the third and fourth of these. If we analyse the plot of, say, 'Lady Maisry' we can see how these elements are realized and how important is the role of dialogue in their realization (see the words in italics). Lady Maisry is wooed, but she rejects her suitors by *revealing* her love-contract with Lord William; a boy overhears this and *reports* it to her brother, who then *interrogates* Maisry and *forbids* her to carry on with her lover. Maisry *refuses*, he *orders* her to be burnt, she *dispatches* a boy to her lover. The boy *reports*, Lord William *orders* his horses to be saddled in preparation for the journey to rescue her; she *requests* the fire to be built up; Lord William *vows* to avenge her and then to commit suicide. In this ballad, JOURNEY is necessary because of the prior absentation of H; the TEST sequence occupies both Maisry's interrogation and her subsequent punishment; the REUNION is realized by their (implied) mutual death. In contrast, the same elements are realized in 'Willie O Douglas Dale' by different means. Willie, a Scot, contrives to woo the king of England's daughter at her father's court; she *expresses* her love for him; they make love; she *laments* her pregnancy, then *warns* of her family's revenge; he *requests* her to accompany him to Scotland; they set out together. On the journey he *asks* her what she lacks, then builds her a shelter; she *expresses* a desire for roddins and water, which he satisfies; she goes into labour, and *requests* that he *summon* her father; he *refuses*. After shooting a deer she gives birth; he then finds a maid in the forest, and *orders* her to accompany them. Dame Oliphant, the king's daughter, *promises* the maid advancement if she will attend her. All three then arrive in Scotland. In this ballad, then, CONTRACT is made explicit after a detailed build-up; JOURNEY is undertaken by both S and H; TEST, as in 'Lady Maisry', involves the exercise of both physical and verbal power; and REUNION is this time comic – we assume Willie and Dame Oliphant live happily as lord and lady of Douglas Dale.

Dialogue has a very wide range of narrative functions across the ballad sample. It is used to give advice and warnings, and either to refuse or accept these; to make contracts, bargains and conditions, and vows; to issue commands, threats, promises; to deliver messages; to report actions; to lament a situation; to interrogate, to greet, to renounce, to plead, to request, to woo, to taunt. Certain functions recur: contracts are explicitly made in GB (5a), YB (53A), FKB (252C), GG (96A); messengers are dispatched in YB (53A), LM (65A), BBL (222A), GG (96A), JS (99A), and accordingly report news as in YB (53A), LM (65A), BBL (222A), GG (96A), JS (99A) and LRR (76D). Reports, of course, are also made by other protagonists; sometimes the audience already knows what is reported (as when the kitchy-boy tells Maisry's brother of her love), but on occasion the audience learns with the protagonist (as when the porter tells Shusy Pye of her lover Bicham's wedding).

In making contracts and in dispatching messengers, dialogue clearly functions to propel the narrative forward; and, from our discussion of pragmatics in section 2.2, it should also be clear that this is the major plot-function of ballad dialogue. When H in 'Fair Annie' and 'Young Bicham' renounces the new bride, we infer that a whole series of actions and events will follow. Occasionally, however, we find a stretch of dialogue in which two people plan an immediate, short-term action, as so often occurs in drama; the unhappy Gil Brenton goes to his mother and laments his marriage to 'a woman great with child', and his mother replies:

> 'O stay, my son, intill this ha,
> An sport you wi your merry men a'.'
> 'An I'll gang to yon painted bowr,
> An see how't fares wi yon base whore.'
>
> (stanzas 36 and 37)

In the same ballad, however, a great deal of dialogue is used to report actions that occurred long before the time-scale of events that are depicted in the actual discourse. After the stanzas just quoted the mother learns from her son's new wife of the latter's 'Hard wierd' – a report occupying some seventeen stanzas. And this section is followed, as we have already seen, by the mother challenging her son to report what he did with the love-tokens she has given him. 'Gil Brenton' stands out from the other ballads in the sample for the leisurely way such 'antecedent' information is given. More characteristic is the deft and economical way in which we learn of Anny's love-contract in 'The Lass of Roch Royal':

> 'Or wha will kemb my yallow hair
> Wi the new made silver kemb?
> Or wha'll be father to my young bairn,
> Till Love Gregor come hame?'

One consequence of the tendency to focus on the final developments of the story is that the ballad-maker faces a choice of ways with which to reveal past events; either she chooses the dramatic mode, and reveals through dialogue, or she presents the information through narrated stanzas (as in JS (99A:2) and CW (63B:9)), a device which emphasizes the presence of a narrating voice.

Occasionally dialogue reveals antecedent information to great dramatic effect. In 'The Lass of Roch Royal' again, stanzas 14–17, in which Anny, challenged by Love Gregor's mother to prove her identity, recounts the time when she and Gregor exchanged love-tokens, contribute little to our understanding of the story. But their occurrence at such a peak in the narrative has the effect of building suspense, of delaying the next development in the plot. Powerless outside the closed door, Anny can only try to answer whatever questions her interlocutor decides to put to her. But, of course, she opens her heart to no avail.

We might legitimately ask what exactly it is that the mother is doing in the sequence mentioned above. I would argue that she is *testing* Anny, even though it appears that her mind is already made up and that she has no intention of allowing Anny inside. Her question, as we have seen, is a way of exercising power over someone else. I have argued above that TEST, a central narrative function in the ballads, can have a physical manifestation (imprisonment, abduction) or a verbal one, such as the example above. According to Taylor (1971), traditional riddles were sometimes used by ballad-makers to serve the self-same function. There are no riddles in the sample, but sometimes what we might call a testing question, similar to the one in LRR (76D) discussed above, is used to intensify a physical ordeal. The pregnant Dame Oliphant, journeying with Willie through the greenwood, begins to cry. Willie asks:

> 'O want ye ribbons to your hair?
> Or roses to your shoone?
> Or want ye as meickle dear bought love
> As your ain heart can contain?'

> (stanza 15)

It is not only questions that are used to test people. Above it was argued that Lord John's words to Burd Ellen as they approach his castle may constitute a kind of test. The issue of what motivates the tester, and how the tested responds, brings us to the next part of this paper.

## 2.4 Ballad dialogue and character

We have already noted the widely-held view that the ballad is a genre of action rather than character. Like the Homeric epic and many works of the medieval period, it concerns 'doing' rather than 'being'. We do not expect a sustained exploration of the psychology of the doers and it is for this reason that the term 'character' is in this context actually rather misleading. The term suggests a human subject with a unified self, a set of individual peculiarities and the propensity to act in accordance with conscious intentions. Such a notion of character, of course, is far removed from the *dramatis personae* proposed by Propp in relation to another traditional genre, the fairy-tale. These are conceived in terms of particular 'tale-roles' within a predetermined sequence of narrative functions – Hero, Villain, Donor, Helper, and so on – and might better be described as actants rather than characters.

The applicability of Proppian 'tale-role' analysis to the ballads studied is, however, questionable. In a recent typology of the whole Brown corpus, Buchan (1982) proposes that for the ballads studied here (which he groups along different lines) the appropriate tale-roles would be Upholder, Opposer and Partner. The Upholder corresponds with the actant who actively promotes the union with his or her partner; the Opposer is the one opposed to the union; and the Partner is the passive member in the amatory relationship. While Buchan's scheme has the advantage of economy and elegance, it does not do justice, I think, to the range of tale-roles to be found in the sample. The eponymous actants in 'Gil Brenton' and 'Child Waters' do not oppose the union with their partners in the same way, say, as the heroine's father in 'Johnie Scot'; while in both 'Lady Maisry' and 'Bonny Baby Livingstone', respectively, the brother and Glenlion function like the Villain in Propp's analysis. Moreover, it is the ambiguity in the role of such actants as Child Waters that may contribute to the appeal of many of these ballads, as I shall discuss later.

How are we given information about ballad actants? Obviously, we are shown what they *do*: Lord William in 'Lady Maisry' reacts instantly to the news of his sweetheart's seizure and gallops immediately to her rescue; finding he is too late he vows vengeance. All we have is a name (generic, rather than individual) and a sequence of actions (including what he says) from which we can infer only the most minimal of character traits: Lord William is a man of action. In other ballads, however, we are sometimes *told* about an actant in a narrated stanza or line; Johny Scot and Willie O Douglas Dale are both 'brave', the mother of Love Gregor is 'fa'se', Johny in 'Bonny Baby Livingstone' is 'angry'. So conventional are the epithets (to the point of formularity, as in the 'proud porter' in YB (53A)) that we are positively discouraged from trying to individualize them. Occasionally, however, the narrating voice goes further and is openly condemnatory about an actant; of the eavesdropping kitchy-boy in 'Lady Maisry' we find 'An ill death may he dee!'

Inevitably, another source of information about actants is what they themselves *say*. A trait 'defiant' can be inferred from Lady Maisry's refusal to give up her lover and her taunting of her brother even as she burns. Before pursuing this line of argument, however, a number of general observations need to be made. Ballad actants seldom talk about themselves or each other in such terms, and ballad discourse makes no attempt to differentiate actants by inventing particular speech-styles to match certain traits. Neither are differences of social status indicated by linguistic markers, and actants do not adjust their ways of speaking to suit different addressees (although in YB (53A), WODD (101A) and BBL (222A) there is extensive use of terms of address, such as Christian names, honorifics (as in '"O what's your will wi mi, Sir Knight?"' in WODD (101A: 4) and kin-terms). Kitchy-boys talk like kings, and even share the same words; as we have seen, different ballads recycle the same dialogue, attributing it not only to different actants but assigning it differences of illocutionary force. And sometimes, as is well-known, a stretch of dialogue may be attributed to no actant at all: who is it, for example, who utters the interdiction at the beginning of 'Child Waters', or the final taunt in 'Bonny Baby Livingstone':

> 'Awa, Glenlion! Fie for shame!
> Gae hide ye in some den!
> You've letten your bride be stown frae you,
> For a' your armed men.'

(stanza 41)

Such unattributed stretches of dialogue might be described as *choric*.

In an important sense, then, ballad dialogue could be said to transcend character. For this reason it is necessary to resist the modern tendency to view all dialogue as having been shaped by the individual personality interacting with another in an enclosed exchange. And as I argued above, we should also not expect that the depiction of actants be necessarily consistent. Consistency of character is an expectation originating in post-Renaissance notions of the character as a centred, individual subject; and such a perspective may be as inappropriate in relation to the ballad as it is to Homeric epic (for an example specially relevant to this paper, see

Kirk (1976), p. 74). To say that ballad actants are shaped by, rather than shape, the words that they speak is only to recognize a crucial aspect of our social lives that is as relevant today as it has ever been.[16]

In some of the ballads we have been looking at, however, the strategy of the dialogue could be said to strain against this conception of character as actant. There are questions to be asked, for instance, about how much the mothers in both 'Gil Brenton' and 'The Lass of Roch Royal' know and suspect (the same question that Bronson asked of the mother in 'Edward'). Furthermore there is an apparent indeterminacy in the role of the leading male actant in 'Gil Brenton', 'Child Waters' and perhaps 'Willie O Douglas Dale'. Finally, it appears that some actants can actually *change*: like so many of the leading female protagonists in the ballad sample, Burd Ellen at the beginning of 'Child Waters' seems so quick-witted, so stoical; later, her nerve seems to falter, though she still plays the role she has been cast in.

What I am arguing is that there is a level of complexity in many of Anna Brown's ballads to which modern audiences, experienced in 'character-centred' dialogue conventions, respond and which prompts the kinds of questions discussed above. My analysis suggests that many interactions in these ballads are moving beyond the traditional conception of character as actant towards what Kennedy (1983, p. 62) called the duologue of personal encounter, in which what 'the speakers say goes beyond any speech that might be predicted from the preceding action, from the logic of relationships or from the formal or rhetorical conventions of the dialogue'. And I would suggest that it may have been precisely this quality that Child (1965) recognized when he wrote that 'No Scottish ballads are superior in kind to those recited in the last century by Mrs. Brown, of Falkland'.

## 2.5 Conclusion

The analysis suggests that there is *some* validity in depicting ballad dialogue as the speech of action, where protagonists do not dither but speak and act in a direct, immediate and non-manipulative manner. Indeed, this quality may go some way towards explaining one aspect of the genre's contemporary aesthetic appeal; that in societies increasingly dominated by remote and bureaucratic institutions it is pleasurable to find people able and willing to take personal responsibility for their words and deeds and to seek to resolve problems and conflicts by face-to-face encounter, as in the genre of the Western. But as we have seen, this image needs to be seen as background, as a property of ballad *langue*; for once we investigate particular ballad-versions, instances of *parole*, we find such generalizations less appropriate. This is particularly true in the case of the Anna Brown ballads analysed; even within such a small sample we can find considerable variety (between say, 'Lady Maisry' at one extreme and 'Child Waters' at the other) and a sense that in Anna Brown we have a ballad-maker of some literary sophistication.[17]

There are, however, some other generalizations that might be made. Not only is ballad dialogue often 'beyond' character but it is also extremely unlike most kinds of 'everyday' conversational speech.[18] The fact that we find the same verbal structures, even whole stanzas, appearing in the mouths of different protagonists across different ballads or even within the same ballad-version contributes in no small measure to the quality of impersonality so often noted in the literature. Like the speech of law, ballad dialogue often has a formulaic solemnity: '"I warn ye all, ye gay ladies,/That wear scarlet an brown/That ye dinna leave your father's house/To follow young men frae town."' This ritualistic flavour is also reinforced – though not determined – by ballad melody; as Bronson says, the pace of dialogue is slowed right down since 'the whole length of the tune is allotted to a single speaker'.[19] These characteristics can be found in Anna Brown's repertoire and contribute, in my opinion, to the power of balladry in that, within a highly stylized and conventional pattern of words, a multiplicity of events, existents, human emotions, motivations and actions are rigorously constrained.

The high proportion of commissive and directive speech acts in ballad dialogue also contributes to this effect. As Fish (1976) says, such illocutions as promises and requests are attempts 'to get the world to match the words' (as opposed to reports, explanations and assertions which attempt 'to get the words to match a state of affairs in the world'). It is partly because some utterances have the power to shape the world that so much of ballad dialogue, stripped as it is of all conversational realism, has something of the ritual quality characteristic of legal discourse. It is as though ballads are enactments of a kind of legal process which exists outside specific institutions of law (see, for a useful overview of legal language, Danet (1980)).

Another aspect of ballad dialogue may contribute an element of stability and continuity in the processes of transmission. Certain sequences such as question/answer, interdiction/commitment-to-violate-interdiction may become conventionalized and afford the ballad-maker another of the kinds of structuring patterns proposed by Buchan.[20] The same could be said of more abstract, or 'meta-sequences' such as the plea/rebuttal pattern in the 'Lass of Roch Royal' or even, perhaps, those sequences which constitute what I have called tests. It has not been my intention to explore this possibility in this paper, but it is clear that there is scope here for further analysis of a linguistic kind.

A final point concerns the issue of genre. I believe that my analysis shows that there is a value in treating the ballad as a kind of drama rather than as narrative or lyric (although this is not to say that drama cannot also be song, or that it doesn't also have a story to tell). To see the ballad as drama is to take seriously the notion that it is a *performed* artefact in which the needs and interests of the audience are of paramount importance. This perspective, furthermore, may help stylisticians get over the feeling that traditional material is not amenable to analysis because it is unfixed. Shakespeare's drama, for instance, was not based on the notion of the fixed text, but stylisticians ought nevertheless to have something to say about it!

# NOTES

1 Structuralism, with its roots in linguistics and the formalism of, among others, Propp (1968), has influenced the study of folklore; see, for instance Hendricks (1973). Many folklorists, particularly in the USA, have in recent years supplemented older approaches (e.g. the comparison of variants, collection of analogues, reconstruction of the Ur-type) with more 'performance'-oriented analyses: see, for instance, Ben-Amos (1972) and Bauman (1977). Some recent studies of balladry, however, still retain older perspectives; see Andersen *et al.* (1983, especially Pettitt's Introduction). On the notion of textual instability, see Pettitt (1979).

2 Buchan (1972a). This writer's insistence on the 'orality' of Anna Brown's ballads is, however, open to criticism: see note 17. A useful edition of ballads which contains the Brown corpus is Buchan (1972b).

3 The centrality of dialogue to oral narrative (so widespread that it could be described as a narrative 'universal' – see Grimes (1972)), is also noted by Kirk (1976, p. 106) in relation to Homeric epic, which is

'essentially dramatic in conception'; see also Tedlock (1972). Kekäläinen (1983) has chapters on dialogue, on questions, and on commands and wishes, but her approach is philological and descriptive rather than pragmatic. I am grateful to David Buchan for drawing my attention to this book.

4  This writer, clearly moved by ballad dialogue, notes its 'trenchant pertinency, not to be matched except in highly developed drama' (pp. 6–7). I make some comments on the dramatic character of the ballad below.

5  Buchan (1972a, pp. 238–9) cites the opening stanzas of 'Jellon Grame' (90B) to demonstrate what he calls the plodding rationalism in the dialogue of the ballad of literacy:

> 'I wonder much,' said May Margerie,
> At this message to me;
> There is not a month gone of this year
> But I have made him three.'

He also argues (p. 236) that the proportion of dialogue diminishes as the ballad is affected by literacy; see further note 9 and Buchan (1982).

6  There is an obvious danger in using linguistics mechanically, and therefore trivially, as a mere cataloguing device (see Fish, 1976).

7  These symbols are adapted from Buchan (1972a) and (1982); my *T* corresponds in some sense to Buchan's 'Opposer'; see further p. 57.

8  The analysis offered here is only tentative, since the study of ballad morphology is complex and difficult (see Turner (1972), Porter (1980); see also section 2.4 below). It is possible that my analysis, which suggests affinities with the persecuted-heroine story-type – see Dan (1972) – fits other ballads in the Anna Brown corpus. I should like to stress that my conclusions from the sample are only indicative; reasons of time and space prevented a more comprehensive analysis. See also Buchan (1982).

9  Since modals and negatives indicate possible or hypothetical circumstances or outcomes, their use within narrated stanzas tends to signal the presence of a narrator and therefore to undermine the centrality of the dialogue. The greater complexity of dialogue grammar is also noted by Kirk (1976, p. 108) discussing Homer.

10  Kekäläinen (1983, p. 39), working from a very large sample of ballads from all periods, concludes that the use of dialogue stanzas peaked in the late seventeenth and early eighteenth centuries, with the overall percentage for all periods as 61 per cent. She also singles out Anna Brown's ballads for their use of unintroduced dialogue stanzas.

11  See Goffman (1976), Coulthard (1977, especially p. 70). For a recent and full discussion of pragmatics in general, see Levinson (1983, especially pp. 289ff.), a study which has proved invaluable in writing this paper.

12  See his introduction to Andersen *et al.* (1983, p. 6). See also Gerould's
    remarks quoted above. The 'one speaker–one stanza' pattern is not
    however invariant; Dame Oliphant in stanza 9 of WODD (101A)
    announces (in six lines, not four) her pregnancy and then goes on to
    warn, in the next stanza, of the likely action of her family.

13  See Austin (1962), Searle (1969), Hancher (1979). Illocutionary force
    refers to the kind of action performed by an act of speaking, e.g.
    ordering, requesting, promising, etc. The notion of speech as action is
    absent in Kekäläinen (1983), but implicit in Bold's (1979, p. 31ff.)
    discussion of nuncupative testaments, and in Buchan's (1972a) use of
    the term 'plaint' to describe the narrative function of stanza 1 of LRR
    (76D).

14  It is argued that in the broadside ballad a 'narrating voice' is present
    to address the audience directly and to comment on the action
    (usually by means of a more emotive vocabulary). According to Pettitt
    in his introduction to Andersen, F., Pettitt, T. and Holzapfel, O.
    (1983, p. 8), this device is a legacy of the minstrel, who, unlike the
    traditional balladmaker, expected a financial reward for his singing
    and could therefore 'intrude' into the narrative. It is interesting that
    some nineteenth-century commentators on the novel (e.g. Flaubert
    and James) recommended authorial de-personalization and scenic
    presentation – often in the name of realism.

15  My own selection of these scenes is necessarily personal; it would be
    interesting to know if other audiences found them particularly
    memorable and whether they could be described as Tableaux scenes
    in the sense established by Olrik (1972). For a relevant discussion of
    narrative 'peaks', see Longacre (1976).

16  Such a view is associated with recent post-structuralist theories of
    language and the human subject (cf. Wales, Geyer-Ryan, this volume).
    For a useful introduction, see Belsey (1980).

17  In support of this conclusion, see Bronson (1969b), Fowler (1968),
    Andersen and Pettitt (1979). Gammon and Stallybrass (1984) mention
    the novelistic 'psychological realism' in the Brown ballads. Kekäläinen
    (1983) points out the similarities between Anna Brown's ballad style
    and that of the earlier 'romance' ballad of print. The 'oral-formulaic'
    theories of Buchan and others have recently been criticized in a more
    general way by Finnegan (1977). For another illuminating discussion,
    see also Scribner and Cole (1981).

18  This is true of all represented speech, of course, which could be
    described as *triadic*, designed to be 'overheard' by an audience. Literary
    dialogue, moreover, must tell us about past events and future
    possibilities, and convey information about protagonists and settings;
    many conversational markers are omitted from such representations,
    but ballad dialogue is singularly lacking in most of these markers. And
    the fact that ballad dialogue is beyond character distances it still
    further, making it more close to the dialogue of many pre-

Renaissance kinds of drama (see Williams, 1984). Contemporary oral performances of folk-tales on the other hand sometimes take a more 'realistic' view of dialogue (see Bruford, 1982).

19  Bronson's (1959) argument that ballad dialogue is governed by the melody seems as deterministic as the orality thesis, which argues that the characteristics of ballad language owe much to the 'limited resources of the singer performing without written text' (Pettitt in Andersen F., Pettitt, T. and Holzapfel, O., 1979, p. 10). In my view attention might more profitably be focused on the rhetorical effect of balladry rather than the supposed conditions of production and transmission (but see below).

20  A further, rather tangential, example might be the use made of the plea/refusal sequence in both ballad and newspaper versions of the Pearl Bryan murder story (see Cohen, 1973).

# BIBLIOGRAPHY

Andersen, F. and Pettitt, T. (1979), 'Mrs Brown of Falkland: a singer of tales?', *Journal of American Folklore*, vol. 92, pp. 1–24.

Andersen, F., Pettitt, T. and Holzapfel, O. (1983). *The Ballad as Narrative*, Odense, Odense University Press.

Austin, J. L. (1962), *How To Do Things With Words*, Oxford, Clarendon Press.

Bauman, R. (ed.) (1977), *Verbal Art as Performance*, Rowley, Mass., Newbury House.

Belsey, C. (1980), *Critical Practice*, London, Methuen.

Ben Amos, D. (1972), 'Toward a definition of folklore in context', in Paredes and Bauman (1977), pp. 3–16.

Bold, A. (1979), *The Ballad*, London, Methuen.

Brahmer, M., Helsztynski, S. and Krzyzanowski, J. (eds) (1971), *Studies in Language and Literature in Honour of M. Schlauch*, New York, Russell & Russell.

Bronson, B. (1959), *The Traditional Tunes of the Child Ballads*, vol. I. Princeton, NJ, Princeton University Press.

Bronson, B. (1969a), '"Edward, Edward" A Scottish ballad, and a footnote', in B. Bronson, *The Ballad as Song*, Berkeley, University of California Press.

Bronson, B. (1969b), 'Mrs. Brown and the Ballad', in *ibid*.

Bronson, B. (1976), *The Singing Tradition of the Child Ballads*, Princeton, NJ, Princeton University Press.

Brown, P. and Levinson, S. (1978), 'Universals in language usage: politeness phenomena', in E. Goody (1978), pp. 56–311.

Bruford, A. (ed.) (1982), *The Green Man of Knowledge and Other Scots Traditional Tales*, Aberdeen, Aberdeen University Press.

Buchan, D. (1972a), *The Ballad and the Folk*, London, Routledge & Kegan Paul.

Buchan (1972b), *A Scottish Ballad Book*, London, Routledge & Kegan Paul.

Buchan, D. (1982), 'Propp's Tale Role and a ballad repertoire', *Journal of American Folklore*, vol. 95, no. 376, pp. 159–72.

Chatman, S. (1978), *Story and Discourse*, Ithaca, Cornell University Press.

Child, F. J. (1965), *The English and Scottish Popular Ballads*, New York, Dover (originally published by Peter Smith in Boston in 1882).

Cohen, A. B. (1973), *Poor Pearl, Poor Girl!: The Murdered Girl Stereotype in Ballad and Newspaper*, Austin, University of Texas Press.

Coulthard, M. (1977), *An Introduction to Discourse Analysis*, London, Longman.

Dan, I. (1972), 'The innocent persecuted heroine: an attempt at a model for the surface level of the narrative structure of the female fairy tale', in Jason and Segal (1972), pp. 13–30.

Danet, B. (1980), 'Language in the legal process', *Law and Society Review*, vol. 14, pp. 445–565.

Dundes, A. (ed.) (1972), *The Study of Folklore*, Englewood Cliffs, NJ, Prentice Hall.

Finnegan, R. (1977), *Oral Poetry*, Cambridge, Cambridge University Press.

Fish, S. (1976), 'How to do things with Austin and Searle: speech act theory and literary criticism', *Modern Language Notes*, vol. 91, pp. 938–1,025.

Fowler, D. C. (1968), *A Literary History of the Popular Ballad*, Durham, NC, Duke University Press.

Gammon, V. and Stallybrass, P. (1984), 'Structure and ideology in the ballad: an analysis of "Long Lankin"', *Criticism*, vol. 26, no. 1, pp. 1–20.

Gerould, G. (1974), *The Ballad of Tradition*, Oxford, Gordian Press (originally published by Oxford University Press in 1932).

Goffman, E. (1976), 'Replies and responses', *Language in Society*, vol. 5, pp. 257–313.

Goody, E. (ed.) (1978), *Questions and Politeness: Strategies in Social Interaction*, Cambridge, Cambridge University Press.

Grimes, J. (1972), *The Thread of Discourse*, The Hague, Mouton.

Hancher, M. (1979), 'The classification of co-operative illocutionary acts', *Language in Society*, vol. 8, pp. 1–14.

Harker, D. (1985), *Fakesong*, Milton Keynes, Open University Press.

Hendricks, W. O. (1973), *Essays on Semiolinguistics and Verbal Art*, The Hague, Mouton.

Jason, H. and Segal, D. (eds) (1972), *Patterns in Oral Literature*, The Hague, Mouton.

Kekäläinen, K. (1983), *Aspects of Style and Language in Child's Collection of English and Scottish Popular Ballads*, Helsinki, Suomalainen Tiedeakatemia.

Kennedy, A. (1983), *Dramatic Dialogue*, Cambridge, Cambridge University Press.

Kirk, G. (1976), *Homer and the Oral Tradition*, Cambridge, Cambridge

University Press.

Labov, W. (1972), 'The transformation of experience in narrative syntax', in W. Labov, *Language in the Inner City*, Philadelphia, Pennsylvania University Press.

Levinson, S. (1983), *Pragmatics*, Cambridge, Cambridge University Press.

Longacre, R. (1976), *An Anatomy of Speech Notions*, Lisse, Peter de Ridder Press.

Olrik, A. (1972), 'Epic laws of folk narrative', in A. Dundes (1972), pp. 131–41.

Paredes, A. and Bauman, R. (eds) (1972), *Toward New Perspectives in Folklore*, Austin, University of Texas Press.

Pettitt, T. (1979), 'When the text won't stand still: the study of traditional genres', *Pre-publications of the English Institute of Odense University*, no. 15, October 1979.

Porter, J. (1980), 'Principles of ballad classification: a suggestion for regional catalogues of ballad style', *Jahrbuch für Volksliedforschung*, vol. 25, pp. 11–26.

Propp, W. (1968), *Morphology of the Folktale*, Austin, University of Texas Press (originally published in Leningrad in 1928).

Scribner, S. and Cole, M. (1981), *The Psychology of Literacy*, Cambridge, Mass., Harvard University Press.

Searle, J. (1969), *Speech Acts*, Cambridge, Cambridge University Press.

Taylor, A. (1971), 'The English riddle ballads', in Brahmer *et al.* (1971), pp. 445–51.

Tedlock, D. (1972), 'On the translation of style in oral narrative', in Paredes and Bauman (1972), pp. 114–33.

Todorov, T. (1977), *The Poetics of Prose*, Ithaca, Cornell University Press.

Turner, J. (1972), 'A morphology of the true love ballad', *Journal of American Folklore*, vol. 85, pp. 21–31.

Williams, R. (1984), 'On dramatic dialogue and monologue (particularly in Shakespeare)', in *Writing in Society*, London, Verso.

Würzbach, N. (1983), 'An approach to a context-oriented genre theory in application to the history of the ballad; traditional ballad – street ballad – literary ballad', *Poetics*, vol. 12, pp. 35–70.

# 3

# Speech presentation, the novel and the press

*Michael Short*

*As Dick Leith showed in the previous chapter, underlying the dialogues in a text is some purpose of the genre. The presentation of oral language as a form of discourse is also conventional in the sense indicated by Mary Louise Pratt. The linguistic modes of such conventional representation of speech can be highlighted, however, by means of a limited number of descriptive categories. To study these, and their concrete manifestations in different text types, is the aim of Michael Short's chapter.*

*Starting from the five modes of speech representation ('direct' and 'free direct', 'indirect' and 'free indirect' speech, and 'narrative report of speech act') developed systematically in his earlier work, Short investigates the question whether these categories are typical for the novel only (in the context of which they were originally designed) or whether they can be said to be of wider relevance. As their application to newspaper texts reveals, all categories occur in them. However, this statement is in need of further qualification. The interpretation (of occurrences of the categories in newspapers) follows slightly different rules, especially with respect to the faithfulness conditions involved in rendering someone else's speech.*

*This throws further light on the fact that the interpretation of discourse-conventions is at least partly dependent on the text type to which they apply. It furthermore appears that the categories initially started from are* not *sufficient to account adequately for all data found in the newspaper corpus. A further category of 'speech summary' is tentatively added to the proposed system of speech representation. Finally, it is suggested that intricate relationships may exist between a writer's selection of a particular mode of speech representation and his own position and attitudes* vis-à-vis *the text's topic. As such the article presents an effort to lay the foundations for a more general theory of speech representation that will allow for both invariant categories and variants across text types.*

## 3.1 Introduction[1]

Over the last few years I have argued that no firm formal linguistic distinction can be made between literary and non-literary language (see, for example, Short (1986) and Short and Candlin (1986)). Literature, as Henry Widdowson says in *Stylistics and the Teaching of Literature* (1975), contains many different varieties of language (though, presumably, not necessarily *all* possible varieties). In the past, this kind of argument has usually been used to justify the use of techniques of general linguistic analysis on literary texts. And I would certainly want to support such arguments. But, if literature and other forms of language are not obviously distinct in terms of their 'linguistic ingredients', it is also possible to argue in a different direction and suggest that the tools which linguists interested in literature have developed for (rhetorical) analysis might also be usefully used on texts not normally thought of as literary. This is the view that I take in this chapter, in which I take a particular form of analysis usually reserved for the novel and apply it to newspaper reports.

Stylisticians working on the novel have focused a good deal of attention on the choices available to authors when they present the speech of their characters. News reporting also often involves the reporting of speech, and so I decided to explore this area of overlap between newspapers and the novel. There are a number of accounts of speech presentation in the novel (see McHale (1978) for a good representative account). I decided to use the descriptive characterization with which I am most familiar, namely that developed in Chapter 10 of Leech and Short (1981). For reasons of space, and because it is now reasonably well-known, I will not re-outline the speech presentation analysis to be found there, but will merely assume that the reader is familiar with it, and refer to particular aspects of that original account where it is necessary for clarity of argumentation. In addition to the above reference, an abbreviated account of the approach can be found in Short (1983).

The reasons for using this (relatively explicit) analysis were:

1  to check whether the categories discovered in the novel occur in newspaper writing and if they differ in any way; and
2  to see what the analysis of this particular area of linguistic choice shows us about the newspaper articles concerned.

## 3.2 The sample

I collected the weekday English national newspapers for two weeks during June 1984 and then selected as data three stories reported in those newspapers.

1  The incident during the miners' strike when, depending upon which account you accept, the miners' leader, Mr Arthur Scargill, slipped or was pushed over by the police.
2  The scandal when Mr Ron Atkinson, then manager of Manchester United Football Club, left his wife for his mistress.
3  The discussion of a commissioned portrait of the British prime minister, Mrs Margaret Thatcher, which was declared to have a squint.

These stories were chosen:

1  because they contained instances of speech presentation in their headlines as well as their texts (this paper will concentrate on speech presentation in newspaper headlines); and
2  because they represent a range of types of story – the first concerns a matter of considerable political impact during the miners' strike, the second combines sex scandal and sport, and the third amounts more or less to gossip-column trivia.

## 3.3 Preliminary results

The three general results of my examination of the data are:

1  The rather obvious point that, by and large, only speech is presented in the newspaper data, whereas in the novel

character thought is also often enacted. Newspaper reporters do not have direct access to the thoughts of the people they interview, whereas novelists, who make up everything that they write, can allow their narrators to have this sort of privileged access to a character's mind. This does not mean, of course, that thoughts, or putative thoughts, will never be represented in newspapers. It is, after all, possible to infer what someone else is thinking from their actions, facial expression, etc., and then report it to a third party. None the less, one would expect thought presentation to be relatively rare in news reporting, and, indeed, there is none in my data.

2  The range of types of speech presentation categories (free direct speech (FDS), direct speech (DS), free indirect speech (FIS), indirect speech (IS), narrator's report of speech acts (NRSA) all occur in the newspaper articles I examined, and there are no new categories, with the possible exception of a category which I will describe later as 'speech summary'. Hence it appears that there is no formal linguistic difference between the novel and newspaper writing with respect to this system, in the sense that all the categories appear in both 'text types'. Instead, the value of the particular linguistic structures varies because of varying contextual conditions (see 3 below). The amount of data analysed is not really large enough to compare in quantitative terms the incidence of occurrence of particular categories with their incidence in the novel, although that would be a fruitful avenue of further research which might bear interestingly on the arguments concerning whether or not there is such a thing as a special literary language.

3  The semantic correlates of the presentation types are similar to those found in the novel, but are not exactly the same because the discourse situation is different. In particular, contrary to canonical expectations, when DS and FDS are used in newspaper headlines they do not always report verbatim what the original speaker said; and 'speech summary' becomes a more likely interpretative possibility in news reporting. Both of these points are related to the fact that in the novel there is no anterior speech situation for the report to relate to (because novels are fictions), whereas with respect to news reports there are. As a consequence it is possible in a news report, but not in the novel, to perceive

discrepancies between the original and the report, providing one has access to the relevant information (see sections 3.4 and 3.8 below).

Because it affects the direction of future possible research, a further important general finding is also worth making, even though it does not follow in a simple way from mere examination of the data. If a good general account of speech presentation is to be established, the phenomenon needs to be examined in a much wider range of text-types than has been the case hitherto. The majority of work in this area has been on the novel, which is unrepresentative, as I have said in 3 above, because most novels are fictional and speech presentation in them is not related to an anterior speech event. Moreover, the fact that DS or FDS strings in headlines do not always present faithfully the words and structures used by the original speaker (see section 3.4.2 below) raises the possibility that the conventions for the interpretation of the use of a particular speech presentation category might vary from text type to text type. For example, within news reporting, it may be the case that faithful and accurate representation of the original is more strongly adhered to in political and legal reporting than in accounts of what football managers say and do. Similarly, one might expect that faithfulness is more strictly adhered to in the minutes for meetings than in a letter to a friend describing a row in a bar the previous evening. These suggestions are only informed guesses. Empirical analysis is needed if we are to be able to ascertain the facts and see the overall picture.

## 3.4 Direct speech and free direct speech in headlines[2]

### 3.4.1 Distribution

First of all we should note that only these two speech presentation types, DS and FDS, occur in the headlines in the data. Indirect and free indirect speech, for example, do not occur. This is presumably because the less direct forms are less eye-catching. Headlines need to attract the reader's attention and so IS, for instance, is unlikely to occur. The second point of interest is that the DS and FDS forms do not appear in my data in the headlines from *The Times*, *The Guardian*, *The Financial Times* and *The Morning Star* (for a fuller discussion of headlines in *The Times*, see Simon-Vandenbergen, 1981). What possible reasons can we adduce for this? The most striking fact is that the three 'quality' newspapers do not use the

DS or FDS forms in these data. This may well be because they wish to play down the notion that they are 'sensationalist'. In this respect, the use of FDS and DS in headlines is stylistically akin to the very large type, exclamation marks and exclamatory words of the 'popular' newspapers (cf. **UGH! GET RID OF MY SQUINT** from *The Sun* (see section 3.4.2 below)). I am not, of course, suggesting that the 'quality' newspapers will never have DS or FDS in their headlines; it is easy enough to find counter-examples to such a claim. However, I would suggest that they are likely to use them more sparingly. A correlate of this would be that when DS and FDS are used in these newspapers they will be foregrounded relative to the norm for the paper concerned. There are, in any case, other possible motivations for using FDS and DS which work against the motivation suggested above. One obvious factor is that in using these direct forms the writer claims to represent faithfully exactly what the original speaker said. When it is particularly important to indicate that the words are those of the original speaker and not the writer (see below), this consideration might outweigh other factors. In any case, the sample discussed here is too small to be reliable and hence this analysis can only be suggestive. The comparative use of the different forms in different newspapers would seem an ideal topic for further research.

In the above discussion I have been careful to put scare quotes around the word *quality* when referring to the 'quality' newspapers. This is because I do not want to prejudge the issue as to whether the *Times, Guardian* and *Financial Times* are necessarily any better or more reliable than the other newspapers. Whilst many would assume a real distinction between the 'quality' and 'popular' press in terms of truthfulness, fairness, etc., others would want to argue that the 'better' newspapers also slant their reporting to a large degree and merely pre-select a different readership. The issue as to whether the 'quality' papers tend to forgo the direct forms of speech presentation because they are more serious or because they merely wish to affect seriousness is thus a difficult one to decide in absolute terms. It is interesting to note, however, that the Communist Party newspaper, *The Morning Star*, also avoids the more direct forms in the headlines of the stories examined, in spite of the fact that the establishment would not regard it as an equivalent to *The Times* or *The Guardian*. Whichever view one takes on the seriousness or seeming seriousness of *The Times*, for example, consistency would seem to demand that with respect to my data, characterization of the non-appearance of DS and FDS in that newspaper would have to be the same as that for *The Morning Star*. Perhaps it should also be accorded the notorious 'quality' label. The only newspaper which has pretensions to being a 'quality' daily which does use one of the direct forms in the data is the *Daily Telegraph*:

**ATKINSON 'TO STAY WITH UNITED'**                                    [3.1]
*(Daily Telegraph*, 11 June, p. 2)

### 3.4.2 Truthfulness in reporting

The usual assumptions that readers make about DS and FDS have to do with veracity. If someone reports the speech of another using either of these two modes, it is normally the case that the reporter (the narrator in the novel) claims to represent faithfully:

(a)  the illocutionary force;
(b)  the propositional content; and
(c)  the words and structures used by the original speaker.

In contrast, the use of indirect speech (IS), for example, only commits one to faithfulness in terms of (a) and (b) above. But in some of the newspaper headlines in this small corpus, the writers appear to ignore the faithfulness maxims to some extent, so that the DS and FDS strings often have the characteristics canonically associated with IS:

**UGH! GET RID OF MY SQUINT**                                    [3.2]
*(The Sun*, 21 June, p. 11)

**You've given me a squint, said Maggie**                        [3.3]
*(Daily Express*, 21 June, p. 7)

In both of these cases it would seem at first sight that Mrs Thatcher was heard by the reporter to utter the two sentences [3.2] and [3.3]. However, it becomes apparent in the main body of the articles that she was not interviewed at all. The artist was interviewed, but his characterization of Mrs Thatcher's words appears to have been less dramatic than the flavour suggested by the headlines.[2] Below is the relevant extract from *The Sun*'s article.

**PREMIER Margaret Thatcher took one look at her new portrait and said: 'Get rid of that squint!'**
    For the painting, which went on show yesterday in London's National Portrait Gallery, shows the Prime Minister with her gaze decidedly awry.

And artist Rodrigo Moynihan admitted last night: 'Mrs Thatcher is not entirely happy with it.'

Mr Moynihan, 74, a former professor at the Royal College of Art, confessed to 'quite a lot of trouble' over Mrs Thatcher's eyes.

And he added: 'I could be quite happy with one more sitting and I know she would be.'

The problems began when Mrs Thatcher asked him to put more grey in the blue eyes in the portrait.

'She also noticed a squint – though she pointed it out fairly diplomatically,' Mr Moynihan said.

(*The Sun*, 21 June, p. 11)

*The Sun's* headline is not only not a faithful reproduction of the words Mrs Thatcher actually used; it also borders on being unfaithful in other respects. We do not know what Mrs Thatcher actually said, but given Mr Moynihan's remarks in the body of the article to the effect that she made her criticism 'fairly diplomatically', it would appear that not only the words used, but the illocutionary force and maybe even the propositional content of the original utterance, have not been faithfully reproduced. Similar remarks apply to the opening sentence of the article itself. In addition, on a first reading, the headline is somewhat ambiguous as to whether the squint belongs to the painting or to Mrs Thatcher herself.

There are other examples from the headline data where the original words and expressions are not strictly adhered to:

**I wish for everyone's sake Scargill would
stay away**                                              [3.4]
(*Daily Express*, 19 June, p. 3)

**'Police hit me on the head'**          claims Scargill          [3.5]
**'He fell, we were nowhere near him'** say the police
(*Daily Mirror*, 19 June, p. 1)

In example [3.4] the quotation given in the main text is:

'I wish for everyone's sake that you would stay away. Your presence is always provocative, and someone could get killed.'
(*Daily Express*, 19 June, p. 3)

At first sight the change from *you* to *Scargill* in [3.4] is innocent and merely provides the reader with the information needed to identify the addressee. But of course it also allows the  writer to choose the item he or she wants from within the name-referring system (in this case, last name only – *Scargill* – instead of *Mr Scargill* or *Arthur*, for instance), hence helping to indicate distancing from Mr Scargill (and perhaps disapproval) on the part of the writer.

It transpires, with reference to example [3.5], that in spite of the locution 'say the police', only one policeman was interviewed. In addition, the relevant part of the in-text quotation has the same gist as the headline, but the words used vary:

> 'He slipped and fell and hit his head on a railway sleeper,' he said. 'The police were nowhere near him. The nearest bobby was 20 yards away.'

In effect, then, it appears that in the headlines of the 'popular' press at least, journalists are relaxing to some extent the faithfulness principle with respect to the words and structures used which is normally associated with DS and FDS. Consequently, faithfulness to propositional content is also in danger. What is going on in all of these examples is, of course, the striving for dramatic eye-catching headlines to attract readers. Strict adherence to the truth is subordinated to these demands. To put it in Grice's (1975) terms, the maxim of strikingness appears to be more important in this genre than the maxim of quality.

It is difficult to know exactly how to characterize what we have just noticed. It is possible that the changes are innocent attempts to make sure that the reader can correctly identify the speakers involved. On the other hand, it may be that the news reporters are manipulating the truth for reasons of strikingness or in order to control the reactions and views of their readers. Alternatively, it may be that neither writers nor readers expect newspaper headlines to obey the faithfulness rules canonically associated with the relevant speech-report categories because eye-catchingness is thought to be more important in headlines than the maxim of quality. It is difficult to tell from this evidence alone whether the faithfulness principle attached to speech presentation is changing gradually or whether there is (as I suspect) some variation in their employment from one text-type to another. Larger-scale empirical work in this area, particularly in terms of informant testing would be of obvious value.

## 3.5  The direct/free direct speech distinction

In section 3.4.2 above I suggested that in direct speech the reporter claims to represent faithfully three properties of the original speech act:

(a)  the illocutionary force;
(b)  the propositional content;
(c)  the words and structures used in uttering the propositions concerned.

This set of distinctions gives rise to a set of functional differences which support the formal distinctions made between direct speech, indirect speech, free indirect speech and the narrator's report of speech acts:

1  DS claims to represent faithfully (a), (b) and (c) above;
2  IS claims only to represent faithfully (a) and (b);
3  NRSA claims to represent faithfully only (a) above;
4  FIS claims to represent faithfully (a) and (b) but is indeterminate with respect to (c), and so becomes a semantic halfway house between DS and IS.

As Jones (1968) has pointed out, the categories of speech presentation are best thought of as being points on a cline rather than completely discrete entities. This allows for sentences which are difficult to assign definitely to one category or another. The FIS category is in a sense an example of this phenomenon as functionally it is to some extent indeterminate with respect to claim (c). Another example would be the difference between the following two (fabricated) sentences:

*Mary gave Fred some advice.*                                              [3.6]
*Mary gave Fred some advice on how to keep greenfly off his roses.*      [3.7]

In [3.6] we have prototypical NRSA, where all that is represented from the original utterance of Mary's is the speech act force. Example [3.7], on the other hand, also specifies the subject matter of the advice, and therefore gives at least some remnant of the propositional content. The functional definitions of the categories are thus prototypical, and examples can be found of utterances which edge towards the next category on the speech presentation cline, or are on the borderline between categories.

Although a formal distinction has been made for some time between direct and free direct speech, it is difficult to see a reasonable functional distinction between them in the data that I have examined. Instances [3.2] and [3.5], for example, are examples of free direct and direct speech respectively, but there appears to be no difference between the two utterances in terms of the scale of faithfulness, or indeed any other functional difference which could be associated with the difference in speech presentation category. It may be, then, that there is no functional reason for keeping the free direct/direct distinction. The presence or absence of quotation marks and reporting clauses may merely be motivated by competing concerns, like the wish for writing clarity on the one hand and the saving of space (especially important in headlines) on the other (for a discussion of this and related matters, see Simon-Vandenbergen (1981), Chapter 13). Certainly if a DS/FDS distinction is to be maintained, rather more work needs to be done in showing what the functional differences are. A formal difference for its own sake seems rather pointless. Perhaps the most reasonable approach would be to reserve the FDS category for what has so far been thought of as its most extreme form, namely for sentences where only the original speech is represented, with no accompanying reporting clause or quotation marks (i.e. item [3.11] in the list of possibilities below):

| | |
|---|---|
| *Mary said, 'Spray them with washing-up water!'* | [3.8] |
| *Mary said spray them with washing-up water!* | [3.9] |
| *'Spray them with washing-up water!'* | [3.10] |
| *Spray them with washing-up water!* | [3.11] |

Traditionally, [3.8] and [3.10] would be said to be DS, while [3.9] and [3.11] would be characterized as FDS. Leech and Short (1981) suggested a somewhat different typology, whereby [3.9]–[3.11] are all FDS. The motivation for this was that they all represent a movement away from the canonical DS form, in that one or both of the residual indications of the narrator, i.e. the reporting clause and the quotation marks, are removed. This account allowed for the clinal nature of speech presentation. It now seems to me, however, that the dividing line between one category and the others, if it is to be drawn at all, might be more sensibly made between [3.11] and the rest, as [3.11] is the only example where the reporter (or narrator) has no physical representation whatsoever in the sentence. The original speaker is thus 'on his own', as in example [3.2] in section 3.4.2 above. Whatever the eventual outcome, it is clear that more work needs to be done in this area.

## 3.6 Free indirect speech

In the novel, free indirect speech is usually used for distance and often as a vehicle for irony. So far I have found no such ironic uses in newspapers for possible FIS strings. Although I have no present plausible general explanation for this genre difference, it is obvious that a fully-fledged theory of speech presentation would need to supply one.

It is often difficult to know whether FIS actually occurs in situations where only grammatical markers are used:

> Rotherham District Hospital later said Mr Scargill was being detained overnight. He was not seriously hurt but was being treated for arm, leg and head injuries.
>
> (*Financial Times*, 19 June, p. 12)

The second sentence can be seen as:

1  FIS (as there is no introductory reporting clause);
2  IS (on the grounds that the reporting clause in the first sentence is 'understood' in the second); or
3  as a statement of fact (the equivalent of narrator report in the novel).

### 3.7 Projections concerning hypothetical speech acts

At first sight, the following headline constitutes another instance of unfaithful reporting:

> **Your job is safe, soccer boss told**                    [3.12]
>
> (*Daily Mail*, 11 June, p. 9)

The relevant portion of the text following the headline is:

> MANCHESTER UNITED manager Ron Atkinson will face the chairman of his club today, only 24 hours after revelations that he has left his wife for another woman ...
>
> But yesterday, as thousands of fans learned about what had been an 'open secret' in the soccer world United chairman, Martin Edwards was planning to tell 45-year-old Atkinson: 'Your job is safe.'
>
> Their meeting was planned before a Sunday newspaper told how Atkinson had left his blonde-haired wife, Margaret for his mistress, divorcee Maggie Harrison. Mr Edwards said he had known about the affair for months. 'Our discussions will be about football, not his personal life,' said Mr Edwards. 'He has two years of his contract to run and as far as I am concerned he will be seeing it through.

'He rang me on Saturday to warn me that his personal life was going to be exposed.

'As far as I am concerned, it doesn't affect his job and I want him to continue as manager of Manchester United.

'He has been a success so far and I want him to carry on the work he has started.'

(*Daily Mail*, 11 June, p. 9)

In effect speech presentation is being used in the headline here to report a future event. The evidence suggests that the headline does represent the gist of what Mr Edwards intended to say, but, as it stands, what the headline says is strictly false. How should we deal with examples like this? They are rarely, if ever, found in the novel, of course, as novels relate what has happened or is happening in a fictional world. Predictions as to what might happen are somewhat rare, particularly with respect to future speech events. It is for this reason, presumably, that scholars working on speech presentation in the novel have not taken such examples into account. Once we have noted this example, however, it is easy to construct plausible parallel instances. For example:

*Your father's very angry with you. If you go in there now*    [3.13]
*he will say, 'Get out and never darken my door again.'*

In cases like this, the faithfulness is to an imagined event in a hypothetical world which the speaker expects to be like the future state of the real world. Hence the instance in the text of the *Mail's* Atkinson story is not illegitimate because it is not strictly an example of speech report but something else, which we might call 'hypothetical report', and because the evidence suggests that something very like what is indicated will be said by Mr Edwards. The future reference is made clear in the body of the text by the modal 'will'. The headline, on the other hand is somewhat dubious in that the use of the past participle 'told' as a reporting verb leads the reader to assume unreasonably that the speech event has already taken place. The motive, as before, is presumably to be startling and eye-catching. If we relate this matter to the issue of faithfulness in the reporting of headlines raised in section 3.4.2, it would appear to give added credence to the idea that the canonical expectations related to the speech-presentation categories as seen in descriptions of the novel are suspended to some extent in newspaper headlines. It seems intuitively plausible to suggest that the faithfulness principle is less likely to be suspended in the text of articles than in headlines, and the *Mail*'s treatment of the Atkinson story appears to confirm this. But it is interesting to note that *The Sun*'s article on Mrs Thatcher's squint (see section 3.4.2) quotes her as saying something almost exactly the same as the headline, in spite of the fact that Mrs Thatcher was not interviewed at all. Work with a larger database obviously needs to be done in this area.

## 3.8 Speech summary

We have noted already that it is the change in discourse conditions that produces the changes in value that the speech presentation types have in newspapers as opposed to novels. In the novel the author makes up the fiction, and so there is no possible veracity difference between the DS or FDS string and what the character 'actually said'. Because the world described is the novelist's fiction, he must by definition be telling the truth about it. Speech report in novels, where it has been most extensively examined, would thus appear to be untypical of many speech-report situations, precisely because novels are fictions. In newspapers, as in most other text types where speech report occurs, the report of a speech event always has the possibility of being different from what occurred in the anterior speech event itself. One result of this is that what in the novel would normally be thought of as indirect speech, might in fact be speech summary. By speech summary I mean a string which reports in an abbreviated form some longer piece of discourse. Hence the following, fabricated, example:

*He told me that he did not like his sister*          [3.14]

could be an indirect report of an original string like 'I don't like Mary' or of a whole series of propositions which can be summarized by:

*Mary really gets on my nerves. She's always bossing me around*
*and whenever I say something she says I'm too young to have*          [3.15]
*an opinion. I'll be glad when she goes to university next month.*

In fact the speech summary interpretation of indirect speech strings is possible in the novel too. It is just that it is a relatively unlikely reading, as evidence of an abbreviated account will tend to be difficult to come by. Unless you have direct evidence of the original speech, the only real clue is how detailed the indirect string is or if there is specifically provided co-textual information (e.g.

locutions like 'the gist of what she said was that ...'). Many newspaper examples of IS are interpretable as speech summary, including the emboldened portions of the following quotations:

> A new portrait of Mrs Thatcher was unveiled yesterday. Then artist Rodrigo Moynihan immediately admitted **he may have to go back to the drawing board**. For the picture shows the Prime Minister with a distinct hint of a squint. Mrs Thatcher, who missed the unveiling at London's National Portrait Gallery, has already said **she is not too happy with the portrait**.
>
> (*Daily Star*, 21 June, p. 8)

> She also disclosed that **her husband had been unfaithful 10 years ago when he was at Oxford United**.
>
> (*Daily Express*, 11 June, p. 6)

It is mainly the brevity of expression and flatness of tone related to what are likely to have been emotionally-charged anterior speech events that lead us to posit a possible speech-summary interpretation. It seems to me that even DS and FDS strings in newspaper headlines are interpretable as speech summary – see, for instance, examples [3.2] and [3.3] from section 3.4.2, which are reproduced for convenience below:

**UGH! GET RID OF MY SQUINT**                          [3.2]
**You've given me a squint, said Maggie**               [3.3]

In either of these cases the reported speech can be seen as an eye-catching version of a possible macro-proposition representing a group of sentences in the anterior utterance to which the headline alludes. Indeed, given the fact that Mrs Thatcher appears never to have used the relevant sentences in these headlines, the speech summary interpretation looks the most likely. It may well be the case, then, that speech summary is possible in all of the speech presentation categories.[3] If this is indeed so, then 'speech summary' is not really a category on the speech-presentation continuum, but, rather, cuts across it. One could argue, however, that the directness markers in examples like [3.2] and [3.3] effectively rule out a speech-summary interpretation. If this is the case, then a 'speech summary' category could be placed on the cline next to NRSA (i.e. rightmost in Figure 3.1 in section 3.9 below). My intuitions favour the possibility of a speech-summary interpretation for examples like [3.2] and [3.3], if only because it best suits the facts of the case in the story about Mrs Thatcher. But the intuitions of others may well differ, and careful informant testing or clearer attested examples than those in my data will be needed to decide the issue.

### 3.9 Concluding remarks – towards a general account of speech presentation

Choice of speech-presentation category is one way in which a reader's viewpoint can be controlled in a text. But point of view can, of course, be controlled in other ways than by the manipulation of the choice of speech-presentation categories, and in a full account a particular speech-presentation choice would need to be interpreted in the context of other choices and patterns related to viewpoint (on newspapers and matters related to point of view see Trew (1979) and Hodge (1979)). One obvious example is the choice of speech act verbs:

**'Police hit me on the head'** claims Scargill                        [3.5]
**'He fell, we were nowhere near him'** say the police
                     (*Daily Mirror*, 19 June, p. 1)

**I WAS HIT says Scargill**                                            [3.16
**NO HE FELL say police**
                     (*Daily Mail*, 19 June, p. 1)

In this pair of examples it would appear that the *Mirror* implies less credence in Mr Scargill's account of what occurred than the police. The *Mail*, on the other hand, treats the two accounts equally in its headline. Interestingly, *The Morning Star*, in the text of its article, uses the verbs 'claim' and 'say' the opposite way round from the *Mirror*:

'They just rushed in. I didn't know what was happening. I was semi-conscious,' said Mr Scargill ... Assistant Chief Constable Tony Clement said he saw what happened to Mr Scargill – and claimed he had fallen and hit his head on a sleeper. 'I was there. I called the ambulance for him.'
                     (*The Morning Star*, 19 June, p. 1)

The opposing patterns in the use of the two speech-act verbs coincide with the opposing sympathies of the two newspapers with respect to the individuals involved. The *Mirror*, as a pro-Labour Party paper, had an interest in not supporting Mr Scargill, as he was perceived as causing a split within the party. *The Morning Star*, Britain's only Communist newspaper, had an obvious interest in supporting the left-winger.

Another way in which a writer's view towards different individuals might be represented is through the contrasting use of speech presentation categories. In the above example, for instance, some of the police officer's words are reported through indirect speech, and one might therefore want to conclude that the writer is distancing the reader from the police officer's words but not those of Mr Scargill. And such an analysis would probably be permissible if speech-presentation categories were differentially allocated in this way on a systematic basis. But in the above example the matter is by no means that simple. In the portion already presented the police officer is quoted partly directly and partly indirectly. And Mr Scargill's words immediately prior to the portion quoted above are in IS and possible FIS (or alternatively narrative report):

> Mr Scargill said he had been hit on the head with a riot shield.
> He was taken to hospital in an ambulance with another picket.
> *(The Morning Star*, 19 June, p. 1)

In an unpublished working paper, 'Speech reportage and the comment/report distinction in media discourse', Norman Fairclough (1982) points to variation in the use of speech-act-report verbs of the sort I have discussed above. He also makes the important point that the reporting of speech is never mere reproduction, but a representation, even in the case of DS or FDS, because the writer can choose 'what parts of the speech reported to include, in what order, and within what discoursal matrix'. In this paper, Fairclough also makes some interesting suggestions about choices along the speech presentation cline which, although I disagree with them in detail, I find interesting because they help point the way to areas of useful future research.

Fairclough takes the account of speech presentation in Leech and Short (1981) as the basis for his work. Leech and Short suggest that the categories along the speech-presentation cline in the novel

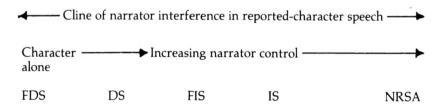

Figure   3.1

can be seen as involving a 'mix' of the contributions of narrator and character, the proportions of which change as you move from one end of the cline to another. We might represent this as in Figure 3.1.

Fairclough replaces this cline of interference with what he calls a 'scale of mediation'. He goes on to suggest in the analysis of an article from *The Guardian* that the writer uses DS in order to make it clear that the words are those of the original speaker, either because accuracy is important or because 'the reporter does not wish to be seen as endorsing the use of that word or expression in that context'. IS is used, on the other hand, if the reporter 'is reproducing words used which (s)he does not feel it necessary to distance or the reporter is rewording what is said'. IS thus appears to indicate agreement on the part of the reporter with what is said.

Fairclough's scale of mediation is rather similar to my own cline of interference, but is different with respect to the claims concerning whether the reporter can be interpreted as endorsing the views of the original speaker or not, depending on what presentation category he or she chooses. This kind of account obviously becomes more plausible when non-fictional data is being interpreted. Although I suspect that what Fairclough suggests may sometimes be the case (his own data is reasonably convincing), I do not think that the situation can be quite as straightforward as he suggests. In the following example, also from *The Guardian* (19 June, p.1), the reporter uses the same mode of speech presentation for speakers with diametrically opposed views:

> Mr Scargill said he believed he was struck by a police shield from behind. The assistant chief constable of South Yorkshire, Mr Tony Clement, said he was standing only a few yards from the miners' president and saw him fall on a railway banking.

The reporter cannot, presumably, believe both accounts. He may be trying to be even-handed in an issue that he cannot decide, or there may be some other explanation. Whatever the case, this example indicates that a simple scale of mediation will not account adequately for the facts. Such an account would also seem to suggest that the choice of a midway category like FIS would imply a half-and-half attitude on the part of the reporter with respect to his endorsement of the reported speech. This looks counter-intuitive, however.

In *The Morning Star* instance quoted earlier in this section, it is not at all clear that the writer is wanting to endorse what is reported when he or she uses IS, but is trying to effect distancing or needing accuracy when DS is used. Rather, it appears that the speech quoted in the direct form is meant to be perceived as highlighted in some way. The IS material in Mr Scargill's speech has already been alluded to in less specific form in both the headline and the main body of the text (**'Scargill injured in worst clashes yet**; MINERS' LEADER Arthur Scargill was injured yesterday . . .'). Hence the IS material gives specific detail to what is an already-assumed piece of information. The direct speech, on the other hand is used when the behaviour of the police is being alluded to by Mr Scargill. Here, then, we have the speech presentation categories being used on some scale of *salience*. Fairclough suggests in his paper that DS, IS and NRSA 'are ordered in terms of the relative degree of importance they impart to parts of reported speech activity, DS implying the greatest importance, NRSA the least'. This appears to be a common-sense characterization of some of his data and also the extract discussed immediately above. But again, on reflection, the situation must be more complex than Fairclough suggests. If there is a scale of mediation and a scale of importance along the same axis, then they would appear, at least in part, to work against one another, as DS will potentially have, from the writer's point of view, the values 'most important' and 'most disagreed with'. If this is to be the case, a reasoned account of how the scales interact in general and how readings are arrived at in particular cases needs to be established. Another possible factor to be taken into account is that the local effect of the occurrence of a particular category may in part be determined by what category has been used immediately before in the text. *The Morning Star* extract quoted above looks to be a fruitful source for such an enquiry as the DS/IS allocation strategy used for the words of Mr Scargill would appear to be different than that used to report what Mr Clement said; in the latter's case what looks like the most important statement, namely his claim that Mr Scargill had merely fallen over, is reported in IS, whereas what appears to be more subsidiary information is reported in DS.

No detailed general theory can be supplied in this paper to the complex issue of how speech-presentation-category allocation strategies are to be interpreted by readers, but it should be clear that examination of newspaper reportage as opposed to fictional data has at least helped to focus our attention on areas of the description which need to be altered slightly in order to provide a more general account. It has also showed that, on the whole, the descriptive apparatus taken from Leech and Short (1981) copes well with the journalistic data. In addition, it has helped to establish one of the areas on which workers in this field will need to concentrate more firmly in the future; namely, how we are to explain the fact that at different locations in the same short text the choice of the same speech presentation category can have different interpretive values and effects. But perhaps the most general conclusion to be drawn from this attempt to apply techniques of speech-presentation analysis developed for the novel to newspaper data is that in order for us to have a properly general and robust theory of speech presentation, we need to examine a considerably wider range of text types and discoursal conditions than has so far been the case.

# NOTES

1  Previous versions of this chapter have been given at the Association Internationale de Linguistique Appliquée (AILA) conference in Brussels, 1984, the Poetics and Linguistics Association conference in Birmingham, 1985, and at seminars in Birmingham and Amsterdam. I would like to thank Malcolm Coulthard, Norman Fairclough, Malcolm Mackenzie, Peter Verdonk, Stef Slembrouck and Willie Van Peer for helpful criticisms. Needless to say, the most interesting parts of this paper derive from their comments and the blemishes are all mine.
   A discussion of an earlier version of this paper can be found in Slembrouck (1986).
2  It should be noted that in the examples which occur in this paper I have emboldened and capitalized headlines (and sometimes running text) where appropriate in order to give a more distinct flavour of the original. It is not, however, possible to represent the differences in the size of lettering in the original texts (which varies in height from 0.5 cm to 4.5 cm). The term 'headline' also needs some explanation. I use it here to mean headlines at the head of any story, no matter where the story concerned occurs in a newspaper, and no matter what size and kind of type. I cannot use it merely to refer to front-page headlines, for example, because the various newspapers do not treat equally the stories I am comparing in terms of the page allocated to them, space given to them and so on.
3  Fairclough (1982) points out that in the texts he examines the category of NRSA reports not so much a speech act as a 'speech event' or an 'activity type'.

# BIBLIOGRAPHY

Brumfit, C. J. (ed.) (1983), *Teaching Literature Overseas: Language-Based Approaches*, ELT Documents 115, The British Council and Pergamon Press.

Brumfit, C. J. and Carter, R. (eds) (1986), *Literature and Language Teaching*, Oxford, Oxford University Press.

Carter, R. (ed.) (1982), *Language and Literature*, London, Allen & Unwin.

Cole, P. and Morgan, J. L. (eds) (1975), *Syntax and Semantics, 3: Speech Acts*, London/New York, Academic Press.

D'Haen, T. (ed.) (1986), *Linguistics and the Study of Literature*, Amsterdam, Rodopi Press.

Fairclough, N. (1982), 'Speech reportage and the comment/report distinction in media discourse', unpublished working paper, University of Lancaster.

Fowler, R., Hodge, B., Kress, G. and Trew, T. (1979), *Language and Control*, London, Routledge & Kegan Paul.

Grice, P. (1975), 'Logic and Conversation', in Cole, P. and Morgan, J. L. (1975), pp. 41–58.

Hodge, R. (1979), 'Newspapers and communities', in Fowler *et al.* (1979), pp. 157–74.

Jones, C. (1968), 'Varieties of speech presentation in Conrad's *The Secret Agent*', *Lingua*, vol. 20, no. 2, pp. 162–76.

Leech, G. N. and Short, M. H. (1981), *Style in Fiction*, London, Longman.

McHale, B. (1978), 'Free indirect discourse: a survey of recent accounts', *Poetics and Theory of Literature*, vol. 3, no. 2, pp. 249–88.

Short, M. H. (1983), 'Stylistics and the teaching of literature: with an example from Joyce's *Portrait of the Artist as a Young Man*', in Brumfit (1983), pp. 67–84; reprinted in Carter (1982), pp. 179–94.

Short, M. H. (1986), 'Literature and language teaching and the nature of language', in D'Haen (1986), pp. 152–186.

Short, M. H. and Candlin, C. N. (1986), 'Teaching study skills for English literature', in Brumfit and Carter (1986), pp. 89–109.

Simon-Vandenbergen, A. M. (1981), *The Grammar of Headlines in The Times*, Brussels, Koninklijke Academie voor Wetenschappen, Letteren en Schone Kunsten van België.

Simon-Vandenbergen, A. M. (ed.) (1986), *Aspects of Style in British Newspapers*, Ghent, Studia Germanica Gandensia 9.

Slembrouck, S. (1986), 'Towards a description of speech presentation and speech reportage in newspaper language', in Simon-Vandenbergen (1986), pp. 44–115.

Trew, T. (1979), '"What the papers say": linguistic variation and ideological difference', in Fowler, R., Hodge, B., Kress, G., and Trew, T. *et al.* (1979), pp. 117–56.

Widdowson, H. G. (1975), *Stylistics and the Teaching of Literature*, London, Longman.

# 4

# Newspaper style and Nazi propaganda

the 'Weekly Mirror' in the German Newspaper
in the Netherlands[1]

## Christoph Sauer

*Newspaper texts not only reveal the categories of speech presentation that one encounters in literary texts. As the following analysis by Christoph Sauer shows, they may also display a number of other stylistic traits. The institutional nature of these texts, something that was already touched upon in the previous chapter by Michael Short, is taken one step further here. Newspapers may also, similarly to landscape descriptions or ballads, present themselves as 'neutral'. In the case selected for analysis by Christoph Sauer, a weekly column in a German Nazi newspaper published in the occupied Netherlands during the Second World War, such neutrality is - contrary perhaps to expectations - a feature of the text's surface. A close investigation, moreover, reveals that this is achieved at the level of presentation through a variety of stylistic means.*

*To study such mechanisms of propaganda, however, it is not sufficient, as Sauer demonstrates, to concentrate on devices of style only. Instead one has to take into account issues of power and of policy. What such passages, based on the Nazi ideology, reveal is the power of texts to provide models of social experience that a reader may be lured into. The totalitarian policy of Nazification is an extreme case, in which social meanings may be prone to a constant reconditioning following the flow of party politics. This is achieved not exclusively through terror, though; language provides means of persuasion and coercion too. In particular, the modelling of experience and the modification of meaning, essential prerequisites for cooperation with the totalitarian plans of Nazi governors, are essential strategies in this respect, depending on the force with which the manipulation of language may be brought home. As Sauer is able to demonstrate, this is done with considerable stylistic sophistication. The analysis thus reveals fundamental issues in the sociohistoric study of political language and its style.*

## 4.1 Prefatory note

In this chapter I would like to draw attention to a complication concerning the concept of style which arises when, rather than basing one's analysis on individual stylistic principles, one views texts as stylistic realizations of verbal *actions*, which, in turn, one relates to the actual historical situation in which the texts originate.

## 4.2 Nazi-style and German language

There exist in the English-speaking world – and not only there – various stereotypes of the mentality of the 'Germans',[2] stereotypes eagerly linked to observations on the German language. Thus for many opponents of German fascism it was a small step to attribute to the German language a complicity in the birth and spread of National Socialism, and indeed to describe it as a causal factor. This foreshortened kind of argument provides an easily grasped 'explanation' for the horrific perversion of political thought and action in the Third Reich. Steiner's voice was especially shrill: 'The German language was not innocent of the horrors of Nazism. It is not merely that a Hitler, a Goebbels, and a Himmler happened to speak German. Nazism found in the language precisely what it needed to give voice to its savagery' (Steiner, 1984, p. 210). If the matter were such as Steiner's grandiose simplification proposes, it would also permit of an exculpation of the German mass approval and acceptance of Nazism; after all, no-one can escape his mother tongue. Steiner himself has recognized this danger, too, and, in consequence, condemned time and again the oblivion that took place in the German countries after the war. The present considerations may help to undermine this oblivion, too.

Undoubtedly Nazism cultivated a very specific manner of handling the tradition of the German language of the nineteenth century, especially that style which, as the so-called academic style, pervaded many popular works and speeches. Here, National Socialist leaders, however wrongly they further developed their techniques of quotation, found points of contact.[3] The analysis of the specific stylistic techniques of Nazi propaganda opens up a perspective which allows for an elucidation of the interrelations of utterance and action in politics that incorporates *sociohistorical* relations. Preliminary studies have long existed, for instance Burke's (1939–40), and have recently been discussed from the vantage point afforded by the recognition that the politics of National Socialism cannot be understood without realizing that it appropriated the rhetoric of art (Sontag, 1981). In presenting here several detailed stylistic examinations, I am indebted to these suggestions.

The level of style is not and was not merely a metaphorical battlefield. I should like to recall the words of Brecht (1967; p. 231):

'Wer in unserer Zeit statt Volk Bevölkerung und statt Boden Landbesitz sagt, unterstützt schon viele Lügen nicht.'[4]

It is stylistic practice which renders possible the linguistic *mise-en-scène* of politics and which it is necessary to understand and to change.

## 4.3 Towards a definition of 'style'

Present-day discussions of style do seem to display (and indeed, in a sense, thus initiate) a growing tendency towards what might be described as an *integration* of different concepts of style; cf. Spillner (1974; 1984), Sandig (1978; 1983), van Peer and Renkema (1984). In particular there seems to be a consensus of opinion that it is especially fruitful to couple general theoretical investigations to concrete stylistic analyses. The plethora of examinations of individual styles is partly superseded now by discussions of the social purposes of texts and their styles. This is the view I should like to move towards in the present study. The fact that the texts I shall analyse were written and printed in a situation characterized by extreme confusion (occupation, state of war, publication within a foreign context) makes the need for an expanded arsenal of instruments for stylistic analysis all the more urgent.

'Style' is the *totality* of textual means realized in any communicative connection, be it conversation or the process of reading or of writing. There is, then, never *one* voice, *one* author alone to be heard speaking in a text; instead, the 'author-agency' is divided into parts. An author employs not one but several 'languages'; political language, ordinary everyday language, poetic language, the language of the past (historical language), etc. An author plays many 'parts' at once; he is a party member, a scientist, a journalist, a private individual, a believer, a participant, etc. In writing a text, the author interweaves several strands of actions; he informs, he alludes to something, he intends to amuse, he threatens, he displays his knowledge, he supplies reasons, etc.

Thus heterogeneity appears in what I wish to term the *multidimensionality* of a text. In terms of style – in terms, that is to say, of the textual means of realization – this multidimensionality entails that in the process of reception this or that element is foregrounded, while the other elements remain present in the background; moreover, it is not inconceivable to have two or more foregrounds.[5] What one refers to in attributing a text to *one* particular style is what one believes to be in the foreground; in other words, what is promoted to the foreground by specific stylistic operations.

The work of the author, his production of the text, remains one-sided and fragmentary until, in the process of reading, the text is animated and completed by the reader. Only in the reader is the communicative connection of the text fully realized. Reception is not at all merely the filling in of spaces left open in the text; rather, it is a comprehensive re-creation, in which the reader, too, possesses a stylistic knowledge which, as the case may be, facilitates, mechanizes or impedes the process of reception. Thus the reader not only needs a 'schema knowledge' of actions (cf. Ehlich and Rehbein, 1977); his knowledge pertains also to whatever textual means of realization are employed. With this knowledge and his experience he is able to reconstruct the text stylistically. The style of the text, then, influences the process of reconstruction. One cannot, of course, expect the whole complexity of the text to be actuated in the process of reading. Differences, misunderstandings, discontinuities and unexploited potential will surely remain.

## 4.4 Language policy, ideology and propaganda

It follows from the above deliberations that stylistic analysis begins with the development of a *search strategy* to be applied to actual texts. Guided by a theory, one needs to select areas upon which analysis can be brought to bear. An initial restriction relates to the *text type*, which provides a 'framework' within which textual processes take place. Stylistic analysis of a poem, for instance, will not be the same as that of a news report, simply because specific textual types entail specific possibilities of content or theme and form. One particularly obvious difference lies in the fact that the analysis is largely restricted to those actions that are characteristic for each type, and that it describes these on the basis of communicative schemata whose operations actually constitute the text.

The question that poses itself next concerns the provenance of textual devices – their social standing. Linguistic forms and formulations do not arise naturally. We are thus called upon to document *sociohistorically* the assumed complexity of the text. This should be possible by employing two different theoretical concepts: a theory of *language policy*, which describes the linguistic *mise-en-scène* of politics and, in doing so, brings to the fore the problem of power; and a theory of *ideology*, which describes power relations as textual acts, focusing on the re-orientation of existing modes of discourse.

Central to the term 'language policy', as it is used here, is the concept of *social experience*. For instance, the expression 'Germany, awake!' can enter my consciousness as 'vulgar saying' and/or as 'summons to enter the party' and/or as 'exhortation' (with Christian-Adventist overtones). Social experience, then, is appropriated in various ways. Analytically, it is possible to make a distinction between the *assimilation* of experiences undergone and their *production*. In short, this concept of language policy (cf. Januschek and Maas, 1981) does not mean that a previously unintelligible 'code' or 'jargon' becomes intelligible; it means that such utterances are understood by absorbing the (modes of) assimilation of social experience which they comprise.

A further example: after the general strike in the occupied Netherlands in February 1941 (following a raid on Dutch Jews in Amsterdam) had been violently quelled by the German occupying forces, the chief Nazi 'Reichskommissar', Seyss-Inquart, proclaimed in a grand speech of justification:

> **I declare that my pledge 'We have no wish to repress Dutch nationhood nor to impose upon it our own beliefs' remains valid now as ever; but only for the Dutch nation. We do not consider the Jews to be part of the Dutch nation. For National Socialism and for the National Socialist Reich, Jews are the enemy**. (12 March 1941; cf. Sauer, 1984)

This excerpt displaces prior experience and foists upon the Dutch new distinctions which they can no longer evade. What is experienced is the situation of occupation, and the racist interference in the assimilation of this experience affects the status of Dutchmen with regard to one another and with regard to the occupier. They cannot simply pretend that the occupier is not there; and they cannot *not* think anti-Semitically. Stylistic analysis of such texts, then, must be prepared to consider a possible language policy and its constituents as a potential for stylistic procedures, forming an additional determinant of textual complexity.

The quotation from Seyss-Inquart is not only a threat addressed to Dutch Jews; it also presents a mode of utterance conventionally judged to be ideological. I wish to conceive of ideology not as a static level of erroneous consciousness, but as consisting of dynamic processes of *actual socialization*. In this view, Nazi ideology is not simply 'wrong' or 'incoherent', and its impact is not just the result of terror, although state terror did indeed affect greatly the docility of the people. The ideology manifests itself in the *manner* in which the Nazis took up existing modes of discourse and political ideas and standardized them, something that has been analysed in detail by Faye (1972). The success of the Nazis consisted of their modification of the determinants of fields of social practice, together with the rewards they held in store for the kind of social behaviour they desired; rewards which defined the status of individuals according to new criteria, namely their proximity to the power of state. It is the ideology which allows the various forms of discourse bearing on different fields of social practice to be connected with each other. To the individual, this was manifest in the intrusion of the ideological in all domains of life. It functioned like a 'text' which, to be sure, had to be 'read' again and again, and which was thus also reconstructed anew in each case. This process adds public violence to the private dimension of a transformation of experience.

Whenever the distribution of an ideology becomes institutionalized, it manifests itself as *propaganda*. The instructions raining down upon editors, journalists and other writers, and the later judgment by the propaganda bureaucracy, encircle the actual process of writing. With regard to the Nazi system of propaganda,[6] this means that, apart from the reference to the assumed or actual reader, there is inscribed in the text a systematic reference to the controlling and directing office of propaganda. In the final resort, the Ministry of Propaganda acts as co-author, and in any case as co-reader. This pluralization of the author (and reader) of a text also affects its style. 'Directives' explicitly concern not only content, but style as well. The texts thus conceived are the result of a balancing-act, which, from the institutional point of view, must satisfy simultaneously these two conditions; the texts must conceal their being regulated by the Ministry, but at the same time obey those regulations. In this way, there emerges a basic pattern for the stylistic analysis of Nazi newspaper texts.

## 4.5  The German newspaper in the Netherlands

The *German Newspaper in the Netherlands* (*Deutsche Zeitung in den Niederlanden*, henceforward *DZN*) was one of twenty-seven (!) German-language occupation newspapers in the various occupied countries: in Belgium, for example, there was the *Brüsseler Zeitung*; in France the *Pariser Zeitung*; in Norway the *Deutsche Zeitung in Norwegen*, which, owing to its financial success, became the model for the *DZN* (cf. Hirschfeld, 1983; Sauer, 1983). The *DZN* had a circulation of approximately 55,000 copies a day, comparable to that of the quality papers in the Netherlands. Half of the copies went to the German troops, the remainder to occupiers' families, to Germans (others than soldiers) in the Netherlands, to the Reich and to newsstands. (On the history of the occupied Netherlands, see Warmbrunn (1963), Hirschfeld (1981)).

The *DZN* occupies, to a certain extent, an 'in-between' position: it is the mouthpiece of the occupier in Holland, it belongs to the Nazi press in general, it addresses German troops in the Netherlands, German and Dutch readers in the Reich, and especially the Dutch people, considered by the Germans to be able to read German. From this follows a *multiple address*, manifesting itself not only in different newspaper articles within the *DZN*, but also in one single press item. Moreover, taking into account their being controlled by propaganda agencies in The Hague ('Presseabteilung'), Berlin (the Ministry of Goebbels and other offices), and Munich (National-Sozialistische Deutsche Arbeiter-Partei (the Nazi Party, NSDAP)), one is able to form an idea of the specific complexity these texts will display. Their analysis builds on extensive preliminary studies of the same material from *DZN* (see especially Sauer (1983, 1985)).

The feature 'Weekly Mirror' ('Spiegel der Woche'), to which we shall further limit ourselves here, is a brief weekly commentary, usually treating three topics which are visually separated one from the other. It addresses the Dutch directly, not only as a people, but also as particular groups of Dutchmen. Hence a relationship of writer and reader is established: *one* German (who also signs his name under each article) addresses *one* or *several* Dutchmen. This form of directness, which is the authentic mark of this column and distinguishes it from all other text types to be found in the *DZN*, delineates more boldly the general contours of the state of occupation. Indeed it is for this very reason that it has been selected here.

The 'Weekly Mirror' appeared weekly in the Sunday edition from 17 August 1941 till 11 June 1944, while the first and last numbers of the *DZN* appeared in June 1940 and May 1945 respectively. The emergence of the new feature is surely connected with a change in Nazi policy. In this respect, the 'Weekly Mirror' marks this change; its first appearance coincides with the decision, after a phase of comparatively gentle methods, to drive forward the Nazification of the Netherlands without further consideration. It seems plausible that, with this new text type, the *DZN* wanted to create for itself an instrument which would enable it to react, more explicitly, or language-politically, to this change.

The feature is set off from other newspaper commentaries, such as the leading article, by appearing on the (fourth) 'page from the Netherlands', a blend of regional and local news (and sometimes also advertisements) relating directly to the Netherlands. The framework thus delimiting the 'Weekly Mirror' is not 'grand politics'; instead, events in the Netherlands are presented as a *'couleur locale'* of the 'New Europe' of the National Socialists. Unobtrusive and indeed hidden away though this rubric may be, it is the only *regularly* recurring feature in the *DZN*, allowing us to scrutinize more closely the events considered worth commenting upon by the occupying forces in the Netherlands.

Formally, the 'Weekly Mirror' conforms to the usual distinction in the press between report (informing) and opinion (commenting), a distinction which it also signals by external features (enframing, different type, etc.). Its further characteristics are as follows.

1 The text arises from an *occasion* which is situated in the reality of occupation of the Netherlands, and which is quite recent (often less than a week ago).
2 The occasion is 'loosely' connected with the main purpose of the text, the *assessment* of specific conditions in the occupied Netherlands (e.g. Nazification or not).

3   What is being assessed are *specific actions* pertaining to virtually all spheres of society in the occupied Netherlands, with the exception of 'grand politics'. The writer divides the matter into different segments of action and arranges them in a sequence; the segments of action thereby appear *reformulated*.

4   The segments of actions are subjected to an *evaluation* or *interpretation* which the writer executes in the reader's place.

5   The evaluation or interpretation takes the form of a perpetual *comparison* of the Netherlands with the Reich, in which the former is always made to appear 'imperfect'; on the other hand an (implicit) registration of the 'Germanization' of the Netherlands is involved.

6   An important procedure is that of *emphasizing*, stressing some elements of information, repressing others and neglecting yet others again.

7   The writer, in having recourse to the general *occupier discourse* and partly actualizing it, applies criteria of comparison (between Germany and the Netherlands) and 'experiences'. This appears as a complex address to readers (multiple address) which also incorporates forms of reinsurance (techniques of legitimation with regard to the institutions of Nazi propaganda).

8   Most of these texts are embedded in wider-ranging *strategies of writing*; communicative schemata of justification, of threat, of confirmation, of appeasement, of wooing, etc., punctuated by journalistic 'ideas' which appear as the writer's 'idiosyncrasies' – allusions, imagery, euphemisms, metaphors, etc.

9   An often-employed subsidiary procedure consists of using *signals of authenticity*; quotations in Dutch, paraphrases, anecdotes experienced at first hand, and other Dutch sources.

10  The reader is partly disconnected from the actuality of the day; he is offered an opportunity to distance himself from it, mainly by means of his memory and especially by the presentation of *what is worth remembering* in general.

As appears from these characteristics, the weekly feature in the *DZN* is considerably more than a commentary by an outside observer. Instead, it is a highly sophisticated device aimed at the political reshaping of Dutch society, in which the confrontation of the two national languages is used to intervene in people's daily experiences. The contact between both languages is therefore not accidental, but politically engineered.

The Dutch case is that the Nazis deliberately blended both languages. Under the common denominator of 'Germanization' they repressed the Dutch language, promoted the instruction of German as a foreign language in continuation of a certain Dutch school tradition, and minimalized, by whatever means they could, the difference between the Dutch and Low German languages. Under the common denominator of 'Nazification' they achieved a competition and disturbance of perception, presented the occupation as the birth of the 'New Order' and the 'New Europe', and transformed established social structures, e.g. the social experience of language forms and meanings. Thus the *DZN*, prior to any further determination of content, is, owing to its use of the German language, fundamentally an *aggressive speech act*, articulating the way in which German domination was taken for granted.

The 'Weekly Mirror' is always written in the form of a *personal* commentary. This permits the writer, who is usually one of the editors of the *DZN*, each time to unfold his German, National Socialist and language-political fantasies. This personal factor enlarges the spectrum of stylistic strategies to be found in the 'Weekly Mirror'. Irritation, irony, attitudes of superiority are added to the inventory of Nazi language policy. Compared to what was otherwise common practice in the *DZN*, the impatience of the occupier in the face of the reserve and rejection by the Dutch, is transformed in the 'Weekly Mirror' into a stimulus of extraordinary stylistic personal 'ideas'. Let us now look in detail at one of these weekly commentaries.

## 4.6 The 'Weekly Mirror' of 7 December 1941

1  *Überall in den Niederlanden fanden in diesen Tagen die Untersuchungen statt für die Aufnahme in den Niederländischen Arbeitsdienst, der am Anfang des kommenden Jahres die zweite Belegschaft auf die Lager in den Niederlanden verteilen wird.*
    All over the Netherlands these days the examinations have been taking place for entering the Dutch Labour Service, which at the beginning of next year will distribute the second shift over the camps in the Netherlands.

2  *Es versteht sich von selbst, dass aus diesem Anlass in den niederländischen Zeitungen mehr über diese Einrichtung gesagt wird.*

Evidently, this has given rise to further comments in the Dutch newspapers.

3   *Doch kann man feststellen, dass die Ergebnisse der ersten Gemeinschaft bestimmt nicht schlecht gewesen sind.*
   Yet one may observe that the results of the first shift have certainly not been bad.

4   *Eine ärztliche Untersuchung ergab nämlich nicht nur einen allgemeinen günstigen Stand, sondern auch Verbesserungen sowohl im Körperbau wie auch im Gewicht.*
   A medical examination revealed not only a generally favourable condition, but also improvements in build as well as in weight.

5   *Wie sich die geistige Schulung auswirken wird, steht heute noch nicht fest, sie kann indessen nicht anders sein, als in allen anderen Ländern auch, die den Arbeitsdienst zu einer Schule der Nation machten.*
   How the effects of the spiritual education will work out is not yet certain, but, for all that, they cannot be any other than as in all other countries that have made the Labour Service a school of the nation.

6   *Da der Arbeitsdienst stärker, als es das Heer kann, die Persönlichkeit berücksichtigt, ist es klar, dass auch die Ergebnisse je nach der einzelnen Persönlichkeit stärker oder schwächer ausfallen.*
   Since the Labour Service takes personality into account in a greater measure than the army is able to, it is obvious that the results will also be stronger or weaker, according to the individual personality.

7   *Eines aber haben alle gelernt, die Handarbeit als eine Arbeit anzusehen, die die Achtung eines jeden Niederländers verdient.*
   But one thing that all have learnt is to deem manual labour a labour worthy of the respect of every Dutchman.

8   *Es taucht wohl hier und da wieder das Problem auf, Arbeitsdienstpflicht ja oder nein.*
   Here and there the problem does indeed emerge as to whether Labour Service should be obligatory or not.

9   *Zu leicht wird dann wohl auch das Wort Pflicht umgewandelt in Zwang.*
   All too easily on these occasions the word obligation is transformed into coercion.

10   *Wer einmal durch den Arbeitsdienst gegangen ist, wird bestätigen, dass der Staat nicht mehr auf diese Erziehung verzichten kann.*
   Anyone having gone through the Labour Service will confirm that the State can no longer dispense with this education.

11  *Wer da aber von einem Zwang redet, missdeutet den Sinn solcher*
    *Einrichtung.*
    He, however, who speaks of coercion in this respect
    misinterprets the purpose of such an organization.

12  *Zugleich gibt er ihr einen Nimbus, der beim Arbeitsdienst vollkommen*
    *unangebracht ist.*
    At the same time, he invests it with an aura which is
    utterly inappropriate to the Labour Service.

13  *Denn trotz aller praktischen Werte, die vom Arbeitsdienst geleistet*
    *werden, spielt die ideelle Erziehung doch immer die erste Rolle.*
    For, despite all the practical results effected by the Labour
    Service, it is the spiritual education that always plays the
    most important role.

14  *Gerade solchen Geist aber braucht der zukünftige Staat.*
    It is just such a spirit that the future State indeed requires.

15  *Hier wächst in einer jungen noch empfindungsreichen Jugend die*
    *Kameradschaft, die einmal das tägliche Leben tragen muss.*
    Here there grows in youth, young and sensitive, the
    comradeship which one day will have to support daily life.

16  *Wirklicher Sozialismus ist diese Kameradschaft eines Volkes überall im*
    *Leben.*
    True socialism is this comradeship among the people
    everywhere in life.

Apart from the last sentence (16), which seems somewhat
surprisingly appended, the text turns out to be easy to understand.
It consists of two sections, the relationship between the two not
being quite clear: while the second section (8–15) defends the
'Labour Service' against critics, the first section (1–7) is concerned
only with a portrayal of the current situation, namely that the first
year's team has completed this 'Labour Service' (3–4) and that the
second year's team has just been examined (1). The occasion for
writing is threefold: the medical examination taking place (1); news
reports in the Dutch press (2); and concluding examinations of the
first year's team (3–4). As early as sentence 3 there is an indication
that this Labour Service is controversial, a fact signalled by the
words 'yet' and 'certainly'. Hence a *portrayal* is immediately
transformed into a *justification*, in the course of which the writer
emphasizes two elements, i.e. the health of those who have already
completed the Labour Service (4) and the respect for manual labour
(7). This argument develops into a more general discussion,
comparing the Labour Service with other countries (5) and the

army (6). It is obvious that the text tries to soften the impact of what was special and new about the Labour Service to the Dutch. This functions as an *appeasement* by means of a generalizing comparison. The addressees of this part of the text, then, are Dutch critics of the Labour Service, including perhaps – this is not altogether clear – parts of the Dutch press. With regard to these critics the text makes a tactical reservation by leaving open further possible effects of the Labour Service: 'spiritual education' (5); or presenting these effects as a problem of the 'individual personality' (6). The final sentence (7) of the first section, which contains a preliminary conclusion, harbours a paraphrase quotation from the ordinance instituting the Labour Service on 27 May 1941. The first paragraph of this ordinance reads:

> **The Dutch Labour Service is a service of honour rendered unto the Dutch people. Its purpose is to teach Dutch youth, in the spirit of the true community of a people, an ethical conception of work, and especially a proper respect for manual labour.** (*DZN*, 27 May 1941)

Within the framework of the ordinance, it is 'youth' that is to be taught respect for manual labour. However, in the newspaper text the target has been enlarged; it now includes '*every* Dutchman' (7). Furthermore, if, in spite of the Labour Service being voluntary, a satisfactory 'generally favourable condition' (4) is observed and underlined by medical authority, the paraphrase quotation functions as a *confirmation* of the text of the original ordinance. Hence the text of the original ordinance proved to be a self-fulfilling prophecy. Thereby the journalist also *flatters* the 'Office of the Reich Commissioner' and *supports* its policy of expediting the Nazification of the Netherlands; everything is said to be happening just as it had been planned by the occupier. In this way the occupier too (and through him the Ministry in Berlin) figures as an addressee.

Before examining the second section of this 'Weekly Mirror', we shall recapitulate which facts the writer introduces and how they can be considered part of the forms of knowledge shared by writer and (historical) reader. In contrast to sentences 1–4, where the writer can appeal to obviousness, Dutch press publications, etc., the propositions in sentences 5–7 are introduced in such a way that the reader is unable to fall back upon his memory, and must instead have recourse to various further mental procedures. This functions as a special stylistic operation in order to regulate the process of reception. Thus the effect on 'spiritual education' (5), as elsewhere, *substitutes* in 5 the mode of certainty ('cannot be any other') for an expected uncertainty. The dependence of the results of Labour Service upon personality in 6 operates a break of expectation; what one expects is a positive statement, yet one finds a qualification, indeed even a playing-down of responsibility for the consequences for the individual. And in sentence 7 the expression 'to deem', instead of, for example, 'to experience' or 'to learn', is quite vague, since it is equally possible to value manual labour without doing it oneself, although this evidently runs counter to the purpose of the Labour Service. These stylistic techniques practically always operate as 'gaps' in a linear course and, over and above the imaginary relation to pseudo-facts, they mobilize in the reader particular mental activities that bring the reader 'closer' to the text. In short, as they appear in the journalist's reformulation, these propositions are indeterminate; though possible and conceivable, they are not really verifiable. They are part of the interpretation undertaken by the writer for the reader, and their effect, maybe, is a disturbance of the reader's 'knowledge system'. He is going to be prepared for further shifts of social meanings.

The second section (8–16) addresses the discussion within the Netherlands on how to react to the obligatory nature of the Labour Service which has been announced, though in 1941 it is still voluntary. The writer's criticism concentrates on the word 'coercion' (9, 11) which he considers a wrong transformation of 'obligation' (8, 9) by Dutch critics. In quoting these critics he uses the word 'aura' (12) as a description of the modification of propositional content. However at the same time, he permits the reader a glimpse of the laboratory of language policy, for at this very point he implements a *displacement of meaning* of the kind he himself has just criticized in the transformation of 'obligation' into 'coercion'. That is, he emphasizes in sentence 13 the 'spiritual education' effected by the Labour Service, as opposed to the 'practical values'; these 'practical values', i.e. the 'manual labour' (7) of the preceding section, are now relegated to a secondary position, thus shifting from the parallelism of 'manual labour' and 'spiritual education', described as the common purpose of the Labour Service, to 'spiritual education' as the first position and 'practical values' ('manual labour') as the second one. 'Spiritual education' thus becomes more important than 'manual labour' with regard to the Labour Service. Now the 'practical values' (the 'manual labour') *alone* are assigned to the term 'coercion' (9, 11); in other words 'coercion' is here viewed exclusively as *physical* coercion. This strategy of bringing together some elements of meaning and reference of 'coercion' and cutting off others, i.e. this *strategy of displacement*, excludes from the argument other kinds – political, psychological, repressive – of coercion. Thus the critics' reproach, which here is reacted to with a *justification*, is transformed from a *whole*/totality (of 'coercion') into a *part*/detail (of only physical coercion) and in this manner *reduced*. This exclusion of the physical aspects of 'coercion' from the others serves a well-known and widespread general stylistic strategy of justification in order to minimize the potential criticism expected by the occupying force because of its measures. While its critics presumably view the Labour Service as a typical institution of collaboration, the commentary makes out that a little 'coercion' in the service of manual labour is not worth all the fuss. The writer further supports his interpretation by reproaching the critics of an insufficient knowledge of the facts; only those who have been 'through the Labour Service' (10) are in a position to judge. The writer thus has recourse to a *commonplace*. This again results in a reduction, and functions as a strategy of *playing-down*.

In the further course of the second section this *reduction* also affects earlier textual components, i.e. components which till now proved incontestable between writer and reader. The 'improvements in build as well as in weight' (4) now appear of slighter importance compared to the spiritual education', which 'always plays the most important role' (13). What had first been adduced as an advantage of the Labour Service that could not be disputed is now devalued in favour of a perspective focusing on influencing the young – which is precisely what invokes once more the critics. There is thus a strong contradiction between the propositions of the first section and those of the second one. What was 'good' with regard to the Labour Service in the first section, namely the young's 'generally favourable condition' (4), is now considered 'not good' enough, because the writer suddenly claims a new 'spirit' (14) to be the very purpose of the Labour Service. Nor is this contradiction resolved by taking into account the fact that the statements made pertain to what is to come, to a 'future State' (14). The attempt to transform the term 'obligation' in 'obligatory' Labour Service (8, 9) into 'education' (10, see below), in order to elude the associations with 'coercion' (9, 11), is tantamount to the writer's confession that, after all, the issue is the National Socialist *reconditioning* of the young. In this way the text intensifies the confrontation with the critics of a Labour Service organized after the German model. Thus the propositional contradiction here is turned out into an ideological confrontation. In order to avoid drawing the attention of the reader to this fact, the writer then draws a veil over the issue by letting it subside in further quotations and modulations of the ordinance text; 'spirit' (14), 'education' (5, 10, 13), 'comradeship among the people' (16), 'true socialism' (16). The writer thus eludes the problem of argument by consciously diving into an ostentatious level of propaganda, the display-side of ideology. This should be interpreted as a *stylistic demonstration* of official National Socialism, intended to show the 'Führer' how far the 'Gleichschaltung' (enforced 'equalization') of the Netherlands has already progressed. The (dis)solution of a problem of *protrayal* and *justification* into *ideology* conjoins events in the Netherlands with the modes of discourse of the Third Reich and is textually operative as an instance of Nazification.

Different stages of the strategy of justification are here acted out. As we could see above, there were appeasement (by means of generalizing comparison), relativization (e.g. by commonplaces), vagueness (by pseudo-facts which the reader could not verify), displacement of meaning (e.g. the shift from 'obligation' to 'education'), counter-reproach (by reproaching the critics of an insufficient knowledge). However, the stylistic regulation of the reader's reception exploits not only those – more or less – 'linear' linguistic means of realization that have just been analysed, but also more 'encompassing' means, distributed over the entire text. The latter function primarily in the service of that reformulation to which the writer subjects the points of fact adduced, i.e. the segmentation and re-ordering of the parts of the original event, action, etc., which, in the commentary are now assessed as specific conditions of life in the occupied country. What we are doing now is to analyse such 'non-linear' means as further stylistic procedures, undertaken within this 'Weekly Mirror'. Thus one frequently finds in texts of this type a vocabulary drawn from the sphere of pedagogic action: 'spiritual education' (5, 13), 'school of the nation' (5), 'personality' (6), 'obligation' (9), 'education' (10), 'spirit' (14), 'youth, young and sensitive' (15). Again we are confronted with a stylistic strategy. Pedagogic knowledge is deployed here in order textually to evade the paramilitary nature of the Labour Service. Since Labour Service and pedagogy, at least at an abstract level, can be related to each other, merging these two spheres leads the reader to view the Labour Service as a concept of 'education', while leaving aside its preparatory military function. It may be worth remembering that initial advertisements for the Labour Service proceeded according to the same strategy, for instance by pointing out that it is better for someone unemployed to enter the Service than to run to seed in the streets. Later, the true nature of this pedagogic style is revealed when, with the introduction of forced labour ('Arbeitseinsatz'), hundreds of thousands of Dutch women and men are put to work in the Reich.

At another place in the text, however, this stylistic demilitarization of the Labour Service is called into question. 'School of the nation' (5), 'army' (6) and 'Labour Service', where they are compared, form a triangle. Since the expression 'school of the nation' is traditionally attached to the army, the equation of Labour Service and army is surprising here: Labour Service does, after all, become a kind of 'army'. The Dutch Labour Service acts as a substitute for the army, which in this period of occupation has *de facto* ceased to exist, having been demobilized or captured. There is thus a persistent *oscillation* between a (para)military and a pedagogic definition of the Labour Service. This oscillation is particularly well suited to create a discursive range of play for subsequent Nazi propaganda, so that, at a later occasion, this or that aspect may be emphasized, according to the aims of the day.

Yet another consequence is entailed by the commentary in this connection. At the centre of the equation there stands the term 'school of the nation', a Prussian synonym of 'army' or 'military' in general, which takes up a Prusso-German tradition that, owing to the absence of a history of militarism, does not exist in the Netherlands. A Dutchman reading this and wishing to understand must have recourse to foreign historical knowledge. If he does not possess this knowledge, he can at best realize 'school of the nation' as a metaphor, or as an equivalent term, for 'Labour Service' (cf. sentence 5). To a German reader, on the other hand, these transitions are perfectly intelligible, and indeed taken for granted. What is involved here, then, is the import of a Prusso-German term into the occupied Netherlands, an exertion of influence in the sphere of language policy which prescribes for subsequent texts the German expression 'school of the nation'. The new experience to which an allusion is thereby made, and in which, from the point of view of the occupier, the Dutch are lacking, is that of militarism.

Earlier in this paper it has been suggested that propaganda is the organizational form of all means of language policy in order to reshape individuals' social experience. One particularly striking illustration of this has been left unmentioned so far. Sentence 10: 'Anyone having gone through the Labour Service will confirm that the State can no longer dispense with this education'. It contains, apart from a criticism of the critics, an *appeal* to those who have completed the Labour Service to view themselves as witnesses for the 'efficacy' of this service. The stylistic proximity in this sentence of individual and state displaces the entire social force-field in favour of the state power to which the individual is henceforth subjected. On the ideological level, this is an expression of the National Socialist deification of the state; at the same time, it is an expression of the actual socialization intended for the Netherlands, for the 'future State' (14) – the incorporation (i.e. subjection) of the individual under a powerful state, which in practice is identical with the occupying power. In this way all textual operations articulate for the German reader a *confirmation* of what he already knows, and *unsettle* the Dutch reader, since he is not yet able, but is forced by the actions of the occupying power and the *DZN*, to judge exactly how his country will develop.

What has been demonstrated here is a small fragment of Nazi language policy with regard to the occupied Netherlands and to the particular sociohistorical situation of the Dutch and German readers of the *DZN*. The stylistic techniques used in making the 'Weekly Mirror', then, reflect the general goal of the Nazi propaganda in Holland, namely to rewrite the Dutch reality as an 'awakening nation' (albeit rudely, by the attacks of the German troops), and as a beginning of the transition from a 'bourgeois' people to an 'Aryan' member of the 'New Europe'. Of course we know that these propagandistic purposes had not been realized at the end of the war. But as analysts of such stylistic features appearing within historical-political language use, we ought to keep in mind the fact that the actual readers in the occupation did not have the same knowledge as we have now. For them the situation consisted of a general lack of knowledge, and they were obliged to build their own reality from whatever elements they could find, for instance in newspapers, even if they were National Socialist ones. The stylistic intervention of Nazi propaganda invaded this widespread pursuit of knowledge, in order to influence, or at least disturb, the readers' reconstruction of what they might think to be a 'social experience', contained in and handed down through words and other language forms.

To conclude this section, a final remark is in order. As far as topics are concerned, the 'Weekly Mirror' could, in principle, react to all matters except – as said before – 'grand politics'. However, in sharp contrast to the ordinary Nazi propaganda and to the other articles of the *DZN*, the 'Weekly Mirror' hardly ever showed an anti-Semitic tendency. The only exceptions were short reports of anti-Semitic activities undertaken by Dutch Nazis, but there was no direct attempt to produce anti-Semitic texts as such. Further, allusions to events in the Netherlands in which anti-Semitic thoughts were involved were very rare too. We might therefore say that the 'Weekly Mirror' takes into account the Dutch rejection of quite explicit anti-Semitic arguments. The commentary does not wish to present itself as a feature which registers all the 'normal' elements of Nazi ideology in underlining its particular type of text. Therefore, the absence of anti-Semitism cannot be considered as a 'mitigation'; at most it can be considered a tactical move. This functions stylistically as a distinction with respect to the other articles of the *DZN*.

## 4.7 Monotony and the Nazi concept of style

The stylistic analysis presented above ought to have shown that Nazi texts can be very complex, varied and rich in reference, and that their strategies of persuasion are quite sophisticated. This observation contradicts the verdict of the 'tediousness', said time and again to be characteristic of Nazi press texts. According to the above analysis, monotony is not an appropriate category at all to describe such texts. Moreover, this diagnosis of 'tediousness' was counteracted by the highest Nazi propagandists themselves, who again and again tried to achieve greater diversity within the whole spectrum of German and occupation press; for instance by founding the weekly paper *Das Reich* in 1940 and by publishing the colour magazine *Signal* for the occupied countries in their respective languages. Therefore, it is not quite clear what a reproach of 'tediousness' means with respect to these 'inner circle' discussions by the propaganda professionals. The inadequate categorization of 'tediousness' could even support a point of view which absolves the Nazi propaganda from all impact, at least as far as the monotonous style is concerned. Monotony, however, became a challenge for the propagandists themselves. The question was how to create an impression of modification to the public without seriously changing the political structure and National Socialist content of the mass media. In this respect, the solution found consisted of a flexible array of stylistic means, i.e. the inner variation of the texts themselves.

It was the aim of the propaganda bureaucracy to implement this stylistic variation by incessantly regulating the production and distribution of texts. Editorial staff were exposed to numerous instructions; the individual directives such as 'Presseanweisungen', 'Tagesparolen' and others have been published repeatedly and are now easily accessible.[7] The fact that these instructions to the press were, of course, 'top secret' in the Nazi years, and that they were accessible only to the editors and the correspondents in Berlin, means that nowadays we still tend to think that there were *real* secrets in this.Thus, although one was able to find out what the most important regulations were by reading and analysing the newspapers, this impression of a 'secret' is still alive. This ought to be interpreted as an after-effect of the image which the Nazi propaganda has established. There is a sense in which the voices of Hitler and Goebbels are still heard if we read the texts. But in doing so, we also re-build this image of Nazi propaganda. In fact, we have to be aware of this vicious circle; 'propaganda' often means that the press is regulated by one 'super-agency'. Reading the texts merely as 'results' of this agency prevents one from seeing which other effects, in the perspective of the language policy introduced above, were also managed. The stylistic analysis of those texts undertaken here provides a strategy for avoiding the re-establishment of this specific image of Nazi propaganda. The notion of 'monotony', therefore depends, among other things, on the expectation that the Nazi regime was a 'never-changing' one, which is obviously untrue, as historical research and more detailed investigations of the Nazi press have revealed.

To come back to the press regulations, their publication after the Nazi period offers a unique chance to reconstruct the *concept of style* upon which the measures of language policy were based. This concept of style, then, has to be considered as a necessary intermediate level between general Nazi language policy and each specific newspaper text, for, as we have seen, the style of a text mediated the specific historical situation by influencing the process of reading. Thus we can say that the style of a particular text printed in a Nazi paper depends, firstly, upon the common concept of style as derived from the institutional context, i.e. the propaganda office, and, secondly, on the specific way in which the text type was used by the journalist, guided as he was by his knowledge and experience. Therefore if we try to examine the stylistic strategies of an article, we have to consider the 'twofoldness' of these strategies. What the writer does, in fact, is to act out stylistically his 'subjectivity' with respect to the concept of style he has learnt to expect in Nazi propaganda. My hypothesis, now, is that the journalists of the *DZN* probably had too many rather than too few ideas in shaping the style of their articles, though in doing so they were limited by the constraints imposed by the general concept of style.

I hope the former, i.e. the journalist's 'subjectivity', has become clear in the above analysis. The latter, however, i.e. the *concept of style*, could be investigated by a closer reading of the language regulations upon which the directives to the press were based. A first rough approximation to this concept of Nazi propaganda style is the view that 'the same' was to be said 'differently' over and over again. This one might term 'variation', albeit always with the proviso that the *basis* that is varied changes according to (political) developments. However, there remains as an additional problem – the question of how large this variation, its latitude and the reader-specific differentiations, might be. It may be obvious that an investigation of this problem presents itself as an onerous task.

Admittedly, I cannot wholly avoid this task, but perhaps I can reduce its complexity by choosing an alternative path, by approaching the concept of Nazi propaganda style *'ex negativo'*, especially with the help of those anti-fascist propagandist forms that achieved their effect by *imitation* and *parody*. One of the most effective imitators of Nazi propaganda style is Rauschning (1973). In his stringing together of Hitler's utterances, of the frightening self-revelations of the 'Führer', and of the thrilling details and frequent observations allegedly made at first hand, Rauschning in his book *Hitler Speaks* captured perfectly the stylistic knowledge, assumed in the preceding analysis to be the background for the writers of the texts and their controllers. He, however, turns this stylistic knowledge against the Nazis themselves. A special feature, which guaranteed Rauschning's success, was that he presupposed in the non-Nazi readership certain *expectations* of content and style. These expectations, namely the usual image of Hitler as a devil and a psychopath, were transformed very cleverly by Rauschning into signals of authenticity by *quoting* a lot of the 'Führer's' ridiculous passages. In his own words, Hitler presented himself as the embodiment of all that fear which lived in the anti-fascist readership. The style exploited by Rauschning and projected on to Hitler counted, and still counts, as the most convincing 'proof' of the authenticity of his portrayal, even though it now appears that Rauschning manipulated, imitated, parodied and invented freely (cf. Hänel, 1984). This case shows that it is those who imitate and, in imitating, parody a style, who use it with the greatest accuracy.[8] Deliberations of this kind provide a starting point from which the further study of stylistic strategies of propaganda and of political language use can be advanced as sociohistorical analysis.

# NOTES

1   An earlier version of this chapter was presented at the Association Internationale de Linguistique Appliquée (AILA) World Congress, Brussels, August 1984. Grateful acknowledgments are due for suggestions and comments made by Willie van Peer. Thanks are also due to Andreas Michael for translating the first version of this article.
2   For a recent overview, see Craig (1982).
3   See the reconstructions in Glaser (1978) and Stern (1975).
4   'He who at present says "population" instead of "people" and "landed property" instead of "soil", already refrains from supporting many lies' (editor's translation).
5   On the theory of 'foregrounding' see especially van Peer (1986).
6   On Nazi propaganda, see Baird (1974), Balfour (1979), Bramsted (1965), Hale (1964), Welch (1983) and Zeman (1973).
7   See, for instance, Abel (1968), Boelcke (1966), Glunk (1966–71), Hagemann (1970), Hoffman (1972), Sänger (1975).
8   See also Lucas (1984), who in BBC broadcasts read fictitious letters of a German infantryman – 'Teure Amalia, vielgeliebtes Weib!' [Dear Amalia, much loved woman!']. Further important contemporary works that discuss the question of the stylistic impact and National Socialist propaganda are Bloch (1937, 1939), Burke (1939–40), Guérin (1966), Münzenberg (1977).

# BIBLIOGRAPHY

Abel, K.-D. (1968), *Presselenkung im NS-Staat* [Directing the Press in the Nazi State], Berlin, Colloquium Verlag.

Baird, J. W. (1974), *The Mythical World of Nazi War Propaganda, 1939–1945*, Minneapolis, University of Minnesota Press.

Balfour, M. (1979), *Propaganda in War 1939–1945. Organisations, Policies and Publics in Britain and Germany*, London, Routledge & Kegan Paul.

Bloch, E. (1937), 'Kritik der Propaganda' [Criticism of propaganda], *Die neue Weltbühne*, vol. 14, pp. 421–5; reprinted in E. Bloch, *Vom Hasard zur Katastrophe* [From Chance to Catastrophe], Frankfurt, Suhrkamp, pp. 195–206.

Bloch, E. (1939), 'Zerstörte Sprache, zerstörte Kultur' [Destroyed language, destroyed culture], *Internationale Literatur*, juni, pp. 132–41;

reprinted in *Vom Hasard zur Katastrophe* [From Chance to Catastrophe], Frankfurt, Suhrkamp, pp. 403–27.

Boelcke, W. A. (ed.) (1966), *Kriegspropaganda 1939–1941*, [War Propaganda], Stuttgart, DVA.

Bramsted, E. K. (1965), *Goebbels and National Socialist Propaganda 1925–1945*, East Lansing, Michigan State University Press.

Brecht, B. (1967), *Gesammelte Werke* [Collected Works], vol. 18, Frankfurt, Suhrkamp, p. 231 (original 1935).

Burke, K. (1939–40), 'The rhetoric of Hitler's "Battle"', *Southern Review*, vol. 1, pp. 1–21; reprinted in M. Shapiro (ed.), *Language and Politics*, Oxford, Basil Blackwell, 1984, pp. 61–80.

Craig, G. A. (1982), *The Germans*, New York, G. P. Putnam's Sons.

Ehlich, K. and Rehbein, J. (1977), 'Wissen, kommunikatives Handeln und die Schule' [Knowledge, communicative action and the school], in H. C. Goeppert (ed.), *Sprachverhalten im Unterricht* [Language Relations in Education], Munich, Fink, pp. 36–114.

Faye, J. P. (1972), *Langages totalitaires* [Totalitarian Languages], Paris, Herrman.

Glaser, H. (1978), *Spiesser-Ideologie* [Philistine Ideology], Frankfurt, Ullstein, (first edition 1974).

Glunk, R. (1966–71), 'Erfolg und Misserfolg der nationalsozialistischen Sprachlenkung' [Success and failure of Nazi language policies], *Zeitschrift für deutsche Sprache*, vol. 22, pp. 57–73 and 146–53; vol. 23, pp. 83–113 and 178–88; vol. 24, pp. 72–91 and 184–91; vol. 25, pp. 116–28 and 180–3; vol. 26, pp. 84–97 and 176–83; vol. 27, pp. 113–23 and 177–87.

Guérin, D. (1966), *La peste brune* [The Brown Plague], Paris, Maspero (first edition 1935).

Hagemann, J. (1970), *Die Presselenkung im Dritten Reich* [Directing the Press in the Third Reich], Bonn, Bouvier.

Hale, O. J. (1964), *The Captive Press in the Third Reich*, Princeton, Princeton University Press.

Hänel, W. (1984), *Hermann Rauschnings 'Gespräche mit Hitler'. Eine Geschichtsfälschung* [Rauschning's 'Conversations with Hitler'. A case of Historical Forgery], Ingolstadt, Verlag der Zeitgeschichtlichen Forschungsstelle.

Hirschfeld, G. (1981), 'Collaboration and attentism in the Netherlands 1940–41', *Journal of Contemporary History*, vol. 16, pp. 467–86.

Hirschfeld, G. (1983), 'Nazi propaganda in occupied Western Europe: the case of the Netherlands', in D. Welch (1983), pp. 143–60.

Hoffman, G. (1972), *NS-Propaganda in den Niederlanden* [Nazi Propaganda in The Netherlands], Munich, Dokumentation.

Januschek, F. and Maas, U. (1981), 'Zum Gegenstand der Sprachpolitik: Sprache oder Sprachen?' [On the object of language policy: language or languages?], *Osnabrücker Beiträge zur Sprachtheorie (OBST)*, vol. 18, pp. 64–95.

Lucas, R. (1984), *Teure Amalia, vielgeliebtes Weib!* [Dear Amalia, much loved woman!], Frankfurt, Fischer, (new German edition from the BBC radio talks during the war).

Münzenberg, W. (1977), *Propaganda als Waffe* [Propaganda as Weapon], Jossa, März (original 1937).

Peer, W. van (1986), *Stylistics and Psychology. Investigations of Foregrounding*, London, Croom Helm.

Peer, W. van and Renkema, J. (eds) (1984), *Pragmatics and Stylistics*, Louvain, Acco.

Rauschning, H. (1973), *Gespräche mit Hitler* [Conversations with Hitler], Vienna, Europa Verlag (original edition Zurich, 1940; English edition *Hitler Speaks*, London, 1940).

Sandig, B. (1978), *Stilistik. Sprachpragmatische Grundlegung der Stilbeschreibung* [Stylistics. Pragma-linguistic Foundation of the Description of Style], Berlin, Walter de Gruyter.

Sandig, B. (ed.) (1983), *Stilistik* [Stylistics], 2 vols., Hildesheim, Olms.

Sänger, F. (1975), *Politik der Täuschungen* [Politics of Illusions], Vienna, Europa Verlag.

Sauer, C. (1983), 'Sprachpolitik und NS-Herrschaft' [Language policy and Nazi-domination], *Sprache und Literatur*, vol. 51, pp. 80–99.

Sauer, C. (1984), 'Nicht drinnen und nicht draussen. NS-Sprachpolitik, die Niederlande und das "Neue Europa"' [Not inside and not outside. Nazi language policy, the Netherlands, and the 'New Europe'], *Diskussion Deutsch*, vol. 78, pp. 408–32.

Sauer, C. (1985), 'NS-Sprachpolitik in der Besatzungsituation' [Nazi language policy and occupation], in F. Januschek (ed.), *Politische Sprachwissenschaft* [Political Linguistics], Opladen, Westdeutscher Verlag, pp. 271–306.

Sontag, S. (1981), *Under the Sign of Saturn*, New York, Farrar, Strauss & Giroux, see especially 'Fascinating Fascism' (originally published 1974).

Spillner, B. (1974), *Linguistik und Literaturwissenschaft* [Linguistics and Literary Theory], Stuttgart, Kohlhammer.

Spillner, B. (ed.) (1984), *Methoden der Stilanalyse* [Methods of Stylistic Analysis], Tübingen, Narr.

Steiner, G. (1984), *The Hollow Miracle. A Reader*, Harmondsworth, Penguin, esp. pp. 207–220 (first published 1959).

Stern, J. P. (1975), *Hitler. The Führer and the People*, London, Fontana/Collins.

Warmbrunn, W. (1963), *The Dutch under German Occupation 1940–1945*, Stanford, Stanford University Press.

Welch, D. (ed.) (1983), *Nazi Propaganda*, London, Croom Helm.

Zeman, Z. A. B. (1973), *Nazi Propaganda*, Oxford, Oxford University Press (2nd ed.).

# 5

# Romeo and Juliet

## The language of tragedy

*Kiernan Ryan*

*Drama is in itself a highly conventionalized mode of presenting speech and discourse, the genre conventions of which allow it to portray human action deviating from the normal, everyday state of the world. As Kiernan Ryan argues, there can be little doubt that such is the case in* Romeo and Juliet. *Significantly, however, as an overview of the common positions in Shakespeare scholarship reveals, most critics seem not to subscribe to this interpretation. Instead an essentially repressive attitude may be discerned towards the fundamentally utopian qualities of the play.*

*This misinterpretation by the literary critics is the starting point for a closer investigation of the kind of discourse that is presented in* Romeo and Juliet. *What emerges is that the violence amidst which the lovers find themselves is inscribed directly in the language, and especially through the use of names. It is language (as a reflection of the social institutions from which it emanates) that is at the basis of the continuous aggression and violence that pervade the lives of men and women in Verona. Not surprisingly, then, the lovers refute this basis (cf. Juliet's 'What's in a name?'). Instead they attempt to escape the deadlock of mutual killings and maimings fed by the family feud by crossing the ideological and linguistic barriers that separate them. Their struggle for sexual freedom on an egalitarian basis demands the undoing of forms of language that their society has ingrained in them.*

*As the analysis by Kiernan Ryan elucidates,* Romeo and Juliet *foregrounds the potential liberation from stifling social norms. This foregrounding takes place against the background, not merely of political issues, but of language controlling and constraining human love and concern. In this sense the play may also, in Sauer's sense, offer an opportunity for creating new experiences, this time not of subjection to a totalitarian racist regime, but of a constructive utopia in the realm of sexual relationships.*

From its first successful performances in Elizabethan London down to our own time, the extraordinary theatrical appeal of *Romeo and Juliet* has made it one of the most enduringly popular of all Shakespeare's plays. But although audiences the world over appear to have had little trouble recognizing the exceptional power and value of the tragedy, most modern Shakespearean critics have found it a play far more difficult to come to terms with. Not only do they tend to be much less enthusiastic about its overall merit, but they are also in fundamental disagreement about the nature of its vision.

Conventional critical opinion seems to be divided at present into three main views of the tragedy. The first sees the fate of the lovers as dictated by an inexorable natural or metaphysical law. J. W. Draper (1961, p. 88) goes so far as to suggest that Romeo and Juliet are the literally 'star-cross'd' victims of astral determinism, 'the puppets of the stars and planets and of the days and times of day'. A more representative argument, however, is that of Lawlor (1961, p. 132), who believes that what defeats them are the 'unchanging limits' of human possibility, of human nature itself. As Frank Kermode (1974, p. 1,057) puts it, 'just as [love] is in its very nature the business of the young, with passions hardly controlled, so it is in its very nature associated with disaster and death'. The fate of Romeo and Juliet is regarded, in short, as a natural and inevitable product of 'the human condition'; cf. Champion (1976, p. 84).

A second line of interpretation, on the other hand, stresses the accidental failure of Friar Lawrence's message to reach Romeo and the unfortunate mistimings of events at the tomb. From these facts it concludes that the play's emphasis 'seems to be, rather more than we should like, on chance', and that perhaps 'we understand the play better if we think of it as a tragedy of "bad luck"' (Spencer, 1967, pp. 21-2). For such critics, as Franklin Dickey (1957, p. 63) observes, the tragic vision of the play is deeply flawed, because the causes of the catastrophe appear to be 'embarrassingly fortuitous ... the accident of chance to which all human life is subject'. The death of the protagonists, in other words, is viewed as nothing more than the random result of arbitrary circumstances, which defies explanation in terms of a coherent pattern or consistent rationale.

From yet another widespread critical standpoint, however, there seems no doubt that the blame for the tragedy lies with the lovers, and with Romeo in particular. This reading tends to rest on the assumption that 'all things considered, the Verona which serves as their testing-ground is not a bad place' (Bryant, 1964, p. xxxiii), and that consequently 'the causes of the tragedy lie in the sufferers themselves', whose 'dangerous fault ... is their extreme rashness' (Stauffer, 1964, p. 30). Whitaker (1965, p. 115), locates the play's chief authority for this judgment in Friar Lawrence, whose orthodox moral perspective serves to establish 'the irrational violence, and therefore the culpability, of the haste with which Romeo acts'; he therefore finds 'Romeo's responsibility for the tragic outcome of the play absolutely clear'. In this reading *Romeo and Juliet* becomes in effect a morality play, depicting the doom awaiting those who demand too much too soon, and who refuse to let their desire be governed by the accepted rules of their society.

Despite the differences between these three approaches to the play, most critics nevertheless agree that, for one reason or another, *Romeo and Juliet* is an immature and imperfectly constructed work, which 'disappoints those critical expectations that the major tragedies arouse and satisfy' (Hamilton, 1967, p. 203).

What I want to argue in this essay is that these standard interpretations of the play are all unsatisfactory because they are based on false assumptions about the central concerns of *Romeo and Juliet* and the objectives of Shakespearean tragedy. The conflicts between the readings I have outlined mask a deeper common allegiance to the same conservative critical ideology. That allegiance commits these critics to the task of interpreting Shakespearean tragedy in ways designed to neutralize its power to question the social and sexual order of both Shakespeare's time and our own. By explaining *Romeo and Juliet* as a timeless and universal tragedy of the 'human condition', as the arbitrary result of mere chance, or as a consequence of the purely personal moral defects of the protagonists, criticism has conspired to evade or obscure the subversive utopian significance of their love and the play's indictment of the specific social forces which deny that love the right to exist and flourish.

The dominant conception of Shakespearean tragedy demands that it should 'purge our emotions of pity and fear by making us acquiesce without bitterness in catastrophe' (Farnham, 1964, p. 22). In the case of *Romeo and Juliet*, therefore, a realization that the catastrophe has been determined by laws beyond human control, or by the characters' failure to obey the moral law of their society, should lead us to accept the necessity of their fate and the folly of protesting against what cannot be challenged and cannot be changed. That is indeed how orthodox criticism would like to see the play, and the reason why it strives to impose upon the text readings consistent with this conservative definition of tragedy. But the problem is that *Romeo and Juliet* obstinately refuses to satisfy such a definition, and it is their frustration at this defiance, I would suggest, which has compelled so many critics to assert, in a perverse contradiction of popular opinion, that 'as a pattern of the idea of tragedy, it is a failure '(Charlton, 1948, p. 61).

Critics can, of course, point to the evidence of the text in support of their conventional readings. The moralistic interpreter can quote Friar Lawrence in order to prove that 'these violent delights have violent ends' (II.vi.9).[1] The protagonists themselves can be cited as witnesses to the view that they are the victims of 'some consequence ... hanging in the stars' (I.iv.107). Nor could anyone dispute that accidental factors play a crucial role in sealing the lovers' final doom. But it is a fundamental mistake to equate a character's perception of the situation with the perspective created by the play as a whole, or to isolate particular incidents from their overall context and construct upon them an explanation of the entire pattern of events. For the total configuration of the text articulates a tragic vision far more penetrating in its analysis, and far more radical in its implications, than the conservative critic is willing to discern.

What the orthodox interpretations have sought to repress are precisely those qualities which alone can account for the profound hold which *Romeo and Juliet* has maintained over the imagination and aspirations of generation after generation of readers and spectators down through the centuries. The source of the play's abiding power lies, I believe, in the way the lovers come to embody the possibility of a more satisfying form of sexual relationship, free of the social and ideological constraints which continue to divide men and women from each other and prevent the full and equal realization of their mutual desire. Far from inducing in us the state of 'intellectual acquiescence' which Charlton (1948, p. 9) requires of Shakespearean tragedy, *Romeo and Juliet* forces us to confront the outrageous contradiction between legitimate human desires and their destructive social repression: between what men and women want to be and could be, and what the barbaric predicament into which they have been scripted by history cruelly condemns them to be in spite of themselves. One of the most remarkable features of the play, moreover, is its recognition of how the social constraints on the lovers are enforced through language, through the words, names and discourses which bind them to the repressive terms of a world with which they cannot compromise, and by which they are therefore finally destroyed.

The first scene of the play establishes the social context within which the subsequent action develops. Verona is depicted as an enclosed, claustrophobic, overheated urban world, dominated and divided by the feud between the Montagues and the Capulets, which consumes both servants and masters, the old and the young alike. The hothouse atmosphere of patriarchal conflict and masculine violence pervades and poisons everything, and especially the realm of sexuality, with which the play is centrally concerned. This is made plain in the opening dialogue between the belligerent Capulet servants:

> SAMPSON:  I will show myself a tyrant: when I have fought
> with the men I will be civil with the maids, I will
> cut off their heads.
> GREGORY:  The heads of the maids?
> SAMPSON:  Ay, the heads of the maids, or their maidenheads;
> take it in what sense thou wilt.

> (I.i.20–5)

Their bragging equivocations persistently identify male aggression with the sexual violation of women, and the male sexual organ with the sword: 'My naked weapon is out' (I.i.33).

That violence and sexuality are synonymous in Verona is underlined by the exclamation with which Romeo himself sums up the situation later in the scene: 'O brawling love, O loving hate' (I.i.174). And it immediately becomes apparent that his own infatuation with Rosaline is no exception to the rule. Her refusal to yield to his attempts at seduction is expressed in terms of a defence against military assault:

> she'll not be hit
> With Cupid's arrow, she hath Dian's wit,
> And in strong proof of chastity well arm'd
> From love's weak childish bow she lives uncharm'd.
> She will not stay the siege of loving terms
> Nor bide th'encounter of assailing eyes.
>
> (I.i.206–11)

As this quotation illustrates, throughout the first Act, while he is still fixated on Rosaline and before he has met Juliet, Romeo is presented as trapped inside the stereotyped role and ossified poetic discourse of the Petrarchan lover. His intensely stylized rhyming speech is paralyzed by the dead weight of clichéd paradoxes and predictable textbook metaphors, rigid with the artificiality of lifeless verbal and rhetorical conventions, which are completely divorced from any genuine experience or feeling:

> She is too fair, too wise, wisely too fair,
> To merit bliss by making me despair.
> She hath forsworn to love, and in that vow
> Do I live dead, that live to tell it now.
>
> (I.i.219–22)

Romeo speaks more truly than he knows when he describes himself as 'shut up in prison, kept without my food,/Whipp'd and tormented' (I.ii.55–6). For he is indeed the prisoner of a degrading sexual ideology, which turns the woman into a sadistic goddess and the man into a tortured slave, condemned to act out a mutually oppressive fiction of domination and subjection. It is significant, however, that even here Romeo seems possessed of an awareness that his true identity exists beyond the confines of his present masochistic role: 'I have lost myself, I am not here./This is not Romeo, he's some other where' (I.i.195–6).

Mercutio's cynical mockery provides a humorously effective means of exposing and puncturing Romeo's artificial persona and fabricated speech:

> Romeo! Humours! Madman! Passion! Lover!
> Appear thou in the likeness of a sigh,
> Speak but one rhyme and I am satisfied.
>
> (II.i.7–9)

But it is soon clear that Mercutio's disillusioned version of love offers no valid alternative. On the contrary, he shares with

Sampson and Gregory a reductive and combative conception of sexuality, which is merely an inverted mirror-image of that which he satirizes in Romeo: 'If love be rough with you, be rough with love;/Prick love for pricking and you beat love down' (I.ii.27–8). From Mercutio's equally stereotyped perspective, love means nothing more than the female sexual organ being penetrated by the male in a simple gratification of animal appetite: 'O Romeo, that she were, O that she were/An open-arse and thou a poperin pear' (II.i.37–8). Both Romeo and Mercutio are governed by the same dominant sexual ideology, which denies men and women the option of a form of love unbridled by subjugation and coercion.

As a young girl, of course, Juliet's subjection to this ideology is much more obvious. The first we hear of her is in Act I scene ii, where her father is discussing the possibility of giving her in marriage to Paris: even before she enters she is defined first and foremost as an object of male choice and negotiation. The following scene dramatizes her condition by showing Juliet herself being pressed by her mother to accept Paris's suit and persuade herself to love him. The terms in which Lady Capulet seeks to secure her daughter's compliance are revealing:

> Read o'er the volume of young Paris' face
> And find delight writ there with beauty's pen.
> Examine every married lineament
> And see how one another lends content;
> And what obscur'd in this fair volume lies,
> Find written in the margent of his eyes.
> This precious book of love, this unbound lover,
> To beautify him only lacks a cover ...
> That book in many's eyes doth share the glory
> That in gold clasps locks in the golden story.
>
> (I.iii.81–92)

The extended book metaphor points to the correspondence between Juliet's situation and Romeo's. Romeo's bondage to the Petrarchan scenario of subjection to a mistress is paralleled by the projected binding of Juliet through marriage to 'the golden story' of her husband's destiny at the expense of her own. It is the husband who is assumed to be both the author and the subject of the 'precious book of love', whose 'content' the wife is expected simply to read, digest and embellish with the beautifying 'cover' of her physical appearance. The prospective marriage submits Juliet, like Romeo, to the power of a set text written in advance by the sexual conventions of their society, which cannot allow them to invent their own script, create their own roles or speak lines of their own devising.

Thus at this stage of the play Juliet performs her prescribed role as the respectful, obedient daughter, diplomatically acknowledging the ultimate subordination of her inclinations to the wishes of her parents:

> I'll look to like, if looking liking move,
> But no more deep will I endart mine eye
> Than your consent gives strength to make it fly.
>
> (I.iv.97–9)

The full extent of that subordination becomes apparent later in Capulet's vicious tirade against his daughter when she dares to resist his command that she marry Paris:

> Look to't, think on't, I do not use to jest.
> Thursday is near. Lay hand on heart. Advise.
> And you be mine I'll give you to my friend;
> And you be not, hang! Beg! Starve! Die in the streets!
> For by my soul I'll ne'er acknowledge thee,
> Nor what is mine shall never do thee good.
>
> (III.v.189–94)

Juliet plainly has no real freedom of sexual choice within the patriarchal structure of the family. Above all, as a daughter who bears the name of Capulet, the independent choice of a man who bears the name of the rival house of Montague cannot even be contemplated.

The play's preoccupation with the controlling power of names provides, in fact, the key to the tragedy. From the first Act onwards we are made increasingly aware of how the members of this society are locked into its regime of division and repression by their very language, by the ruling discourses of their world. The kind of language people use determines the way they see themselves and the way they see their reality: it defines their assumptions, their values, their expectations. One of the most striking achievements of *Romeo and Juliet* is its recognition that the material and ideological forces which overwhelm the protagonists exercise their power primarily through forms of linguistic constraint. Words and names are the chains which bind the lovers to the sexual norms and social imperatives of Verona. Only when we grasp this can we understand why their struggle for sexual freedom expresses itself inseparably as a struggle to free themselves from the limits of the kinds of language which Verona has taught them to speak.

It is no accident that Romeo and Juliet meet and fall in love (I.v) while Romeo is disguised behind his mask and before they know each other's names. For while they are nameless they are untrammelled by the limitations of their social identities, which would otherwise prevent them from meeting simply as a man and a woman. For a brief moment the festive licence of the masquerade not only relieves them of their obligations as Montague and Capulet, but dissolves the strict codes of courtship which would normally make such a direct and intimate first encounter between any man and woman of their class unthinkable. The outraged Tybalt does indeed identify Romeo's voice, triggering once again the mindless machinery of the feud, which will drive its lethal wedge between the lovers in Act III. But meanwhile this privileged interlude allows them to touch and kiss with frank immediacy, and their love is born.

Significantly, their entire exchange (I.v.92–109), initiated by Romeo, takes place within the highly stylized form and idiom of the love-sonnet, whose artificial vision continues as yet to restrict the scope of his emotions and imagination. They complete their first sonnet together with a kiss (I.v.92–105), and at once begin a second (I.v.106–9). But, having played his language-game so far, Juliet now sabotages the sonnet in the fourth line begun by Romeo, turning its second half back upon the speaker in playful mockery of his text-book courtship:

> ROMEO:  Thus from my lips, by thine, my sin is purg'd.
> JULIET:   Then have my lips the sin that they have took.
> ROMEO:  Sin from my lips? O trespass sweetly urg'd.
>               Give me my sin again.    [*He kisses her*]
> JULIET:                              You kiss by th' book.

Juliet's teasing quip reflects the gap already perceived to be opening between actual feelings and this formalized literary discourse which distorts and stuns them in the very act of communication. The impulse to resist predictable formulations of desire and intention is evident right from the beginning of their love.

Within seconds of this exchange, however, each discovers the name of the other, and at once, with the pronunciation of the words 'Capulet' and 'Montague', the licence of the moment is cancelled and the tragic conflict between the lovers and their society begins. From now on they are forced, as the Prologue to Act

II observes, 'to steal love's sweet bait from fearful hooks' (II. Prologue. 8).

The linguistic dimension of the tragedy is made explicit in the balcony scene of Act II. Juliet's main speech is of course famous, and relentlessly quoted. But it is worth quoting again in the context of the present argument, which puts us in a position to gauge the full depth of its significance. Believing herself to be alone, and thus released from the burden of self-censorship which a public statement would impose, she soliloquizes on the problem at the heart of the play:

> O Romeo, Romeo, wherefore art thou Romeo?
> Deny thy father and refuse thy name.
> Or if thou wilt not, be but sworn my love
> And I'll no longer be a Capulet ...
> 'Tis but thy name that is my enemy:
> Thou art thyself, though not a Montague.
> What's Montague? It is nor hand nor foot
> Nor arm nor face nor any other part
> Belonging to a man. O be some other name.
> What's in a name? That which we call a rose
> By any other word would smell as sweet;
> So Romeo would, were he not Romeo call'd,
> Retain that dear perfection which he owes
> Without that title.

And Romeo replies:

> Call me but love, and I'll be new baptis'd:
> Henceforth I never will be Romeo ...
> My name, dear saint, is hateful to myself
> Because it is an enemy to thee.
> Had I it written, I would tear the word.
>
> (II.ii.33–57)

These passages spell out the stifling contradiction between being simply a 'man' and being a 'Montague', between a potentially unshackled self and the disabling controls and commitments socially inscribed in such a family name. The verbal labels 'Capulet' and 'Montague' fix Romeo and Juliet within a patriarchal power-structure, whose demands directly conflict with their naturally sanctioned desires as human beings. 'The tradition of the dead generations', as Marx pointed out, 'weighs like a nightmare on the minds of the living' (Fernbach, 1973, p. 146). What *Romeo and Juliet* makes us realize is the extent to which that inherited weight of history is experienced as the weight of words, the programmed network of signs designed to pin us to the habitual terms of a given way of life.

For it is not only their names from which Romeo and Juliet are straining to cut themselves loose. As the quotation from the balcony scene shows, Romeo's love for Juliet has begun to generate a radical transformation of his language into a fresh mode of self-expression which is more simple, direct, personal and resolute. The transformation is far from complete and sustained, and traces of the old Petrarchan discourse, with all it implies, will cling to both his language and Juliet's to the end. A clean and full break with the normative idioms of their world is impossible. But they have already moved far enough away from them to reveal their 'stony limits' (II.ii.67) and define the distance which separates their present from their former selves.

Thus Juliet consciously rejects the impulse to conceal the intensity of her desire beneath the inhibiting formalities of polite public speech: 'Fain would I dwell on form; fain, fain deny/What I have spoke. But farewell, compliment' (II.ii.88–9). She explicitly waves aside the role of the manipulative Petrarchan mistress, along with its obligation to be reserved, distant and 'strange' (II.ii.101–2), 'to frown and be perverse and say thee nay' (II.ii.96). And she forbids Romeo likewise to cast himself in the corresponding role of devoted worshipper at her shrine. When he threatens to slip back into the routine posture of submissive suitor by swearing the usual elaborate oath of allegiance to his lady, she cuts him off abruptly with 'Do not swear at all' (II.ii.112). For to accept these roles and the discourse which confirms them would be to accept the prevailing conditions of sexual relationship, which Romeo and Juliet have already begun to transcend. 'Love goes toward love', observes Romeo, 'as schoolboys from their books' (II.ii.156). The new kind of union developing between them means tossing aside the prescribed texts of the oppressive school of love in which they have been educated, and setting out to learn through their own experience what real love might be like.

What they discover, however fleetingly, is a genuine, mutual form of love, which drives them not only beyond the divisive social structure epitomized by the feud, but beyond the established sexual order and thus beyond the conventional modes of language which serve to perpetuate that order. They discover that the words and names and idioms which previously contained them within the *status quo* do not fit what they are now experiencing and their new perception of themselves. The way of life which had hitherto seemed normal and unquestionable is exposed as a prison-house of language contrived to lock them within its walls of words. Those walls prove in the end too strong. But through their very struggle to demolish them and set their love at liberty they open up a dimension of alternative possibility, which demonstrates that what Verona understands as normal is neither desirable nor inevitable.

The utopian quality of their love is stressed right from the start of Act II. Its subversive implications proceed from the fact that it is founded on equality and reciprocity rather than subservience. As the Chorus puts it: 'Now Romeo is belov'd and loves again,/Alike bewitched by the charm of looks .../And she as much in love' (II. Prologue. 5-6, 11). Romeo himself constantly employs symmetrically balanced syntax and diction in order to express the perfect equivalence of power and emotion which distinguishes their relationship: 'One hath wounded me/That's by me wounded' (II.iii.46-7); 'As mine on hers, so hers is set on mine' (II.iii.55); 'her I love now/Doth grace for grace and love for love allow' (II.iii.81-2). It is, moreover, a mutually expanding, limitless love, whose value defies selfish quantification. In Juliet's words:

> My bounty is as boundless as the sea,
> My love as deep: the more I give to thee
> The more I have, for both are infinite.          (II.ii.133-5)

> They are but beggars that can count their worth,
> But my true love is grown to such excess
> I cannot sum up sum of half my wealth.          (II.vi.30-4)

Romeo and Juliet's 'true-love passion' (II.ii.104) goes much further than simply dramatizing the pernicious effects of the family feud. It embodies a revolutionary assertion of the fundamental human right not only to love whoever one chooses, regardless of such social divisions, but to do so in a relationship uncontaminated by the drive to use and dominate, by the predatory self-interest and calculating hierarchical mentality which pervert the love between men and women into an instrument of mutual exploitation and oppression.

Their tragedy is that they live in a society which denies them this right. It is the pressure to conform to the normative practices and civil regulations of Verona which is 'the true ground of all these piteous woes' (V.iii.179), not some inherent flaw in the nature of young love or the human condition, and not some mysterious metaphysical compulsion governed by the stars, whatever the Friar may say or Romeo believe. Moreover, the accidental confusions which result in their suicides could not even have arisen without these institutionalized pressures which split and isolate the lovers, leaving them utterly vulnerable to such chance adversities. The question is not whether their doom might have been averted if the protagonists had simply had better luck, but why two quite innocent lovers should find themselves driven to a point where their lives are at the mercy of mere luck at all.

It is thus far from accidental that the first decisive step towards catastrophe is taken when Romeo is compelled by Mercutio's death to reassume the obligations of the name he had abandoned for Juliet, re-enter the arena of the family feud and kill Tybalt in revenge (III.i). As a consequence the lovers must undergo the torment of separation, inflicted once again by the power of a single word:

> JULIET:  Some word there was, worser than Tybalt's death,
> That murder'd me ...
> That 'banished', that one word 'banished',
> Hath slain ten thousand Tybalts ...
> ... Romeo is banished,
> There is no end, no limit, measure, bound,
> In that word's death.
>
> (III.ii.108–26)

> ROMEO:           'Banished'?
> O Friar, the damned use that word in hell.
> ... How hast thou the heart
> To mangle me with that word 'banished'?
>
> (III.iii.46–51)

A word can maim or kill as surely as poison or a bullet. But even as they writhe under this realization, Romeo and Juliet continue to insist on the gulf between what they perceive as their real selves and the intolerable identities which the language of their world mercilessly persists in weaving round them:

> JULIET:  Hath Romeo slain himself? Say thou but 'Ay'
> And that bare vowel 'I' shall poison more
> Than the death-darting eye of cockatrice.
> I am not I if there be such an 'I'.
>
> (III.ii.45–8)

ROMEO:                As if that name,
          Shot from the deadly level of a gun,
          Did murder her, as that name's cursed hand
          Murder'd her kinsman. O tell me, Friar, tell me,
          In what vile part of this anatomy
          Doth my name lodge?

                                        (III.iii.101–6)

Through this conflict between their secretly emerging and their prescribed public selves, Romeo and Juliet demonstrate the potential of men and women to live and love each other on terms quite different from those by which they themselves are doomed to be defeated in their particular world and time. This tragic sense of being inexorably forced, despite oneself, to play a character in a script over which one has no control is precisely caught in Juliet's reflection that 'My dismal scene I needs must act alone' (IV.iii.19). It likewise informs Romeo's remarkable extension of his sympathy to the dead Paris, in whom he recognizes a fellow victim of the same relentless historical narrative: 'O, give me thy hand,/One writ with me in sour misfortune's book' (V.iii.81–2).

The final chapter of that misfortune follows directly from Capulet's demand that Juliet obey the word of the father and marry the husband he has chosen for her. The drug plot is a last desperate attempt to rewrite their story and give their truly 'precious book of love' a happy ending. But by now the odds are stacked overwhelmingly against them. The final scene is played out appropriately in the Capulet crypt, the repository of the dead generations and symbol of the patriarchal family, whose inherited structures of repression have imprisoned Romeo and Juliet from the start. In this sense both of them have all along been a 'poor living corse, clos'd in a dead man's tomb' (V.ii.29), and their self-inflicted deaths at the end simply turn that virtual entombment into a fearful reality.

At the same time, the fact that Romeo and Juliet are prepared to kill themselves rather than face life without each other gives us the measure of the extraordinary depth and value of their love. That they can only find peace and unity in death constitutes, furthermore, a devastating indictment of the society which would not let them be united on their own terms while alive. The completeness of Romeo's disillusionment with that society, whose perversion of authentic human values he now sees all too clearly, is crystallized in his bitter words to the poverty-stricken apothecary from whom he seeks the means of death:

> The world is not thy friend, nor the world's law;
> The world affords no law to make thee rich ...
> There is thy gold – worse poison to men's souls,
> Doing more murder in this loathsome world
> Than these poor compounds that thou mayst not sell.
> I sell thee poison, thou hast sold me none.
>
> (V.ii.72–83)

The whole thrust of the tragedy is to question the legitimacy of a world whose law deprives men and women of unbounded love as surely as it deprives the poor of their right to the world's wealth. The closing reconciliation of the families and the promised erection of golden monuments to the lovers cannot begin to compensate for the fact that Romeo and Juliet were driven by the injustice of 'the world's law' into an impossible dilemma which resulted in their pointless deaths by their own hands.

The play compels us to face without illusions the appalling cost in possible human happiness of the material and ideological constraints responsible for the lovers' destruction. But by foregrounding the conflict between the rebellious lovers and the verbal conventions which encode and enforce those constraints, the play also makes it clear that what defeats their utopian desires is not the universal and immutable tragedy of the human condition, but a particular social construction which is open to dispute and therefore open to be changed.

It is in this sense, that *Romeo and Juliet* may be described as a radical tragedy, whose vision is subversive and protesting rather than conservative and acquiescent. Moreover, in so far as social divisions and sexual inequalities continue to sabotage the relations between men and women in the modern phase of patriarchal society, this tragedy still has the power to speak constructively to us, to educate our imagination in the need to further the struggle for social and sexual liberation in our own world today.

# NOTES

1   Textual references are to the Arden edition of Shakespeare's works: Brian Gibbons (ed.), *Romeo and Juliet*, London, Methuen, 1968.

# BIBLIOGRAPHY

Bryant, J. (ed.) (1964), *Romeo and Juliet*, New York, New American Library.

Champion, L. S. (1976), *Shakespeare's Tragic Perspective*, Athens, Georgia, University of Georgia Press.

Charlton, H. B. (1948), *Shakespearean Tragedy*, Cambridge, Cambridge University Press.

Dickey, F. M. (1957), *Not Wisely But Too Well: Shakespeare's Love Tragedies*, San Marino, California, Huntington Library.

Draper, J. W. (1961), *Stratford to Dogberry*, Pittsburgh.

Farnham, W. (1964), 'The tragic qualm', in A. Harbage (ed.), *Shakespeare: The Tragedies*, Englewood Cliffs, NJ, Prentice Hall, p. 22.

Fernbach, D. (ed.) (1973), *Marx: Surveys from Exile*, Harmondsworth, Penguin.

Hamilton, A. C. (1967), *The Early Shakespeare*, San Marino, California, Huntington Library.

Kermode, F. (1974), '*Romeo and Juliet*', in G. B. Evans, *The Riverside Shakespeare*, Boston, Houghton Mifflin, p. 1057.

Lawlor, J. (1961), '*Romeo and Juliet*', in J. R. Brown and B. Harris (eds), *Early Shakespeare*, London, Edward Arnold, p. 132.

Spencer, T. J. B. (ed.) (1967), *Romeo and Juliet*, Harmondsworth, Penguin.

Stauffer, D. A., (1964), 'The school of love: *Romeo and Juliet*', in A. Harbarge (ed.), *Shakespeare: The Tragedies*, Englewood Cliffs, NJ, Prentice Hall, p. 30.

Whitaker, V. K. (1965), *The Mirror Up To Nature*, San Marino, California, Huntington Library.

# PART II

## Models and methods

---

TAILOR: But how did you desire it
should be made?
GRUMIO: Marry Sir, with needle and
thread.

(*The Taming of the Shrew*, IV. iii. 120–1)

# 6

# Styles as parameters in text strategy

*Nils Erik Enkvist*

*Texts present themselves as complex linguistic structures, the meaning of which must be (re)constructed in the act of reading itself. Traditionally, such processes of constructing meaning on the basis of a text are studied by stylistics. As the term indicates, this discipline confronts the idea of 'style' as a concrete manifestation of textuality. In this essay, Nils Erik Enkvist first addresses the notion of style as such. To begin with, two classic definitions of the concept are examined: style as related to a linguistic norm; and style as choice. Each of these definitions creates its own problems. A situation-bound definition may surmount these problems. The question, however, is how to elaborate further such a definition. In this respect, recent developments in discourse analysis and text linguistics provide fruitful insights.*

*As Enkvist shows, texts are aimed at particular goals and are affected by the specific situation in which writer and reader find themselves. This requires them to employ a dynamic text strategy. However, this in turn involves several forces and principles at once. For instance, in writing a poem, the poet has to obey rules of metre and rhyme, and principles of composition and thematic develop-ment, over and above the rules of the language, which of course have to be obeyed too. As the examples provided in the essay show, such different forces may conspire, but they may at other times also conflict with each other. Consequently, the ultimate surface structure of the text is the result of the weightings allocated to various structural elements in the text strategy. The weight given to a specific element, and its subsequent selection and inclusion in the text, is thus the outcome of a complex decision-making process in which the importance given to one textual parameter is held against the value estimated for other parameters.*

*The ultimate decisions made are dependent on text type too. This calls for a flexible notion of style. In other words, style is intimately tied to social acting. Both writer and reader must estimate the appropriateness of linguistic structure to contextually-relevant norms deriving from the situation, the particular goals aimed at, and the specific text type under consideration. By assigning weightings to the various decisions made in these respects, the notion of style as situationally determined may be given further development. What emerges is a more powerful model of literary communication, in which the social forces do not only form the 'context' for the text, but are directly involved in its ultimate shaping and functioning.*

### 6.1

In this chapter my purpose is to bring together a number of points made in a set of other contexts, but in the overall perspective of stylistics. Therefore the first question that arises is: What is style?

Style – so goes the classic commonsense definition – is one way of saying or writing something (assuming that we are interested in styles in language, not in other fields). But once we speak of one way, we acknowledge the existence of other ways. For a style to arise, there must be *one* way of expressing oneself that contrasts with *other* ways.

If this is right, we can only experience styles by comparing a text or piece of discourse with something else. And what is 'something else'? Apparently other texts or pieces of discourse, which say more or less similar things, though in another way.

Against this view, objections have been raised. There are 'monists' who say that a given meaning can only be expressed in one single way. Once you start tinkering with expressions you also start tinkering with meanings. This used to be one of the basic tenets of the New Critics in the 1940s. But there are also 'dualists' who claim that the same underlying meaning can be dressed up in different surface forms. So for instance certain classic, though now outdated, schools of generative-transformational grammarians used to insist that transformations do not change meanings though they do change surface forms. For a linguist it would be nice to escape responsibility by referring to reliable judges outside the stylistic debate for an ultimate verdict on such metaphysical problems. But in spite of persistent efforts, semanticists and philosophers have failed to give us simple, valid and reliable rules for deciding once and for all whether two utterances mean the same or not. And of course a phrase such as 'more or less similar in meaning' has already introduced fuzz into the argument.

This time I shall leave such questions alone. I shall once again assume that our experience of style arises when we match an emerging text with past experiences of other texts which we regard as worth comparing with the emerging one (Enkvist, 1964, 1973, 1974a). It is through assessments of similarities and differences between the emerging text and what we compare with it (call it 'norm' for brevity, though 'norm' here does not involve value judgments) that stylistic impressions arise.

This view rests on a specific conception of our knowledge of language (one might like to say 'linguistic competence' but the term has been usurped for another, more technical purpose). A person who knows a language has accumulated a vast store of experience of its use in many social practices. He will match the texts he hears or sees with his available norms. And he does so with great intuitive ease, just as he copes intuitively with the structures of sound and syntax in the languages he masters, though he is unable to explain in technical detail what its structures are. This matching process, then, leads to stylistic responses. But if a person lacks experience of a certain type of text and discourse, that type of text and discourse cannot possibly be part of his norm. To feel the characteristically Shakespearean texture of a poetic passage we must have experienced both characteristically Shakespearean and characteristically non-Shakespearean poems. Otherwise how could we spot what makes Shakespeare stand out as Shakespeare? This argument is not invalidated by the fact that when we absorb texts in a foreign language we can sometimes respond successfully, even to their styles. When this happens, we are matching foreign texts with norms we transfer from our native language and its culture. In so doing, however, we take great risks: we may, and often do, go terribly wrong.

One of the prime tasks of linguistic stylistics is to simulate the matching of text and norm through explicit linguistic procedures. A precise methodology for doing just this has been developed, for instance, for author-attribution studies. The linguist begins by analysing and describing the text. He then circumscribes and analyses and describes a representative sample of a carefully selected norm. And he then compares text with norm, noting significant similarities and differences and describing them at a suitable level of abstraction and delicacy. Thus he arrives at an inventory of style-markers, of those features whose occurrence and density are significantly similar to, or significantly different from, the corresponding features in the norm. Intuitive judgments of significance can be supported with statistical calculations if need be. The style-markers are what makes up the characteristic style of the text.

There are of course many pitfalls built into this simplistic simulation of an extremely subtle aspect of human text comprehension. One of the hazards is the selection and circumscription of the norm. It is not in itself a linguistic procedure, but one determined by sociocultural considerations. All the same, it will determine the results. Ultimately the choice of norm must rely on a competent and knowledgeable investigator's judgments as to what is worth comparing with what in a particular investigation.

**6.2**

Such models simulate what happens in the receptor when he responds to the style of a text. Should we wish to move from the receptor to the producer of discourse in order to model the genesis of styles in texts, the first idea that springs to mind is, of course, style as choice. A speaker or writer has a vast repertoire of linguistic devices as his disposal. He must sift and choose among them, and his choices will result in a style.

All choices? Certainly not. The choice between 'it's raining' and 'it isn't raining' should not be labelled as stylistic. It is a matter of truth rather than of style. If we go on to contemplate what choices actually qualify as stylistic, we shall once again be tempted to say that stylistic choices are those that do not affect the truth value of an utterance. 'My wife is a children's doctor' and 'My wife is a paediatrician' presumably qualify as two different utterances which have the same truth condition: if one is true, so is the other. If you accept this kind of argument and believe you are a competent arbiter of truths, you can accept differences such as that between 'children's doctor' and 'paediatrician' as stylistic.

This view of style as choice also has a built-in difficulty, however.

When we hear or see a text, all choices have already taken place. How can we ever reconstruct the repertoire of alternatives that was actually available to the person who produced the text?

Therefore many students of style have tried another route. They have noted that styles are situation-bound modes of expression. We know from experience that people express themselves differently in different types of situations. Sometimes we use solemn language, sometimes colloquial expressions and even slang; sometimes we need the convolutions of legal language, sometimes the insistent staccato of a leading article in a popular newspaper. If we try to merge such observations with the view of style as choice, the merger will produce definitions of the type 'Styles arise through the situation-bound choice between expressions that have a certain similarity of meaning'. Think of the language a clergyman uses when admonishing his flock and of the language a sergeant uses when ticking off a platoon of recruits. Both operate within stylistic traditions. They may conform and stay within the tradition, but they may also rebel against conformity (at least in a thought experiment). And such rebellions can be very striking; think of the clergyman using the language of the sergeant, and vice versa! The suprise effect here does not reside in the language as such but in its transfer into a novel context or situation. Note, by the way, that there are certain situations in which expressions are completely frozen (as in performative formulae such as prayers, military commands and other rituals), and other situations in which stylistic shocks through transfer may even be at a premium (as in, say, advertising or some types of modern poetry). It is easy to see why. Information theorists have taught us that unpredictability is information, and what is unpredictable to the point of shock will carry even more information than a mere slight surprise. Such observations will lead us to an aesthetic of probabilities; the classical temper was fond of satisfied expectations such as symmetries in architecture of poetry, whereas romantics – like some modern architects – found their beauty in surprises, in thwarted expectations.

## 6.3

To summarize this, I once suggested that styles come into being as aggregates of probabilities of expressions in situational contexts, or, more briefly, as aggregates of contextual probabilities (Enkvist, 1964, p. 28). It did, however, take me a long and intricate essay to explain in what sense I was using terms such as 'contextual probability'.

Instead of once again rehearsing these arguments conceived a quarter-century ago, it seems more opportune to try to relate them to more recent developments in linguistics. Most notably, the rise of text and discourse linguistics since the early 1970s has given us various text theories and text models which are potentially interesting to the student of style. As many style-markers may consist, not of features within individual sentences but of ways in which sentences are linked into texts, the study of intersentential linking is thus of obvious relevance to stylistic description. And as students of discourse-as-interaction have widened our views on relevant situational factors, interactional discourse linguistics, pragmalinguistics and conversation analysis are of obvious relevance too. They take us further than a mere listing of stylistically interesting situational factors (Enkvist, 1980b). In this paper I shall stay with one particular text model, however; the one I have called predication-based.

In a predication-based text model, the input consists of a set of 'text atoms', symbolized as propositions or predications (in a predication, something is said about something), and of a text strategy which steers the textualization of these predications into a text. It is easy enough to draw box diagrams showing the essence of such models (cf. Enkvist, 1975, p. 19). Figure 6.1 shows one. Of course such a diagram solves nothing unless it has been proved right by psycholinguistic evidence or set to work through a computer, or other, simulation of text production. What virtues such diagrams have lie entirely in their helping us to visualize an argument and in revealing deficiencies in our knowledge.

As this box diagram shows, the input into the textualizer consists of a set of predications (which van Dijk and Kintsch (1983) call a 'text base') and a text strategy. Different text strategies can

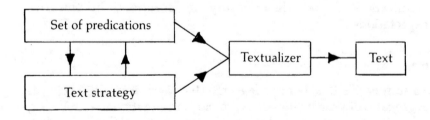

Figure  6.1

lead to different textualizations of the same input. Compare for instance:

(a) My sister Susie has a dog. It is a collie. It is        [6.1]
    called Winston. Winston is brown and white.
    Winston is eight years old. Susie takes Winston for
    walks in the park. She does this every morning.
(b) Every morning my sister Susie takes her
    brown-and-white collie Winston, who is eight,
    for a walk in the park.
(c) You ought to know about Winston, the
    eight-year-old brown-and-white collie who
    belongs to my sister Susie. She takes him for
    walks in the park every morning.

The reason for the arrows between the predication box and the strategy box in Figure 6.1 is one of the many problems raised by such models. Are discourse elements such as 'You ought to know about $x$' in example [6.1] (c) predications, or have they been added by the strategy? Anyway, as composition teachers have noted in the methods known as 'sentence combining', textualizing the same set of predications with different strategies is a useful stylistic exercise and a good instance of stylistic choice in action. Textualizations can vary through different use of metatext (text explaining the text), different groupings of predications into syntactic units, different linearization and embedding. The text strategy is what steers the lexical and syntactic operations of textualization.

### 6.4

This was the background against which I shall take up the central problem of my essay: What goes into a text strategy? First, however, a set of authentic examples to support and augment what so crudely emerged from the fabrication in [6.1].

First let us contemplate the verb 'to put'. With 'put', an indication of place – a locative adverbial – is necessary; a sentence such as:

(3) John put his hat and his umbrella        [6.2]

is awkward to the point of rejection. It is a characteristic of English syntax that obligatory adverbials, which are tightly bound to their verbs by meaning ('put' for instance implies place), like to stay close to their verbs and thus resist moving to the front of the sentence, unless there are very strong reasons for doing so.

Now if we look at the collections of texts known as the Brown and LOB corpora, which together consist of some 2 million running words of text (1 million from American and 1 million from British sources), with a controlled sampling of different text types, we shall find that there is a total of four instances in which a locative used with 'put' occurs in the front of the sentence. Two occur in each corpus. There are some 409 sentences in the Brown corpus and some 500 in the LOB corpus which have frontable locatives. Why, then, so few actual frontings?

Of the four instances, two involve anaphoric adverbs (such as 'here' in 'Here John put his hat'). What is more interesting is that the remaining two come from a very specific text type, namely the cookery book:

(a) Peel, core, and slice across enough apples to          [6.3]
    make a dome in the pie tin, and set aside. In a
    saucepan put sufficient water to cover them, an
    equal amount of sugar, a sliced lemon ...
                    (Brown Corpus, E.11.1,620)

(b) Into a champagne glass put a lump of sugar, an
    egg-spoonful of brandy ...
                    (LOB Corpus, E.19.139)

Why should a cookery-book writer be especially prone to fronting locatives with 'put', which seem to resist such fronting in other text types? One reason is the principle of end weight; long and heavy constituents tend to go last in a written English sentence, and the lists of things the cook ought to put into his saucepan or champagne-glass are long. The locative itself also expresses 'old' information, in the sense that saucepans and champagne-glasses are part of the equipment taken for granted in a cookery-book. And such 'old' information usually comes early in the sentence.

But an even more interesting conspiring reason for the fronting of these locatives can be deduced from the fact that cookery books are written in a style we might call 'terse operational'. A cookery book should not be like a family Bible; it should be easy to handle. Its expressions must therefore be brief and to the point (which is not to deny that there are cookery books containing chatty bits beside the terse operational ones). One good way in which a writer can save space is to make use of what I have called 'experiential iconicity' (Enkvist, 1981). The text is made into a picture, an icon, of experience by ordering the elements of the text in the same order in which they occur in reality. This is a very common principle; we all know that

(a) Sue and Peter got married and had a baby.          [6.4]

does not mean the same as

(b) Sue and Peter had a baby and got married.          [6.4]

A terse operational text will profit from such experiential iconicity (or 'natural order' as rhetoricians used to call it). 'Into a champagne glass put $x$, $y$ and $z$' is cookery-book short-hand for 'First take a champagne glass and then put into it $x$, $y$ and $z$'. A structure such as 'Put $x$, $y$ and $z$ into a champagne glass' would not reflect the actual order of operations in the kitchen. Experiential iconicity is even more common in guidebooks, for the same reason. Sentences such as:

(a) Behind the altar is the tomb of Cardinal X.          [6.5]

are short for the 'Next please go behind the altar and there you will find a tomb of Cardinal X.' A sentence of the type:

(b) The tomb of Cardinal X is behind the altar.          [6.5]

answers the question 'Where is the Cardinal's tomb?' but does not expressly tell the visitor how he should organize his guided tour. Such locative strategies are common whenever we have to explain a layout, for instance the appearance of a house or a flat (Linde and Labov, 1975). The interplay of spatial fact and temporal organization in language is reflected in text strategy and exposed through word order. The principle, or text-strategic parameter, of iconicity is especially important, and therefore heavily weighted, in the terse operational style of a cookery book or a guidebook.

### 6.5

Under the spell of Wonderland – not an uncommon condition among linguists – M.A.K. Halliday has produced a set of permutations of the first two lines of the White Rabbit's accusation:

(a) The Queen of Hearts, she made some tarts,          [6.6]
    All on a summer day;
    The Knave of Hearts, he stole those tarts,
    And took them quite away!

In a paper ironically entitled 'It's a fixed word order language is English', Halliday (1985) goes on to permute:

(b) Upon a summer day the Queen of Hearts    [6.6]
    made some tarts.

(c) The one who made some tarts upon a summer
    day was the Queen of Hearts.

(d) Some tarts were made by the Queen of Hearts
    upon a summer day.

(e) It was upon a summer day that the Queen of
    Hearts made some tarts.

Once again, such permutations neatly demonstrate how 'word order consideration can override other tendencies in the grammar', as Halliday puts it. But what is even more interesting is: What precisely is it that prompts such word-order considerations? Of course they are not a purpose in themselves. They are motivated, not by forces within the sentence but by the need for adapting the sentence to its textual environment, the need for giving the sentence the textual fit (to speak with Enkvist, 1977a, p.6) required by the text strategy. Permutations such as Halliday's should therefore be contextualized if we are to understand what motivates their use in each individual instance. In other words, the function of a given syntactic variant only becomes understandable if we look at its job within the discourse.

We might also note in passing that if we are to explain in a generative grammar what triggers off such processes as topicalization, clefting, extraposition, or the kind of passivization which is motivated by information dynamics (theme-rheme or topic-comment or focus patterning), we must build representations of the relevant textual forces into our grammar. If we refuse to deal with text strategies as such, we must devise explicit formatives that introduce textual forces into the description of single sentences.

Back to textual fit. Some ten years ago I did some experimenting, both in Swedish and in English (Enkvist, 1977a, 1978), permuting sentences and asking informants to produce the kinds of contexts into which these permutations seemed to fit snugly. Let me repeat my report on one of them. The text, adapted from Winston Churchill's *History of the English-Speaking Peoples*, and the permutations went like this:

Like Lee, Stonewall Jackson had served gallantly in    [6.7]

the Mexican War. He had devoted himself to the
theoretical study of the military art.

1  At the Virginia Military Institute, Jackson was at
   this time a professor.
2  A professor at the Virginia Military Institute
   Jackson was at this time.
3  Jackson was at this time a professor at the
   Virginia Military Institute.
4  At this time Jackson was a professor at the
   Virginia Military Institute.
5  A professor Jackson was at this time at the
   Virginia Military Institute.

He came of Ulster stock, settled in Virginia

To go on quoting from my report (Enkvist, 1978, p. 66–9):

Twelve native-speaker lecturers in English from six different
universities in Finland were asked to rate the contextual
acceptabilities of the test sentences, first ranking them in order
of preference, and then placing them on a three-point scale of
acceptability. Half of the subjects regarded (4) and half (3) as
their first choice, and the second choice was also evenly divided
between (4) and (3). The third choice was (1), unanimously; the
worst sentences were (2) and (5). The acceptability ratings
went like this:

| Sentence | All right | Doubtful | Unacceptable |
|----------|-----------|----------|--------------|
| 1 | 2 | 7 | 3 |
| 2 | 0 | 1 | 11 |
| 3 | 9 | 3 | 0 |
| 4 | 10 | 2 | 0 |
| 5 | 0 | 0 | 12 |

This experiment is suggestive and can teach the investigator
a lesson. The subjects were asked to comment and justify
their judgments and to try to write contexts into which the
ill-fitting sentences could be placed more snugly than into
the context actually given. The comments showed that some
of the subjects (professional teachers of English to
foreigners) may well have worried about grammatical
correctness and aired their own linguistic prejudices. The
context given was also said to have been too short to provide
a basis for firm judgments. When asked to provide plausible

contexts improving the acceptability of the awkward
sentences, the subjects ventured solutions such as:

> Like Lee, Stonewall Jackson had served gallantly in the
> Mexican War. He came of Ulster Stock, settled in Virginia.
> At the Virginia Military Institute, Jackson was at this time
> a professor.

This justifies the topicalization by linking 'Virginia Military
Institute' to 'Virginia' in the previous sentence and to 'war' in
the preceding one. Some of the recontextualizations were
fairly elaborate and show that the subjects were willing to
adjust to the spirit of the game:

> Jackson was meanwhile pursuing his Jekyll-and-Hyde
> existence with unremitting energy. At the Virginia
> Military Institute, Jackson was at this time a professor. In
> Baltimore, Md., he was a dealer in antiques, while in
> Philadelphia, Pa., he was masquerading as a gynecologist.

> In the course of his life Jackson ran through a number of
> careers. A bootblack boy in his childhood, a bank
> messenger in Baltimore in his teens, a professional soldier
> as a young man and subsequently a yeoman farmer in
> Tennessee. A professor at the Virginia Military Institute
> Jackson was at this time. Later he played the roles of
> politician and judge, before retiring as a decadent
> aristocrat.

These solutions try to justify the topicalization through
iconic parallellism with neighbouring sentences. Several
informants also ventured comments such as:

> On sentence 1: 'He made a slow start at Yale, but then
> made rapid progress: at the VMI Jackson was ... a
> professor.' In this case, though, the following sentence
> scarcely fits. And in none of the sentences is it clear what
> 'at this time' refers to – surely not the Mexican War?
> More context needed.

The subjects were also asked for comments on the test itself,
without being told precisely what the purpose of the exercise
was. Several of the testees made critical suggestions: there
was not enough context, the style was not controlled
(several informants volunteered that some thematic variants
looked like Irish or Welsh English), many sentence variants

were so flagrantly unacceptable as to be hardly worth including, and so forth. 'My most serious worry about this kind of test,' one subject wrote,

> is whether suitable native speakers can be relied upon to evaluate some of these examples, and especially to suggest contexts ... It may be that naive native speakers, and especially those of other language backgrounds (e.g., immigrants of first or possible second generation) would be somewhat more lenient than a 'good' prose writer in what they would allow and rather at a loss when trying to make up contexts for examples – an 'unnatural' text-creation process.

There is, then, no ideal informant: the naive are too naive, the sophisticated are too sophisticated. This conflict between norms and usage has also been anticipated by Joseph Grimes, who wrote in his book *The Thread of Discourse* as follows, having included structures such as 'Saw the play did John', 'Saw the play did John?' and 'The play did John see?' among the normal paradigms of English:

> Before he reacts to the examples ... as bad English, as many do the first time they encounter them, the reader should observe his own thematizing behaviour for a day or so. Our grammatical tradition is heavily biased toward regarding unmarked thematization as well behaved and proper, and marked thematization as aberrant. Not so; it is part of the language, used constantly, related systematically to the rest. In fact, many of the phenomena written off in grammars as free word order are in contrast with each other thematically. (Grimes, J. E., 1975, *The Thread of Discourse*, p. 330–331).

However crude such acceptability experiments may be, they do show that groups of suitably selected informants can rate acceptabilities of thematic sentence variants with a reasonable degree of agreement, and that they can be coaxed to produce contexts which improve the acceptabilities of specific, otherwise doubtful thematic variants. Iconic parallelisms and the manipulation of old and new information were the two devices resorted to in the experiment referred to here.

Such elicitation studies are a healthy antidote to the study of acceptabilities in decontextualized isolation. There are sentences that look weird in isolation but which are all right in a suitable context, even in writing. A sentence such as Wyndham Lewis's

Be touched by this woman he must on occasion. [6.8]

from *The Revenge of Love* (Penguin Books, 1972, p. 55) would hardly win praise from an English teacher in a class for foreign students, at least not if it stood by itself. And then of course any thorough glance at transcripts of authentic impromptu speech will show word-order patterns which apparently did their job nicely but which seem most awkward and unacceptable, not only in isolation but also in writing.

And what, let us ask once again, is it that motivates these departures from 'normal' or 'basic' or 'least marked' or 'canonical' word order? Obviously, the text strategy, the need for adapting the sentence to the text, the need for coaxing the information to flow through the text in the desired fashion; in brief, giving the sentence the textual fit which seems optimal in the light of the text strategy adopted.

This leads to a model assuming the existence of a normal, basic, least marked, canonical word order, which is then modified if there is adequate justification for such modifications. In English the canonical order is subject-verb-object. If we wish to add adverbials to the canonical pattern, matters get more complicated. This is because different types of adverbials go into different places in the linear sequence of constituents. But the placing of adverbials too can be subject to textual forces, as we saw in the instance of locatives with 'put'.

We are now in a position to return to Halliday's example, the permutations of Lewis Carroll's Queen of Hearts. Let us assume a set of input predications, a text base, symbolized like this:

REFERENCES: [6.9]

    EXISTS: Queen of Hearts (with attributes)
    EXIST: tarts (with attributes), more than one but
        unspecified in number; one attribute of tarts
        is that they are artefacts made by baking

PREDICATION: make (Queen of Hearts, some tarts)

TIME OF PREDICATION: a summer day

From our knowledge of the world (which might be modelled in

schemata or frames or scripts or other kinds of cognitive networks) we infer that in the collocation 'make tarts', the verb 'make' stands for a sequence of operations such as getting flour and jam and other ingredients, producing dough, shaping the tart, and baking it in an oven. The collocation 'to make tarts' thus functions like an allusion because it activates a new semantic schema or script in which we have stored our knowledge of the processes of tart-making. Other schemata or scripts are activated in chains if necessary; thus 'to bake' would activate a schema involving dough, an oven, heating, temperature, baking time, and so forth. Relevant parts of such knowledge can thus be drawn into the set of predications, into the text base, for textualization if called upon by the text strategy.

Lewis Carroll was writing for contemporary English readers, notably his favourite young ladies. But had he written a science fiction story where the White Rabbit had been speaking at a law court on the planet Mars, he might have had to adapt his strategy to an audience innocent of tart-baking:

The aforesaid Queen of Hearts then, on a summer          [6.10]
day, made some tarts, a process which involves
several sub-processes, the first of which is getting
some flour, which is a white meal used for
making edible things and which is produced from
grain which is part of plants that grow in fields . . .

Martians might well need explanations of lots of concepts, even 'summer day', 'grow' and 'fields'. Nor did the White Rabbit in Wonderland bother to add 'aforesaid' which would be indicated in real-world legal style to show that the Queen of Hearts of the accusation is the same Queen of Hearts who had been spoken about before and who was present at the hearing.

In the spirit of the previous experiment, it is easy enough to invent contexts justifying the other permutations cited by Halliday and repeated in [6.6]:

The Wonderlanders were fond of seasonal dishes. On          [6.11]
winter evenings they used to mull their dandelion
wine. And on a summer day the Queen of Hearts
made some tarts.

The justification of fronting 'on a summer day' is the temporal text strategy, which makes sentences often begin with temporal expressions. Then what about the passive?

> The best culinary products of the Wonderlanders were    [6.12]
> pie-crust, gravy, meat, mock-turtle soup, and
> lobster. Pies were baked by the Owl and the
> Panther. Lobsters were especial favourites with
> the Gryphon. And some tarts were made by the
> Queen of Hearts.

The passive here makes it possible to begin the sentence with a noun phrase which is semantically a patient and which, in the corresponding active sentence, would be an object and only come after the verb. And this would be too late for the strategy, where successive sentences are made to begin with names of foods.

In a similar manner we can try to produce contexts justifying the use of clefted variants:

> A: 'I seem to remember that the Pussycat made    [6.13]
> some tarts on a summer day.'
> B: 'You're wrong. The one who made some tarts
> upon a summer day was the Queen of Hearts.
> The Pussycat only got interested in baking
> around Christmas.'

> A: 'The Queen of Hearts, I seem to remember,
> once made some tarts for Christmas.'    [6.14]
> B: 'You're wrong. It was on a summer day that the
> Queen of Hearts made some tarts. She never
> did any baking during other times of the year.'

The clefted constructions serve a definite text-strategic purpose. The pseudo-cleft in [6.13] makes it possible to move the subject, the Queen of Hearts, to the end of the sentence. And the cleft in [6.14] makes it possible to mark the information within the cleft as new, though it comes early in the sentence. In both constructions, the back-shifted or front-shifted noun phrase signals the choice of one, unexpected, alternative from those in a presuppositional set, a set of reasonable possibilities only one of which is correct. Hence the 'contrastive' character of clefts (cf. Enkvist, 1980a).

Out of all these examples, trivial though they seem at first blush, there emerges a very fundamental view of text strategies. A strategy is always directed towards a goal. The goal is affected by the situation, by what a speaker or writer wants to achieve. He must adjust his strategy to the situation. Among other things he has to estimate what his receptor already knows and how much information the receptor can process within a given span of discourse. He has to give the receptor the right information, both in quality and in quantity (Grice, 1975). He has to give it in the right concentration, putting in enough redundancy but not diluting the text too much (Enkvist, 1983). And he has to organize the text according to certain principles. His major strategy can have unity of actor or hero, as often in narrative; a chronological or temporal strategy, as in chronicles and chronologically organized narrative; or a unity of place leading to a spatially-motivated linear patterning of a text, as in a guidebook. These different strategic principles of unity can of course also be combined in different ways.

Within the sentence and the clause, one well-known strategy is to choose the words and arrange the syntax so that old, given, thematic information goes into elements that occur early in the sentence, and new, rhematic information goes into elements that come later. A corollary is that weighty elements usually come late; they are weighty precisely because they tend to contain a lot of new information. If there is no old, given, thematic information, special structures are used, such as existential 'there' or the narrative 'once upon a time'. An alternative strategy, very common in impromptu dialogue, might be labelled as 'crucial information first' (as in 'What would you like?' 'A double scotch'.) Here the new, important information goes first, and old information, if given at all, is added as an afterthought. All these strategies are exposed through the choice of words ('Susie is John's daughter'/'John is Susie's father') and through the choice of syntactic structures. Lexis and syntax offer the repertoire of structures from among which a speaker or writer can look for the best tactical solutions to his strategic problems.

## 6.6

Particularly strong are the textual forces that compel syntax into a bound metre, a form characterized by phonologically definable isomorphy or iconicity between positionally specified text units. Thus alliteration is phonological iconicity at the beginning of words, usually stressed ones; rhyme is phonological iconicity or isomorphy in unit-final syllables; rhythm is iconicity or isomorphy between stress and/or tone patterns of text units. Lewis Carroll's original:

(a) The Queen of Hearts, she made some tarts,        [6.6]
    All on a summer day.

The Knave of Hearts, he stole those tarts,
  And took them quite away.

owes its tactical arrangements to a strategy which prescribes a
metre:

$$
\begin{array}{ll}
\text{x x́ x á, x x́ x á} & \qquad\qquad \textbf{[6.15]} \\
\text{x x́ x x́ x b́.} & \\
\text{x x́ x á, x x́ x á} & \\
\text{x x́ x x́ x b́.} &
\end{array}
$$

To fill the pattern of the first two lines, Lewis Carroll had to add
some extra syllables to the canonical structure – 'she', which makes
the structure a so-called front dislocation (as in 'John he is a nice
chap'), and 'all' in 'all on a summer day' (as also 'quite' in the fourth
line). Ideally, of course, such additions ought to contribute
something more to the poem than mere filling-out of the verse
pattern. A great deal of literary criticism and literary history has
been written on the fine distinctions between suggestive poetic
language, and the kind of poetic licence that involves the insertion
of useless elements or the use of non-canonical word-order
patterns which are not justified by a text strategy. In Milton
criticism for instance, some critics accuse Milton of unjustifiably
warped syntax, whereas others find ample excuses for Milton's use
of marked word-order patterns.

Let me cite another example from poetry (cf. also Dillon (1976,
and 1978) and Verma (1976)). This time I shall leave Wonderland
for George Crabbe, whose *Tales* lend themselves nicely to my
purpose. This one is about Farmer Moss's only daughter in Langar
Vale:

Used to spare meals, disposed <u>in manner pure</u>,    [6.16]
<u>Her father's kitchen she could ill endure</u>;
Where <u>by the steaming beef he hungry sat</u>,
And laid at once a pound upon his plate;
Hot from the field, her eager brother seized
An equal part, and <u>hunger's rage appeased</u>;
The air surcharged with moisture, flagg'd around,
And the offended damsel sigh'd and frown'd;
<u>The swelling fat in lumps conglomerate laid</u>,
And fancy's sickness seized the loathing maid:
But when <u>the men beside their station took</u>,
The maidens with them, and with these the cook:
When one huge wooden bowl <u>before them stood</u>,

Fill'd with huge balls of farinaceous food;
With bacon, mass saline, where never lean
Beneath the brown and bristly rind was seen;
When <u>from a single horn the party drew</u>
<u>Their copious draughts</u> of <u>heavy ale and new</u>;
When <u>the coarse cloth she saw</u>, with many a stain,
Soil'd by rude hinds who cut and came again –
She could not breathe; but with a heavy sigh,
Rein'd the fair neck, and shut th' offended eye;
She minced the sanguine flesh <u>in frustums fine</u>,
And wonder'd much to see the creatures dine:
When she resolved <u>her father's heart to move</u>,
If hearts of farmers where alive to love.

(Tale VII, 'The Widow's Tale', in *The Poetical
Works of the Rev. George Crabbe*, London, John
Murray, 1834, volume IV pp. 287–8)

I have underlined the instances in which Crabbe departs from the canonical world-order patterns of everyday English. We would say 'in pure manner' rather than 'in manner pure'; 'She could ill endure her father's kitchen' rather than 'Her father's kitchen she could ill endure'; 'he sat hungry by the steaming beef' rather than 'by the steaming beef he hungry sat'; and so on. Crabbe's use of marked structures obviously owes to the requirements of metre and rhyme. In English, verbs are a good source of rhymes; if a poet opts for end-stopped lines, rhyming on verbs in fact leads to an object-subject-verb pattern instead of the canonical subject-verb-object. Here metre and rhyme are so important that they are allowed to impinge on normal syntax. This is precisely what is meant by poetic licence: poetic forms are allowed to override the requirements of canonical syntax.

## 6.7

So as not to slight prose altogether, yet another quotation, this time from Paul de Kruif's *Men Against Death*, from a passage on Dr Banting's early work on insulin:

Now at last the chance to test the hunch. Ten in the          [6.17]
morning of July 27 and of course the eight-week
limit Banting had asked for long since past. No
money to pay Charlie Best for his time now, so Best
borrowed money from Banting. A giant tractor

couldn't have pulled Banting away from his little
black bench now. Weeks ago, when work had just
started, Macleod had left for Europe. It's again to
the credit of Professor Macleod that he didn't write
to stop Banting now that the eight weeks are up,
and that he let Banting struggle on, but how he
went on God knows.

This steamy hot day a poor dog, miserably thin,
lies on their table. Nine days before Banting had slit
out his pancreas and with the dog going down hill
like a shot, day after day, Banting had drawn
samples of dark blood from the beast's veins with a
syringe while Best sat before his colorimeter,
watching the sugar in the dog's blood go higher,
higher. It got harder for the dog to stand up. He
could hardly wag his tail when they came for him.
He was horribly thirsty and hungry as a wolf and it
was precisely like a bad case of human diabetes.
Pancreas-less, this beast's body simply couldn't burn
sugar.

The day before they'd given him sugar-water but
not a bit of this glucose stayed in him to help his
starving tissues but all kept running out of him in
rivers of urine.

This morning of July 27 he was dying. His eyes
were glazed over as he lay there hardly able to lift
his head and right here by him was another dog,
frisky, healthy. Weeks before this one had recovered
from Banting's operation to tie off his pancreas
duct, and now . . .
(Paul de Kruif, *Men Against Death*, London and Paris,
                    The Albatross, 1948, pp. 67–8)

The flavour of the style here owes to several salient features.
Three of them are particularly striking. The main text strategy is
chronological, and therefore several sentences begin with
expressions of time: 'now at last', 'ten in the morning', 'weeks ago',
'this steamy hot day', 'nine days before', 'the day before', 'this
morning of July 27' – all these adverbials of time have been placed
to mark the temporal strategy. Secondly, some of the sentences are
incomplete, and there is a contrast between what one might
impressionistically call the frenzied staccato of the fragments and

short sentences, and the drawn-out sentences on the sufferings of the experimental animal. There is obvious iconicity in this contrast. What de Kruif did not give us was a sequence of complete sentences of, say, equal, or otherwise non-iconic, length. Thirdly, the expressions are vivid and they conjure forth images: 'hunch', 'giant tractor', 'struggle', 'miserably thin', 'slit out his pancreas', 'dog going down hill like a shot', 'dark blood', 'beast's veins', 'rivers of urine'. De Kruif did not opt for a factual, image-free, scientific mode of expression. If the reader has been moved to disgust and revulsion, while feeling the tension of research, the style has been a success.

### 6.8

We have now seen examples of various forces that govern text strategies: iconicity at various levels; vivid description as opposed to factual or scientific prose; unmarked canonical word-order patterns versus marked word-order patterns; non-metrical structures versus metrically bound ones; well-formed sentences versus fragments (the norm being, say, the generally accepted well-formedness standard expected of literate expository prose); and so on. For reasons of space I have omitted samples of impromptu speech, which are interesting because they contain features of hesitation and correction prompted by the exigencies of on-line processing. But they too should be remembered in lists such as this.

A contemplation of such textual forces suggests that text strategies are decided upon and texts generated, not through a placid and harmonious process, but rather through the struggle and arbitration between a number of principles, some of which conspire but some of which conflict. The strategy box in Figure 6.1 is thus more like a battlefield than a garden of love. Strategies and their tactical solutions come into being through decisions which weigh against each other the relative importance of incompatible elements; if you cannot have both, you must choose. For instance, is metre more important than canonical syntax? Is iconic word-order more important than the unmarked canonical word-order pattern? Is it more important to indicate a hectic succession of events with a sequence of fragments, iconically, than to produce a sequence of impeccably complete sentences? These are a few examples of the struggles and conflicts that a speaker or writer must referee in his arbitration between incompatible principles. And it is this arbitration that decides the ultimate surface form of the text and its sentences and fragments and other text units. It is this arbitration that selects the structure, from among the total repertoire, which best satisfies the text strategy in each individual instance.

Modelling such an open set of textual forces, whose priorities shift from one text type to the next, in terms of fixed systems of rigidly ordered rules, hierarchic decision-trees or system networks, would be to invite failure. If we want to visualize a model capable of incorporating such dynamic, processual views of style, a better solution is to opt for non-hierarchic parameters. In such a model, styles arise through a generative process steered by a set of heterarchic parameters. Each parameter is set at a value and it carries a certain weight in relation to other parameters. Parameter values can be binary or scalar. The rhyme parameter, for instance, might have the values 'no rhyme – imperfect rhyme – perfect rhyme'. The information-dynamic parameter steering the linking of successive sentences might have the extreme values 'theme iteration only – theme progression only', where theme iteration stands for links from theme to theme as in:

(a) *John* came home. *He* was tired.                    [6.18]

and theme progression for links between an element in the rhematic end-part of one sentence, and the beginning of the next, as in:

(b) On his wall there was *a painting.*                    [6.18]
    *It* was by Canaletto.

Intermediate values on this parametric scale would consist of different proportions of theme iteration and theme progression. High proportions of theme iteration are generally characteristic of passages with unity of hero or actor, as in narrative. And high proportions of theme progression are characteristic of expository and argumentative texts, which proceed from one thing to another (Enkvist, 1974b).

The weight of a parameter, as a concept separate from its value, expresses the importance of the parameter in relation to other parameters. In metrically-regular poetry, the values of the metricality parameter or parameters that steer metre and rhyme are heavily weighted. Their weight is heavy enough to override the resistance and inertia of canonical syntax. In the terse operational style, the weight of the iconicity parameter is sufficient to override the syntactic force tying locatives to the verb *to put*. And so on. We should try to view all the phenomena exemplified in this paper in terms of parameter values and parameter weightings.

In such a view, styles are born out of specific patterns of parameter values and weights. It is for instance characteristic of the terse operational style that the iconicity parameter is heavily weighted and given a value prompting the use of otherwise rare syntactic patterns. It is characteristic of metrically strict styles that the requirements of metre and style may override those of syntax, which means that the parameter of metricality is given the value 'strictly bound' and a weight greater than syntactic canonicity. It is characteristic of legal style that the emphasis on maximally explicit expression, leaving a minimum of opportunity for arbitrary or false interpretation, overrides the ordinary restrictions of sentence complexity, repetition and embedding. Thus parameter weighting is often associated with the style characteristic of an entire text type and not only with that of individual texts.

Conversely, if styles arise through specific patterns of parametric values and weights, such a specific pattern must also become characteristic of specific styles. Another corollary: presumably the best text is the one that best satisfies its ideal strategic weighting pattern. The best impromptu speaker is he who best follows the priorities of impromptu-speech parameters. The best advertiser is he who best attracts attention to his product by weighting what surprises and attracts a customer. The best lawyer is the one who can best bend the specific features of legal language to his own purposes. But we should not expect impromptu speech or advertisements or statutes to follow the requirements we have set for, say, literate school essays. Our stylistic ideals should be relative and flexible. Perhaps the ideal text is one that obeys the ideal text-strategic weighting pattern specific to its own text type, but which at the same time avoids needless departures from the least marked values of those parameters that are less relevant. For instance, even in metrical poetry, the best poets (such as Alexander Pope) succeed in maintaining patterns of canonical syntax. This is what makes their verses so smooth. Only when metre and syntactic canonicity are incompatible should metre win over syntax.

It is perhaps also worth noting that the way in which I have drawn on word-order phenomena for illustrations of my argument is hardly coincidental. I mentioned at the beginning of this essay that the great problem in investigations of style is the relation between expression and meaning. In the dualistic view, where we define style as one of several possible ways of expressing something, we must be capable of deciding whether two different expressions mean the same or not. It is easy to assume, though in fact it is far from self-evident, that those word-order permutations that do not change the basic syntactic roles of constituents, and which do not change quantifier scope, are cognitively equivalent. 'John kicked Mary' and 'Mary kicked John' are non-equivalent because syntactic roles have been switched, and 'Everybody in this room speaks three languages' and 'Three languages are spoken by everybody in this room' are non-equivalent because they differ in quantifier scope. But 'John went at five' and 'At five John went' would more readily count as equivalent because syntactic roles as well as the scopes of existential and all-quantifiers remain the same (assuming that we do not try to explain adverbial placement in terms of quantification). Thus the study of different word-order permutations is a nice heuristic starting-point for those who want to see how different text strategies are exposed on the textual surface. Many word-order arrangements in fact serve text strategies by determining in which ways and in what order information is incremented, and how the textual fit of clauses and sentences can be optimized.

## 6.9

The view of style as arising from conflicts and conspiracies which are resolved through choices of parameter values and parameter weightings is, of course, a dynamic rather than a static one. If we wish to model it in concrete terms, we must borrow a set of concepts from decision theory. A decision thus becomes necessary whenever there is an opportunity for acting in more than one way. Every choice in text production involves a decision (which is not to say that such decisions need be conscious). Decisions are made by referring those factors that affect the decision to a strategy. A strategy in turn is definable as a goal-determined assignment of parameter values and weighting of parameters. To simulate such text-strategic decisions and their tactical implementation we shall need a dynamic, processual model of text generation, and not merely a static model capable of describing texts such as they are.

As the attentive reader has no doubt noticed, the conflicts and conspiracies that decide text strategies are another way of looking at style as choice. The resolution of a conflict is of course only another term for choice. What use, then, is viewing style as parameter values and weightings? Is it simply a new jargon, another pointless exercise in terminological pluralism, pouring old wine into a new bottle? Or does it bring something interesting into stylistics?

Styles have always resided and will always reside in text processing. As we have noted, in text production the stylistic process is a choice between elements which reckons with context of situation. And in text comprehension it is a result of matching an emerging text with contextually relevant norms. Therefore there is a virtue in any method that views styles as processes, and not only as static structures residing in texts. I say 'not only as structures' because all process-models of course presuppose structures. For structures are what processes operate on. A process is definable as the change of one structure into another. Therefore processual stylistics too rests squarely on a foundation of structural stylistics.

But what about the parameters themselves? Are we merely giving pseudo-scientific terms to vague concepts, and perhaps also arguing in a circle? If we make a statement such as 'In this text the iconicity parameter is given a strongly positive value and maximal weight', are we in fact saying anything beyond the fact that we have found iconicity in the text?

First, a parametric model may give a starting-point for actual simulation, by computer or otherwise, of the rise of texts in specific styles. It may also give a base for concrete analyses of styles in specifying what the analyst might be looking for in texts.

Secondly, a parametric view relates the genesis of styles to a specific text model, that based on predications and a text strategy. After the rise of text linguistics and discourse analysis in the 1970s, there has arisen a need to relate stylistics to text theories and text models. And this, it seems, the parametric view of style can do. It helps to bridge the gap between stylistics and text-cum-discourse linguistics. Conversely, it also suggests some contents for the text-strategy box in diagrams such as Figure 6.1, which might otherwise remain a mystical, sealed black box.

Thirdly, a parametric view compels us to see style-governing forces, not in isolation but as values and weightings which contrast with other values and weightings. In other words, it compels us to structuralize the forces that determine style by viewing them as elements in a system. As the structuralists used to teach us, an element is meaningful only if it contrasts with other elements; elements without contrast are meaningless. Conversely, only by setting up a contrast between the element which is actually there in a text, and other elements which might have been but are not, can we grasp the meaning of that element. If, for instance, we find that a certain text is maximally explicit (like a law or statute), we must look for texts with the opposite explicitness value, namely maximal implicitness. And we shall find them for instance in the impromptu dialogue of people who work together and say things like 'Now!' or 'One more inch!'. Such a quest for contrasts is of heuristic use in directing our attention to certain specific features, perhaps one at a time. It leads us from single atomistic observations to attempts at systematization. And it gives us clues as to the character of stylistic choice, though we can never tell precisely what actually went on in the mind of a text-producer.

To sum up. 'How', I asked at the beginning of section 6.2 of this chapter, 'can we ever hope to reconstruct the repertoire of alternatives that was actually available to the person who produced the text?' One way of trying is this. We identify style-markers. We postulate that these style-markers have arisen through specific parameter values and weightings, and we try to figure out what would be the other, or opposite, parameter values and weightings. Of course such processes have to rely on the researcher's stylistic competence and on his intuitions. But as linguists, we cavil at intuitions at our own peril. All descriptions of any natural language, beyond the stage of physical descriptions of sounds or letters, ultimately rest on somebody's instuitions about his language. Why, then, shouldn't stylistics?

# BIBLIOGRAPHY

Dijk, T. A. van and Kintsch, W. (1983), *Strategies of Discourse Comprehension*, New York, Academic Press.

Dillon, G. L. (1976), 'Literary transformations and poetic word order', *Poetics*, vol. 5, pp. 1–22.

Dillon, G. L. (1978), *Language Processing and the Reading of Literature: Toward a Model of Comprehension*, Bloomington, Indiana University Press.

Enkvist, N. E. (1964), 'On defining style', in N. E. Enkvist, J. Spencer and M. Gregory (eds), *Linguistics and Style*, Oxford, Oxford University Press, pp. 1–56.

Enkvist, N. E. (1973), *Linguistic Stylistics*, The Hague, Mouton.

Enkist, N. E. (1974a), *Stilforskning och stilteori*, Lund, Gleerup.

Enkvist, N. E. (1974b), '"Theme dynamics" and style', *Studia Anglica Posnaniensia*, vol. 5, pp. 127–35.

Enkvist, N. E. (1975), *Tekstilingvistiikan peruskäsitteitä*, Helsinki, Gaudeamus.

Enkvist, N. E. (1977a), 'Contextual acceptability and error evaluation', in R. Palmberg and H. Ringbom (eds), *Papers from the Conference on Contrastive*

*Linguistics and Error Analysis, Stockholm and Åbo, 7–8 February 1977*, Åbo, Reports from the Research Institute of the Åbo Akademi Foundation, no. 19.

Enkvist, N. E. (1977b), 'Stylistics and text linguistics', in W. U. Dressler (ed.), *Current Trends in Text Linguistics*, Berlin and New York, Walter de Gruyter, pp. 174–90.

Enkvist, N. E. (1978) (with Marianne von Wright), 'Problems in the study of textual factors in topicalization', in E. Andersson (ed.), *Working Papers on Computer Processing of Syntactic Data*, Åbo, Reports from the Research Institute of the Åbo Akademi Foundation, no. 41, pp. 45–71.

Enkvist, N. E. (1980a), 'Marked focus: functions and constraints', in S. Greenbaum, G. Leech and J. Svartvik (eds), *Studies in English Linguistics for Randolph Quirk*, London, Longman, pp. 134–52.

Enkvist, N. E. (1980b), 'Categories of situational context from the perspective of stylistics', *Language Teaching and Linguistics Abstracts*, vol. 13, pp. 75–94; reprinted in V. Kinsella (ed.), *Surveys I*, Cambridge, Cambridge University Press, 1982, pp. 58–79.

Enkvist, N. E. (1980c), 'Motives for topicalization', in R. Thelwall (ed.), *Linguistic Studies in Honour of Paul Christophersen*, Coleraine, The New University of Ulster, pp. 1–15.

Enkvist, N. E. (1981), 'Experiential iconicism in text strategy', *Text*, vol. 1, pp. 77–111.

Enkvist, N. E. (1983), 'Some thoughts about the role of inference in text concentration or expansion and in text typology', in K. Granström (ed.), *Om kommunikation 2*, Linköping, University of Linköping Studies in Communication, vol. 6, pp. 1–17.

Enkvist, N. E. (1985), 'A parametric view of word order', in E. Sözer (ed.), *Text Connexity, Text Coherence: Methods, Aspects, Results*, Hamburg, Buske pp. 320–36.

Enkvist, N. E. (forthcoming), 'Stil' kak parametral'naja nagruzka', in M. P. Kotjurova (ed.), *Festschrift for M. N. Kozina*, Perm', Universitet im. A. M. Gor'kogo.

Enkvist, N. E. (1986), 'Linearization, Text Type, and Parameter Weighting', in Mey, J. L. (ed.), *Language and Discourse: Test and Protest*, Amsterdam/Philadelphia, John Benjamins Publishing Company, pp. 245–60.

Grice, H. P. (1975), 'Logic and conversation', in P. Cole and J. L. Morgan (eds), *Syntax and Semantics 3: Speech Acts*, New York, Academic Press, pp. 41–58.

Grimes, J. E. (1975), *The Thread of Discourse*, The Hague, Mouton.

Halliday, M. A. K. (1985), 'It's a fixed word order language is English', *ITL: Review of Applied Linguistics*, vol. 67–8, pp. 91–116.

Linde, C. and Labov, W. (1975), 'Spatial networks as a site for the study of language and thought', *Language*, vol. 51, pp. 924–39.

Verma, S. K. (1976), 'Topicalization as a stylistic mechanism', *Poetics*, vol. 5. pp. 23–33.

# 7

# Intercultural writing

## A pragmatic analysis of style

*Ludger Hoffmann*

*The conflicts involved in writing of which the previous chapter spoke are perhaps nowhere as powerful as in the case of intercultural writing. This is the name Ludger Hoffmann gives to a situation in which writer and reader belong to different cultures, involving different languages or different varieties of a language. Apart from requirements on the level of lexis and grammar, such intercultural writing also demands the command of stylistic skills. As with Enkvist's approach, Hoffmann proposes to look beyond what are traditionally-regarded stylistic 'devices', and to concentrate both on the specific actions such devices might fulfil and on the patterns of action which develop socially and historically to realize such aims.*

*A literary competition organized for Turkish immigrant workers in Germany provided the material for the present analysis; what Hoffmann attempts is a description and analysis of the various potential conflicts which arise out of this situation. In essence, the situation presents itself as a problem to a writer. This problem calls for a solution, and hence for a particular action. The resulting text, being grounded in two cultures simultaneously, bears witness to the unavoidable conflicts involved in the process.*

*A distinction is made between processes which bear on the level of expression only, i.e. the local surface form of the text, and on the level of action patterns, i.e. organized and prestructured forms of linguistic interaction such as greeting, narrating, explaining, protesting, etc. On each of these levels, different solutions to the problem of intercultural writing are demonstrated and analysed. The result is a systematic inventory of stylistic solutions to the problem of intercultural writing which is generalizable beyond the corpus investigated. The type of results gained in the exercise, according to Hoffmann's theoretical position, can only be arrived at through a type of discourse analysis which sees language primarily as a way of acting socially and culturally.*

## 7.1 Writing

According to general opinion, writing is secondary to speaking. Chronologically, this holds true. However, for many societies writing becomes the primary medium for the preservation of knowledge and tradition, which can then be passed on with the possibility of objective validation. Historically this usually leads to a corresponding decline of oral traditions in those societies. In this respect the recent rediscovery of oral tradition characteristically coincides with the changing position of the written word in the presence of the new media. At the same time we find attempts to secure a broader base for literature in everyday life, so that it may be used for the production and reproduction of experiences.

The distinguished feature of a 'text' is its detachment from the original context of its formation (see Ehlich, 1982). It requires its own form of language (e.g. another kind of deixis, different syntactic structures, etc.) which ensures understanding independent of the situation. In order to succeed in this, however, the author must explicitly provide points of reference in the text, which are immediately available in oral communication. The author is relieved, however, from the immediate pressure of action in everyday communication; he can plan and develop his product in complex stages. Consequently, it is to be expected that structural principles in the construction of the text are easily recognizable and that it is a self-contained entity. The linguistic devices employed should be chosen with respect to criteria such as suitability, variation and precision. The higher degree of control over the writing process increases the author's responsibility for the outcome. The characteristics of writing are therefore to be gained from the process of action. The enormous potential of textual meaning is a direct result of the dissociation of writing from (repeatable) reading.

## 7.2 Learning to write

Normally, a considerable amount of teaching effort is required in order to create a basic ability to write. But even then a final success is not at all secured. The reasons for this are traditionally looked for in the methods of teaching. This is obviously not the whole truth. After all, since the rules of writing differ considerably from those of speech, the command of a relevant part of standard speech is an actual prerequisite. The transfer into the medium of writing lends the speech action the character of a definite result. This fixation is only possible on the basis of an analytical relationship to the spoken language (cf. Coulmas, 1981, p. 25), such as to the phoneme and morpheme structure. On the other hand, the functionality of writing in linguistic action must be tangibly experienced. In the institution of the school, which has more a cognitive than a practical orientation, this will be taught only in a very restricted sense, e.g. through typically educational texts like the essay. Indeed, we come across the following:

1 illiteracy in the technical sense (to which more attention has been paid recently by public opinion and education);
2 illiteracy in the literary and functional sense (the lack of command of relevant types of text).

Access to writing is therefore always at risk on the grounds of institutional conditions:

1 Individual learning processes cannot be optimally accommodated. Teaching and learning often work against each other.
2 Learning and practice of communication are dissociated.
3 Teaching procedures for creating an analytical relationship to language are lacking.
4 To a great extent there is a lack of attempts to teach in detail a broad spectrum of everyday and literary types of text and their forms of realization. Instead of this, specific school types of text (of a surrogate nature) are passed on.

## 7.3 Writing in a second language

The teaching of foreign languages is based largely on working with texts. Often it is organized around literary models. Some types of text are introduced in this manner, at least *en passant*. But generally more attention is paid to matters of grammar than to text type or linguistic action-patterns. Basic requirements, in the sense of technical literacy, are regularly attained in the foreign language, but it is largely up to the learner him/herself to acquire a literacy in the functional sense. The acquisition of the foreign tongue thus remains controlled by the mother-tongue for a long time. The learning process thereby tends to be completed at a fairly low level, which is reduced even more through non-use – the typical fate of school learning. Only a continuing need for communication can counteract this process.

The bridge to writing can hardly be crossed if a second language is acquired 'naturally' – as under conditions of migration. One may indeed notice that, on the whole, migrants of the first generation remain restricted to linguistic means which are strongly contextually bound. Often this is just enought for what is required to get by for work and consumption. In this way, their writing skills are of a rudimentary character (filling out forms, etc.). Their literary presence is attested only by means of reports and translations, usually provided by non-members of the culture. For second-generation migrants, however, writing is indispensable in order to fulfil their need for literary self-expression. They have not been brought into the country to work. They are there, unwanted, and counted as a burden on the schools and the employment market. They have to struggle for a place in society. Those who do not lose their courage over this, and do not succumb to the culture-shock, often have to realize that successful language acquisition is no guarantee of climbing the social ladder. However, many acquire near-native knowledge of the second language and thus master the prerequisites for more sophisticated attempts at writing.

On the whole, it can be shown that all those who can write in the second language have had an appropriate school education, which lays the foundations for a literary socialization. Members of the second generation are now represented in growing numbers. They often begin with literary writing while still at school. Therefore, an orientation towards the types of texts used in schools is to be expected.

## 7.4 Style

The starting point of almost all theories of style is the variability of linguistic forms of expression. What is to be said seems to be expressible in different ways. Some of these ways are seen as particularly effective (rhetorical tradition), appropriate to a norm (prescriptive stylistics), fitting to situational requirements (functional stylistics), expressive in regard to social factors (sociolinguistic concept of register), or producing the individual aesthetic quality of a text (literary studies). Stylistic analyses are generally restricted to the registration of the various manners of occurrence of linguistic devices as constituents of style, mainly by simple quantification, comparison (characteristic/non-characteristic in relation to the norm) and abstraction to a structure (e.g. 'nominal style'). This repertoire of stylistic devices can then – as in rhetoric – be passed on with normative claims or be used for the further examination of types of text or discourse. Thus structuralist conceptions do not go beyond the establishment of a system of linguistic styles and its internal relations (syntagmatic-paradigmatic). A particular repertoire will be seen at best as a variety which is characteristic for a distinct domain of language-use or an expression of social relationships.

A pragmatic view, however, does not stop at the system of linguistic devices, but develops the system from the quality of action connected with linguistic forms. Sandig (1978), for instance, concerns herself with stylistic rules such as 'repetition', 'variation', 'deviation' as patterns of action; in relation to higher-level 'text illocution' this involves the simultaneous or additional performance of action-patterns. Rehbein (1983) applies the concept of style even more strongly to linguistic devices relating to patterns of action.[2] Such patterns are developed within society in order to come to terms with the needs of individuals in specific social constellations. Depending on the respective constellation in which the patterns are used, specific devices for their realization are formed. Hence they are associated with particular groups of speakers/hearers. Rehbein describes this as 'style' (1983, p. 23). Thus the collective element inherent in most concepts of style acquires a pragmatic precision. It is then possible to ascertain how large the scope for individual variation is. The constraints to such variation, however, are formed by the action-patterns, and – since we are dealing with texts – by text-types.

## 7.5  The corpus

The following analysis is based on a corpus of texts written in a second language. In 1982 the Institute of German as a Foreign Language (University of Munich) organized a literary competition. Foreigners were invited to write in German on the theme *Living in*

*Two Languages*. Publication was offered to the authors. The appeal was very successful. About 340 texts – fifty written by authors younger than eighteen – were submitted to the jury who awarded ten prizes. The literary quality, moreover, exceeded all expectations. Many texts were published in editorial form (Ackermann, 1983, 1984). I had access to the original manuscripts of Turkish authors for the purpose of the present analysis.

It was possible to approach this corpus in a number of different ways; for instance by regarding the results as different types of text – as an essay, as a report of personal experiences, as a story or as a poem. The addressee was primarily the jury, but in a sense it was also the reading public. Whether or not migrants themselves should be considered as addressees as well is not always clear. In any case, it may be clear that whoever writes interculturally in the situation described above, faces serious problems:

1  The writer cannot fall back on familiar patterns of action and types of text.
2  The writer can only presuppose that which is common to both cultures.
3  The text must stylistically comply with the requirements of a literary context.
4  The text must be intelligible to a general audience, on which, however, information is lacking.

In addition, normal writing abilities and a general command of the necessary patterns of action are prerequisites. Note, moreover, that the demands of 1, 2 and 4 may come into conflict with 3. The main question therefore to be addressed in this paper is: How are the intercultural problems of communication treated on the level of style? Underlying this question is the very possibility of intercultural writing as such. In the following, different types of solution to this problem will be demonstrated. It will be shown that it is possible to differentiate between processes which operate solely on the level of expression (section 7.6) and those relating to the level of linguistic patterns of action and text types (section 7.7).

## 7.6 Intercultural writing and the level of expression

Considering the linguistic level of expression, i.e. the local surface forms of the text, four different stylistic possibilities present themselves to an author writing in a foreign language. These will be called *transfer, mixture, integration* and *installation*.

### 7.6.1 *Transfer of stylistic devices*

Transfer[3] is to be understood here as a reproduction or 'imitation' in the second language of an expression belonging to the first language by means of the linguistic repertoire of this second language (see Figure 7.1). The psychological basis of this is a generalization of conditions in the first language. Of course, sometimes a suitable expression simply may be lacking in the second language. In order for such a transfer to be successful, the same text must be produced by the substitution of similar devices of style, so that there is an equivalent on the level of meaning. Indeed there are many cases of transferability that are so obvious that they have not been noticed by any contrastive analysis. One obvious illustration of this principle of transfer may be seen in the following.[4]

**Oral Yilmaz: The bilingual world**

I was in town, wanted to buy something,
I met a father, right among the crowd.
He looked as though he wanted to tear at his hair,
somehow I had an oppressive feeling ...
I have a son, he said, around about fifteen.
Here he was born, here on the Saar.
He speaks very good German, one must see it,
but his knowledge of Turkish is very scarce.

(p.44)

The text-type 'poem' is signalled by the graphic layout and the characteristic amateur rhyme (in the German original). The poem

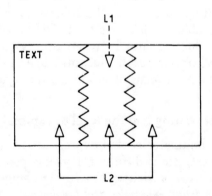

Figure 7.1 Transfer.

consists of three parts. The form is determined by the fact that in each part the 'lyrical I' meets 'a father' who describes the language problems of his son. In the first verse of each part, the father is introduced as someone who has problems, drinks, is ill, etc. This introduction of a person who can then be referred to, however, is not grammatically correct. In German, as in English, the noun 'father' demands that the corresponding relation (father of X, my father, etc.) be expressed. Therefore an introduction with an indefinite article is not acceptable. The Turkish expression 'baba' (combined with an indefinite article in complex noun phrases only), however, can be used in a much wider sense, for example in the sense of 'an elderly man'. It is possible to construct a coherent Turkish version of the text without difficulty, in which the opposition of father and son remains the central stylistic device of the poem and no deviation on semantic grounds occurs. A Western reader, unfamiliar with this, may interpret the deviation as a shortcoming due to lack of competence. It may be different for Turkish readers, though.

In the following examples the process of transfer is consciously used as a stylistic device:

**Melek Baklan: Un-fairytale**

We'll now let Ahmet travel from MOTHERLAND to FATHERLAND.

(p. 136)

The Turkish expressions 'anayurt' or 'anavatan' ('ana' = mother, 'yurt' and 'vatan' = home or country of origin) are brought into opposition with the German word 'Vaterland' (Fatherland). In this context the opposition has the function of irony, alluding to an intercultural contrast. Although this opposition is typographically marked, it remains incomprehensible for readers without any knowledge of Turkish; the publisher of the book therefore added a footnote with reference to 'anavatan' (Ackermann, 1984, p. 136).

In general then, the process of transfer proves to be a highly problematic one and this may also apply to those cases where fluency in the second language is not lacking.

### 7.6.2 Mixture of stylistic devices

Cases where isolated expressions from the first language are taken on into the second language must also be considered. The consequence of this is a mixture on the basis of the second language (see Figure 7.2). There may be several reasons for this:

1  the expression is not translatable (e.g. specific terms);
2  the writer does not know the appropriate expression in L2;
3  the writer considers the expression from L1 to be
   particularly effective (e.g. in order to pass on a particular
   atmosphere).

It is often difficult to identify the exact reason, as may become clear
from the following example.

### Kemalettin Yildirim: Our deal hostel (student in Istanbul)

A big sign. It says, in large letters 'Atatürk Öğrenci Sitesi'. If
you want to go in, you must attach your Yurt-card to your
jacket, then you can go into the modern prison, as we call it
amongst ourselves.

(p. 31)

In this text, we are dealing with a description. The qualities of an
object are to be described exactly to the extent necessary, the
minimum requirement being that the reader is able to identify the
object and to form a picture of it for himself. Here the reader is
partly enabled to imagine the physical conditions of the student
hostel, and also to see it from the point of view of a resident. The
name of the hostel, however, remains unintelligible to the reader.
Names are normally taken over into second-language texts
unchanged, but here we are confronted with translatable terms:
'öğrenci' (students), 'site' (closed town quarter); 'si' is the third
person possessive suffix. The 'yurt-pass' (hostel card) represents
another problem. The expression involves a mixture of language

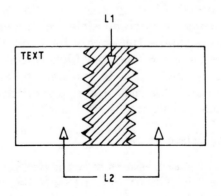

Figure  7.2 Mixture.

that is not transparent for the reader and may therefore be said to be the opposite of an integrated expression (see below). The reader interprets such an expression ('Yurt') to be an untranslatable name. At best, he can make uncertain presumptions on the grounds of his knowledge of the world (about credit cards, etc.). In any case, the expression contradicts the general requirements of a description, which demands precision.

### 7.6.3 Integration as a stylistic device

The device of integration (see Figure 7.3) largely corresponds to that of transfer, with one difference; precautions are taken so as to assure comprehension. This demands a broadly-based competence in the second language; the writer must:

1 reproduce the forms of realization from L1 in L2 (as in transfer);
2 realize that reproduction in L2 is liable to produce problems of understanding;
3 analyse the kind of comprehension problem which may thus arise and find adequate means of solving it.

The writer may adopt various strategies in order to cope with these tasks, e.g.:

1 mark the integrated expression graphically, although, as we have seen (in section 7.6.1), this is by itself not enough to allow a full understanding of the expression;
2 use a paraphrase or explanation of the integrated expression;

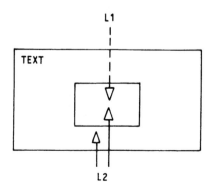

Figure  7.3 Integration.

3  insert the expression in a context which may help the reader in grasping its meaning (see further under 7.6.4).

An example:

### Servet Aksakal: From the diary of a migrant worker

Among them are some that who were often abroad. They often tell stories of which one can only dream of here. They also tell me that I to find some possibility and go as worker abroad. They always say: that one here in mine profession 'will not get shorter but also not get long'. That is: on it you die will not but can't live on it either.

(p.95)

Here a Turkish idiom ('kütü layemut geçinmek'; literally, too short to live eternally) is integrated with a similar non-Turkish idiom (not enough to live on, but too much to die from). The integration is achieved linguistically by using the 'repair' formula 'that is'. The writer believes that the second expression in combination with the first will help the reader to comprehend what the author had in mind. This process is not only used to make comprehension easier; its purpose is, in effect, to pass on the first expression inter-culturally. Integration is thus made simpler. In spite of all the linguistic problems which the author faces, the reproduction of the non-Turkish idiom can make the idea behind the Turkish idiom comprehensible. The context does the rest.

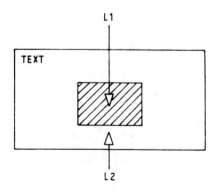

Figure  7.4 Installation.

### 7.6.4 Installation as a stylistic device

The complex process of installation consists of combining expressions from both languages within a text, so that they remain comprehensible in the complete context without translation (see Figure 7.4). An expression from the first language is inserted into a complex expression in the second language. The linguistic pattern of action remains the same; the forms of realization from the other language do not involve any unbearable illocution. It is nevertheless a foreign body in the second language if it cannot be integrated through specific processes which make it comprehensible.

**Birol Denizeri: Dead feelings**

After all the formalities had been carried out, I went excitedly into the waiting room. My parents were already there. I went to them and kissed their hands. 'Hoş geldin, my son. How are you?' my mother said. 'Hoş bulduk. I am well.'

(p.176)

The Turkish expressions here are placed in exactly those positions where greetings are to be expected. In each case they are followed by a ritual non-Turkish greeting formula. In the first instance the Turkish expression is also combined with a non-Turkish form of address. No serious problems of understanding should arise here. The illocution can be reconstructed by taking up the knowledge of greeting patterns and translation of the Turkish formula is therefore unnecessary.

It may be clear that this type of intercultural stylistic device carries its own risks. The writer must *construct* the context in such a way that the reader is not led astray. Easy recognition of the discourse pattern (*and* of the precise position of the expression within the pattern) must be attained. Especially risky are transitional points in the discourse, where different continuations are possible or new patterns may be initiated. Particularly suited are pattern positions which hardly allow any decisions, e.g. the third position in 'request – grant – thank'. A further requirement is that the pattern, or in particular the positions, must not be specific to one culture. The author must therefore have some knowledge of patterns in both languages. Moreover, hypotheses on the understanding of the recipient are essential. If problems are anticipated, additional strategies are required, e.g. the parallel postposition of an L2-expression bearing the same illocution, as 'How are you' and 'I am well' in the example. In this framework it is possible for the

Western reader to categorize the culture-specific form of greeting for respectable persons, i.e. the kissing of hands in Turkey. In the following example we also find an installation by a postponed characterization.

### Alev Tekinay: The homecoming, or Aunt Helga and Uncle Hans

'Another piece of Baklava, please', the hostess says and fills my plate with the sweet flaky pastry pie, 'it certainly tastes better than your apple pie in Germany'.

(p.40)

By the description the properties of taste (sweet), the material (flaky pastry) and the type (pie) of Turkish 'Baklava', which has no direct translation, are given. It is worth noticing that the parallel description is not redundant, but has a syntactic function (prepositional object of 'fill') and varies the text stylistically. Hence, this may be said to be a very good example of the device of installation.

It has become clear that the process of installation requires a great deal of competence in the second language. Yet on the whole, processes of installation form an important linguistic resource for intercultural mediation.

## 7.7 Intercultural writing and linguistic patterns of action

Linguistic patterns of action are socially developed for the realization of specific purposes. Speakers with sufficient linguistic competence can systematically use the knowledge of these patterns to achieve special effects. To this end, linguistic devices typical for certain patterns can be brought together in different ways; the originally initiated pattern can be used throughout or be temporarily abandoned, and a new unity can be formed out of a *combination* of patterns. In this section we will first deal with the combination of patterns in the second language (sections 7.7.1–7.7.3); then we will look at *pattern integration* (7.7.4) and *mixing of patterns* (7.7.5). In principle, we could expect to find something like 'pattern-transfer' and 'pattern-installation' here, but these types are not represented in the corpus under investigation. However, they do occur in oral communication and in aesthetic forms, such as in bilingual theatre as described by Müller (1985). Starting, then, with the *combination* of patterns, one may discern three different types; pattern-*synthesis*, pattern-*implementation* and pattern-*import*. These

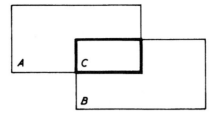

Figure 7.5 Pattern-synthesis.

present themselves as chances or difficulties for writers in their native language too, although of course the difficulties are far greater when writing in a foreign language.

### 7.7.1 Pattern-synthesis

By pattern-synthesis we mean the combination of different patterns of action (in one language) in such a way that they serve a certain purpose (see Figure 7.5).[5] The combination of two patterns $A$ and $B$ for a common purpose can result in a complex pattern $C$. The development of such new patterns depends on whether the social conditions call for it. On the level of linguistic devices, a process of association with which a new unity can be formed or an already-initiated unity can be expanded is required. Juxtaposition seems to be a very simple process, although the recipient must be able mentally to sense the common purpose connecting them, so that relevant knowledge can be built up. Another device is that of the occupation of positions of pattern $A$ by those of pattern $B$, with similar functional requirements. Extensive pattern knowledge, however, is required in order to succeed in such a pattern-synthesis. An example for such a process may be found in the following text.

#### Kadriye Güler: A foreigner abroad

There once lived an eleven year old girl, in a small village, at the Black Sea. She was happy and content, just like the other children. But there was a difference between the others and herself: She had polio and could only walk with the help of two crutches. Although she had been told quite clearly that she would never be able to walk like the other children, she firmly believed in a miracle. Although she was always told by the adults that this was her fate, and she must come to terms with it, she did not think of this, but dreamed of the day when she would run, jump, dance just like her friends. One day she heard news of her father who lived in a foreign country, in two languages ...

(p.171)

[Her hopes are then raised that she might be cured in the foreign country where her father lives. The story ends sadly, however. The girl eventually learns that her illness is not curable in the foreign country. This symbolizes that migration cannot fulfil the hopes of the migrants. He who remains behind will at least not be disappointed.]

The initial pattern introduced is that of the fairy tale, where an unhappy situation may be brought to a happy end by supernatural intervention. Most Turkish and European fairy tales correspond to this type. Thus the introduction of this text-type awakens in the reader the expectations of such a conclusion. However, this expectation of a happy end is not borne out by the story. Instead, it takes on a different turn altogether and develops into a different type of story, i.e. one in which the protagonist gradually emancipates herself from the false illusions she initially had. Thus two different linguistic patterns merge.

Pattern-synthesis has thus a calculated stylistic effect. However, it requires extensive competence in the second language, i.e. knowledge and command of the synthesized patterns, including their respective stylistic devices, as well as insight into their compatibility in relation to a specific propositional content.

An additional characteristic of pattern-synthesis is that patterns A and B are not completely realized. Instead, it is necessary to break down the text into those elements which can be synthesized in view of a stylistic purpose. Within the framework of a comprehensive plan, which may include aesthetic aspects, the elements are then to be linked together so that a new unity is formed.

### 7.7.2  Pattern-implementation

A 'pattern-implementation' (cf. Rehbein, 1983, p. 83) is produced when a speaker changes within a linguistic pattern A for another pattern B, whereby it becomes possible to achieve aims which were not attainable by the sole use of A (see Figure 7.6). This type is often to be found in second-language texts, because it is sometimes the only way to ensure that the recipient is able to understand. The following example illustrates this.

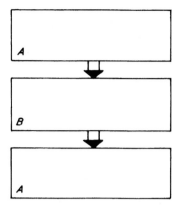

Figure 7.6 Pattern-implementation.

### Özgür Savaşçı: On a Friday evening

I like Friday evenings, because although Friday is a holy day for muslims, it is the only day for me – and also for many of my countrymen here – on which one gets together and can be a little cheerful in the evening. Saturday is yet merely shopping day for many and on Saturday evenings one makes obligatory visits, so that one cannot really be as free as on Fridays. On the holy German Sunday one is very well-behaved, i.e. one does nothing much, because the next working day is coming up.

Well, it was a normal Friday evening and we – three good friends – had decided to go to a Greek pub this time ...

(p.92)

The narration of a story requires what Labov and Waletzky (1967) have called 'orientation'. In the above example this part begins only with 'Well, it was a normal Friday evening and ...'. What comes before does not really belong to the story. The narrator expresses his view of Friday evenings and bases it on a cultural background. This clearly is not yet the pattern of 'narrating'. Its purpose is to provide some information to the non-Turkish reader, who might otherwise encounter problems of understanding. The usage of a 'supportive pattern' is a characteristic solution to problems of understanding which arise or are expected to arise in intercultural communication. One drawback of such supportive patterns, however, is that they take up valuable story-time. Therefore it can lead to hampering the flow of communication and the processing of the core of the text. Indeed, in this example the information given in the implemented pattern plays no role in the events to follow. At the same time it is difficult to decide whether it is redundant in an intercultural context. In any case, texts such as these appear more as cultural documents and for that reason may sometimes not be taken seriously in a literary sense. Particular functions – here didactic – can open up or close down the text's potential.

### 7.7.3 Pattern-import

A 'pattern-import' (see Figure 7.7) is produced when the stylistic repertoire of a linguistic pattern *A* is realized in the framework of another pattern *B* (cf. Rehbein, 1983, p. 38). Pattern *A* is then partially superimposed on to pattern *B*. Hence *A* is not fully realized but brought to attention by characteristic devices. In this case, *A* and *B* serve completely different purposes. The stylistic devices must be specific for *A* and *B* respectively and are therefore incompatible, so that a conflict of style arises. This may be witnessed in the following text.

**Alı Çıracı: Hopeless?**

In the year 1960, a boy comes on to the world, in an Anatolian town. At the Black Sea, Sinop/Ayancik. When was 3 Years old, his mother deceased. The boy had had three other brothers and sisters. That was very difficult for them father as the brothers and sisters. The father maried so many times until he had found the right mum to his children, when he was 6 Year old he was sent to his step-uncle to karabük there his uncle sent him to a religion school. After one year he comes home to the locality . . .

(p. 93)

The author tries to tell a life-story with the help of rather limited

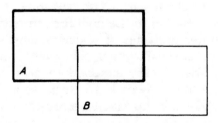

Figure   7.7 Pattern-import.

linguistic resources. As a result, conflicts of style arise repeatedly. The pattern of literary narration is broken by stylistic elements belonging to:

1  bureaucratic institutions – 'deceased', 'Sinop/Ayancik' (=postal address of birth place), 'locality';
2  family communication – 'mum'.

These stylistic devices remain isolated in the text. They do not prevent comprehension of the text, but make it clumsy and show the author not to be aware of the stylistically harmful effects of pattern-import.

### 7.7.4 *Pattern-integration*

By the term 'pattern-integration' (see Figure 7.8) we mean the complete or partial reproduction of an L1-pattern in the second language. In this case, particular arrangements must be made in order to make the integration understandable. If the L1-pattern has a great deal in common with that of the second language, a more or less 'organic' insertion is possible. The context and surrounding patterns must then be considered as aids to understanding. Where L1- and L2-patterns do *not* match easily, however, the task of integrating them demands considerable skill on the part of the author. Of course the pattern knowledge to be passed on to the recipient can also be directly brought in by an explanation or comment. Stylistically, this is not a particularly elegant solution, but at least it indicates that the problem has been recognized. Knowledge of patterns in both languages is thus necessary, to allow for a comparison of the patterns. In order to bridge the gap

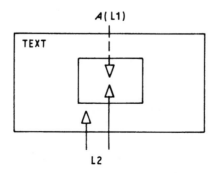

Figure  7.8 Pattern-integration.

between them, the integration requires detecting the differences between L1 and L2 resources which go beyond straightforward translation.

### Melek Baklan: Un-fairy tale

But now back to the girl Ayşe, who grew up in this village ...
We'll now let Ahmet travel from MOTHERLAND to
FATHERLAND and see what is going on in the village in the
mean time, we will see what Ayşe is doing ... Let us now leave
Ayşe alone with her worries and watch the new life of Ahmet
for a while ...
   Let us now go back to the village with Sadik's letter and have
a look at what has happened since Ahmet's departure ...

(p. 136)

This narration shows the experiences of migration from the viewpoint of Ayşe, who remains at home while her husband works in West Germany. The story is at the same time defamiliarized and generalized through the use of the oriental fairy-tale type of text. In the passages reproduced here, the narrator addresses himself directly to the reader and orientates him towards a different space of imagination, in which further scenes can be developed, accessible through deictic expressions.[6] In this way, chronologically parallel story-lines are tied up with each other. The point of transition can be chosen such as to increase the tension (e.g. 'we will see what Ayşe is doing'). This produces an elaborate narrative structure. At the same time the narrator is made explicit, whereas in Western fairy tales the narrator remains mostly concealed.

This narrative procedure of explicit reorientation is characteristic of the oriental (including the Turkish) fairy tale,[7] that lies at the basis of this text; Persian and Arabic literary fairy tales have had a strong influence on oral tradition in Turkey. A procedure such as reorientation may thus not be new to readers who are familiar with oriental fairy tales. It puts no great demands on understanding, and – coming from oral tradition – actually makes reception simpler.

The critical question here is whether or not the patterns are compatible (*integration* versus *transfer*). The intercultural common ground of the fairy tale makes understanding easier. Integration is therefore achieved by such linguistic means of the fairy tale, which are also common in the second language and thus clarify the connection of the patterns. The elements of the fairy tale enable the text to achieve a particular stylistic effect; the inherent contrast between wishes and reality is ironically increased.

### 7.7.5 *Mixing patterns*

In this type (see Figure 7.9) a complete pattern *A*, realized in the first language, is inserted into a second language framework. No precautions to ensure comprehension are taken here. Thus the part in the first language is isolated in relation to the whole; in some cases it is supposed to have a phonetic effect and to create a desired feeling of 'foreignness'. No example of this type was found in the corpus. But this type can be illustrated by a verse from a song by Metin Oz (from Anhegger, 1982, p. 15):

**Metin Oz: Chiefo**

| | |
|---|---|
| I work at Ford'ta. | (I work at Ford Company) |
| We fall asleep yurtta. | (We sleep in a hostel) |
| Hayatim mantar oldu, | (My life (or, my firm) has become mindless for me) |
| Bir kil var bu yoğurtta. | (There is a hair in this yoghurt) |

On the one hand, the text contains mixtures on the level of expression ('ta' as Turkish locative suffix); on the other hand, realizations of assertions in L1 (final lines). The context in which the song was written must be considered for an explanation; the song developed on the occasion of a strike at Ford in Cologne and was addressed to Turkish and German colleagues as well as to the company management, which was attacked in later verses. All in all the song is full of breaks between passages from the first and the second language and also contains imitations of 'immigrant-worker German' (like 'chiefo'). More aggressive passages are expressed in Turkish, thus possibly offering Turkish

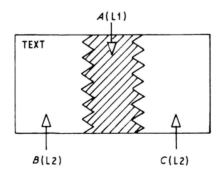

Figure  7.9 Mixing patterns.

colleagues a certain protection against the management. In this respect, the mixture can be completely functional. Such direct functionality might not apply to literary contexts, although similar cases of pattern-mixing may be found in the works of Ezra Pound, T. S. Eliot, Thomas Mann and others.

## 7.8 Conclusion: the possibilities of intercultural writing

The texts which have been analysed in the previous sections reveal the nature of intercultural writing as a specific type of problem. They are written by immigrants or their children in a situation of cultural conflict manifested by themselves. At the same time, to fulfil the conditions of the actual occasion (competition, prospect of publication), they must somehow bridge the gap to the second language and the culture of the country of immigration. This situation can be dealt with in different ways.

1  One solution lies in taking on completely the perspective of the second language. The long-term goal would be to form *a new type of literature.* The linguistic requirements of this goal are now met by some members of the second and third generations. Recent developments would seem to make this possibility realistic. This is apparent in complex stylistic processes, to which the synthesis of patterns belongs. The texts can be regarded as the success of individual learning processes; whoever is able to write in this way has overcome the barriers.

2  Another solution consists of taking the second language as an instrument of mediation. The situation between the cultures is taken up with the aim of broadening the perspective of the majority culture, of giving information and furthering understanding. Its starting point was *a literature of distress,* concerning itself little with literary standards. Overcoming speechlessness was crucial. The style of this type of literature is characterized by linguistic breaks, pattern-import, pattern-implementation, the mixing and transfer of stylistic devices. The texts give the impression of being patched together. The reader approaches these texts as documents of social experience of a specific quality that could not be attained through statistics or economic analysis. At best the texts are seen

as politically serious, while their literary quality remains in doubt.

The second language remains dominant even in *a literature which sets out to mediate between cultures*. It tries not only to express individual experiences, though, but also to make them transparent in the second language and to reproduce them by means of this second language. The stylistic devices of integration and installation are characteristic features of this. The cultural background of L1 is not renounced, but neither can one escape from the absorbing culture of L2. The barrier continually opposing foreign norms is already evident in the very concept of mediation. The main danger lies in the fact that the text is assigned to a cultural tradition, to which the author belongs, but which (s)he cannot continue without severe breaks when in exile or immigration. Consequently, allocation can serve as an exclusion; the text falls into the gap between the cultures.

3 Finally, a new form of literature, being an *authentic expression of minority cultures*, may be expected. This type of literature no longer devotes itself to the domestication of the strange nor to the integration into the majority culture. Instead, the function of mediation is rejected as restrictive. This literature can dispense with any mediator introducing, commenting or elucidating. The texts speak for themselves, and for those they have been written for. And they speak their own language (probably a specific variety of the second language). Something new arises; forms of knowledge and action which reflect exactly the situation *between* the cultures. What exactly these will look like will come to light.

# NOTES

1 I wish to thank Irmgard Ackermann (University of Munich) for providing the majority of texts analysed in this chapter, Wolf Gewehr (University of Münster), who has made stylistic corrections and Willie van Peer for suggesting many valuable improvements on the final version of this paper.
2 This concept belongs to the theory of linguistic action developed by Ehlich and Rehbein (1979). An empirical analysis can be found in Rehbein (1984).

3   The term 'transfer' has become common in the field of research in
    second-language acquistion. In the method of 'contrastive analysis',
    which has recently been strongly criticized, this means the conversion
    of structures from a language L1 into a language L2. This can lead to
    errors in L2 ('negative transfer'). If one disregards the behaviouristic
    basis (speech acquisition as habit formation) of this approach and
    considers new cognitive theories, the concept of transfer can be given
    a more precise sense. The starting point of this is the linguistic
    knowledge which speakers have acquired in the first language and
    which, in a complex way, determines later linguistic experiences and
    learning processes. Such knowledge refers to the kinds of linguistic
    devices, their action quality, etc. Recourse to such knowledge can lead
    to very complex strategies of learning and ways of usage in L2, which
    are not to be illuminated by means of a simple comparison of
    structures. At present too little is known about this.
4   The following analyses are based on the original manuscripts as they
    were submitted to the jury. The translations (also stylistically) are as
    near to the original as possible (provided by and under the
    responsibility of the editor only). The published versions, from
    Ackermann (1983), are identified by their page number at the end of
    the quotes.
5   Rehbein (1983, p. 42) describes this phenomenon as 'compatibility of
    styles'. The basis of this is the 'technique of synthesizing of different
    linguistic devices fitting the patterns'.
6   In reference to deictics in general and to the concept of 'deictic space',
    see Ehlich (1982).
7   This text type is analysed by Eberhard and Boratev (1953).

# BIBLIOGRAPHY

Ackermann, I. (ed.) (1983), *In zwei Sprachen leben* [Living in Two Languages],
    Munich, Deutscher Taschenbuch Verlag (dtv).
Ackermann, I. (ed.) (1984), *Türken deutscher Sprache* [Turkish Speakers of
    German], Munich, Deutscher Taschenbuch Verlag (dtv).
Anhegger, R. (1982), 'Die Deutschland-Erfahrung der Türken in ihren
    Liedern' [The experience of Germany by Turkish people in their songs],
    in H. Birkenfeld (ed.), *Gastarbeiterkinder aus der Türkei* [Immigrant Children
    from Turkey], Munich, Beck, pp. 9–26.
Coulmas, F. (1981), *Über Schrift* [On Writing], Frankfurt, Suhrkamp.
Eberhard, W. and Boratev, P. N. (1953), *Typen türkischer Volksmärchen* [Types
    of Turkish Fairy Tales], Wiesbaden, Steiner.
Ehlich, K. (1982), 'Anaphora and deixis: same, similar, or different?', in R.
    J. Jarvella and W. Klein (eds), *Speech, Place and Action*, Chichester, Wiley,
    pp. 315–38.

Ehlich, K. and Rehbein, J. (1979), 'Sprachliche Handlungsmuster' [Linguistic action patterns], in H. G. Soeffner (ed.), *Interpretative Methoden in den Text- und Sozialwissenschaften* [Interpretative Methods in Text Linguistics and Social Sciences], Stuttgart, Metzler, pp. 241–74.

Labov, W. and Waletzky, J. (1967), 'Narrative analysis', in J. Helm (ed.), *Essays on the Verbal and Visual Arts*, Seattle, University of Washington Press, pp. 12–44.

Müller, F. (1985), 'Theater mit italienischen Jugendlichen als Praxis interkultureller Kommunikation' [Theatre with Italian youths as a practice of intercultural communication], in J. Rehbein (ed.), *Interkulturelle Kommunikation* [Intercultural Communication], Tübingen, Narr.

Rehbein, J. (1983), 'Zur pragmatischen Rolle des Stils' [The pragmatic function of style], in B. Sandig (ed.), *Stilistik, vol. 1*, [Stylistics], Hildesheim, Olms, pp. 21–48.

Rehbein, J. (1984), 'Remarks on the empirical analysis of action and speech', *Journal of Pragmatics*, vol. 8, pp. 49–63.

Rehbein, J. (ed.) (1985), *Interkulturelle Kommunikation* [Intercultural Communication], Tübingen, Narr.

Sandig, B. (1978), *Stilistik* [Stylistics], Berlin/New York, de Gruyter.

Tannen, D. (ed.) (1982), *Spoken and Written Language: Exploring Orality and Literacy*, Norwood, N. J., Ablex.

# 8

# Back to the future

## Bakhtin, stylistics and discourse

*Kathleen Wales*

*Within the fields of stylistics and of literary theory, the work of the Russian scholar Mikhail Bakhtin has recently attracted wide attention. The major reason for this, as Kathleen Wales argues in this chapter, is his constant emphasis on the living nature of language and literature. Contrary to what some models might want us to believe, language is not profitably studied in a highly idealized and abstract way. The avoidance of any empirical reality of the language is even more detrimental if it is employed in the study of literature. At any one point in the novel (the genre analysed and emphasized most in Bakhtin's works) there are multitudes of voices and sociolects, dialects and idiolects, registers and styles to be heard. It is this essentially composite and dynamic nature of language, termed heteroglossia in Bakhtin's works, that Kathleen Wales finds of high value for the study of literature. It is this dialogic quality which lays bare the essential characteristic of the literary model of communication.*

*It further appears from this chapter that the position taken by Bakhtin more than half a century ago also ties in with a number of recent developments in stylistics, such as Roger Fowler's 'linguistic criticism', the recent work in novel theory by Genette and Lanser, Hoey's and Edmondson's approaches to text and discourse, Halliday's functional approach or speech act theory. As the literary texts (by Larkin, Joyce, Shakespeare) analysed as examples show, these ideas are not merely grandiloquent schemes without much relation to the text themselves. On the contrary, it is their very applicability to textual analysis (along with its theoretical insights) that Wales takes to be the primary importance of Bakhtin's work. His most fundamental contribution, then, lies in his breaking away from one-dimensional models of literary communication, and providing methods of analysis which take into account the multi-layered nature of human language and, consequently, of literary works of art.*

The work and ideas of the Russian philosopher-linguist-critic Mikhail Bakhtin, first formulated in the 1920s, have in recent years gradually become more widely known in the West. The 1980s indeed, have produced a number of important (re-) publications by or about Bakhtin, and also his associates (see lists 8.B.1 and 8.B.2 in the Bibliography for full details). However, despite some recent isolated articles (list 8.B.3), the impact of this dynamic and revelatory writer has yet to be fully felt in stylistics. In this chapter I do not propose to summarize all Bakhtin's ideas, but simply to discuss those insights which are of some direct relevance to contemporary stylistics, to the way it is developing and should develop. It is a remarkable, if ironic, fact that although we must readily assess Bakhtin's ideas in the whole context of early twentieth-century thought, and in relation to pre-war Formalism and Marxism, for example, none the less Bakhtin indisputably heralded developments in linguistics and literary criticism of some half a century or so later. If there is thus a danger of over-stating his originality from our sense of familiarity, there is also re-assurance; that certain trends were desirable, even inevitable. Moreover, Bakhtin's ideas remain, like his whole mode of writing, very stimulating. This is not to say that we must revere them; this would lead to the very 'fossilization' that Bakhtin himself abhorred. Undoubtedly there are many weaknesses in his theories, which he himself re-worked over and over again in his lifetime. But out of the necessarily critical but constructive 'dialogue' with his poetics, an important sociostylistic theory is in the process of emerging

Strictly speaking, Bakhtin's constant and central critical pre-occupation is with a (diachronically biased) poetics of the novel. However, for Bakhtin there is no 'strictly speaking'; it is precisely because of what he saw as the generic nature of novel discourse that led him inevitably to ponder the nature of literary language, and of language generally.

For Bakhtin, Saussure's opposition between the abstract or systematic *langue* and the concrete individualistic *parole* belies an understanding of language as a living, diversified construct between living, diversified speakers; language as 'utterance' in a social, and historical, context:

> at any given moment of its historical existence, language is heteroglot from top to bottom: it represents the co-existence of socio-ideological contradictions between the present and the past, between differing epochs of the past, between different socio-ideological groups in the present, between tendencies, schools, circles and so forth, all given a bodily form. These 'languages' of heteroglossia intersect each other in a variety of ways, forming new socially typifying 'languages'. ('Discourse in the novel' (DIN); see Bakhtin, 1981, p. 291).

Bakhtin continually stresses the 'internal stratification' of a language into:

> social dialects, characteristic group behaviour, professional jargons, generic languages, languages of generations and age groups, tendentious languages, languages of the authorities, of various circles and of passing fashions, languages that serve the specific sociopolitical purposes of the day, even of the hour. (DIN, p. 263)

What Bakhtin makes us sense in these and his many similar remarks is the very 'three-dimensionality' of language, its 'distinction between levels and distances', whose re-creation he sees quite rightly as the goal of stylistic analysis, especially of works of older periods (DIN, p. 417). Re-creation should be the goal, of course, of sociolinguistic analysis; what Medvedev calls a 'sociological poetics', without which the stylistic descriptions of older texts must inevitably suffer.[1] Literary language, most particularly the language of the novel, is itself basically 'stratified and heteroglot' (DIN, pp. 272, 288), open to the generic and social diversity of the living language around it, as well as creating its own stratification. Thus rooted in discourse, the novel lends itself to a kind of stylistic analysis which Bakhtin does not yet believe exists:

A stylistic analysis of the novel cannot be productive outside a profound understanding of heteroglossia, an understanding of the dialogue of languages as it exists in a given era. But in order to understand such dialogue, or even to become aware initially that a dialogue is going on at all, mere knowledge of the linguistic and stylistic profile of the languages involved will be insufficient: what is needed is a profound understanding of each language's socio-ideological meaning and an exact knowledge of the social distribution and ordering of all the other ideological voices of the era. (DIN, p. 417)

In Kristeva's words, here is 'no vulgar sociologism' (1973, p. 108). But what Bakhtin is saying may well evoke the recent 'critical linguistics' approach of Fowler and his colleagues (e.g. 1979, 1981), who argue strongly for a more probing type of sociolinguistics which investigates the (inseparable) relationship between language, social meanings and ideologies.[2] Transformed into stylistics, this suggests the kind of 'radical' approach to textual forms and meaning adopted by Burton (1982). For her, stylistic analysis should not simply be concerned with effects, but should be a powerful method for understanding the ways in which realities are constructed through language. Ironically, however, it is Burton's earlier study of discourse and drama (1980) which is perhaps in principle closer to the kind of stylistic approach that Bakhtin is advocating for the novel.[3] But precisely because of the fact that, although 'one of the main subjects of human speech is discourse itself', this has not 'up to now been sufficiently taken into consideration, nor has its crucial importance been appreciated' (DIN, p. 355), then 'all the categories and methods of traditional stylistics remain incapable of dealing effectively with the artistic uniqueness of discourse in the novel' (DIN, p. 266).

Clearly, the recent work in novel theory, e.g. of Genette (1980) and Lanser (1981) has done much to open our eyes to the rhetorical and pragmatic strategies of the novel as discourse and as speech act, rather than as a repository or texture of poetic symbols. But the idea of language as discourse is explored by Bakhtin in many other ways which suggest possibilities of application, not only to the novel but to other literary genres. They also, in the process, invite some reassessment of critical attitudes. I shall restrict discussion here to just two aspects.[4]

As a result of the work done 'by all these stratifying forces' in language, Bakhtin says there are

> no 'neutral' words and forms – words and forms that can belong to 'no one'; language has been completely taken over, shot through with intentions and accents … Each word tastes of the context and contexts in which it has lived its socially charged life; all words and forms are populated by intentions … Language is not a neutral medium that passes freely and easily into the private property of the speaker's intentions; it is populated – overpopulated – with the intentions of others. (DIN, pp. 293–4; cf. also Bakhtin (1973), *Problems of Dostoevsky's Poetics* (PDP), p. 195)

What Bakhtin is saying here is not only significant for sociologists, but for all who use language: 'The word in language is half someone else's. It becomes "one's own" only when the speaker populates it with his own intention, his own accent' (DIN, p. 293):

> The transmission and assessment of the speech of others … is one of the most widespread and fundamental topics of human speech … in the everyday speech of any person … no less than half (on the average) of all the words uttered by him will be someone else's words. (DIN, p. 337)

So much for Chomsky's human 'creativity' – at least in performance. If we may sense here a certain Bakhtinian exaggeration, none the less we are equally jolted by his acuteness of observation, which has salutory implications for sociolinguistic and stylistic analysis, as well as literary theory generally. Scholars who study the techniques of composition of oral literatures have been telling us for years that literary value for many cultures and periods is not necessarily dependent upon originality of idea or expression; and plagiarism has only in modern times acquired its pejorative associations. To take and use another person's thoughts as one's own, acknowledged or unacknowledged, is, as Bakhtin emphasises, the natural pattern of our linguistic behaviour, and distinctly marked for many types of verbal activity – writing articles like this, for instance (Bakhtin himself refers to this kind of discourse in PDP, p. 188). Characteristically, as we shall see below, he sees it as an essentially dynamic process; citation for refutation, confrontation or supplementation, etc.[5]

Borrowed words and citation come significantly together in the (post-)structuralist notion of *bricolage*, and of the 'sedimented' or 'layered' text, even also the Derridean 'trace'; and more generally, the concept of the 'other' or 'alien' (*cuzoj*) word/discourse gave rise to Kristeva's own appropriation of it for the broad and currently popular notion of 'intertextuality'. But Bakhtin's idea of language as a kind of public property suggests a method of stylistic analysis far removed from that largely associated with mainstream stylistic tradition: the analysis of the odd practitioner, the highly deviant text, of E. E. Cummings and the like. Eliot's *The Waste Land* is an obvious and extremely marked illustration of a text woven from allusions, quotations, alien voices and registers, whose very markedness, of course, has attracted critical attention. In contrast, Larkin's poems appear ordinary, even banal, although Larkin's technique is in part similarly based on the notion of borrowed speech or structures. Bakhtin's vivid imagery of the 'taste' or 'accent' of words seems particularly apt for many of Larkin's lines, which are 'shot through' with appropriations from diverse registers, often foregrounded in a kind of ironic silent quotation:

> Standing under the fobbed
> Impendent belly of Time
> 'Tell me the truth', I said,
> 'Teach me the way things go.'
> All the other lads there
> Were itching to have a bash,
> But I thought wanting unfair:
> It and finding out clash.
>
> So he patted my head, booming 'Boy,
> There's no green in your eye:
> Sit here, and watch the hail
> Of occurrence clobber life out
> To a shape no-one sees –
> Dare you look at that straight?'
> 'Oh thank you,' I said, 'Oh yes please',
> And sat down to wait.
>
> ('Send no money')[6]

Here colloquial idioms (indicated by the broken lines) such as 'the way things go', 'no green in your eye' and 'clobber' are re-contextualized, strikingly juxtaposed with distinctly literary or formal phrases (underlined) like 'fobbed impendent' and the metaphor, itself striking, of 'hail of occurrence'. The phrase 'itching to have a bash' evokes not only colloquial speech generally, but a particular speech, of the 'lads' themselves. From Bakhtin's own work on the complexity of speech-representation in literary discourse, we can see it as an example of 'concealed speech', or of 'hybridization', of the mixing within a single utterance of two different 'voices' or consciousnesses, the narrator's and the boys' – a quotation within a quotation.

Bakhtin's ideas of the 'quotation marks' of discourse referred to in his unpublished notes (1959–61) make an apt analogy for the texture of Larkin's poetry, with his appropriation of phrase and the dialogic or polyphonic nature of his discourse:

> The word used in quotation marks, that is felt and used as alien
> ... The infinite gradation in the degrees of strangeness ...
> between words, their different degrees of distance in relation
> to the speaker. Words are set on different planes, at different
> distances, in relation to the plane of the author's words.
> (Bakhtin, cited in Todorov, 1984, p. 74)

If phrases like 'He walked out on the whole crowd' and 'Take that you bastard' leave the poet-narrator 'flushed and stirred' ('Poetry of departures'),[7] time and again in Larkin's poems phrases and words are flaunted, world-views and values held up for questioning:

> When I see a couple of kids
> And guess he's fucking her and she's
> Taking pills or wearing a diaphragm,
> I know this is paradise.
>
> ('High Windows')[8]

Here 'fuck' and 'paradise' are ironically contrasted; the idiom and values of the street-wise juxtaposed with, yet critically distant from, his own.

An extreme and more explicit kind of ironic appropriation is illustrated in parody, to which Bakhtin devotes attention repeatedly in his work. What parody, in fact, very vividly illustrates through its process of quotation-yet-distortion is the essentially dynamic nature of speech borrowing.[9] But the dynamic nature of speech generally is continually stressed by Bakhtin:

> another's word will be the subject of passionate
> communication, an object of interpretation, discussion,
> evaluation, rebuttal, support, further development and so on
> ... people talk most of all about what others talk about – they
> transmit, recall, weigh and pass judgment on other people's

words, opinions, assertions, information; people are upset by
others' words, or agree with them, contest them, refer to them
and so forth. (DIN, p. 337)

Here Bakhtin depicts the essentially 'dialogic' nature of discourse,
and anticipates in the process much of the speech act theory of
Austin and Searle. The words of others are not only handled
reverentially (as in quotation) but are used, abused, tossed around
like a rugby ball. To my mind, the only recent linguist who has
grasped any comparable sense of the physicality, the objectivity of
speech is Halliday (1985), in his chapter on the clause as 'exchange',
where he develops the notion of language as a 'commodity' in a
style with a distinctly Bakhtinian ring; in the exchange of
information the proposition becomes something that 'can be
argued about ... affirmed or denied, and also doubted, contradicted,
insisted on, accepted with reservation, qualified, tempered,
regretted and so on' (p. 70).

The significance of words like 'dialogic' and 'dialogue' in the
thought of Bakhtin must not be underestimated, however loosely
and contradictorily they are used at times. For Bakhtin any and
every utterance is dialogic, an inner polemic, in the sense that it
engages with itself in the process of engaging with appropriate
words and other utterances. And it is this 'dialogical principle'
(Todorov) which is the second aspect of his work that I wish to take
up here, with particular reference to the traditional notions of
'dialogue' and 'monologue'.

Bakhtin's claim that speech is dialogic, oriented towards
another's words, refers not only to utterances already uttered, but
also to those yet to come; speech engages with words that have not
yet been spoken, as well as those which have: 'every word is
directed toward an answer – it provokes an answer, anticipates it'
(DIN, p. 280).

> In every style, properly speaking, there is an element of
> internal polemic, the difference being only in its degree and
> character. Any literary discourse more or less keenly senses its
> listener, reader or critic, and reflects anticipated objections,
> evaluations, points of view. (Bakhtin (1971), 'Discourse
> typology in prose' (DTIP), p. 189)

In his notes of his last years Bakhtin evokes even an existential
projection, reminiscent of Winnie in Beckett's *Happy Days*; it is the
nature of discourse that it 'always wants to be heard ... always is in

search of responsive understanding ... For discourse (and, therefore for man) nothing is more frightening than the absence of answer' (Bakhtin, 1974; cited in Todorov, 1984, p.111).

The traditional approach towards discourse of any kind has been to treat it as monologic, 'single-voiced', although reader-response criticism and reception theory, with the notion of 'implied readers', have made a decided impact on novel theory in particular. And since the 1970s research in the fields of discourse analysis and pragmatics has led to increased understanding of many kinds of conversational and formalized interaction and their underlying implicatures. But it is dialogue in the narrow pragmatic sense of an exchange between (at least two) speakers that tends to be the object of attention. What is needed is a kind of analysis for any type of text or discourse that arises from the focus on inherent or internal dialogism, the interaction of word with word, and which probes deeper than traditional concerns of 'tenor' of discourse at the interpersonal level. Admittedly, Bakhtin's own liberal use of the terms 'dialogue' and 'dialogic' lead him to some apparent contradictions and debatable judgments, compounded by his general view of the 'superiority' of the novel over the other main genres of poetry and drama, both of which he sees as largely 'monologic' (see also note 3). But I follow the (re-)assessments of Bakhtin by Booth (Bakhtin, 1984 PDP, Introduction), and Todorov (1984), namely that inherent dialogism may be repressed in some contexts (in lyric poetry, for example) in the interests of a different kind of aesthetic valorization to that of prose. It is also possible, as we shall see, to speak of degrees of dialogization.

Actually Bakhtin himself does hint at a possible procedure for analysing dialogism:

> Imagine a dialogue between two persons in which the statements of the second person are deleted, but in such a way that the general sense is not disrupted. The second speaker's presence is not shown; his actual words are not given, but the deep impression of these words has a determining effect on all the utterances made by the only one who does speak. (DTIP, p. 189; PDP, p. 197)

To 'reconstruct' the dialogue then, the 'deletions' can be 'recovered'. This is the sort of process which happens in the dramatic monologues (sic) of Browning, or the sketches of the American comedian Bob Newhart. Bakhtin also imagines another situation; an utterance and counter-utterance superimposed, made into a single utterance (PDP, p. 209); and he also re-writes a passage from Dostoevsky into the form of a dialogue with another person (PDP, p. 210).

Working on the very basis that monologue is a 'specialized form' of dialogue, Hoey (1983) adopts precisely this kind of operational procedure in his analyses of different types of discourse. Monologues are 'projected' into dialogues by means of posited questions in order to reveal the inner or overall structure of the text. Interestingly, Hoey acknowledges Bakhtin's seminal discussion of this kind of procedure in his annotated bibliography, but his own work is an extension of Winter's 'contextual grammar', which itself is based on the pragmatic view that 'for every clause there must be a question to which it represents an answer' (Winter, 1982, p. 7). Certainly Winter's own discussion of apposition and interpolation, for instance, illustrates very clearly the way evaluation and anticipation can be built in to apparent mono-tone texts. And in Edmondson's work on spoken discourse (1981) he devotes some attention to such 'anticipatory strategies', as what he calls 'grounders', 'expanders' and 'disarmers', as in 'Could I ask you something', 'I just wanted to tell you', 'I'm sorry to bother you, but . . .', etc. In Bakhtin's words, with such devices 'speech literally cringes in the presence or the anticipation of someone else's word, reply, objection' (PDP, p. 196). Edmondson too 'rewrites' one turn at talk (a doctor to patient) into a dialogic structure on the basis of its anticipatory strategies (pp. 196–7). And both he and Hoey refer to Gray's work on 'implied dialog' (1977), in which he states that 'in a composition the basic semantically complete unit of discourse will be an answer that contains its question – that is, an assertion' (p.286).

It seems to me that such an approach to discourse raises interesting possibilities for further study, and for more extensive stylistic analysis and evaluation of non-literary and literary texts. As Edmondson merely hints, the 'creation of a complex text – be it a novel, a sermon or whatever – is . . . to be seen as a complex manipulation of (such) discourse structures' (1981, p. 136). What we need to know, for example, are the number and range of questions that can be elicited at each stage of the 'argument'; whether these vary significantly for different discourse types, or different writers (Orwell vs. James, for example);[10] what they reveal about coherence, point of view, ideology, etc; and how these constructs relate to the 'real' question likely to be asked by real readers.

One very practical application of the ideas of monologue-as-dialogue could be the reassessment of these very terms themselves and what they stand for, and the related terms of 'interior monologue' and 'soliloquy'. If the notion of single speaker/thinker is over-stressed, as in Crystal and Davy's definition of monologue (1969) as an 'utterance with no expectation of a response', we can miss the element of address to Self, but as Other. Just as Bakhtin's and Voloshinov's important work on the heteroglossic language of the novel breaks down any rigid categories of speech represent-ation, so it might be possible, again following Bakhtin's own suggestions, to set up a scale of 'dialogization' according to the degree or intensity of question-response polemic. Seen in this way, the distinction between speech and thought may not be so especially significant, nor the physical presence of an addressee. Certainly many modern novels, particularly those associated with the 'stream of consciousness' technique (e.g. Joyce's *Ulysses*), have challenged traditional modes of representation and provoked contradictory classifications.[11]

Actually what is interesting in *Ulysses* about Stephen Dedalus, for example, is the consistency with which he is presented as engaged in address. Indeed, he epitomizes the Bakhtinian figure in search of 'responsive understanding'. At one extreme he expounds his (multi-accented, re-appropriated) theories on *Hamlet* to his friends in the most 'dialogized' of dialogues, namely the Platonic Dialogue mode of question and answer, which is also discussed by Bakhtin, in PDP (pp. 109ff.).[12] At the other extreme (and in the same chapter) Stephen ponders and assesses what he hears and sees around him:

> [Mr Best:] It's the very essence of Wilde, don't you know. The light touch.
> His glance touched their faces lightly as he smiled, a blonde ephebe. Tame essence of Wilde.
> You're darned witty. Three drams of usquebaugh you drank with Dan Deasy's ducats.
> How much did I spend? O, a few shillings.
> For a plump of pressmen. Humour wet and dry.
> Wit. You would give your five wits for youth's proud livery he pranks in. Lineaments of gratified desire.[13]

Here, as the pronouns underlined indicate, Stephen turns critically from interlocutor to self, and to self as Other.

Self-criticism is the very basis of Hamlet's own self-communion, and a detailed analysis of his soliloquies, and a comparison with those of other Shakespearean 'heroes' (e.g. Macbeth, Richard II) might reveal interesting dialogical similarities and differences. Yet common to many soliloquies generally, and also dramatic monologues (cf. Tennyson's 'Maud', for instance), as Bakhtin's own discussion of Dostoevsky reveals, is the exposure of a double self, an *alter ego*. Again, the Bakhtin and Voloshinov preoccupation with social diversification introduces helpful refinements for this 'interior dialogue'. If normally our 'second voice' is typically the social norm which we confront (either to agree or disagree with), instability can arise if this voice loses its frame of reference (cf. Voloshinov's *Stylistics of Artistic Discourse* (1930), cited in Todorov, (1984, p. 70). Hamlet, the social misfit, is in continual danger of losing his mind; or is he? In a play where answers are publicly sought but also evaded, where no-one understands let alone trusts one another, his own cross-examination of himself at regular intervals reveals an underlying recurring norm of an Other not afraid of responsibility – for the burden of life, for his own death, for accusation, for revenge.

In his soliloquy in Act II, Scene 2, for instance, a series of explicit direct questions ('What's Hecuba to him, or he to Hecuba?' 'Am I a coward?' 'Who calls me villain ...?') reveals his self-torture, at the same time as demanding agreement with his self-condemnation. But out of the recognition there can come resolution, if only temporary:

> Ha! 'Swounds, I should take it: for it cannot be
> But I am pigeon-liver'd ...
> [*Yes, you are: but why are you?*]
>               ... or ere this
> I should ha' fatted all the region kites
> With this slave's offal ...
> [*What is this slave?*]
>               ... Bloody, bawdy villain!
> Remorseless, treacherous, lecherous, kindless villain!
> [*Yes, yes, I get the point: what follows from this?*]
> O, vengeance!
> [*A good idea: why not?*] etc.

In this play, the very device of soliloquy is an essential catalyst for the audience's own recurring question: 'Why does Hamlet not act?'

That all understanding is dialogical is perhaps a truism; but there are still many truisms left that would repay detailed (stylistic) analysis. Voloshinov, taking up the well-known 'le style, c'est l'homme', states 'Style is, at least, two men, or more precisely man and his social grouping, incarnated by its accredited representative, the listener' (*Discourse of Life and Discourse in Poetry* (1926), cited in Todorov, 1984, p. 61). In so far as postwar stylistics, with its characteristic protean eclecticism, has responded to developments in linguistics and literary theory, then it seems both inevitable and desirable that it should integrate itself more closely with sociolinguistics and pragmatics, following recent trends in these areas. And as White (1984) acutely observes, it is precisely the failure of Deconstruction to recognize and grasp the 'positive, socially constitutive role' of discourse diversity that ultimately renders it sterile. Stylistics should also, taking again the tone of the Bakhtin circle, be more dynamic, more searching in its procedures: on the one hand discriminating between the multiple voices charged with their ideological accents; on the other adopting a more flexible, procedural approach akin to Enkvist's 'process' model of style, or contextual grammar.

# NOTES

1  On the need, within sociolinguistics, to adopt a broader approach to the study of linguistic variation in earlier periods, and so to give fuller recognition to differences of register, sociolect, etc. see, e.g. Kytö and Rissanen (1983). For a modest illustration of the complex interplay of stylistic and sociolinguistic variation in respect of sixteenth–seventeenth–century syntax, see Wales (1985).
2  Fowler (1979) himself makes a connection between Bakhtin and his own work, and adopts some Bakhtinian ideas in an analysis (1983) of the speech styles in *Hard Times*.
3  I emphasize the 'in principle'. One problem arising from Burton, as Taylor and Toolan indicate (1984, p. 65) is the extent to which any model of non-dramatic 'dialogue' can be matched to the dramatic. In Bakhtin's terms, in fact, as we shall see below, drama is not 'authentic' dialogue in the sense that it is not truly 'dialogic'; like poetry, he generalizes, it is really 'monologic', i.e. single-voiced, unified, sealed off from the influences of living heteroglossia, and also controlled by the dominant voice of the author (see DIN, *passim*).
4  Many of Bakhtin's ideas therefore cannot be dealt with here. But as the Bibliography reveals, critical attention has rightly focused on, for example, 'carnival' (see Hayman, 1983; Jones, 1983) and modes of speech representation in the novel (see especially McHale, 1978).
5  Sanctified authoritative citation has, of course, a long history. The

unwelcome aspect of relying on 'dominant viewpoints' in criticism, and in science, which can lead to instability and uncertainty in ideology, is noted by Voloshinov (1973); see Todorov (1984, p. 94).

6  Philip Larkin (1964), *The Whitsun Weddings*, Faber & Faber, p. 43.
7  Philip Larkin (1955), *The Less Deceived*, Marvell Press, p. 34.
8  Philip Larkin (1974), *High Windows*, Faber & Faber, p. 17.
9  For a recent theoretical reappraisal of parody, which actually assimilates Bakhtin's ideas (especially in Chapter 4), see Hutcheon (1985). Hutcheon rightly stresses the element of 'critical distance', and also parody's 'active' nature.
10  On the 'dialogic' nature of Orwell's prose, for example (and his ironic and subversive use of official discourse), see Good (1984).
11  For an interesting discussion of some of the problems of 'monologue' in *Ulysses*, see Sandulescu (1979). Attridge and Ferrar (1984), in a mere footnote (p. 13), conclude that 'Joyce's monologue is anything but monological'.
12  As Bakhtin notes, it depended for its effect on *syncrisis* (the juxtaposition of points of view) and *anacrisis* (the means of eliciting opinions). It is out of this process, of course, that true understanding can occur, agreement from (potential) disagreement. As Gray notes (1977, p. 284), dialogue was an important mode in the Greek theory of meaning. It was also, in the Middle Ages, a popular pedagogical tool. In this respect, other 'catechistic' modes of discourse warrant further study. We may ponder, for example, why in ballads (see Leith, this volume) there is not only a high proportion of 'dialogue', but also question-answer sequences.
13  The Bodley Head edition (1968), pp. 254-5.

# BIBLIOGRAPHY

## 8.B.1  Works of Bakhtin and his circle

The authorship of some of these works is notoriously a matter of dispute. I have adopted the conventional attributions, while acknowledging Bakhtin's probably extensive influence overall.

Bakhtin, M. (1968), 'L'énoncé dans le roman', *Langages*, vol. 12, pp. 126–32.
Bakhtin, M. (1971), 'Discourse typology in prose', A translation of a section of the original 1929 (Leningrad) text of *Problems of Dostoevky's Poetics*, in L. Matejka and K. Pomorska (eds), *Readings in Russian Poetics: Formalist and Structuralist Views*, Cambridge, Mass., MIT Press, pp. 176–96.
Bakhtin, M. (1972), *Rabelais and his World* (Translated by H. Iswolsky; first written 1940; first published 1965), Cambridge, Mass, MIT, Press.
Bakhtin, M. (1973), *Problems of Dostoevsky's Poetics* (translated by R. W. Rotsel), Ann Arbor, Ardis.

Bakhtin, M. (1981), *The Dialogic Imagination: Four Essays* (ed. M. Holquist, and translated by him and C. Emerson) Austin, University of Texas Press. Contains translations of four of Bakhtin's essays from the 1930s which were collected and published after his death as *Questions of Literature and Aesthetics* (1975): 'Epic and novel', 'From the prehistory of novelistic discourse', 'Forms of time and chronotope in the novel', 'Discourse in the novel'; this last essay (DIN) is cited extensively in this chapter.

Bakhtin, M. (1984), *Problems of Dostoevsky's Poetics* (ed. and translated by C. Emerson, Introduction by W. C. Booth) Manchester, Manchester University Press. Appendix I contains three fragments from the 1929 edition which he altered or deleted in his later revision (1963); Appendix II 'Toward a reading of the Dostoevsky book' (1961) is a guideline for the revised 2nd edition, on which Emerson's translation is based.

Bakhtin, M. *School Papers* (1983) (with an introduction by A. Shukman), Oxford, RPT Publications. Includes Voloshinov/Bakhtin (1926), 'Discourse in life and discourse in Poetry'; (1928), 'Latest trends in linguistic thought in the West'; Medvedev/Bakhtin (1925–8), 'Three papers on Russian Formalism, Marxism and sociology of literature'; Voloshinov (1930), 'Three papers on a Marxist stylistics'.

Medvedev, P. and Bakhtin, M. (1978), *The Formal Method in Literary Scholarship* (translated by A. J. Wehrle; first published 1928), Baltimore, Johns Hopkins University Press (also by Harvard University Press 1985).

Voloshinov, V. N. (1971), 'Reported speech' (a translation of a portion of *Marxism and the Philosophy of Language*, below), in L. Matejka, and K. Pomorska; (see Bakhtin, 1971), pp. 149–75.

Voloshinov, V. N. (1973), *Marxism and the Philosophy of Language* (first published 1929, translated by L. Matejka and I. R. Titunik), New York and London, Seminar Press; reprinted as paperback, with new Preface, by Harvard University Press, 1986.

Voloshinov, V. N. (1976), *Freudianism: A Marxist Critique* (first published 1927; translated by I. R. Titunik), New York, Academic Press.

*Writings by the Circle of Bakhtin* (forthcoming) (translated by W. Godzich), Minneapolis, Minneapolis University Press. This will include Voloshinov's 'Discourse in life', and also his 'On the borders between poetics and linguistics' (1930), as well as Bakhtin's 'Preface' to Tolstoy's *Resurrection* (1929).

### 8.B.2 Commentaries

Clark, K. and Holquist, M. (eds) (1985), *Mikhail Bakhtin*, Cambridge, Mass., Harvard University Press.

Kristeva, J. (1973), 'The ruin of a poetics', in S. Bann and J. E. Bowlt (eds), *Russian Formalism*, Edinburgh, Scottish Academic Press, pp. 102–19.

Pateman, T. (1982), 'Discourse in life: V. N. Voloshinov's *Marxism and the*

*Philosophy of Language*', *UEA Papers in Linguistics*, vol. 16–17, pp. 26–48.

Pomorska, K. (1978), 'Mixail Bakhtin and his verbal universe', *Poetics and the Theory of Literature*, vol. 3, pp. 379–86.

Todorov, T. (1981), *Introduction to Poetics*, Brighton, Harvester Press, Chapter 3 (first published in French in 1968).

Todorov, T. (1984), *Mikhail Bakhtin – the Dialogical Principle* (translated by W. Godzich), Manchester, Manchester University Press (first published in French in 1981).

White, A. (1984), 'Bakhtin, sociolinguistics and deconstruction', in Gloversmith, F. (ed.), *The Theory of Reading*, Brighton, Harvester Press, pp. 123–46.

## 8.B.3  *Articles influenced by Bakhtin and/or Voloshinov*

Fowler, R. (1979), 'Anti-language in fiction', *Style*, vol. 13, pp. 259–78.

Fowler, R. (1983), 'Polyphony and problematic in *Hard Times*', in R. Giddings (ed.), *The Changing World of Charles Dickens*, London, Vision/New York, Barnes & Noble, pp. 91–108.

Frow, J. (1980), 'Discourse genres', *Journal of Literary Semantics*, vol. 9, no. 2, pp. 72–81.

Hayman, D. (1983), 'Towards a mechanics of mode: beyond Bakhtin', *Novel*, Winter, 1983, pp. 101–20.

Jones, A. R. (1983), 'Inside the outsider: Nashe's *Unfortunate Traveller* and Bakhtin's polyphonic novel', *English Literary History*, vol. 50, no. 1, pp. 61–81.

Lodge, D. (1983), 'Double discourses: Joyce and Bakhtin', *James Joyce Broadsheet*, no. 11, pp. 1–2.

McHale, B. (1978), 'Free indirect discourse: a survey of recent accounts', *Poetics and the Theory of Literature*, vol. 3, pp. 249–87.

## 8.B.4  *Other references*

Attridge, D. and Ferrar, D. (eds) (1984), 'Introduction' to *Post-Structuralist Joyce*, Cambridge, Cambridge University Press.

Burton, D. (1980), *Dialogue and Discourse*, London, Routledge & Kegan Paul.

Burton, D. (1982), 'Through glass darkly: through dark glasses', in R. Carter (ed.), *Language and Literature*, London, Allen & Unwin, pp. 195–214.

Crystal, D. and Davy, D. (1969), *Investigating English Style*, London, Longman.

Edmondson, W. (1981), *Spoken Discourse*, London, Longman.

Fowler, R. (1981), *Literature as Social Discourse*, London, Batsford.

Fowler, R., Hodge, B., Kress, G., and Trew, T. (1979), *Language and Control*, London, Routledge & Kegan Paul.

Genette, G. (1980), *Narrative Discourse*, Oxford, Basil Blackwell.

Good, G. (1984), 'Language, truth and power in Orwell', *Prose Studies*, vol. 7, no. 1, pp. 55–69.

Gray, B. (1977), 'From discourse to dialog', *Journal of Pragmatics*, vol. 1, pp. 283–98.

Halliday, M. A. K. (1985), *An Introduction to Functional Grammar*, London, Edward Arnold.

Hoey, M. (1983), *On the Surface of Discourse*, London, Allen & Unwin.

Hutcheon, L. (1985), *A Theory of Parody*, London, Methuen.

Kytö, M. and Rissanen, M. (1983), 'The syntactic study of early American English: the variationist at the mercy of his corpus?', *Neuphilologische Mitteilungen*, vol. 84, no. 4, pp. 410–89.

Lanser, S. (1981), *The Narrative Act*, Princeton, NJ, Princeton University Press.

Sandulescu, C. G. (1979), *The Joycean Monologue*, Colchester, A Wake Newslitter Press.

Taylor, T. and Toolan, M. (1984), 'Recent trends in stylistics', *Journal of Literary Semantics*, vol. 13, no. 1, pp. 57–79.

Wales, K. (1985), 'Generic "Your" and Jakobean drama: the rise and fall of a pronominal usage', *English Studies*, vol. 66, no. 1, pp. 7–24.

Winter, E. (1982), *Towards a Contextual Grammar of English*, London, Allen & Unwin.

# 9

# Heteroglossia

## in the poetry of
## Bertolt Brecht and Tony Harrison

*Helga Geyer-Ryan*

*This chapter by Helga Geyer-Ryan takes issue with an aspect of Bakhtin's work which has already been hinted at in the previous chapter, i.e. its one-sided emphasis on the novel as a literary genre. How then must we interpret poetry? Is it the case that heteroglossia is by and large a phenomenon applicable to the novel only? Or is it possible to extend Bakhtin's analysis into the realm of poetry? As the analysis reveals, Bakhtin's theory must be called defective vis-à-vis the lyrical genres. This does not mean, however, that devices traditionally described in the fields of poetics must be re-interpreted dialogically. As the chapter shows, this will not do. Instead one must concentrate on the intentional semantic hybrid which is essential to Bakhtin's concept of literature.*

*In this chapter, Helga Geyer-Ryan demonstrates this concept with reference to poems by Bertolt Brecht and Tony Harrison. Heteroglossia appears in the works of both poets. More importantly, though, in both authors the dialogic character is installed as a central artistic device pointing to the social and ideological constructs which underlie the uses of language in various situations. As such, both authors deal explicitly with language and its (social) mechanisms. In Brecht's 'Questions from a worker who reads' it is the medium of writing, especially its use in historiography, which constitutes the exclusion of individuals from their own history. The literary text presents a pluriformity of linguistic organization here; the questions of the worker undermine the validity of the historiography, thence forming a new text which is a critique of political forms of language-use (see also Sauer's chapter in this volume). In the case of Tony Harrison's poetry, the phonologically-based discriminations of spoken language are transferred into the written medium. By means of a detailed investigation of the various heteroglossia in this poetry, Helga Geyer-Ryan points to the central role played by this device and its function in laying bare the power structure upon which the social uses of language are based. Both the analyses of Brecht and of Harrison raise fundamental issues regarding the functions of poetry in present-day society.*

The 'rhetoric of silence' has become an established part of twentieth-century poetics; see, for instance Hart-Nibbrig (1981), Steiner (1969). When poets seek to articulate not only the emotional and communicative aspects of experience but equally the imprints left by the bureaucratic power-structures of the system surrounding them, they find themselves on the verge of silence. Faced with a reality which destroys humanity, the language of the poem is ashamed of its own inadequacy. Adorno's statement that poetry was impossible after Auschwitz has its place in this context, as does Karl Krauss's poetic reaction to Fascism, or Brecht's movement away from the poetry of nature.

The thing threatened with silence, however, is not actually the language itself but rather a quite particular lyric voice, which nevertheless constitutes the dominant tradition in European poetry of the modern age. It is, in a general sense, the linguistic expression of one kind of idiosyncratic subjectivity which presents itself as an autonomous and absolute entity. This points to the existence of a self in the world and, conversely, it represents the heterogeneous and centrifugal dynamics of the world as being focused and filtered, as they are, through the perspectives of a synthesizing and unifying linguistic agency. Behind this, despite techniques of fragmentation, there is still the ideological construct of a monadic subject. Whether this is called 'author' or 'lyrical self' or 'text' or 'language' or 'the imaginary' does not really matter. What does matter is that it is still a monological agency. Its job is to unify the heterogeneity of performative language. The poet's technique demands exclusion. Just as the idea of the subject is oriented towards monadic substantiality, so the idea of lyricism is oriented towards monological inwardness. In the ideology of the subject its essence is seen precisely as the result of its being set apart from that which is other. Likewise the heteroglossia of the world, its plurality of discourses, is expected to reappear in lyrical poetry in that one authentic voice after its journey through the soul. Describing the relationship between the subject, the world, language and poetry in such a way nostalgically presupposes a state of richness in the past, and the ever-worsening states of privation in the course of the modern era are expressed, as far as poetics are concerned, in ever more radical hermetic techniques. Such a description does indeed present poetry as critique, but runs the risk of ontologizing it outside the context of history, since any such description is based on a particular anthropological and philosophical view of mankind.

## 9.1 Heteroglossia as a principle of alterity

The homogenization of the language of poetry has probably been analysed most impressively by Mikhail Bakhtin (1981). For him it serves as a foil to his pioneering theory of the novel in the 1930s. In this theory, he takes the dialogic nature of language as a basic principle. He thus replaces the traditional poetic model of language as a medium of expression and impression, characterized by saturated subjectivity, with a model of language seen as communication between subjects. In Bakhtin's theory every word bears the traces of the social and ideological contexts in which it has been used. These social, ideological and historical shadows which the linguistic units automatically cast when they are actualized in speech represent in Bakhtin's theory the dialogic principle inherent in language. Each word is inextricably bound up in the dissemination of its social contexts.

Although the heterogeneity of language is seen as a 'natural' feature in speech, it can be accentuated in different ways. While in the reality of daily life the social heterogeneity of language spreads across various speakers, groups and texts, in literature it always appears within one and the same text. The extent to which the dialogization of language is expressed in this one text is for Bakhtin both a systematic criterion, which can be used to differentiate between poetry and the novel form, and a historical criterion, which can be used to describe the novel's development through history (Bakhtin, 1981, pp. 366–426). For Bakhtin, the actualized social diversity of the word is a constituent element of the novel as a genre, while monologization is a principle of poetic form. Thus, from the point of view of linguistic pragmatics, Bakhtin here follows exactly the same line of argument as that put forward in traditional aesthetics.

> In genres that are poetic in the narrow sense, the natural dialogization of the word is not put to artistic use, the word is sufficient unto itself and does not presume alien utterances beyond its own boundaries ... In poetic genres, artistic consciousness – understood as a unity of all the author's semantic and expressive intentions – fully realizes itself within its own language; in them alone is such consciousness fully immanent, expressing itself in it directly and without mediation, without conditions and without distance. The language of the poet is *his* language, he is utterly immersed in it ... The language of the poetic genre is a unitary and singular Ptolemaic world outside of which nothing else exists and nothing else is needed. The concept of many worlds of language, all equal in their ability to conceptualize and to be expressive, is organically denied to poetic style. (Bakhtin, 1981, pp. 285–6)

Where philosophical aesthetics talks of the silencing of poetry in a hardened world, the linguistic theorist Bakhtin talks of ossification, or the replacement of natural language by an artificial one.

> As a consequence of the prerequisites mentioned above, the language of poetic genres, when they approach their stylistic limit, often becomes authoritarian, dogmatic and conservative, sealing itself off from the influence of extraliterary social dialects. Therefore such ideas as a special 'poetic language', a 'language of the gods', a 'priestly language of poetry' and so forth could flourish on poetic soil. It is noteworthy that the poet, should he not accept the given literary language, will sooner resort to the artificial creation of a new language specifically for poetry than he will to the exploitation of actual available social dialects. (*ibid.*, p. 287)

It is only in the 'low' satiric and comic genres that Bakhtin admits a certain latitude for social heteroglossia. Yet even here the other language is never that of the writer, but rather an object which is described in the writer's own language.

> Nevertheless, heteroglossia (other socio-ideological languages)

can be introduced into purely poetic genres, primarily in the speeches of characters. But in such a context it is objective. It appears, in essence, as a *thing*, it does not lie on the *same* plane with the real language of the work: it is the depicted gesture of one of the characters and does not appear as an aspect of the word doing the depicting. Elements of heteroglossia enter here not in the capacity of another language carrying its own particular points of view, about which one can say things not expressible in one's own language, but rather in the capacity of a depicted thing. Even when speaking of alien things, the poet speaks in his own language. To shed light on an alien world, he never resorts to an alien language, even though it might in fact be more adequate to that world. Whereas the writer of prose, by contrast ... attempts to talk about even his *own* world in an alien language. (*ibid.*, p. 287).

It will be seen that this last criterion, that is, talking about one's own world in an alien language, does indeed appear in poetic forms which are in no way comic.

It is worth considering therefore whether it would not be possible to posit two poetic traditions which differ in their 'social style' on an analogy with the 'two stylistic directions in the European novel' which Bakhtin's theory sets up. When Bakhtin was writing, the novel had developed to make use of heteroglossia in the fullest sense, including self-criticism of novelistic writing as such which reached a high level of refinement (Joyce, Döblin, Dos Passos). It is possible that being a much more personal genre, poetry is only just beginning to universalize the strategies of 'low' and 'comic' sub-genres. The threat of becoming too rigid and authoritarian, too exclusive and hermetic, or speechless and finally silent, would thus serve as an indication of the current level of historical development, not only of poetry but also of the concept of the subject underlying it.

Adorno called poems 'sun dials of the philosophy of history'.[1] It would thus not be going too far, perhaps, at a time when the concept of the subject is undergoing a sweeping process of reconstruction in philosophical discourse, to posit an analogous reconstruction in poetic discourse. The notion of relational subjectivity at the basis of Habermas' theory of communication, or the definition of identity as involving the inclusion of the other and his language found in Lacan's work,[2] have their counterpart in Bakhtin's investigations into the dialogization of the word. If I am my language, then at any time I am also an ensemble of heterogeneous speech.

Just like the stylistic phenomena in Shakespeare's epic theatre, in the drama of the German *Sturm and Drang* and Büchner, there are also epic structures to be found earlier in poetry, as for example in the popular song or ballad. Here too the specifically epic element can be defined as the integration of diverse social discourses. It is that element which we generally refer to as popular. Yet here the different ways of speaking are assigned to different speakers, and are brought together not in dialogizations of themselves but rather in dialogic speech acts. For Bakhtin, these are nevertheless still legitimate manifestations of heteroglossia or polyphony. But they are not necessarily the product of the author's conscious desire to create a polyphonic text. The artistic realization of such a desire is intentional hybridization, as Bakhtin calls the fusing together of different languages.

> It is a mixture of two social languages within the limits of a
> single utterance, an encounter, within the arena of an
> utterance, between two different linguistic consciousnesses,
> separated from one another by an epoch, by social
> differentiation or by some other factor. Such mixing of two
> languages within the boundaries of a single utterance is ... an
> artistic device ... that is deliberate. (*ibid.*, p. 358)

As unintentional hybridization is part of the dynamics of language change in life, so the purpose of the writer's creative act is to produce 'an image of language', a constellation of representing and represented language based on two levels of linguistic consciousness: 'Indeed, if there is not a second representing consciousness ... then what results is not an *image* [*obraz*] of language but merely a *sample* [*obrazec*] of some other person's language, whether authentic or fabricated' (*ibid.*, p. 359). Because of the intentions and desires behind the linguistic utterances, 'it is the collision between differing points of views on the world that are embedded in these forms. Therefore an intentional artistic hybrid is a *semantic* hybrid; not semantic and logical in the abstract (as in rhetoric), but rather a *semantics that is concrete and social*' (*ibid.*, p. 360). It is typical for a semantic hybrid 'to fuse into a single utterance two utterances that are socially distinct. The syntactic construction of intentional hybrids is fractured into two individualized language-intentions.' (*ibid.*, p. 361).

This social semantic hybrid is the cornerstone of Bakhtin's

theory of the dialogization of the word. In this respect, Renate Lachmann's (1982) views on the dialogization of the poetic word seem to me to be open to attack. Phenomena such as ambiguity and ambivalence arising from particular stylistic figures which Lachmann chooses to interpret as dialogic structures in the Bakhtinian sense are not only not overlooked by Bakhtin himself but are explicitly analysed by him as non-dialogic. They do not belong to the orchestra of social heteroglossia but rather to the register of rhetoric.

> The double-voiced prose word has a double meaning. But the poetic word, in the narrow sense, also has a double, even multiple, meaning. It is this that basically distinguishes it from the word as concept, or the word as term. The poetic word is a trope, requiring a precise feeling for the two meanings contained in it. But no matter how one understands the interrelationship of meanings in a poetic symbol (a trope), this interrelationship is never of the dialogic sort; it is impossible under any conditions or at any time to imagine a trope (say, a metaphor) being unfolded into the two exchanges of a dialogue, that is, two meanings parceled out between two separate voices ... The polysemy of the poetic symbol presupposes the unity of a voice with which it is identical, and it presupposes that such a voice is completely alone within its own discourse. (Bakhtin, 1981, pp. 327-8)

Elsewhere Bakhtin even stresses the mutual exclusivity of the two stylistic processes.

> No matter how multiple and varied these semantic and accentual threads, associations, pointers, hints, correlations that emerge from every poetic word, one language, one conceptual horizon, is sufficient to them all; there is no need of heteroglot social contexts. What is more, the very movement of the poetic symbol (for example, the unfolding of a metaphor) presumes precisely this unity of language, an unmediated correspondence with its object. Social diversity of speech, were it to arise in the work and stratify its language, would make impossible both the normal development and the activity of symbols within it. (*ibid.*, pp. 297-8)

I have chosen to quote so comprehensively as a way of making it quite clear that the now ubiquitous theory of intertextuality cannot be traced back to Bakhtin's theory of social dialogization. On the contrary, Bakhtin explicitly places intertextuality beyond the sociolectic word, namely as a criterion of the poetic word, which for him is monologic. 'Everything that enters the work must immerse itself in Lethe, and forget its previous life in any other contexts: language may remember only its life in poetic contexts' (*ibid.*, p. 297). If we were not to make a distinction between intertextuality and social heteroglossia, the latter would lose its force as a criterion of stylistic genre. It would then be impossible to characterize mixed genres or 'deviations'.

I shall use Bertolt Brecht's 'Questions from a worker who reads' and some poems by Tony Harrison to show how the principle of social and ideological dialogization, which for Bakhtin is a formative element of prose style only, becomes a central artistic device in poetry too. Even in the titles of Brecht's poem and the perhaps best-known poem by Tony Harrison, 'Them & [uz]', there is a noticeable tension between two languages.

Whereas Brecht confronts the written discourse of historiography, that fundamental pillar of the tradition which reflects how a society sees itself, with the representative of a social class largely excluded from the written word, Harrison transposes the scandal of phonologically-based social differentiation in the spoken language into the medium of writing. The worker is not only excluded from the written language but from any form of discourse recognized in public life. Both poems demonstrate that the so-called standard languages, written or spoken, operate on a basis of class distinction, that is, exclusion. The poems therefore set out to find the voices which have been silenced in the process of monopolization and monologization of speech perpetrated by the social powers that be.

> The category of common language is the theoretical expression of historical processes of linguistic unification and centralization, the expression of the centripetal forces of the language. The common language is never given but in fact always ordained, and at every moment of the life of the language it is opposed to genuine heterology.[3]

The lost voices are recovered on two different levels; they consistute both the theme and the language of the poems. It seems to be symptomatic that these two poets themselves are socially dialogized. The writer Brecht, who as a bourgeois intellectual pursues a practical political standpoint from the perspective of the proletariat; and the proletarian Harrison, who in the course of a policy of school reform expands his linguistic and cultural competence to such an extent that he becomes a writer. That which is negatively termed 'falling between two classes', 'leaving' or even 'betraying one's class' turns out to be the advantage of social polyphony. Only by constructing social polyphony is it possible to recognize and represent the losses of monologic speech.

Put into linguistic terms, we could say that techniques of defamiliarization always involve the dialectization of a monological medium by means of dialogization. Dialectization has two meanings here. On the one hand, it is the relativization of a monopolistic dominant language. By holding it up to the mirror of another, underprivileged language, it is made to take on an equal status as a dialect itself, one language among many. But dialectic also means that the two languages do not stand in opposition to one another in an antagonistic configuration, but rather stand together as evidence of the fact that the whole wealth of experience of a socially diversified society can only be conveyed in polyphony. Only in that way is the *status quo* of culturally, politically and linguistically established patterns brought into tension and movement.

## 9.2 Bertolt Brecht

### Questions from a worker who reads

Who built Thebes of the seven gates?
In the books you will find the names of kings.
Did the kings haul up the lumps of rock?
And Babylon, many times demolished.
Who raised it up so many times? In what houses
Of gold-glittering Lima did the builders live?
Where, the evening that the Wall of China was finished
Did the masons go? Great Rome
Is full of triumphal arches. Who erected them? Over whom
Did the Caesars triumph? Had Byzantium, much praised in song
Only palaces for its inhabitants? Even in fabled Atlantis
The night the ocean engulfed it
The drowning still bawled for their slaves.
The young Alexander conquered India.
Was he alone?
Caesar beat the Gauls.
Did he not have even a cook with him?

Philip of Spain wept when his armada
Went down. Was he the only one to weep?
Frederick the Second won the Seven Years' War. Who
Else won it?

Every page a victory.
Who cooked the feast for the victors?
Every ten years a great man.
Who paid the bill?

So many reports.
So many questions.[4]

Before Brecht's text actually begins in the narrower sense, it is already framed in three ways: Svendborg Poems – Chronicles – Questions/reading. All three headings thematize forms of language or discourse and thus form a plurilogic complex of reference. Thus the poem works from inside outwards. Its linguistic dynamics are set in motion by the linguistic and pragmatic oxymoron of the 'worker who reads'. From this stems the critical view of historical records (Chronicles) and thus doubt is cast on the rationale of the entire cultural tradition (*Svendborger Gedichte*). The poem talks of the strange disappearance of those who really made history and culture and, what is more, had to bear the cost, as Benjamin describes in his theories *On the Concept of History*:

> without exception the cultural treasures he [the historical
> materialist] surveys have an origin which he cannot
> contemplate without horror. They owe their existence not only
> to the efforts of the great minds and talents who have created
> them, but also to the anonymous toil of their contemporaries.
> There is no document of civilization which is not at the same
> time a document of barbarism. And just as such a document is
> not free of barbarism, barbarism taints also the manner in
> which it was transmitted from one owner to another.[5]

Both Benjamin and Brecht are writing about the same phenomenon, the ideologically dictated repressions and exclusions of bourgeois historiography. Yet, whereas Benjamin presents us with the result of a process of discovery, Brecht dramatizes this process itself in the form of a conflict between languages: the smallest linguistic unit is the reading worker. The worker attacks a text which is written neither for him nor by him but rather against him, using his own text in the form of questions. He picks holes in something which is presented as an unassailable, coherent whole. It is a 'conflict between one's own word and an alien word' as Bakhtin puts it, because the word is never

> in a neutral and impersonal language (it is not, after all, out of a dictionary that the speaker gets his words) but rather it exists in other people's mouths, in other people's contexts, serving other people's intentions: it is from there that one must take the word and make it one's own. (Bakhtin, 1981, p. 294)

The process of transcribing history from one mouth to another is further emphasized by the archaic-sounding 'Chronicles' of the Middle Ages. Historiography is the modern way of writing history, a 'universal' history which structures particular events from a centralized perspective. It is this choice of a unifying and monologizing perspective around which historical discourse is organized and which determines what is included in it. What is included are monuments. 'Monumental historiography'[6] tells of great buildings, men and battles. They are the vestiges of power in the collective memory, even of those people who had no share of it.

The 'chronicle' form turns against this colonization of historical memory. It structures events in a purely chronological way without giving more importance to some things over others or setting up a hierarchy such as the unifying centralized perspective involves.

The 'questionable' nature of official historiography is emphasized by the central position of the word 'questions' at the beginning (title) and end of the text, and by the actual syntactic arrangement of the text: of twenty-five sentences, fourteen are questions; the very first sentence is a question. Normally one reads a text to obtain answers. In this case it is the other way round, as the last two lines of the poem neatly point out: 'So many reports./So many questions'.

In this inverted dialogue between reader and book appears the 'displaced' relativization of a historiographical discourse which has become second nature. Since history is primarily conveyed in the form of a text, historiography and history seem to become identical. This conglomerate, in which a contextually defined form of narrative appears to be transformed into reality, is torn apart by the worker's questions.

Anyone who does not recognize the central stylistic principle of heteroglossia in Brecht's composition necessarily reaches erroneous conclusions. In the following quotation it is clear how literary criticism continues to see Brecht the politician and not Brecht the writer, whose stylistic means are in the vanguard of his time and whose political impact springs from his *avant garde* method of writing.

> It would of course be naive to expect an exhaustive reflexion upon the difficult relationship between the great individual and the 'masses' in history from this poem. By continually using the question form Brecht has avoided the real problem. In 1934/35 he was not concerned with contributing to the theory of history in the form of a poem. This is a political poem. In posing question after question which, as it were, give their own answer and are in this respect rhetorical, the poem draws on a politically fatal way of viewing history which has deteriorated into ideology. (Mennemeier, 1982, pp. 166–7)

This poem has nothing to do with the relationship between the individual and the masses, nor does Brecht avoid the real problem by asking questions. Nor are the questions rhetorical, as we shall see, nor is there necessarily a contrast between politics and the theory of history. The fact that Brecht is associated at all with such an impossible cross-breed as 'contributing to the theory of history in the form of a poem' shows that Brecht is not taken seriously enough as a linguistic artist.

What Brecht actually makes in this poem is a profound linguistic critique of particular stylistic devices employed in certain discourses of power-politics. The questions are the centre-piece in his lyrical staging of social heteroglossia. Within the questions the various social semantic horizons are fused into an ideological semantic hybrid in the Bakhtinian sense. Here the language of the worker clashes with the quotations from the history books, and in such a way that the political dimension inherent in the apparently objective devices of classical rhetoric comes to the surface. Brecht shows how historiography produces ideology by making use of particular devices from the resources of classical eloquence.

In the first part of the poem the centralizing effect of the polished *epitheton ornans* is disrupted ('Thebes of the seven gates', 'Babylon many times demolished', 'gold-glittering Lima', 'the Wall of China', 'great Rome', 'Byzantium much praised in song', 'fabled Atlantis'); Brecht demonstrates how the origin and development of the thing mentioned disappears behind the stereotypical and formulaic nature of the noun-plus-epithet construction. The *epitheton ornans* underlines the factuality of something, the fact of it being so. The process by which it came about is made invisible, and with it those who produced it and the conditions under which it was produced. Such epithets have a dehistoricizing effect by virtue of constant repetition of the construction; it takes history back into the realm of myth.

Because the worker's reading of the text does not follow the conventions for reading myth – rather he takes the myth literally, treating Byzantium, Atlantis and Thebes as if they were Berlin, Essen and Frankfurt – the *epitheton ornans* is dislodged by the cold wind of everyday reality. It tumbles down from the realm of the mytho-historic into the history of simple people. Suddenly the interest in these marvellous fabled cities shifts to banalities, such as building, hauling, living, walking, drowning. This strategy is most clearly seen in the last sentence of the first verse in the juxtaposition of 'fabled Atlantis' from the history book and 'the drowning still bawled' from the language of the worker.

In the second part the focus shifts from the monumental buildings to the monumental men. Where in the first part the worker's two-eyed view and double-edged way of putting things served to repopulate the otherwise empty squares around the mythical monuments, so in the second verse he brings out the workers from behind the kings and the troops from behind the generals. He changes the stylistic figure of metonymy back into everyday language. (Is it perhaps also a feature of fine arts that the mythical dimension can only be achieved in the absence of people? Consider de Chirico for example). The proposition containing the metonymic subject of the general representing the troops is the part of the text which is taken from the history book; the questions are asked by the worker. The definitions of the rhetorical device of metonymy – 'renaming', 'changing names around', 'figurative speech', 'replacement of the actual word by another related to it in real terms'[7] – clearly show the possibilities it offers for an ideological cover-up. The linguistic moves which are permissible in poetic discourses in order to avoid repetition take on the power to shape reality in historiography.

In this process of deconstructing particular rhetorical devices to expose the interests of a dominant class, a third device from the classical armoury is also used in a different way – the question itself. The series of questions which make up the poem seem to be rhetorical as the answers appear to be so obvious. But they are only obvious because the question presents a particular rhetorical way of speaking in such a way that something concealed or forgotten within it comes to light again. This is not, however, the characteristic feature of a rhetorical question but rather the hallmark of the maieutic question. In this kind of questioning, the person asked the question 'talks only of something he already knows and has merely forgotten. The dialectician's questions help him to remember'.[8] Whereas the rhetorical question is for one voice only, accentuating the monologue of one speaker referring only to himself, the maieutic question speaks in two languages. It operates on the basis of the visible text and yet finds its way to the palimpsest concealed beneath it.

The worker in Brecht's poem is an artistic device. He poses the questions and is asked the questions at the same time. This is possible because the worker is the textual expression of Brecht's heteroglot position. We hear the voices both of the cultured bourgeoisie and of a politically aware working class. Only a crudely realistic approach, seeing not the polyphonic construction (of Brecht the artist) but the pure agitation (of Brecht the politician), would then say 'Thus a bourgeois intellectual who would like to stop being one models a worker on the image of his own desires, and sees the purpose of history, even the history of civilization, as a way of realizing a myth, namely the removal of all class barriers in the rise of the proletariat, (Ueding, 1978, p. 71). It is even less true to say that '"Questions from a worker who reads" thus brings Brecht to the limits of his artistic capabilities', nor is 'the worker the device used to salve his own social conscience'.

On the contrary. The brilliance of the text becomes apparent in the tension between prosodic, semantic and syntactic simplicity and interphrasal complexity. The language is predominantly colloquial. The usual poetic devices such as metre, rhyme, regular rhythm, and line and verse construction are replaced by parallelisms, a semantically dynamic counterpoint of line and syntax units, clearly meaningful radicalizations of the *enjambement* and careful orchestration of social polyphony.

In the poem as a whole the speaker is neither a worker nor Brecht. It is the artistic combination of three social speech positions which sets, and keeps, the semiosis in motion. Brecht's presence is only felt in the way the words are constructed, the breaks where the different types of speech are encapsulated in hybrid constructions, and where this craftsmanship exploits the phenomenon of contrasting elements to produce a critique of monologic power, a critique of ideology.

## 9.3 Tony Harrison

For Tony Harrison, born more than a generation later, social polyphony as a stylistic device is the central principle upon which all his poetry is based. Harrison himself talks of 'the ironies of language' and his method: 'I play one form of articulation off against the other'.[9] Just like Brecht, he too walks the borderline between political classes. Through a grammar-school education and the study of classics, Harrison moved away from the proletarian petit-bourgeoisie (his father was a baker) into the intellectual middle class. The heteroglot attitude to language in Brecht and even more so in Harrison thus draws its energy from their own linguistic experiences.

This heterogeneous linguistic and social identity was condemned by Brecht's critics as being an egoistic and therefore insincere strategy devised to compensate for the limited experience of a member of the bourgeoisie. Conversely, Harrison is criticized for having abandoned and betrayed linguistic and social solidarity with the realms of his social origins to gain a higher position on the social ladder.[10] Both writers are envied for their differential identity, since, although Harrison, for instance, makes no secret of the alienation, hostility and love lost as a result of extending the discourses open to him,[11] it is clear that it is to their advantage that both writers are equally at home in two social spheres which are mutually exclusive in the experience of a monological social identity. Brecht's and Harrison's critics see these spheres in the following terms: the sphere of the proletariat is a kind of 'pre-'linguistic symbiotic cavern of intersubjective solidarity from which will flow a privileged power of political renewal; the sphere of the bourgeoisie is characterized by a higher linguistic competence and higher social status obtained at the cost of cold and deprivation and an immediate power which is nevertheless condemned to decline.

At the basis of such a conceptualization, there is a quite specific narrative pattern which may incorporate the most diverse parameters of tension between powerlessness/authenticity and power/alienation, and which, sadly, does indeed incorporate them (men and women, non-whites and whites, children and adults, the insane and the sane, workers and middle class). In psychoanalytical terms, this model is based on the transition from symbiosis with the mother through the various processes of separation into the realm of the father which rests on castration, language and power.[12] The shortcoming of inscribing into underprivileged groups an imaginary sphere of fullness is that a model which posits an ontogenetic pre-linguistic state is applied metaphorically to groups who have in fact always used language; and that a further radicalization transforms and consolidates social differences within speech as a whole into antagonistic linguistic oppositions between groups of speakers.

Whether the universalists propagate the extension of the dominant sociolect to all as an element of reform, or whether the particularists see the purity of local varieties of speech as a potential form of resistance, the arguments remain within the bounds of monological exclusivity. It is precisely this which Brecht's and Harrison's polyphonic poetic procedures fight against. In seeking to remonologize these procedures by accusing them of class treachery on a biographical level, their critics are taking up precisely those positions which Brecht and Harrison describe in their poems as inadequate and power-conscious. The poetic fusion of discourses does away with a theory which says that class politics should be dug in along the demarcation lines between linguistic spheres. Preserves of this kind are forced open as a means of extending reality for all speakers.

Harrison too breaks up the language of cultural tradition, above all that of poetry, by using words and sentences which otherwise never occur in this medium. This has the effect of making it clear, as happened in Brecht's work, that we are not dealing with different languages but with different discourses. Discourses are pragmatic linguistic fields, the identities of which are institutionalized and safeguarded by exclusion and the creation of a positive hierarchy (see Cameron, 1985, p. 152). Thus, in themselves, French, Spanish, Portuguese and English are value-free idioms. But they immediately become the discourses of imperialist power when they are seen in relation to the native languages of the colonized peoples.

### Dichtung und Wahrheit

for Marcelino Dos Santos (Frelimo)
Dar-es-Salaam 1971

Frelimo's fluent propagandist speaks
the cloven tongues of four colonial powers:
French and Spanish, Portuguese and ours,
plus Makonde *one* of Mozambique's,
and swears in each the war will soon be won.
He speaks of 'pen & sword', quotes Mao's phrase

about 'all power' the moment his guests gaze
on the 14-18 bronze with Maxim gun.

Dulciloquist Dos Santos, swear to them
whose languages you'll never learn to speak
that tongues of fire at 1,000 rpm
is not the final eloquence you seek.

Spondaic or dactylic those machines
and their dry scansions mean that truths get lost,

and a *pravda* empty as its magazines
is Kalashnikov PK's flash Pentecost.[13]

Here, Harrison brings together the title of Goethe's autobiography, the dedication to Marcelino dos Santos, the classical topos of 'sapientia et fortitudo' as 'pen and sword' which was valued so highly precisely in the Spanish tradition (cf. Curtius, 1967, pp. 186-7), the revolutionary chant 'power to the people', and '*pravda*'. The result is a mosaic fusion of the linguistic fields 'pen' and 'sword'. The bursts of machine-gun fire are 'spondaic and dactylic' but in them there is no sign of the truths which may still be conveyed in the other 'fighting machines' made up of spondees and dactyls, that is, linguistic constructs. Poems and guns are 'tongues of fire', guns and newspapers can have 'empty magazines'.

These linguistic areas which Tony Harrison continually rearranges from poem to poem to form new sociolinguistic patch-works and pastiches embrace all the discourses which have been invested with power and domination. Bakhtin and Brecht are still both concerned with the heteroglot realm of meaning, the signified. Harrison, a generation later, brings out in all cases the discursive nature, or perhaps better, the susceptibility to discourse of the signifier.

For this reason, the social markers of oral speech in Great Britain have a central place in Harrison's texts. Taking it as his theme, he presents the linguistic conflict between the north, signifier for industry, workers, and now unemployment, and the rich south, signifier for a genteel way of life, wealth, social privilege and education – 'a dreadful schism in the British nation' as it is described in 'Classics Society'.

The linguistic schism in Harrison's own life, as it continued to shape him as a son, schoolboy, student and writer, is the source from which all his poetry draws its energy, above all the hundred sonnets in the *School of Eloquence*. In these poems there speaks repeatedly, almost obsessively, a first person whose identity never comes to rest because it is construed in the difference between two normally mutually exclusive social linguistic worlds. That identity is characterized not only by the guilt feelings of the social climber towards family and friends ('Book ends', 'Self justification,) and the hostility of the dominant cultural system, above all the grammar school, towards the intruder, but also the feelings of happiness, euphoria and freedom arising from the mastery of a variety of languages transcending the limitations of convention and achieved against all social obstacles.

Harrison experienced the social gulf in the spoken language, and for this reason it is the spoken language which dominates in his work (not, as in Brecht, the worker who *reads*). Because of this, the body of the speaker moves more visibly into the foreground. The inability to speak, the socially-determined silence, is not only a linguistic mutilation but also a physical one. The interlinking of body and language is most incisively drawn in 'Self justification'. There is a close parallel between the physical handicap of the daughter, the physical speech defect of the stuttering Uncle Joe and the linguistic uncertainties of the novice poet. This reaches its climax in the zeugma in the second verse: 'Those cruel consonants, *ms, ps* and *bs*/on which his *jaws and spirit* almost broke/flicked into order with sadistic ease' (my emphasis).

Furthermore, the material and physical character of under-privileged speech is especially accentuated in the shift of the signifying matter from the stuttered spoken word to the fluently printed word. The physical torment of a kind of speech which does not come up to an objectively evolved standard of language and speech for social reasons is blatantly expressed in the word 'sadistic' and is repeated in many different images of physical torture: 'Coarser stuff than silk they hauled up grammar/knotted together deep down in their gut' ('Fire-eater'); 'I doffed my flat a's (as in "flat cap")/my mouth all stuffed with glottals, great/lumps to hawk up and spit out ... E-nun-ci-ate!' ('Them & [uz]'); 'The stutter of the scold out of the branks/of condescension, class and counter-class/ thickens with glottals to a lumpen mass/of Ludding morphemes closing up the ranks' ('On not being Milton').

The poetic process of signifier polyphony is demonstrated in the techniques which Harrison uses to transpose the auditory differences into the written medium: non-grammaticality ('Sir, I Ham a very Bad Hand at Righting' ('On not being Milton'); spaced type, phonetic script ('Them & [uz]'); capital letters, inverted commas, iconography ('aggression, struggle, loss, blank printer's ems/by which all eloquence gets justified' ('Self justification'). In an ironic reversal it is precisely the technique of printing which otherwise shows the flow of the lines of the poem in the form of line spacing ('blank printer's ems') by having the same length of print, which becomes the marker in the written language for an absence of linguistic flow, namely the flow of oral speech. Thus the purely aural effect of stuttering becomes visible, readable.

**Them & [uz]**
for Professors Richard Hoggart & Leon Cortez

I

αἰαῖ, ay, ay! ... stutterer Demosthenes
gob full of pebbles outshouting seas –

4 words only of *mi 'art aches* and ... 'Mine's broken,
you barbarian, T. W.!' *He* was nicely spoken.
'Can't have our glorious heritage done to death!'

I played the Drunken Porter in *Macbeth*.

'Poetry's the speech of kings. You're one of those
Shakespeare gives the comic bits to: prose!
All poetry (even Cockney Keats?) you see
's been dubbed by [ʌs] into RP,
Received Pronunciation, please believe [ʌs]
your speech is in the hands of the Receivers.'

'We say [ʌs] not [uz], T. W.!' That shut my trap.
I doffed my flat a's (as in 'flat cap')
my mouth all stuffed with glottals, great
lumps to hawk up and spit out ... *E-nun-ci-ate!*

II

So right, yer buggers, then! We'll occupy
your lousy leasehold Poetry.

I chewed up Littererchewer and spat the bones
into the lap of dozing Daniel Jones,
dropped the initials I'd been harried as
and used my *name* and own voice: [uz] [uz] [uz],
ended sentences with by, with, from,
and spoke the language that I spoke at home.
RIP RP, RIP T. W.
I'm *Tony* Harrison no longer you!

You can tell the Receivers where to go

(and not aspirate it) once you know
Wordsworth's *matter/water* are full rhymes,
[uz] can be loving as well as funny.

My first mention in the *Times*
automatically made Tony Anthony!

In this process a third level of heteroglossia after the semantic (signified) and the phonetic (signifier) is brought to the surface, namely that of the written language as a signifier of the second degree. Apart from the examples already given, I should mention two strongly socially-marked cases of a kind of heteroglossia of writing. In 'Self justification' we can read 'their aggro towards me, my need of them's/what keeps my would-be mobile tongue still tied' (the physical torment once again); and in 'Them & [uz]' we read 'All poetry (even Cockney Keats?) you see/'s been dubbed as [ʌs] into RP'. Here, a spoken language with contracted 's' forms, which are normally only written down in prose, if at all, is introduced into the printed form of the poem.

The wholly unorthodox placing of the apostrophes at the beginning and end of lines in itself demonstrates that the printing conventions of poetry are such that certain conventions of speech cannot be expressed in them. The poem form itself is exclusive. It is not printing but rather pronunciation that the teacher refers to when he says the same thing to the lyrical self in 'Them & [uz]': 'I played the Drunken Porter in *Macbeth*./"Poetry's the speech of kings. You're one of those/Shakespeare gives the comic bits to: prose!"' From the excess of language arising here from the overloaded lines, with all the colloquial speech crammed in, comes the 'picture' of the language of poetic form, the representation of the one language in and by means of the other, as Bakhtin puts it.

In other poems, Harrison uses Gothic script for German words. This is unfamiliar to English writing, and in general has connotations of the foreignness and the enigmatic, cranky and speculative aspects of German history and culture. In Harrison's poems it reminds us of the German philosophies of origin and the death policy of the Fascists. The Gothic letters, set against the international Latin script, mark the anachronistic, antiquated and pseudo-archaic element inherent in such a philosophy and policy, and the deadly dangers latent within them which are also high-lighted by the Gothic characters with their aura of the uncanny.

Thus Harrison takes the identification of linguistic schisms beyond the realms of his own life into the areas of history, culture

and politics, areas which are always seen as one in his work. In
'Them & [uz]' the speech difficulties experienced by a working-class
child at grammar school are mirrored in the tortuous elocution
exercises performed by the stutterer of antiquity, Demosthenes, in
the rules of decorum for comedy and tragedy and of the comic and
tragic elements in Shakespeare's dramas, in the colonization of
poetry by the standard language, or in the received pronunciation
which is even contrary to the spoken language of the poets
themselves, e.g. Keats. And in the play on words of 'Received
Pronunciation' and 'Receivers' the semantic spheres of cultural
hegemony and regimentation and financial receivership are
projected into one another.

Finally, I want to look at 'The Ballad of Babelabour', which
corresponds linguistically and politically to Brecht's 'Questions
from a worker who reads'. Whether Harrison refers to Brecht here
unconsciously or consciously is immaterial. More important is the
affinity in theme and linguistic combination, which mainly comes
to the fore in terms of Bakhtin's concept. The only thing that can
be said about the origin of the poem is that in the two texts a
similar political and linguistic disposition is expressed.

### The Ballad of Babelabour
'This Babylonian confusion of words results from
their being the language of men who are going down.'
(Bertolt Brecht)

What ur-𝕾prache did the labour speak?
ur ur ur to t'master's 𝕾prache
the hang-cur ur-grunt of the weak
the unrecorded urs of gobless workers

Their snaptins kept among their turds
they labour    eat and shit
with only grunts not proper words
raw material for t'poet

They're their own meat and their own dough
another block    another
a palace for the great Pharaoh
a prison for their brothers

Whatever name's carved on those stones
it's not the one who labours
an edifice of workers' bones
for one who wants no neighbours

Nimrod's nabobs like their bards
to laud the state's achievements
to eulogize his house of cards
and mourn the king's bereavements

The treasurer of Sprache's court
drops the bard his coppers
He knows that poets aren't his sort
but belong to the ur-crappers

Ur-crappers tongueless bardless nerks
your condition's shitty
no time for yer Collected Works
or modulated pity

but ur ur ur ur ur ur urs
sharpened into Sprache
revurlooshunairy vurse
uprising nacker starkers

by the time the bards have urd
and urd and urd and Sprachered
the world's all been turned into *merde*
& Nimrod's Noah'sarkered

sailing t'shit in t'ship they urd at
no labour can embark her
try and you'll get guard-dog grred at
the shitship's one class: Sprache

Bards & labour left for dead
the siltworld's neue neue
bard      the HMV doghead
in that *negra negra* Goya.

After the epigraph to Brecht, Harrison too begins his poem by questioning the cultural presence of those who do the work. Syntactically, his question is identical to Brecht's 'Who built the Thebes of the seven towers?': 'Whar ur-Sprache did the labour speak?' Not only is there this parallel between Brecht's German text and Harrison's English text, but there is also an explicit juxtaposing of the two languages, German and English.

In this sentence we see, at the very beginning, a perfect semantic hybrid in the Bakhtinian sense. As the word 'Sprache' is printed in Gothic type, it is not the only fusion into a German-English compound. The archaic signifier makes the 'ur', written in lower case, also bilingual, dialogic. The German 'Ur-', so consciously superior in its obsession with genealogy, is only recognizable as being German because of the word '𝕾𝖕𝖗𝖆𝖈𝖍𝖊' following and is obscured at the same time by being written in the English way with a small letter (a fine example of Derrida's critique of *origine*, namely that the first only comes about because of the second; therefore the first is never really the first but rather the second). This German 'Ur-' is fused with a transcription of the English interjection indicating hesitation (generally spelt 'er'). 'ur' is the written signifier of an oral signifier of linguistic deficiency, not of absence, but of the borderline case of a fading, threatened type of speech, yet one which is now emerging after being silent, making its presence felt. In any case it is a fragile kind of speech.

The fusion of competence, fullness in the German 'Ur-' and of incompetence and deficiency in the English 'ur-' is ironically reproduced in the 'ur-grunt', where 'language' becomes the 'grunting' of those who are excluded from language but who hanker after it ('hang-cur'). Yet at the same time there is an association with 'ur-grund' (reason, cause). The reason the weak are weak lies in the apartheid of their 'ur ur ur' from 't'master's 𝕾𝖕𝖗𝖆𝖈𝖍𝖊', the master language. This state without language is an inhuman, i.e. bestial, state which can be seen in 'grunt' (pigs) and 'hang-cur' (dogs) and in the link set up between 't'master's voice' in the first verse and the last verse which is dominated by the picture of the dog (Goya's picture, HMV His Master's Voice).

The German word '𝕾𝖕𝖗𝖆𝖈𝖍𝖊' appears in Gothic type throughout the poem. Both signifiers, the word and the typeface, reinforce one another to form a semantic field in which the obsession of German Fundamental philosophy is set into the hazy regions of German as a master language, where 't' master's 𝕾𝖕𝖗𝖆𝖈𝖍𝖊' leads further by association to 'master race'. The poem 'A piece of cake' begins with the lines 'This New York Baker's Bread's described as Swiss/though it's said there's something Nazi in their past' and ends with the description of how a cake is iced: 'the frosting comes out Gothic and reads "Tod!"' The word 'TOD' appears in Gothic type.

But there is yet another nuance to the word 'ur', which comes across, particularly in the line 'ur ur to t'master's 𝕾𝖕𝖗𝖆𝖈𝖍𝖊'. Admittedly, the restriction of this language almost to the point of silence shows the inhuman side of this state. Yet Harrison makes it clear that this is the result of cultural violence. The weak are deprived of their own language, they are linguistically dispossessed; 'the language of the powerful ruling classes always kills off the language of the class beneath it'.[14] To the ears of the powerful elite, the speech of those who are socially less privileged becomes a chaotic and repetitive stream of signifiers ('ur ur ur').

In a similar way the Greeks, our forebears in their ethnocentric linguistic policy too, in an arrogant process of reduction recognized only the bar, bar, bar of the barbarians in all non-Greek languages. Theories of so-called 'subhumanity' which are devised to give an ideological basis to imperialist policies rest upon perverse linguistic theories. Derrida points to this in his critique of Lévi-Strauss:

> With the help of a simple analogy in the mechanisms of assimilation/ethnocentric exclusion, we should remind ourselves here with Renan that 'in the oldest languages the words used to describe foreign words derived from two sources: either from verbs meaning *babble* or *stammer* or from words meaning *dumb*'.[15]

In 'Rhubarbarians' Harrison gives a picture of the construct of social 'barbarianism' in the nameless masses whose mumblings of 'rhubarb, rhubarb' (nowadays used in films, theatre and TV) provide the auditory background for the public presentation of the great speeches of great men. In the title he brings together the racist verdict of barbarianism and the purely acclamatory function of a mass degraded to the level of mere decoration in power-political or cultural spectacles; and in the same way in 'Babelabour' he combines the toil of the silenced workers building the Tower of Babel with the (social) confusion of languages which divides mankind even today. This picture of Babel as an exploitative project of utter futility (an early mythological Star Wars undertaking) comes up again explicitly in 'Questions from a worker who reads'.

Both poems criticize a tradition of which they are nevertheless still a part, yet the contradiction is merely on the surface. Only the exclusive, monologic tradition is singled out as being an instrument of domination which is particularly manifest in the written language. The underprivileged are silent and faceless because, like the colonized nations, they have no written language.

Yet the lack of a written medium, incredibly significant in power-political terms, has a retroactive effect, casting a dark, devastating shadow back onto the spoken language of earliest times, the 'archi-écriture' in Derrida's terminology. This 'archi-écriture', which is later split into written and oral language, is overshadowed by the social demarcation-lines set down in the 'real' written culture, which in Brecht is represented by the history books and in Harrison's 'Babelabour' by the 'Collected Works'.

The 'Collected Works' are traced right back to the figure of the bard, and it is only the privileged position of written works later which makes it clear that even the culture we call 'oral' bore the hallmarks of privilege. For the oral memory, the writing on Freud's magic slate[16] which caused Derrida to conceptualize language as an 'ur-script', is already in the service of those in power if we locate it in the figures of bard, singer and seer.[17] Stanzas 4 and 5 make this particularly clear.

But it is not only because the bard ensures the continued existence and legitimation of those in power in the written language, the memory, that he fulfils a profoundly ideological function, but also because he is involved with the selection of the signifiers. The bard is the one who constantly filters the language, monologizing and unifying it into the so-called standard language, the 'received pronunciation' – 'the shitship's one class: 𝔖𝔭𝔯𝔞𝔠𝔥𝔢'. Here we have a nice correspondence between the continual use of the German morpheme '𝔖𝔭𝔯𝔞𝔠𝔥𝔢' and the typically German tradition of receiving poets as seers, harbingers and prophets.

For this bard the speech of the crowd is merely the material upon which he imposes his form and which he thus appropriates as an object (stanzas 8 and 9). This monomaniacally rarefied language becomes as exclusive as Noah's Ark and at the same time the guard dog controlling who has the privilege to enter: 'no labour can embark her/try and you'll get guard-dog grrred at'. Here there is a bold fusion of the 'dog' and its growling in such a way that the growling is at the same time the morpheme which is used to verbalize the noun. A similar heteroglot fusion links the noun '𝔖𝔭𝔯𝔞𝔠𝔥𝔢' with the English verbalizing morpheme of the past tense: '𝔖𝔭𝔯𝔞𝔠𝔥𝔢red'. The traditionally refined language of the poem is now brought crashing down by Harrison through the use of everyday expressions and vulgar language, especially the polyphonic use of 'turd', 'crap', 'shit', 'merde' into which the world is gradually sinking.

Nevertheless, objectively speaking, the bard's place is on the workers' side since he too is merely paid off by the rich (stanza 6). As long as bard and worker are mutually exclusive, their demise is a foregone conclusion (stanza 11). Contrary to this viewpoint, Harrison once again presents a polyphonic staccato in the last stanza: English, German and Spanish language; Gothic, spaced and normal typefaces; capital letters and symbols from the language of business (&).

The threefold framing of the Brecht poem – Questions/ Chronicles/Svendborg Poems – in which the questions about history become questions about poetry, the insistence with which Harrison says 'I' in his poems, the thematic nature of the bard figure in 'Babelabour' – all these are aspects which bring us to a final type of heteroglossia; the self-criticism of the literary word.

The reflexivity which is so pronounced, particularly in the twentieth-century novel (but also in *Don Quixote* and *Tristram Shandy*), is likewise a feature of polyphonic poetry. Bakhtin (1981) says (admittedly only with reference to the novel):

> a critique of literary discourse as such ... this *auto-criticism of discourse* is one of the primary distinguishing features of the novel as a genre.
>
> Discourse is criticized in its relationship to reality: its attempt to faithfully reflect reality, to manage reality and to transpose it (the utopian pretenses of discourse), even to replace reality as a surrogate for it (the dream and the fantasy that replace life). (p. 412)

Only through polyphony and the self-criticism of the literary word can the situation be prevented where even a poem which is designed to let the silenced speak becomes a cultural monument which is repressive towards these silent masses because it uses their silence as material for its own eloquence. Benjamin's dictum of barbarity as the other side of culture is mirrored in Brecht's and Harrison's poetry in the piles of bones – the only remains of the nameless masses above which the statues of history are so prominent. Harrison calls a group of three poems – of which 'The Ballad of Babelabour' is one – the *Bonebard Ballads*. In the poem the pyramids are described in these terms: 'an edifice of workers' bones/for one who wants no neighbours'.

However, this ossification cannot simply be broken down by a naive reversion to the remains of an expropriated and suppressed culture. The intra-ethnic colonial territories of society cannot be directly inherited. Fanon (1967) speaks for all of those suffering colonization and their culture:

> a continued agony rather than a total disappearance of the preexisting culture. The culture once living and open to the future becomes closed, fixed in the colonial status, caught in the yolk of oppression. Both present and mummified, it testifies against its members ... the cultural mummification leads to a mummification of individual thinking ... As though it were possible for a man to evolve otherwise than within the

framework of a culture that recognizes him and that he decides to assume. (p.34)

## 9.4 Polyphony and writing

The medium of polyphony in the Bakhtinian sense is the written language. If it is true that the monopolized written language as a symbol of social power has silenced the bearers of oral culture, then they can only regain the power of speech in and through the medium of the written language.

Any attempt to celebrate the spoken language for the sake of authenticity ends merely in a priestly gesture of hermetic silence, which strives to defy any kind of hermeneutic approach in an absolutist way. Silence and silencing are set in opposition to one another. In silence a subject is apparent, in silencing an object is affected. Silence radically destroys the signifier which is liable to corrupt one's own intention, and preserves the illusion of pure meaning no longer deformed by linguistic material concerns. Silence is absolute logocentricity.

Heteroglossia strives vehemently in the opposite direction, for in writing, printing and the media the levels of signifiers are pluralized to form ever-more-numerous possible combinations. The paradox is this: oral polyphony can only be recognized in the written language. Only the written language can draw us a 'picture' of the universe of oral speech. In these innumerable dispersions, arrangements and reflections, any centralized meaning is diffused. The truth is eccentric and differential, never quite there and always distributed along a time axis.

Thus the mirror, by its mingling of presences with representations, is anathema to all those who seek the authentic, present and logocentric. But it is a seismograph for polyphonists and heteroglots, for whom truth is divided up between endless mirror-images. Bakhtin (1981) says:

> Languages of heteroglossia, like mirrors that face each other,
> each reflecting in its own way a piece, a tiny corner of the
> world, force us to guess at and grasp for a world behind their
> mutually reflecting aspects that is broader, more multi-leveled,
> containing more and varied horizons than would be available to
> a single language or a single mirror. (pp. 414–15)

# NOTES

1 Theodor W. Adorno (1958), 'Lyrik und Gesellschaft', in *Noten zur Literatur I*, Frankfurt am Main, Suhrkamp, p. 92 (my translation).

2 In the negativity of Lacan's terminology regarding the constitution of an identity which includes the image of the other, we can still detect the implicit regret at the loss of a concept of undifferentiated identity.

3 Quoted after Tzvetan Todorov (1986), *The Dialogic Principle. Theory and History*, vol. 13 (Wlad Godzich and Jochen Schulte-Sasse, (eds)), Manchester, Manchester University Press, pp. 57–8.

4 The German version of the poem is from Bertolt Brecht (1967), *Gesammelte Werke*, vol. 9, Gedichte 2, Frankfurt am Main, Suhrkamp, pp. 656–7. The English version is translated by Michael Hamburger (1981), *Bertolt Brecht. Poems 1913–1956*, (John Willet and Ralph Manheim (eds)), London, Eyre Methuen.

5 Walter Benjamin (1974), 'Über den Begriff der Geschichte', in Walter Benjamin, *Gesammelte Schriften* vol. I, 2 (Rolf Thiedemann and Hermann Schweppenhäuser (eds)), Frankfurt am Main, Suhrkamp, p. 696. English translation from Walter Benjamin (1973), 'Theses on the philosophy of history', in *Illuminations* (edited and with an introduction by Hannah Arendt), London, Suhrkamp, p. 258.

6 See Nietzsche on 'monumentalische Geschichtsschreibung' in 'Vom Nutzen and Nachteil der Historie für das Leben', in Freidrich Nietzsche (1976), *Werke* (Karl Schlechta (ed.)), Frankfurt-Berlin-Wien, Ullstein, vol. I, p. 223.

7 Gero von Wilpert (1964), *Sahwörterbuch der Literatur*, Stuttgart, Alfred Kröner Verlag, p. 424.

8 Gerd Ueding (1976), *Einführung in die Rhetorik*, Stuttgart, Metzler, p. 26.

9 John Haffenden (1984), 'Tony Harrison. An interview', *Poetry Review*, vol. 73, no. 4, January, p. 21.

10 See for instance Ken Worpole (1985), 'Scholarship boy: the poetry of Tony Harrison', in *New Left Review*, no. 153, p. 244.

11 Haffenden, *op. cit.*, p. 22.

12 At its most general level it is a narrative dealing with the transition from nature to culture. The various disciplines such as anthropology, sociology, psychology, theology and philosophy can put their own specific terms in place of 'nature' and culture.

13 All poems are quoted from Tony Harrison (1984), *Selected Poems*, Harmondsworth, Penguin.

14 Haffenden, *op. cit.*

15 Jacques Derrida (1967), *De la grammatologie*, Paris, Editions de Minuit, p. 180:

> Par simple analogie dans les mécanismes d'assimilation/exclusion ethnocentrique, rappelons avec Renan que 'dans les langues les plus ançiennes, les mots qui servent à désigner les peuples

étrangers se tirent de deux sources: ou des verbes qui signifient *bégayer, balbutier,* ou des mots qui signifient *muet'.*

16 Sigmund Freud (1975), 'Notiz über den "Wunderblock"', in Sigmund Freud, *Studienausgabe,* vol. III, *Psychologie des Unbewussten,* Frankfurt am Main, Fischer, pp. 363–70.

17 For instance:

> Homer sang not even for nobles but for princes, and was concerned almost entirely with them. The bards whom he depicts in the *Odyssey* are the servants of kings, at whose court they live and for whose pleasure they sing ... Being of humble position as the servant of princes, Homer says nothing about himself and passes no moral judgment.

C. M. Bowra (1937), 'Sociological remarks on Greek poetry', *Zeitschrift für Sozialforschung,* Jahrgang VI, Heft 2, p. 387.

# BIBLIOGRAPHY

Bakhtin, M. (1981), *The Dialogic Imagination. Four Essays* (ed. by M. Holquist), Austin, University of Texas Press.

Cameron, D. (1985), *Feminism and Linguistic Theory,* London, Macmillan.

Curtius, E. R. (1967), *Europäische Literatur und lateinisches Mittelalter* [European literature and Latin Middle Ages], Bern/Munich, Francke.

Fanon, F. (1967), *Toward the African Revolution. Political Essays,* New York/London, Monthly Review Press.

Hart-Nibbrig, C. (1981), *Die Rhetorik des Schweigens. Versuch über den Schatten literarischer Rede* [The Rhetoric of Silence. Essay on the Shadow of Literary Discourse], Frankfurt am Main, Suhrkamp.

Lachmann, R. (1982), 'Dialogizität und poetische Sprache' [Dialogue and poetic language], in R. Lachman (ed.), *Dialogizität,* Munich, Fink, pp. 51–63.

Mennemeier, F. N. (1982), *Bertolt Brechts Lyrik. Aspekte-Tendenzen* [Brecht's lyrical poetry. Aspects and Tendencies], Düsseldorf, Bagel.

Steiner, G. (1969), 'Silence and the poet', in G. Steiner (ed.), *Language and Silence. Essays 1958–66,* Harmondsworth, Penguin, pp. 57–76.

Ueding, G. (1978), 'Fragen eines lesenden Arbeiters' [Questions from a worker who reads], in W. Hinck (ed.), *Ausgewählte Gedichte Brechts mit Interpretationen* [Selected poems from Brecht, with Interpretations], Frankfurt am Main, Suhrkamp.

# PART III

## Form and interpretation

---

I pray you tell me what you meant by that.
(*The Taming of the Shrew*, V.ii.27)

# 10

# Discourse and drama

## King Lear's 'question' to his daughters

*William Downes*

*How complex the interaction between form and interpretation may be becomes clear in William Downes' chapter. In it he analyses a brief passage from the opening scene of* King Lear. *By concentrating on the famous 'question' of Lear, the analysis gains considerable depth as to what constitutes the various alternative routes in the interpretative process. In a number of successive steps, Downes investigates its linguistic form (i.e. syntax), meaning and rhetorical devices. As is shown, Lear's question throws up a multitude of factors which cause the utterance to be basically indeterminate with respect to its status as a question. Its meaning (or rather its illocutionary force) essentially oscillates between a question and a command, and the linguistic form by itself does not provide a ground for resolving this pragmatic ambiguity. It may, indeed, be resolved by the reader, but this will occur mainly on the basis of further information, gained from the specific situation in which the utterance occurs.*

*It is only by seeing Lear's utterance as a specific form of action, involving beliefs, intentions and goals, and grounded in the institutions of the family and of kingship that one is able to trace the origin both of the conflict Lear is involved in and of the paradoxes it generates. In the context of the drama, the action involves different beliefs as to the meaning of the word 'love'. Again, as we saw in Kiernan Ryan's essay (Chapter 5), the play seems to be preoccupied with* linguistic *issues. This is perhaps less the result of the author's interest in language as such, but rather the product of language itself being constitutive of social norms and conventions. The tragic fate of Lear is set in motion by a linguistic game, i.e. a competition in filial love, which the audience - together with some protagonists (Cordelia, Kent, France) - may notice as absurd but which Lear himself soon becomes a prisoner of.*

47          Tell me, my daughters,
48 (Since now we will divest us both of rule,
49 interest of territory, cares of state)
50 Which of you shall we say doth love us most?
51 That we our largest bounty may extend
52 Where nature doth with merit challenge. Goneril,
53 Our eldest born, speak first.

*King Lear*, I.i[1]

## 10.1 Action and belief in drama: the process of interpretation

Lear's 'question' is our starting point. And a question is the name of an action performed with words, an illocutionary act (Austin, 1962; Searle, 1969). A speaker performs an utterance. He has done something. Besides issuing those sounds, with that linguistic form, he has also performed an action such as 'stating', 'promising', 'questioning', 'commanding', and so on. These terms package up a great deal of information. Such illocutionary acts are of the class of intentional human actions, performed as a means of attaining a goal and therefore having reasons which explain or rationalize them. Characterization essentially involves the manifestation of inner states, desires, motives, intentions, beliefs, through action, including speech acts. We can ask 'why' a speaker said what he did and propose an intentional description as an answer.

Faced with an action, we can say that the agent intended to achieve a goal and, believing this particular action would achieve that goal in this context, set himself to perform it. If the action is a standard way of achieving that goal in a culture, then the action has that meaning-potential and can be quite easily understood. If the act is an utterance and the goal is communicative, then it is the 'literal' meaning of the words which directly conveys communicative intent. Very often, however, the connection between intention, goal and how the action facilitates the goal, is much more indirect and requires considerable inferencing work to interpret.

Whether direct or indirect, this model of understanding applies equally to all intentional actions, whether verbal or non-verbal. The two are so interwoven that in many cases one can achieve a communicative goal both or either way. A speaker/agent can intend an utterance, a gesture or an action, for example, to count as a warning, threat, dismissal or greeting. He expects his meaning to be inferable from what he says and does equally. What he intends is calculable from what he does – including what he says.

Thus behind every illocutionary act is an intention, or network of intentions, that the utterance count as such and such. And the process of understanding the utterance as an illocutionary act is, in essence, that of trying to determine these intentions (achieving uptake) on the evidence of the utterance, its linguistic form and the context. What is directly or literally conveyed depends on the linguistic form. What is indirectly conveyed must be inferred from the linguistic form and the context taken together (Searle, 1975).

Beliefs are crucial in this process. We can distinguish two kinds of speaker-belief relevant to utterance-understanding. First, there are those beliefs about the context which are the conditions necessary and sufficient for the utterance to count as a particular illocutionary act (Searle (1969), pp. 54ff.; Austin (1962), pp. 14ff.). Such beliefs, combined with other factors, are sometimes called the felicity-conditions of the act. Second, there are those beliefs of the speaker which we infer he holds by virtue of his utterance of the sentence itself, both by virtue of its very form and by virtue of being uttered in a particular context. Of this second type of inference we can distinguish two types. There are those things we infer by virtue of the literal meaning of the sentence uttered (semantically-warranted inferences) and there are further things we infer by virtue of its utterance in this particular context (pragmatic implications), (Grice, 1975; Sperber and Wilson, 1982). This last type is of particular importance in determining the force of indirectly-conveyed acts, since the speaker may pragmatically imply that the felicity-conditions of an act are satisfied in the context, although this act is not the same as the one literally conveyed by the linguistic form he utters. In this way, we come to understand the beliefs of the speaker, and what he intends to convey and to do by virtue of what he utters.

To interpret Lear's utterance, then, we must analyse its linguistic form and literal meaning. But this is just the first step. We also have to see what we can infer from the use of this form in this context.

The discourse of drama has a particularly complex set of contexts. If we take a context to be those hearer's beliefs or assumptions about the world required to draw the inferences necessary to understand the text, then we can distinguish a number of different contexts required to interpret drama. These are:

1   context of *dramatis personae*;
2   context of audience or reader;
3   synchronic vs diachronic context;
4   local vs global context;
5   context of critical interpretation.

There is the context of the *dramatis personae*. We treat the characters as persons and determine what beliefs they bring to the utterance in order to enact and comprehend the fictional speaker's communicative intentions. By determining such patterns of putative character-beliefs, we construct fictional personalities embedded in fictional social contexts. By understanding how they take the utterance, we constitute the minds of the characters. But we do this from our point of view, in the context of the audience. As overhearers of a discourse designed to be overheard, the audience is in a privileged position with respect to the characters. The audience usually has more and different information about each character than the characters have about each other. Furthermore, the audience draws on its assumptions about the actual world in constituting the world of the text. These two worlds may diverge, as they do in *King Lear*, but the very process of audience interpretation guarantees that the text world is an analogue of the actual world and this is why the text is relevant to an audience. Each utterance of the text world is interpreted as relevant to the world in which we 'really' live.

This process is made more complex by two further distinctions, between local and global contexts and between synchronic and diachronic contexts. As for the former, the audience can interpret each utterance locally in its immediate context of utterance or it can utilize its privileged global position with respect to the 'play as a whole'. As for the latter distinction, interpretation can take place synchronically, using background knowledge from the time of performance or reading. Alternatively, the time of the play's composition, its diachronic context, can be used in interpretation. Diachronic context is important if linguistic changes have occurred between the two times. It is in this temporal hiatus that the text is mediated to audiences by editors, historically-oriented critics and specialists in the history of the language. A text is established from available variants and glossed so that synchronic interpretation does not diverge unwarrantably from what scholars surmise to be the original sense. In our case there is the 'textual problem in *King Lear*', arising from the differences between the Quarto and Folio texts (see Clayton (1983), pp. 123ff.; Stone (1980); and Taylor and Warren (1983)). The Arden text, which is adequate to our purposes, is based on the Folio text.

Finally, there is the context of critical interpretation. To comprehend an utterance in performance is a different process from submitting a text to the practice of criticism. In the latter, the theories brought to an interpretation reflect the interests of criticism and will generate as products different kinds of readings of the same utterance. Literary texts warrant a wide range of implicatures, for which the reader, rather than the author, takes the responsibility (Sperber and Wilson (1986), pp. 199ff.). A dramatic text is not strictly communicative in this sense. Although we attempt to determine Lear's intentions in speaking, we are not out to determine Shakespeare's intentions in putting the utterance in Lear's mouth; rather, we interpret the text world as relevant to our own critical and personal interest. In this sense, although there are constraints imposed by the text's literal meanings and obvious or 'strong' implicatures if any, there is no correct, intended critical interpretation. In this essay, I will move from the literal, through more obvious textual interpretations and conclude with a global critical interpretation of Lear's utterance and the significance of the fictional personality which I construct.

## 10.2 Lear's utterance: critical comments

Lear's 'question'? In the critical literature, Lear's utterance in lines 47–53 of Act I scene i is usually referred to as a question, but sometimes alternatively referred to as a demand or a request for speech. However it is taken, there is rough agreement that this is a crucial utterance and that this scene embodies a problem of values from which the action of the play follows. For Brooke ((1963), p. 18) it is rather a prologue than a scene: 'it provides the data from which the play develops' and 'directs our attention forward into what follows'. (He, mistakenly in my view, discourages 'quaint speculation' into the aberrant logical structure of the scene itself.) Similarly, for Martin ((1984), p. 7) it provides a *'donnée'*, a sort of thought-experiment, 'a given narrative premise' from which the consequences are developed.

As for the utterance itself, Heilman ((1963), p. 160) refers to it as Lear's 'demand for avowals of affection', but then, in the same paragraph, characterizes the utterance by writing, 'Lear asks, "Which of you etc?"', the form of a question. Van Laan ((1974), p. 60) takes 'Lear's repeated requests for speech as formal cues', within a pre-arranged ritual. The ritual nature of the scene is a recurring theme of the critics (Brooke, (1963), p. 19; Kozintsev (1967), pp. 56ff.; Van Laan (1974), pp. 59ff.).

But perhaps the standard glossing of Lear's utterance is as a questioning. Ewbank ((1971), p. 111) sees it as a 'typical speech mode' of the play: 'very simple but also very basic questions in *King Lear* – which not only set the mood for the play but express in epitome its spiritual core'. Nowottny ((1982), p. 35) places the utterance as part of a pattern of questions posed by Lear,

> King Lear . . . is a passive hero, but at the same time he is
> himself the active cause of what is tragic . . . in his experience,
> and is indeed more truly the maker of his own tragedy, by
> virtue of the questions he himself raises than any other
> Shakespearean tragic hero. The play opens with the *locus classicus*
> of Lear's questioning: 'which of you shall we say doth love us
> most?'

Within this view, the traditional problem of the king's question has been summarized succinctly by Hawkes ((1959), in Kermode, (1969), p. 179), 'The first scene of *King Lear* has been described as improbable, Lear's question, "How much do you love me?" has been called imponderable and improper, and his equation "so much love = so much land" is said to be immoral.' For a similar view see Heilman ((1963), pp. 160ff.). With this in mind, let us turn to the language, starting with the syntactic form.

### 10.3 Syntactic analysis

The first clause of Lear's utterance is a grammatical imperative, with its understood subject explicitly addressed by means of the vocative NP, 'my daughters'. This is followed by a parenthetical adverbial clause of reason. At this point problems begin. The third clause, introduced by the wh-question phrase 'which of you' appears to be syntactically indeterminate – that is, susceptible of two alternative syntactic analyses. These are illustrated in Figure 10.1. Alternative A I term the direct-question analysis and alternative B the indirect-question analysis.

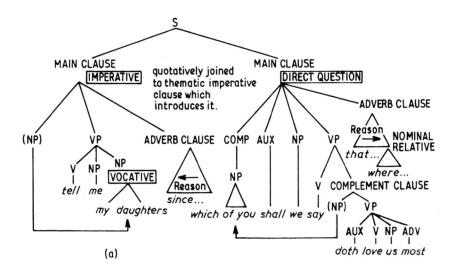

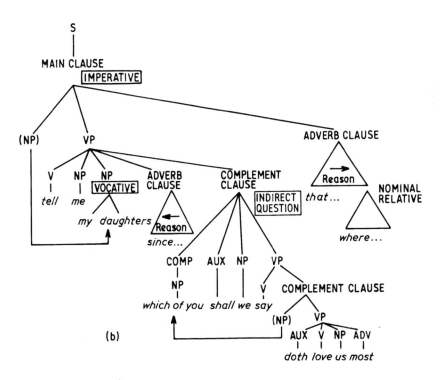

Figure 10.1 Syntactic analysis. (a) Alternative A: the direct question analysis. (b) Alternative B: the indirect question analysis.

In alternative B, the wh-clause is taken to be a complement of the verb 'tell'. 'Tell' is subcategorized for such a complement as in sentences like, 'Tell me who came'. The principal justification for alternative B is that, by itself, the first clause does not form a complete sentence. It requires the wh-complement to complete it. 'Tell me, my daughters', is ungrammatical.

There is a rub here, however! Such wh-complements, called indirect questions, normally do not have the auxiliary verb preceding their subjects. Contrast:

Tell me where you have put it. (no inversion)
Tell me where have you put it. (inversion)

However, both Quirk *et al.* ((1973), p. 318) and Jesperson ((1909–49), Vol. III, pp. 39ff.) point out that such inversion, the retention of the form of a direct question, does occur in literary style. Also, such wh-complements are not separated from their matrix verb by comma intonation. However, in this case, where the complement is separated from the verb by an intervening parenthetical clause, the intonation can be seen as due to the parenthesis rather than being attributable to the relation of complement and verb.

Nevertheless, the effect of the retained inversion and the parenthesis together here produces something more like alternative A, the direct-question analysis. Referring to the construction in *The Merchant of Venice* (III.ii.63) also with 'tell':

Tell me where is fancy bred,

Jesperson notes that it might as well have been written:

Tell me: Where is fancy bred?

The effect of the inversion, accompanied by the comma intonation, promotes the wh-clause into a direct question, which is introduced by an imperative semi-sentence which frames it, as if the speaker were subsequently 'quoting' himself.

Both the imperative verb and the question word in alternative A are separate themes; that is, they are both equally issues which the sentence is about and separate starting points for a complex message (Halliday, (1985), pp. 38ff. and 128ff.). But at the same time the wh-clause also retains something of the dependent status of alternative B, because the 'tell' clause requires it in order to be syntactically complete.

Both indirect and direct forms with 'tell' occur back-to-back in *As You Like It* (III.ii.200):

tell me who it is ... tell me, who is it quickly

Again, both 'tell' and 'who' are thematic. Together the imperative and interrogative conspire to foreground (in this case) the urgency of the question.

The retention of inversion permits us, as a first hypothesis, to propose that Lear's utterance is a question by virtue of its interrogative form. As Searle ((1979), p. 14) points out, questions are a subclass of directives; that is, they are attempts by the speaker to get the hearer to do something; namely, to provide the information which the speaker seeks. Now what about our first imperative clause? What is its illocutionary point? Although the categories of sentence type and illocutionary force must be kept distinct, in unmarked cases the imperative is also used to issue directives, such as requests, orders, commands and so on. In this case the directive is to 'tell me X'. The meaning of this directive is, strictly speaking, tautological, since it is simply making overt the directive force of the following question; namely, its essential feature – the attempt to get the information from the hearer. Questions are often paraphrased by the formula (Karttunen (1977), p. 165):

I DIR. you (tell me) wh—

where DIR. is an abstract semantic predicate representing directive force. The imperative first clause has precisely this directive force. It is therefore redundantly a directive to answer a question, redundant because the question has the same force. The redundancy foregrounds the directive element of the question; and we can ask why it does so.

The syntax of this single utterance epitomizes two major forms which recur throughout the play, questions and commands (see Burton (1968) p. 22, note 10, on sentence types as a source of interpretative hypotheses; also Doran (1976)). I will return later to a more detailed analysis and interpretation of the linguistic form.

## 10.4 Analysis of Lear's utterance as a question

The next step is to find out if the utterance is in fact a genuine question. There are two things we can do to approach this. First, we can look at the semantic structure of the interrogative sentence and see what inferences it warrants. This will make explicit the content of the question. Second, on the hypothesis that Lear's utterance is a question, the felicity-conditions for the successful performance of this illocutionary act will have to be satisfied in the context.

First, let us examine the logic of the question. Lear has uttered a wh-question of the alternative kind (Quirk *et al.* (1973), p. 198). The wh-item, 'which of you', specifies the unknown information, X, within the proposition, 'we shall say X doth love us most', the alternatives for X being Goneril, Regan and Cordelia. Following Hamblin's (1973) semantics for questions, we can express the denotation of Lear's question as the set of propositions expressed by possible answers to it. As a three-term alternative question this set becomes, 'we shall say Goneril loves us most' *or*, etc. Since the sentence also involves comparison, the full set of possible true answers can be unpacked as in Figure 10.2.

Let's see what Lear is presupposing here. It is that one of his daughters loves him more than the other two. One of the disjuncts is true and after the information is supplied he or he and his daughters will say, and will be able to say, which daughter that is. (Note that 'we' is ambiguous as between a singular imperial reading, that is Lear himself, and a plural inclusive reading, in which all four participants together will be able to say publicly who loves Lear most). Note also, very significantly, that there is a deeper presupposition behind the superlative 'most', that each daughter loves Lear in any case. This is just assumed to be true. (For a play of comparatives see I.iv.115–25).

From this we begin to learn what Lear believes about love. He believes, for instance, that it is quantitatively gradable. Note the use of 'most' as opposed to 'best'. There is a quantitative hierarchy

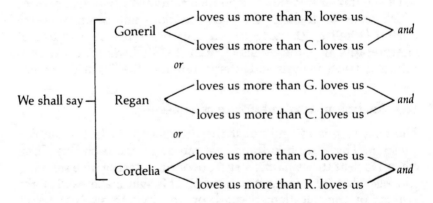

Figure 10.2

of love and it must be possible to truly calculate from a verbal response (a question requires a speech act as an answer) a person's relative position in this hierarchy. But within Lear's sentence this first hierarchy does not stand alone. The final adverbial clause, which rationalizes the question, explicitly relates this scale to two others, a quantitative hierarchy of bounty, and also one of merit. Bounty and merit are both gradable. And all three scales are interlocked. The most love merits the extension of the largest bounty. Thus, degree of love is calculable. This linkage establishes the motif of calculation as an interpretative norm within the text. It recurs not only explicitly in terms like 'self metal ... prize me at her worth', 'ponderous', 'dower', and, of course, the quantity 'nothing', the cipher 'O' (I. iv. 189), but in the rational calculation of their self interest by Goneril, Regan and Edmund, the individualist 'new men' of the play (Heilman (1963), Ch. IX).

Lear's assumption that love is quantitatively gradable reifies love by turning it into a measurable thing. But there is nothing semantically odd about the question in itself. The word 'love' is often used in a gradable way, to characterize preferences. 'He loves her more than she loves him' does not entail any contradictions. If non-gradability were part of the meaning of 'love', then Lear's question would be semantically ill-formed and we could not assign it a true answer. Morally, however, most of us would not condone love's gradability.

Shakespeare here reveals a clear distinction between the meaning of the word 'love', as coded in the semantics of English, and beliefs about love. Lear's sentence establishes a link between the gradability of love and that of merit and bounty. In our culture, differentiation on the latter quantitative scales is not morally problematic, as it is on the former. A moral disjunction is revealed in the audience as they interpret this, and two systems of value are implicitly established. The hierarchies of merit and bounty are later partially resolved, driven by the moral, rather than the semantic, conception of love: 'Poor naked wretches, whereso'er you are' (*equality of merit*); 'Take physic; Pomp/... That thou mayst shake the superflux to them,/And show the Heavens more just' (*equality of bounty*) (III. iv. 28–36).

Now to turn to the felicity conditions for the act of questioning. If the utterance is to be a genuine question, the speaker must not know the answer but must believe that the hearer is likely to be able to provide it. He must also sincerely want the information and intend his utterance to count as an attempt to elicit it from the hearer. As Lang ((1978), p. 313), following Bolinger (1957), points out, one consequence of these conditions is that the asker of a real question is subordinating himself to his hearer. Therefore, in the act of uttering a real question another hierarchy would be formed, that of the possession of information.

Are these conditions satisfied by the context of Lear's utterance? As the context develops we learn from Lear himself (I. i. 122–3), from France (I. i. 213–15) and from Goneril (I. i. 288–9) that Lear loves Cordelia most. In France's terms, 'the best, the dearest'; 'most' in Goneril's and in Lear's own terms. Furthermore, there is some evidence from the use of the second-person pronouns, 'thou' and 'you', between Lear and his daughters that Lear has a special relationship to Cordelia. Although the overall interpretation of pronominal usage is rather complex (see Fowler (1986), pp. 96ff.), Lear employs the second-person 'you' to Cordelia, and switches to a harsh use of 'thou' in dismissive condescension after her refusal. The significant contrast is between the 'you' used to Cordelia, and the 'thou' of authority used to Goneril and Regan (Aers and Kress (1981), p. 79), which distinguishes between them. Here diachronic context is relevant since this distinction in pronominal usage is now obsolete in English, although current in other European languages (Brown and Gilman, 1960). Quirk moreover notes that the use of the less-decorous unmarked form to Cordelia conveys 'a special feeling Lear has for the girl he calls "our joy"' (Quirk (1971), p. 71). There is evidence then that the obverse of Lear's hierarchical question is that Lear himself loves Cordelia most.

Can we also say that he believes that this is reciprocated; that, of his three daughters, Cordelia loves him most? In fact, he has already acted on this belief. This is the contextual relevance of the well-known puzzle of the division of the kingdom into thirds. We know from Gloucester (I. i. 3–6) that Albany and Cornwall have received equal shares. We learn that Regan and Cornwall have been allocated an 'ample third', 'no less in space, validity and pleasure/than that conferred on Goneril' (I. i. 78–81). Hence two thirds, each of equal value, are distributed. There remains a third. It is, in Lear's words, 'A third more opulent than your sisters' (I. i. 85). This exercise in the motif of literally quantitative calculation (again note the comparatives) is evidence that he has acted on a belief that Cordelia loves Lear most, if we take his equation of love and bounty seriously. He has retained the largest bounty for his youngest daughter. Therefore, he believes she loves him most.

Since Lear believes this and already has to his satisfaction the information required to complete the proposition truly, the utterance can hardly count as a sincere attempt to elicit unknown information. Furthermore, since the overtly-given reason for the question is fraudulent, the results being predetermined, true answers to it as a question become irrelevant in this respect. From Lear's point of view, the true answer is already known. So whatever else its relevance may be, Lear's utterance is not a real question.

There is something darker implied by this structure. We now see what Lear believes. He has addressed the question collectively to the three daughters, with the knowledge that his true answer, Cordelia, will be revealed to the court. He conversationally requires three individual replies, in serial order, ranked by precedence of age. This is further evidence that the utterance is not a sincere question, since it invites not a true answer as a reply, but evidence from each daughter that she loves Lear most. (This in spite of the foregone conclusion.) In fact, is a truthful answer relevant by Lear's lights?

Consider Goneril and Regan. A truthful reply by Lear's lights would require these daughters to act against their own interests, since he believes Cordelia loves him best. The only rational response for Goneril and Regan is not to tell the truth, but to competitively claim 'I do' and by this exhibition gain merit. In fact, from Goneril and Regan, Lear does not invite the truth that they love him less than Cordelia does, although this is what he believes. So, for them, we have an equation of falsehood, merit and rational calculation in pursuit of their interests constituted by Lear's interrogative. This is precisely the character of Goneril, Regan and Edmund as regards rational calculation noted by Heilman ((1963), Ch. IX, pp. 225ff.). They are the 'new men', the rationalists of Machiavelli's *The Prince*, representatives of a new individualistic social order (Aers and Kress, 1981). But this position becomes available to them through Lear's use of language. He relativizes truth to interests.

Consider further the case in which it is common background knowledge that Goneril and Regan love their father less than Cordelia does, known to both audience and characters. (In fact this is the truth and Lear is correct in his belief.) In this case, the former daughters are required by self-interest to speak falsely, not only by Lear's lights, but by their own. This is darker still. Conversely, and ironically, only Cordelia can speak the truth, and only for Cordelia would this be rationally in her interest. But this speculation may not be correct. Goneril and Regan may not know that they love

Lear less than Cordelia does, not knowing this sense of the word 'love'. And, but slenderly knowing themselves, may sincerely profess dutiful love by their lights, being sincerely false as required, without knowing it. This raises the issue of character self-deception (from the point of view of the audience). We have argued that Lear's utterance, despite its literal force, is not a real question. But does Lear know this? Might it be a question on some other level? I shall consider this later. Interpretative doubt remains.

## 10.5  Analysis of Lear's utterance as a command

If the interrogative is not a real question, how is it to be taken? We return to the foregrounding of the directive force of the question encoded in the redundantly-directive first clause. The question element of this has now been factored out. What remains is the directive to 'tell me X'.

Searle ((1979), p. 13) notes that attempts to get the hearer to do something can be arranged on a scale of intensity, from very modest attempts such as suggestions and invitations to 'very fierce attempts' such as commands. This scale relates to a dimension of the overt or covert exercise of power. In commands, 'the authority relation infects the essential condition because the utterance counts as an attempt to get the Hearer to do the Act in virtue of the authority of the speaker over the hearer' (Searle (1969), p. 66). So there is the presupposition, on the scales of kingship and fatherhood, of another hierarchy; the hierarchy of power. This interlocks with other assumed hierarchies of love, merit, bounty and information.

The authority of a king can compel competitive statements of love, on the evidence of which he can assess its quantity; How much love! On this basis, he claims merit is earned and bounty distributed relative to the degree of love expressed. But, on the hierarchy of information, far from there being any subordination of king/father to subject/daughter, the truth that all his daughters love him and Cordelia loves him most is simply assumed. Truth itself is thus also infected by authority. The reasons given for the competition are false, but commands, unlike requests, have no preparatory condition that the act should be done for a purpose. A king, especially, need not give reasons. The force flows simply from Lear's will and his power. These override logic itself within the motif of calculation – three thirds constitute one kingdom. Two of the thirds are equal, and already pre-distributed. The reserved third is 'more opulent'. Nevertheless, we command you to compete for this prize you cannot win. Power requires that you obey. As audience, however, the force of the logic is so great that we must look for some *other reason* for the command. We will examine such other reasons later on.

Alternatively, we can conclude that Lear is mad. This is because logic formalizes necessary truth and this gives us linguistic access to what we conceive of as the structure of reality in the deepest way. It underpins rationality. When socially-constituted power relations create norms which violate rationality, normal human behaviour becomes irrational and therefore confronts the structure of reality in this sense. Lear's authority imposes his presuppositions on the other characters. They must accept that his presuppositions hold, or act either to fulfil them or as if they hold, by virtue of the institution of kingship. The sanction, as always in power relations, is legal violence, exclusion from society or deprivation of bounty. Thus, in Lear's utterance a social world and its values are constituted; from his will, through his tongue, by virtue of his power. It is this world that provides the irrational framework for the rational calculations of Goneril, Regan and Edmund. When authority passes to Goneril and Regan, and the will exercising power becomes theirs, the violence which is its sanction becomes endemic and Lear is forced to bargain numerically in his own interest regarding his retinue of knights (II. iv. 229ff.). Self-interest in this framework is the attainment of social roles which maximize power and therefore access to bounty. In this society, the social role of king is the apex of all the hierarchies and its power controls them all.

Directives also have an ability conditional on their felicitous performance. The hearer must be able to perform the act. Cordelia twice questions whether this presupposition fails (I. i. 61–2, 76–7) and her explanation of her response is explicitly put in terms of the failure of the ability condition (I. i. 90–1): 'Unhappy that I am, I cannot heave/My heart into my mouth'. The crux here is that there is a conflict between the ability- and the authority-conditions on commanding. Cordelia does not believe that she is able to comply. Lear has assumed in the act of commanding that his daughters are able to comply. Obedience to the king requires that his hearers/subjects/daughters accept his assumptions, imposed on them by virtue of his authority. This authority is grounded in institutions; the institution of kingship on the one hand, and that of the family on the other.

Within these institutions of the social order, Lear's command constitutes the central part of a particular language game in Wittgenstein's (1953) sense. It is an 'obedience game'. I introduce this terminology to highlight the arbitrary originality of Lear's stipulation. He commands his daughters to do something linguistic – to provide verbal evidence of their degree of love in public competition with one another. This act of commanding defines a norm of relevance for replies. A relevant reply is compliance. The relevance of any other kind of reply is non-compliance. The command is the central move on which pivots a highly schematic pattern of formal filial compliance and kingly endowment, to be thrice repeated. The overall function of the obedience game, Lear's stated purpose and 'fast intent' (I. i. 35–40), is to facilitate the public transfer of power. So although the language game is arbitrarily created by Lear's will and his words, it ultimately rests on the power relations of the state, and secondarily of the family. That is the source of his authority, and the form of life which the game enacts. As such, it structurally corresponds to any such power-laden exercise of arbitrary power and can thus be viewed as an analogue model of this social form.

Within this grounding, Lear's language game is teleological, each utterance controlled by his power and realizing a move in a structure intentionally designed as a means of publicly accomplishing a purpose of state in a court context. Cordelia's inability to comply stems from meanings outside this context. It is therefore appropriate that the sanction is exclusion. In her refusal, personal and metaphysical contexts, from which alternative meanings of the word 'love' are derived, meet and conflict with institutional contexts.

### 10.6  Rhetorical performances and the language of the court

Cordelia may be unable to reply, but Goneril and Regan have no difficulty in complying. The form of language appropriate for compliance is given by the register in which Lear's own utterance is put. It is the register of 'high style' enacting the meanings of the court. It is a realization of an underlying code of power relations, with its hierarchic and depersonalized public roles of authority, submission and institutional obligation (Halliday (1978), pp. 35, 110ff., 123). The appropriate reply is to be as rhetorical, in the sense of decorous and eloquent, as the command, encoding formal public submission to it. There is no sincerity condition on such formal submission in a court context. (Just as there is no sincerity condition on greetings or the register of advertising!).

Critics have described the language of Lear's speeches in this scene as 'ceremonial utterance' appropriate to 'a ritual of the royal prerogative', exhibiting 'confident amplitude' (Brooke (1963), p. 19). Zitner ((1974), pp. 66ff.) recognizes Lear's utterance as a form of 'high style' – formal eloquence – which is 'decorous', that is, appropriate to his kingly station and the court setting. But, he adds, 'the decorum of the high or court style ... is undercut ... Its magniloquence cloaks Lear's self indulgence, its *copia* the sister's disloyalty'. Elsewhere, 'the appropriate sententiousness of Goneril and Regan' is referred to. Van Laan ((1974), pp. 59ff.) notes 'the highly artificial rhetoric of Lear's own speeches, especially when he indulges an apparent tendency for formal balance and excessive amplification'.

The court register is rhetorical in that it utilizes the figure of the arts of rhetoric (Vickers (1971); Joseph (1966)). The linguistic features of the high style can be seen quite clearly if we return to Figure 10.1. The balance, parallelism and contrasts are striking. I will discuss the rhetoric under nine headings.

1  The parallel imperative and interrogative clauses contrast these two sentence types, and their differing but both directive meanings. The imperative precedes and might dominate the interrogative. But the form releases the latter from the former, promoting it into the position of a quotation. Lear quotes his own direct question. In a sense the imperative clause is thus incomplete. As such it is a *figure of defect or omission*. The sentence has two contrasting themes, commanding and interrogating.

2  The two verbs of speaking, 'tell' and 'say', balance and contrast within the two clauses. In the two clauses, the two verbs lead to an interchange of participant roles. Halliday ((1985), pp. 129ff.) specifies distinct participants for verbal processes. Employing these we get the structure in Figure 10.3. The whole structure is verbal; even the question is self-quoted. Its verbal answer is itself to be evaluated or reported as the complement (verbiage) of the verb 'say'. Speech roles are what matter and they are to be interchanged, modelling the transfer of power and its interchange of social roles. It is a world of words.

3  We have already noted the importance of pronominal usage

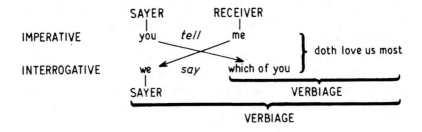

Figure 10.3

and the ambiguity of 'we' in the interrogative. The power-marked royal 'we' can progressively expand in reference to include all the participants in the social structure created by that power. The alliterative 'me' and 'my' of the imperative (line 47) parallels the plural 'we' and 'us' of the question (line 50). The question, which subordinates the questioner, uses the power-laden form. In balanced contrast, the command, which subordinates the one commanded, uses the form unmarked for power. The person-oriented and power-oriented are interchanged. Lear is the Receiver 'me' of what the Sayer 'you' is directed to 'tell' him (line 47) about themselves ('which of you' (line 50)), but at the same time is the Possessor of that Sayer, 'my daughters' (line 47), in control of their response. Finally, the Receiver 'me' (line 47) of what is told, Lear, rhymes with the Sayer 'we' (line 50) of who loves 'us' most. On one reading of the power-marked 'we', he is included as a Sayer, and in a sense he is, since his authority controls the response. Similarly the reflexive 'we ... divest us' (line 48) recapitulates the reflexive, controlling nature of the command and compliance and, at the same time, contrasts with the act of divesting which it is supposedly accomplishing.

4  Neither the imperative nor the interrogative clause has a superficial subject. 'We', that is Lear himself, is the only overtly-realized personal subject in the sentence. In particular, the subjects of 'tell' (line 47) and 'love' (line 50) are understood. They are commanded and interrogated. There is a nice pun on 'subjects' here, linking syntax and social role. His daughters are the understood subjects in both cases. Reference to them is made explicit by the wh-interrogative

phrase. They are the theme of his question, escaping from a clause subordinate to his saying by virtue of this question. In the imperative clause, reference to them is made by the vocative noun-phrase. This highlights the relation of possession and social and filial dependence between them.

5  The traditional rhetorical forms and hence the register of high style is even clearer in the two adverbial clauses. It is here that the Quarto and Folio most diverge, the former omitting the first adverbial clause altogether and thus not having either the parallelism or *copia* of the latter (*Pied Bull Quarto*, 1608). The two adverb clauses are balanced, yet contrastive. The first *since* clause follows the imperative. The second *that* clause follows the interrogative. Both clauses give the reasons for the clause preceding. The first points backwards to Lear's intended renunciation of power, immediately following the exercise of power in the imperative. The second points forward to the distribution of rule according to the result of the replies to the interrogative. The second clause is false and the truth of the first is incompatible with the act being performed by the sentence which contains it. The first adverb clause is an example of the figure, *parenthesis*, and since it repeats redundant information, *pleonasmus*. This redundancy is added to the tautology of the directives discussed above. Both clauses are also figures of defect: the first interrupts the imperative first clause, leaving it suspended during the parenthesis; the second is added after the closure of the interrogative completes the sentence. There is a great deal of redundant quantity here, and syntactic disruption.

6  Both pleonastic clauses employ figures internally. The first clause thrice paratactically iterates the complement noun phrases after 'divest us both of —' (lines 48–9), eliding the latter two instances of 'of' – (of) interest, (of) cares. In each of these latter two instances another 'of' phrase is embedded, namely 'of territory' and 'of state' (line 49). This is both *parallelism* and *ellipsis*. The sentence also contains a vice of language, *solecism*, because 'both' (line 48), which has always referred to exactly two in English, is misused to refer to three. This is perhaps a structural allusion to number and quantity in the scene.

7  The second pleonastic clause contains two instances of *anastrophe*, or marked word order. Both of its clauses are verb

final, establishing a linkage between the two verbs 'extend' and 'challenge'. This leads, in the last clause, to a balance between the two antithetical abstract nouns 'nature' and 'merit'. These are *personified*, since 'challenge', in the relevant senses, selects an animate, not an abstract, subject. The verb itself is *ambiguous*. The *Oxford English Dictionary* (*OED*) entries which are current in the sixteenth century are:

|  |  |  |
|---|---|---|
|  | LAW | *(i)* To assert one's title to, to demand as a right. (Now obsolete) |
|  | LAW | *(ii)* Accuse, bring a charge against, impeach. (Last attested 1693) |
| CHALLENGE | MILITARY | *(iii)* To call to account, as of a sentry. |
|  | LAW | *(iv)* Law – to object or take exception to (a juror etc). |
|  | COMPETITIVE | *(v)* To summon or invite defiantly to a contest or any trial of daring or skill (first attested 1513). |

The relation of nature and merit thus established figuratively recapitulates the authority-laden legal, political or military nature of the verbal competition which Lear requires in order to make his judgment.

8  The alliterative wh-items 'which of you' and 'where', which begin lines 50 and 52 respectively, are linked. They are co-referential and both refer to the daughter who loves Lear most and who therefore will be the locus of his largest bounty. She is, at the same time, the locus of best outcome in the challenge between nature and merit. In another solecism, she is referred to as a place by the locative wh-word 'where' (line 52). She is a locus of competitive conflict.

9  A possible *pun* on two senses of the word 'love' has been noted by Hawkes ((1959), in Kermode (1969), pp. 179ff.). There is a distinct lexical item 'love', a homophone of, but historically unrelated to, 'love' in synchronic use. This word is glossed by the *OED* (Vol. VI, p. 467) as:

|  |  |  |
|---|---|---|
|  | VERBIAGE | *(i)* Praise, extoll, to give praise, flatter. |
| LOVE | CALCULATION | *(ii)* To appraise, estimate or state price or value of. |

'Love in this sense' is not attested after 1530 – close enough to the diachronic context to be used by Shakespeare. It almost exactly expresses the literal sense of Lear's use of the word. The contrasting side of the pun is Cordelia's understanding of 'love'. This wordplay would focus the fundamental conflict in the meeting of these two senses in one phonetic form.

The rhetorical register analysed in this section, and the cultural code it realizes, preselects the form an appropriate response must take. Goneril and Regan's replies (I. i. 54-60 and 68-74) are therefore transparently relevant to Lear's utterance. They convey that they understand it as a command for a rhetorical performance and are complying to the best of their ability. It is also clear that high style is appropriate in another way. If quantity of love is verbally expressible, it must be so in terms of rhetorical complexity, cleverness of style and sheer quantity. The one who loves Lear most will implicate this by rhetorical excellence or extravagance. The daughters' replies are studies in quantity and comparison. So we have another quantitative hierarchy, this time of rhetoric, which is interlocked with our earlier hierarchies. In all this speaking the truth is made strictly irrelevant. Indeed, the truth or falsehood of the assertion 'I love you' remains the same, no matter how it is rhetorically put.

One of the remarkable features of *King Lear* is its self-consciousness about linguistic issues; see, for example, the debate between Kent and Cornwall in II. ii. The characters themselves judge the significance of registers. For Kent and Cordelia the 'semantic style' of Goneril and Regan's replies is read as 'flattery' which masks ulteriorness of intention and to which truth is irrelevant: 'that glib and oily art to speak and purpose not' (I. i. 223-4). In its most extreme form it becomes lying; that is, 'intending your statement to mislead' irrespective of its actual truth or falsity (Bok (1978) p. 6). This and a moral use of deception are explored in the Edmund-Edgar-Gloucester subplot. Kent and Cordelia recognize ulteriorness as a potential of the court code, inherent in and fostered by its hierarchy of power. Utterance and its apparent intention clothe an ulterior intention to justify, manipulate or serve the power structure. A metaphor of clothing develops this in the play. But there is no easy equation of rhetorical styles and falsehood, or plainness and truth.

Lear's single sentence syntactically and semantically recapitulates the structural problem of the play. In point 8 above, I noted that 'which of you' and 'where' are co-referential. This use of locative reifies a person, who already has the role of daughter, into a place – a social locus. This locus is the outcome of a challenge, a term of law, conflict and competition. The two pleonastic clauses frame the competition in the language of politics. Quite literally, in the tree diagrams of Figure 10.1 the imperative precedes and/or dominates the interrogative, just as the command utilizes the question. The grammar models the social hierarchy it enacts. The sentence summarizes the whole game device, of which it is the pivotal action, within itself. And at the centre of this reifying device is the word 'love'. The central act of the language game is a command to provide verbal evidence of how much the king is loved. This is to be the mechanism by which power is transferred.

## 10.7  Further interpretations: a network of paradox

Our interpretation thus far has been fairly narrow. We have argued that the question is not a real question. Rather it is a command to provide evidence of love. This is just one step beyond the literal meaning. But there is more interpretative work to do. Why is the command about love? We need to ask why Lear is commanding this in this way.

Poetic effects are the result of a wide range of 'weak implicatures' (Sperber and Wilson (1986), pp. 199ff.). These are contextual inferences for which the hearer takes the greater part of the responsibility. They can be contrasted with those strong contextual effects which clearly originate with the speaker and are what he intends to communicate. In a literary text, a hearer can derive many interpretations, but can be much less sure that any or all of these were intended. This is the source of the relative irrelevance of the author's intentions in the process of reading a literary text.

Thus, critical interpretation breaks free of the words on the page. Depending on what background assumptions we bring to bear, we are warranted in deriving a wide range of relevant implications from the text. For example, Aers and Kress (1981) interpret *King Lear* in terms of the confrontation of a conservative order of values and a new assertion of self based on the ideology of individualism typified by Edmund, Goneril and Regan. They are applying a model of sociohistorical change to the text from their background assumptions, and interpreting the text accordingly.

So, I will now ask why Lear has issued the command and what the implications of this might be. It generates a network of paradox or inconsistencies. These are the locus of insights which Lear's utterance yields to critical interpretation.

Lear's stated intention is the renunciation of power. Overtly, this is why the game exists at all. But the very form of the central act is the exercise of power. Lear is exercising his power in his command, as indeed he must, since only one who has something possesses the power to renounce it.

But the manner of this exercise, in its very ferocity and illogicality, perhaps implicates that there is a conflict in his fast intent. Is there not a reaffirmation of power in the act of its renunciation? There is evidence of an intention to demonstrate his power by demanding its confirmation through obedience, beyond what would be strictly sufficient to transfer his authority. To obtain power, his daughters must dance to his tune.

This casts a shadow of uncertainty over the truth of the first pleonastic clause and this is a continuing anxiety for Goneril and Regan (I. i. 303–5): 'if our father carry authority with such disposition/ as he bears, this last surrender of his will but offend us'. A continuing conflict is initiated between Lear and his two daughters. This externalizes both the above paradox of the renunciation of power and the conflict within Lear himself. Goneril and Regan in their insecurity attempt to secure their power over and against him and 'strip' him of the authority which he cannot non-paradoxically renounce. They are Lear's conflict and quantitative hierarchical values objectified against him.

The play is much concerned with questions of identity. Lear's identity is socially constituted by the structure of power (Aers and Kress (1981), p. 84). There are two such structures and roles unified in Lear's person: state and kingship; and family and fatherhood. To renounce only his royal authority will be to divide the role, and renounce the power-constituting part of his identity, while retaining the power of the other part. Like the kingdom, his identity will fracture.

His attempt to renounce actual kingly power is an act of self-renunciation. This self and its identity with the structure of power is intrinsic to the linguistic form which recapitulates what it is attempting on one level to renounce. In renouncing power, he will be renouncing himself as a social being. He doesn't intend to do this, and this is another paradox. It generates Lear's passage through madness, or loss of self, in the course of the play.

Lear not only demonstrates power, but demands a public confirmation of it. But it does so in terms of love. For Lear, obedience is the symptom of love. We have seen above how for him love is embedded in hierarchies of power. This is true both in the kingly and paternal structures of state and family. A term like 'love' is vague, and its actual reference must be fixed in context, relative to other background assumptions. It is therefore arguable that Lear is not using the word inappropriately in these power-laden contexts. His sense of the word might be called 'institutional love' and could be glossed as the respect and obedience due to those in authority in hierarchies, the love due to a monarch by a subject, or a parent by a child. And, as Aers and Kress ((1981), p. 91) point out, Lear is an almost totally institutional figure at this stage of the play. But such institutional love also requires the reciprocal due fulfilment of the social roles involved, and this Lear himself violates by his arbitrary and unloving rhetorical game, as Kent points out.

Lear does not understand his obligation to love his subjects. And the rhetorical measure of institutional love enunciated by Goneril and Regan in pursuit of power, a mirror of his failure to love them as subjects, paradoxically exhibits lack of love in its very expression. The love of ruler and subject breaks down in the process in which these roles are being exchanged.

What is missing is the sense of 'love' on a more intimate and individual level. This is excluded by the power relations of the court context. Is personal 'love' possible in a hierarchical context? Love on a personal level would be the positive counterpart of the individualistic ideology of Edmund, Goneril and Regan. Also missing is love in a metaphysical sense, as charity or concern, as a relation between persons within the moral order of the universe. It is these senses which Cordelia's action of refusal, but not her words, implicate. Paradox hangs between the two senses of the word love. Lear's hierarchical position makes him identify obedience and love. Cordelia, in enacting another sense of love, must repudiate the hierarchy. At the same time paradoxically she is also loving the king truly in the institutional sense, by disobeying him. So the two senses of love are not incompatible. It is Lear that has divided them in his arbitrary identification of love and obedience, his misuse of power in the very act of renouncing it. He demonstrates power by demanding a confirmation of love through obedience. From the point of view of personal or metaphysical love, which must be freely given, this is paradoxical.

Why should love, in whatever sense, be relevant to Lear? If obedience is the symptom of love and Lear is implementing his renunciation of power, then, once the transfer is complete, he will not be in a position to command obedience and therefore guarantee love. He is in the process of facing the potential autonomy of his daughters, both in love and potency.

He therefore commands them to confirm their love through obedience. But there is another paradox here. When a speaker seeks confirmation of something, his position is less authoritative than if he commands. Asking a hearer to confirm something grants privileged access to the truth to the hearer. If I say 'Tell me that you love me', no matter how sure I am that the answer will be yes, I have granted some autonomy to my hearer. Only hearers can say with authority that they love me. This subordinates me, who tacitly admits there might be some question about their love. The paradox is that Lear's command is weakened by its very content. The command indirectly conveys a weaker request that they confirm their love (Searle, 1975).

Therefore, by hypothesis, on another level Lear is genuinely requesting, through his royal command, evidence that he is and therefore will be loved in spite of his intended resignation. Obedience to his command will do this. So the command to avow love indirectly implicates a request to confirm love. It is transformed into a request on this level because his authority is about to be abdicated. In fact, when he is confronted with Cordelia's autonomy, he interprets her disobedience as conveying that she does not love him, in spite of her clear and literal claim that she does. The transfer of power is cracked open by the exercise of autonomy in the one to whom most power is to be transferred. A command (infected by authority) and a request (which transfers authority to the hearer) conflict here, and embody the contradictory nature of the king's renunciation.

We have now introduced uncertainty into Lear. This leads us to reinterpret the command at a higher level. Lear believes his daughters love him. But he cannot *know* this. Belief always admits of some degree of uncertainty and, in the case of love, only the one who loves can, at least partially, alleviate this. By obedience to his command his daughters can respond to his request and publicly confirm their love. At the same time, it will confirm his power since the two are identified. But this deeper Lear is a more uncertain Lear.

The converse of this act also potentially holds. That is, Lear may intend to affirm his love for his daughters by endowing them with his power since the two are identical. This is a reified affirmation. It will demand gratitude in return (II. ii. 175-9).

Now, however, we can go back to the original question and ask ourselves if, after all, on some level it may not be a real question. We argued before that the question interpretation was defective because Lear already acted on his belief. As a question, it was insincere.

But now we have introduced uncertainty into Lear as he faces the abyss opened up by his intended renunciation of power. If love and obedience are one, there is an abyss of both powerlessness and loss of love before him. Also, if Lear's kingship constitutes his identity, he confronts both that loss and also the ultimate loss of self, 'while we/Unburthen'd crawl toward death' (I. i. 39–40). It has been noted that this sentence touches an otherwise ceremonial utterance with 'more ominous and sensitive ... implications ... "crawl" is the action of the *over*-burdened, the exhausted animal; a private not a ceremonial experience' (Brooke (1963), p. 19). The autonomy of the structure of reality parallels the real autonomy of his daughters. In the issues of death, or logic, or the ultimate autonomy of others, on which their sincerity rests, the writ of power doesn't run. We experience this as ontological anxiety, the anxiety of fate and death. In this context, Lear's question might be felicitous. The command indirectly conveys a genuine question (Searle, 1975).

In Figure 10.4 I have placed the above interpretations on a scale, with the defective pseudo-question at the bottom and the real question at the top. Where readers place Lear on this scale depends on their evaluation of his degree of uncertainty. This depends in turn on the degree of autonomy he grants his daughters. And this will be related to the strength of his fast intent to renounce power in the face of age and death. The more uncertainty and anxiety the reader is prepared to grant Lear, the more they will interpret him as asking a real question on some level. This is the traditional act of interrogating reality (in the guise of his daughters). Conversely, the less uncertain Lear is felt to be, the more institutionally blind he is, the more likely the reader is to take the question as defective, enacting only the command.

However, both mutually-incompatible interpretations might be the case in different contexts. Both terms in the paradox could be true. The more transparent command interpretation might be viewed as Lear's conscious intent, while the genuine question might arise from paradoxes in his position. Lear may intend to interrogate reality without being aware of it. In this reading, the very ferocity of the game may 'clothe' the uncertainty of the 'naked'

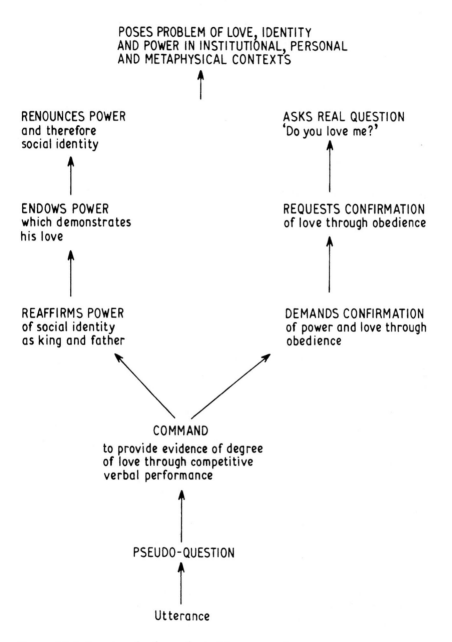

POSES PROBLEM OF LOVE, IDENTITY
AND POWER IN INSTITUTIONAL, PERSONAL
AND METAPHYSICAL CONTEXTS

RENOUNCES POWER
and therefore
social identity

ASKS REAL QUESTION
'Do you love me?'

ENDOWS POWER
which demonstrates
his love

REQUESTS CONFIRMATION
of love through obedience

REAFFIRMS POWER
of social identity
as king and father

DEMANDS CONFIRMATION
of power and love through
obedience

COMMAND
to provide evidence of degree
of love through competitive
verbal performance

PSEUDO-QUESTION

Utterance

Figure 10.4  A network of paradoxical interpretation.

Lear, as a manifestation of the social identities that 'clothe' us from 'naked' anxiety in the face of the human situation. The more uncertain he is, the more fierce in demonstrating his power. He commands an answer to an unconscious real question, which undermines the command and conflicts with it. But both are genuine. From this starting point, in the course of the play Lear moves to an awareness of the question he has posed, and finally to experience and insights which begin to answer it.

## 10.8 The psychological disruption of Lear's utterance

This interpretation gives us another Lear behind the personality derived from the institution of kingship. The interaction of these paradoxical intents generates the conflicts and contradictions in language noted above, including the central act of questioning love through commanding compliance. This also accounts for Lear's seeming capriciousness and inconstancy. Since something within him is cracking open the structure, there is the potential for change.

There is linguistic evidence of psychological pressure acting through the high style and disrupting the register. This was evident in our analysis of the rhetoric in section 10.6 above. The way in which the interrogative clause escapes the domination of the imperative reflects the way the question escapes the command. In alternative A the question has a quotative effect that distances it from the urgent authority of the imperative, at the same time as making it more direct. The very structure is indeterminate as between two analyses. And it is also rhetorically inflated and has figures of defect, which counter its balance and parallelisms. The framing imperative is incomplete, interrupted by a redundant parenthesis. After the syntactic closure of the interrogative, the utterance again continues with a redundant pleonastic clause. There is the tautology of the directives. There are the solecisms. Even as it realizes the high style, the utterance is fractured and inflated. This is arguably evidence of psychological pressure towards dismantling the purely verbal structure in which Lear's identity as King is institutionalized, and is a manifestation of the paradoxes we have described.

## 10.9 Global critical interpretation

One may object to my use of the term 'intention' in describing this last set of paradoxical interpretations. Thus, Lear couldn't have intended to pose a genuine question without being aware of it. There are two general senses of intention which are relevant to this problem. In the first sense, an intent is a conscious mental act oriented to a goal, and it would be incoherent to speak of an unconscious intention. I am not suggesting that the fictional character Lear has a communicative intention of conveying the paradoxical intents described above; that his goal is explicitly to demonstrate his power, for example.

The second sense of intention contrasts with the first. It refers to the ways in which human behaviour can be made intelligible in context. It is the sort of intentional answer an interpreter can get when asking 'why' a person performed a certain action or utterance. Presumably no agent is ever conscious of why he performs each detail of the chains of behaviour required to achieve some goal. Indeed, he may not be conscious of the goal until he interprets his own behaviour and realizes the pattern which makes it intelligible in intentional terms. His insight is then into 'why' he did or said something. Much behaviour is motivated below the level of conscious awareness.

In this sense, 'intention' is a term in a kind of interpretative discourse (Downes (1984), pp. 337ff.). It is a subtype of the broader intentionality or other directedness of human mentality. When I interpret Lear's utterance in this way, I am constructing a personality for the fictional entity Lear, and I am construing the utterance in such a way as to make it adequately relevant in the context of criticism. A real person is a theoretical entity for his interpreters, to which they assign those intentions that make sense of what he does. A character in drama is an analogy of a person and is interpreted in the same way. Then this fictional analogue of a person can be the source of insightful inferences about the situations of actual persons, e.g. the interpreter. The personality I propose for Lear is built of the weak implicatures I draw from the language of the play.

To conclude, we can try to formulate a global critical interpretation of Lear's utterance, including the paradoxes. Lear does not seem to be aware that what he has compelled is insincere ulterior conformity and not love. If indeed he is asking a real question about love, he is doing so within a context which makes a true literal statement of love – even institutional love – irrelevant as a reply (I. i. 91–2) (see Figure 10.5). To Lear, the relevance of this reply is disobedience and therefore for him it implicates the

Figure 10.5

contradictory of what its first clause states. By contrast, the rhetorical compliance of Goneril and Regan satisfies him, although false and insincere. His institutional identity and its codes of quantitative hierarchy blind him to Cordelia's use of the word.

Now say on another level, from his anxiety and urge to authenticity, he is asking a genuine question about love. The answer will lie outside his institutional framework and his identity. (That is why he is trying to renounce it!) But at this stage he doesn't know what those senses of the term are. A valid response, the response in Cordelia's action, makes relevant the other personal and metaphysical senses of the term and, as we have seen, these are congruent with the true sense of institutional love (filial and political obligation; Cordelia and Kent). He seeks this sense of 'love', but misnames it 'love', identifying it with obedience in his code. This is his greatest solecism. But he is trying to fill this semantic space. That is 'why' he attempts to renounce power by commanding this in this way.

So what is foregrounded here (Mukařovský, 1932)? It is the problem of institutional love in a context where social identity is constituted in hierarchies of authority, and the reliability of language in this context. The conservative social meanings of the term are unreliable in the face of social change (Aers and Kress, 1981). But beyond that, the human bond of love in a personal context, the unselfish face of individualism, is also raised and placed in the deepest context of all. This is a metaphysical context in which we face an implacable reality to whom we are 'As flies' (IV. i. 36). In this context, all other institutional and personal contexts fail and even love as concern is tragic. It is outside verbal and social structures.

'Come, good Athenian.'
'No words, no words: hush.'

(III. iv. 177-8)

## NOTES

1  I employ the Arden edition of *King Lear* (Muir, 1972) in this paper. I
would like to thank the staff and students of the programme in
literary linguistics at the University of Strathclyde for their
challenging comments on an earlier version of this paper, and W. van
Peer for his invaluable advice.

## BIBLIOGRAPHY

Aers, D. and Kress, G. (1981), 'The language of social order: individual,
society and historical process in *King Lear*', in D. Aers, B. Hodge and G.
Kress, *Literature, Language and Society in England 1580-1680*, Dublin, Gill &
Macmillan.

Austin, J. L. (1962), *How to do Things with Words*, The William James
Lectures, 1955, Oxford, Clarendon Press.

Bok, S. (1978), *Lying*, London, Quartet Books.

Bolinger, D. (1957), *Interrogative Structures of American English*, Publication of
the American Dialect Society 28, Tuscaloosa, University of Alabama
Press.

Brooke, N. (1963), *Shakespeare:* King Lear, London, Edward Arnold.

Brown, R. and Gilman, A. (1960), 'The pronouns of power and solidarity',
in J. Laver and S. Hutcheson (eds) (1972), *Communication in Face to Face
Interaction*, Harmondsworth, Penguin.

Burton, D. (1968), *Shakespeare's Grammatical Style*, Austin and London,
University of Texas Press.

Clayton, T. (1983), '"Is this the Promis'd end?": revision in the role of the
King', in Taylor and Warren (1983).

Cole, P. and Morgan, J. (eds) (1975), *Syntax and Semantics, Volume 3, Speech
Acts*, London, Academic Press.

Colie, R. and Flahiff, F. (eds) (1974), *Some Facets of* King Lear: *Essays in
Prismatic Criticism*, London, Heinemann.

Doran, M. (1976), *Shakespeare's Dramatic Language*, Madison, The University
of Wisconsin Press.

Downes, W. (1984), *Language and Society*, London, Fontana Paperbacks.

Ewbank, I-S. (1971), 'Shakespeare's poetry', in Muir and Schoenbaum
(1971).

Fowler, R. (1986), *Linguistic Criticism*, Oxford, Oxford University Press.

Grice, H. P. (1975), 'Logic and conversation', in Cole and Morgan (1975).

Halliday, M. A. K. (1978), *Language as Social Semiotic*, London, Edward Arnold.

Halliday, M. A. K. (1985), *An Introduction to Functional Grammar*, London, Edward Arnold.

Hamblin, C. (1973), 'Questions in Montague English', *Foundations of Language*, vol. 10, pp. 41–53.

Hawkes, T. (1959), '"Love" in *King Lear*', *Review of English Studies*, May, 1959, in Kermode (1969).

Heilman, R. (1963), *This Great Stage: Image and Structure in* King Lear, Washington D.C., University of Washington Press.

Hiz, H. (ed.) (1978), *Questions*, Dordrecht, D. Reidel.

Jesperson, O. (1909–1949), *A Modern English Grammar on Historical Principles, Part III, Syntax*, Vol. 2, London, Allen Unwin; reprinted 1956.

Joseph, Sister M. (1966), *Shakespeare's Use of the Arts of Language*, New York and London, Hafner.

Karttunen, L. (1977), '*Syntax and Semantics of Questions*', in Hiz (1978).

Kermode, F. (ed.) (1969), *Shakespeare:* King Lear, London, Casebook Series, Macmillan.

Kozintsev, G. (1967), *Shakespeare: Time and Conscience* (trans. by J. Vining), London, Dennis Dobson Books.

Lang, R. (1978), 'Questions as epistemic requests', in Hiz (1978).

Martin, G. (1984), *King Lear* (A361 Shakespeare Course, Block VI), Milton Keynes, The Open University Press.

Muir, K. (1972) (ed.), *King Lear*, The Arden Shakespeare, London, Methuen.

Muir, K. and Schoenbaum, S. (eds) (1971), *A New Companion to Shakespeare Studies*, Cambridge, Cambridge University Press.

Mukařovský, J. (1932), 'Standard language and poetic language', in P. Garvin, (ed.), *A Prague School Reader on Esthetics, Literary Structure and Style*, Washington, (Washington) D.C., Georgetown University Press, 1964.

Nowottny, W. (1982), 'Lear's question', in K. Muir and S. Wells (eds), *Aspects of* King Lear, Articles Reprinted from *Shakespeare Survey*, Cambridge, Cambridge University Press.

*Pied Bull Quarto: King Lear* (1608), London, the Shakespeare Association and Sidgwick & Jackson, 1939.

Quirk, R. (1971), 'Shakespeare and the English language', in Muir and Schoenbaum (1971).

Quirk, R. and Greenbaum, S. (1973), *A University Grammar of English*, London, Longman.

Searle, J. (1969), *Speech Acts*, Cambridge, Cambridge University Press.

Searle, J. (1975), 'Indirect speech acts', in Cole and Morgan (1975); also in Searle (1979).

Searle, J. (1979), 'A taxonomy of illocutionary acts', in J. Searle, *Expression and Meaning. Studies in the Theory of Speech Acts*, Cambridge, Cambridge University Press.

Sperber, D. and Wilson, D. (1982), 'Mutual knowledge and relevance in theories of comprehension', in N. Smith (ed.), *Mutual Knowledge*, London, Academic Press.

Sperber, D. and Wilson, D. (1986), *Relevance*, Oxford, Basil Blackwell.

Stone, P. (1980), *The Textual History of King Lear*, London, Scolar Press.

Taylor, G. and Warren, M. (1983), *The Division of the Kingdoms: Shakespeare's Two Versions of* King Lear, Oxford Shakespeare Studies, Oxford, Clarendon Press.

Van Laan, T. (1974), 'Acting as action in *King Lear*', in Colie and Flahiff (1974).

Vickers, B. (1971), 'Shakespeare's use of rhetoric', in Muir and Schoenbaum (1971).

Wittgenstein, L. (1953), *Philosophical Investigations* (translated by G. E. M. Anscombe), Oxford, Basil Blackwell.

Zitner, S. (1974), '*King lear* and its language', in Colie and Flahiff (1974).

# 11

# Poetic discourse

## A sample exercise

*John Sinclair*

*As was demonstrated in William Downes' contribution, interpretation does not solely depend on linguistic form. Yet the interpretation cannot do without information on linguistic form. Hence any interpretation which aspires to a minimal degree of adequacy will have to study in detail the contribution structural features make to the text's overall meaning. This is also the viewpoint taken by John Sinclair in his analysis of a poem by the Asian writer, Edwin Thumboo.*

*A detailed observation of the various poetic devices employed by the poet leads to the insight that the final sentence is in various ways set off from the rest of the text, and that there is a sense in which the poem 'prepares' the reader for the final sentence. This is indicated first in terms of a general commentary and then elaborated in subsequent sections, listing the various devices and patterns of equivalences and contrasts – layout and punctuation, metrics, syntax, grammetrics, lexis, information structure and discourse structure. Such a division has the advantage of allowing a detailed scrutiny of the poem's formal structure. By adding the results of this enterprise together and by linking them to the general commentary, one is able to draw some conclusions as to the interpretation of the text as a whole. In particular the poem's mimetic effect, i.e. the reflection of the theme in its structural organization, and the surprise effect of the last line are major elements in such an interpretation.*

## 11.1

This chapter describes the main structural features of a short poem, and then considers the contribution they make to the meaning and effect of the poem. The terms of the description are those of language as *discourse*.

The choice of poem was unusual. The opportunity occurred to interest a leading writer in SE Asia, Edwin Thumboo, and he picked one of his own poems. No contact was made with him until the analysis was complete, and then a carefully-structured interview focused on the following topics:

1  points of potential ambiguity (section 11.5.5);
2  points of interpretation of the Hindu myth (sections 11.2, 11.5.5.4, 11.5.5.6, 11.8.4).

### Krishna

1  Before he became a god
2  To tidy up the world, Krishna
3  Searched a thousand years,
4  Along the peaks, the lesser hills,
5  Each sudden plain, persistent star,
6  The columns of his thought,
7  Down deeply anxious limbs
8  And great inclines of the heart
9  To the rim of the world at sunset...
10  Searched among the maidens of the day,
11  The maidens of the night,
12  A face for Bindavan.

13  Under her consequential sun,
14  The computations of every rising moon,
15  That face grew, asserted
16  All his love, his dreams,
17  Destinations, softly magical.
18  She gazed upon him
19  With a look of morning lotus,
20  Till each stood within the other.
21  So the blue god, his votive flute
22  Multiplying his love, the gopis,
23  Sporting with them all,
24  He sported with but one.

25  Perched upon a chord of time,
26  His yearning flute unfolds

27  The lovely burden of her eyes
28  To feed his nimble fingers.
29  Within the radiance of each note
30  So bound to her answering look,
31  The world revives, quickens,
32  Renews itself, turns whole,
33  Adores their love unparalleled.
34  And so they sit, ever moving,
35  Ever still, in stone,
36  In ivory, in us.

Edwin Thumboo

## 11.2 General commentary

This section is an informal commentary on the poem as a whole. Each statement arises from the consideration of the detailed analysis presented in the succeeding sections. Forward references are given, where a point is summarized.

The poem concerns Krishna, his lover or lovers, the effect on the world, and the effect on the reader (11.8, 11.9). The love relationship is permanent. The first stanza is a dramatic expression of the long and careful search that Krishna made (11.9). The second stanza tells about their developing relationship (11.5.2, 11.5.6.2), and points out that there is no distinction between a single lover and many lovers (11.8.3, 11.8.5). The third stanza concerns the typical manifestation of the myth in statuary (11.8.4), its value to the world, and particularly to the reader (11.5.5.4, 11.9).

The poem shows an alternation of predictive structuring, where the reader's attention is held because something important is yet to come, and continuative structuring, where a potentially complete structure is extended by the addition of optional items (11.5.1, 11.5.2, 11.5.3, 11.5.6, 11.6, 11.8.1). Additionally there is no clear structure to stanzas (11.4), and the late position in the clause of continuative structures suggests that syntax does not provide the skeleton of the poetic form (11.5.1).

Meaningful units in the poem vary greatly in size, but average just under one line length (11.3.2.) Later units tend to be shorter than earlier ones, and there is a marked contrast in the two halves of stanza 3. The effect is of a quickening of pace (note the verb 'quicken' in line 31) especially in the last sentence. Whereas other runs of short units lengthen towards their end (e.g. lines 4–9, 15–

17, 31–33), the units in the last sentence do not, and get very short indeed.

The poem may be interpreted structurally as, in general, preparing for its final sentence. It begins with the word 'and', which has only occurred once before (line 8). It is normal in a list like lines 3–8 for the last item to be prefaced by 'and', but the other lists do not have this feature (11.5.1, 11.9). This fact correlates with the absence of other linking adjuncts except for the concluding signal 'so' (line 21). In the last sentence is the only combination of two such adjuncts, 'and so'. It is appropriate as an introduction to the concluding statement in the poem.

The main clause subject is 'they' (11.8), which refers to the protagonists of the narrative, and their coming together in one pronoun has been heralded in a dramatic way in line 20. The verb 'sit' has a meaning which contrasts with the activity-oriented verbs that mainly occur elsewhere, and particularly those of the previous sentence. The contrast is eventually consolidated in an interpretation that the mythological story lies outside time (11.5.5.2), reminiscent of Keats's 'Grecian Urn'.

'Ever moving' contrasts with 'sit', and 'ever still' contrasts with 'ever moving' (11.5.6.1). When such incompatible statements occur, we seek an interpretation that resolves their incompatibility. The poem has already given us some practice in this. Line 20 implies two statements which are incompatible (11.8.5) (compare 'each was bigger than the other'), and lines 23–4 are paradoxical, but serve to resolve the lover/lovers problem (11.5.5.4, 11.5.6.1, 11.8.4).

'Ever moving' and 'ever still', form a minimal list of two items (11.5.1). They are followed by another list, consisting of two similar items ('in stone, in ivory'), and a final odd one ('in us'). Although 'in stone' and 'in ivory' do not contrast, they form a parallel pair to the preceding list, and further isolate 'in us'.

If the lovers are statues in stone or ivory, they cannot be moving. Our first level of interpretation is that a well-carved statue can appear to be alive; beyond this the incompatibility reinforces the notion of 'outside time' (11.5.5.2).

The final two words appear superficially to make a third item in a fairly trivial list (11.5.6.2), but there are surprises.

1  The word 'in' has a different meaning from 'in stone'; it can be paraphrased as 'within', where the other can be paraphrased as 'out of' (11.7.3). The contrast is sharp. There has been some earlier indication of this kind of switching,

e.g. the move from literal to figurative in lines 5–6.

2  The poem in its very last syllable changes from objective narrative to subjective ('us' involves both writer and reader) (11.9). The reader is pressed to participate, but has not been warned in advance and so has to readjust his perspective of the entire poem, and to take a personal message from it.

## 11.3  Layout and punctuation

### 11.3.1  Constant features of layout

Constant features of layout are:

1  three stanzas with twelve lines in each;
2  left-alignment;
3  capital letters initial in the line.

### 11.3.2  Punctuation   ·

#### 11.3.2.1

There is end-line punctuation in twenty-six out of thirty-six lines, evenly distributed.

There is mid-line punctuation in thirteen lines.

Lines which both mid- and end-line punctuation increase in frequency as the poem proceeds, and stanza three shows a contrast between the first half and the second half – see Figure 11.1

#### 11.3.2.2 Chunking

We can count the number of syllables between punctuation marks, noting separately the line breaks (see Figure 11.2). Note the long chunk in stanza one, lines 7–9, and stanza two, lines 14–16 and 17–18.

0 0 0 0 0 0 1 1 0 1 1 1

1 = line has both mid- and end-line
    punctuation

Figure 11.1 Stanza 3.

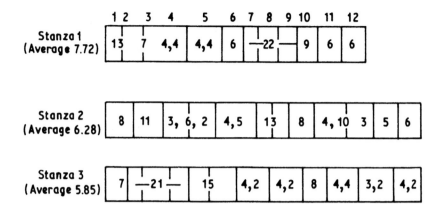

Figure 11.2 Syllable distribution relative to punctuation. Each box represents a line. A break in the dividing line between boxes means that there is no end-line punctuation. Mid-line punctuation is shown by commas. The numbers refer to syllables between punctuation marks.

Average no. of syllables in a chunk = 6.5
Average no. of syllables in a line    = just over 7

## 11.4 Metrics

### 11.4.1 Line length

Line length varies between five and eleven syllables, most commonly six or eight. Stressed syllables on my reading vary between two and five per line, with a strong tendency towards three. There is no rhyme.

There is a suggestion of a stanza form, in that the last two lines of each stanza are shorter than the average, and noticeably shorter than the preceding two lines (see Table 11.1).

### 11.4.2 Commentary

Stanza and line are features mainly of layout rather than of metrical form, though lines are commonly end-stopped. There is considerable variety in the chunking, as shown by the distribution of punctuation marks.

The distribution of these features over the poem shows little patterning, but we should note:

1  the hint of stanza form in the length contrast between lines 9–10 and 11–12 in each stanza;

| | Line average (whole poem) | No. of syllables 7.11 |
|---|---|---|
| Stanza 1 | 9 | 9 |
| | 10 | 9 |
| | 11 | 6 |
| | 12 | 6 |
| Stanza 2 | 9 | 8 |
| | 10 | 9 |
| | 11 | 5 |
| | 12 | 6 |
| Stanza 3 | 9 | 8 |
| | 10 | 8 |
| | 11 | 5 |
| | 12 | 6 |

Table 11.1 Syllable distribution in final lines to stanzas

2 the tendency towards smaller chunks as the poem proceeds, with a marked pattern in stanza three. The average length of a chunk in lines 25–30 is 14.3 syllables, and in lines 31–36 is 3.5 syllables.

## 11.5 Syntax

The main characteristics of the syntax are as follows.

### 11.5.1 Lists

A list is defined as a replacement of a syntagmatic choice by a paradigmatic one. The syntactic structure is not developed, but instead there is a reselection of the same element of structure. The lists are shown in Table 11.2.

List I features adjuncts occurring late in the clause; the adjuncts are realized by prepositional phrases and so the major surface effect is the introduction of strings of nominal groups. List II is similar; in list III the same structures occur, but initially in the clause.

Lists IV and V feature predicators and their transitivity options. List IV moves from a second choice of predicator to three choices of nominal groups as object. List V lists predicators, moving from intransitive to transitive.

**List    Items**

I along    the                      peaks
           the     lesser          hills
           each    sudden          plain
                   persistent      star
           the                     columns of his thought
    down           deeply anxious  limbs
           and     great           inclines of the heart
    to     the                     rim     of the world

---

II among   the     maidens of the day
           the     maidens of the night

---

III under  her     consequential   sun
           the                     computations of every rising moon

---

IV that    face    grew
                   asserted all his love
                            his dreams
                                destinations

---

V the      world   revives
                   quickens
                   renews itself
                   turns whole
                   adores their love unparalleled

---

VI they    sit     ever moving
                   ever still
                            in stone
                            in ivory
                            in us

Table 11.2 Lists

So in all the lists except III the extension occurs late in the clause structure (late means after the minimum required choices of mood and transitivity have been made).

### 11.5.2  Arrest

Whenever an element of structure can be predicted (from normal rules of syntax) but does not occur immediately, the elements which do occur are said to *arrest* the progress of the syntax. Arresting elements can be the realizations of optional choices, or positional choices. Arrest can be initial or medial in a structure (see Table 11.3).

| Stanza 1, | lines | 1–2 | Subordinate clauses arrest main clause |
| Stanza 2, | lines | 13–14 | Prepositional phrase arrests mood choice |
| Stanza 3, | line | 25 | Subordinate clause arrests main clause |
| | lines | 29–30 | Prepositional phrase and subordinate clause arrest main clause mood choice |

Table 11.3 Syntactic arrest

The last sentence of stanza 2 will be discussed below. At present we note that each stanza is initially arrested, and there is very little subsequent arrest.

The pattern of arrest is enhanced by the selection of verbs which have objects in the text, but are not decisively transitive. At this point only 'searched' in stanza 1 is relevant. In a weakly predictive fashion, the whole of stanza one apart from the last line thus has the quality of arrest.

When listing occurs in an arresting pattern, the effect of arrest is intensified, and this is found clearly in stanza 2, line 14 and stanza 3, line 30. It is called *stretch*.

### 11.5.3  Continue

A label is needed for a grammatical structure which just goes on, beyond the minimal needs of a complete unit. In an earlier account (Sinclair, 1982) this category and that of *list* were together labelled *flow*; but the effect of developing a text by means of paradigmatic choices (list) is quite different from development through further syntactic choices (continue).

Clear instances of *continue* in this text are stanza 2, lines 18–23, and stanza 3, lines 26–28.

### 11.5.4

Continuing the point about *search* and its transitivity (made in section 11.5.1 above) we must note:

1  there are three other verbs of indecisive transitivity at line ends:

   15   *asserted*
   26   *unfolds*
   31   *quickens*

2  there are very few decisively transitive verbs anywhere in the poem; 'adores' (line 33) is the only clear case among the finite verbs, and 'tidy' (line 2) is the only other example. The verbs 'grow' (line 15), 'multiply' (line 22), 'feed' (line 28), 'revive' (line 31), 'renew' (line 32) and 'turn' (line 32) all have an ergative quality (cf. 'He turned the wheel', 'The wheel turned') which they share with 'assert', 'unfold', 'quicken'. The other verbs in the poem are intransitive (if we overlook the rather infrequent use of 'sport' as transitive in, e.g. 'He sported a tartan tie' and 'stood' in 'He stood a round of drinks.')

### 11.5.5 Obscurity

This is not intended as a pejorative term. It covers areas of potential ambiguity, and areas where normal expectations are not confirmed. In the ambiguities, the various options are set out below with my own decisions. In poetry, it is not necessary to decide upon a particular option; more than one can be held as relevant, even if they are incompatible with each other. In some cases one's overall interpretation will assign priorities without excluding less likely possibilities.

The places which merit consideration are as follows.

#### 11.5.5.1 Stanza 1, line 2

'To tidy up the world'

This is a subordinate clause introduced by an infinitive, and it can be associated with the previous line, also a subordinate clause, or the main clause starting 'Krishna'. The question is whether we understand that Krishna became a god in order to tidy up the world, or whether Krishna searched a thousand years in order to tidy up the world. My preference, and the author's, is for the first reading. It may be significant that a comma at the end of line 1 would have tipped the balance towards the second reading.

### 11.5.5.2 Stanza 1, line 3

'Searched a thousand years'

Because of the absence of 'for', it is possible to consider this as a transitive structure. Priority is given to the obvious meaning of 'searched for a thousand years', but the secondary meaning is worth attention. Someone godlike could be located outside time, and so 'a thousand years' could be the location of his search as well as the time it took.

### 11.5.5.3 Stanza 1, line 5

'persistent star'

This is taken as a branched structure; read as 'each persistent star'. Alternatives, like apposition or vocative, seem irrelevant.

### 11.5.5.4 Stanza 1, lines 10–12

'Searched ... a face for Bindavan'

Again there is no 'for' to guide the reader, so we have several possible interpretations following structural choices. The two questions are whether 'searched' is transitive or not, and whether 'for Bindavan' is part of the noun group 'a face for Bindavan' or a separate adjunct in the clause, meaning roughly 'on behalf of Bindavan' or 'to find Bindavan'.

A   **Transitive verb, final adjunct**
   1   'Krishna looked all over a face on behalf of Bindavan'.
   2   'Krishna looked all over a face to see if he could find Bindavan there'.

B   **Transitive verb, with line 12 a single noun group**
   3   'Krishna looked all over a face which was destined for Bindavan'.

C   **Intransitive verb (meaning 'searched for') and final adjunct**
   4   'Krishna searched for a face on behalf of Bindavan'.
   5   'Krishna searched for a face to give to Bindavan'.

The fourth possibility (intransitive verb with line 12 a single noun group) does not yield a sensible interpretation.

The meaning of the A and B choices seems secondary though not entirely irrelevant; the main choice is between 4 and 5. Since Bindavan is a garden, 5 is the preferred choice, though there is a residual ambiguity centred on the meaning of 'for'.

5 (a)  'a face to stand as a symbol of Bindavan'. Krishna has a vision of Bindavan that could be matched in a face.

5 (b)  'a face that would grace the garden'.

### 11.5.5.5 Stanza 2, lines 16 and 17

This is a branched structure capable of several interpretations depending on the branching. List IV in Table 11.2 gives one version, which I prefer; others are in Table 11.4. The author prefers list A.

| A all his love | B all his love | C all his love |
|---|---|---|
| all his dreams | all his dreams | his dreams |
| all his destinations | destinations | his destinations |

Table 11.4 Interpretations of lines 16–17

A list of this kind can be interpreted as a simple concatenation, each item being separate, or an appositional list, where items in that relationship have the same referent, or a mixture of both. The only likely ambiguity here is whether or not 'dreams' and 'destinations' are appositional, that is his dreams are his destinations. I am not tempted towards this meaning, nor is the poet.

This decision clarifies the clearly appositional relationship with 'softly magical'; only the destinations are.

### 11.5.5.6 Stanza 2, line 22

'The gopis'

The gopis were milkmaids who sported with Krishna in Bindavan. Krishna is the blue god, and played a flute. So presumably 'the gopis' is appositional to 'his love', despite the clash of grammatical number; the clue is in 'multiplying', and the interpretation is supported by the paradox in lines 23–4.

The last sentence of this stanza has an unexpected syntactic form. After 'So the blue god' we would expect a verb and the remainder of what is predicted as a main clause. But it never comes, and we have to interpret 'So the blue god' as a complete main clause.

### 11.5.5.7 Stanza 3, line 30

This line is a subordinate clause introduced by a past participle, and could refer either back or forwards. Is it each note (or the radiance of each note) which is so bound, or the world? My preference is for 'the radiance of each note' as referent, suggesting that the quality of Krishna's playing is enhanced by the audience reaction. As in 11.5.5.1 above, a comma at the end of line 29 would have favoured the second alternative.

### 11.5.5.8 Stanza 3, line 32

In 'turns whole', 'whole' could be interpreted as complement ('becomes a unity') or adjunct ('resolves completely'). There is nothing to guide the choice; I prefer the first interpretation, and the author agrees.

### 11.5.5.9 Stanza 3, line 33

'Unparalleled' could be a postmodifier of 'their love', equivalent to 'their unparalleled love'. Alternatively it could be interpreted as an adjunct in the clause, suggesting that the world's adoration was unparalleled. The first, and more straightforward version is preferred, and the syntax also echoes Shakespeare's 'lass unparalleled' (*Antony and Cleopatra*, V.ii.317). The poet confirms the interpretation and the reference.

## 11.5.6 Commentary

### 11.5.6.1 Parallelism

This is a perceived surface effect, brought about by various co-selections of syntax and lexis. One type is based on a list with sufficient similarity among members of the list to invite the effect of parallelism. Lists II and VI in Table 11.2 show such an effect. In list II, the syntax is identical and the actual words are the same except for the antonyms 'day' and 'night'. List VI is in two parts, each of which also varies in just one word: 'moving' and 'still' are antonyms and the sequence 'stone', 'ivory', 'us', is one which has been explicated in section 11.2.

Parts of lists I, IV and V show a less distinct parallelism, but in list III only the striking selections of 'consequential' and 'computations', although in different syntactic positions, suggest any parallel effect.

Another type of parallelism can occur when successive clauses incorporate lexical repetition at similar places of syntax. The only clear case in the poem is stanza 2, lines 23–4, where the pattern 'sport ... with' plus the similar syntax and rhythm, and the antonym 'all-one' make the parallel obvious.

A case could be made for an indistinct parallel effect in stanza 3, lines 26, 27 and 28. Each contains a noun group of similar structure and rhythm.

### 11.5.6.2 *Text shape*

The sentences in this poem, in general, do not have strong endings from a syntactic point of view. If the verb 'searched' in stanza 1 had been decisively transitive, then the last line would appear as a climax of a stretched syntax (list within arrest). However, the reader is certainly anticipating that the objective of the search will be identified, and the last line has a substantial effect. In stanza 2, only the last sentence is rounded off (with a two-line parallelism), and the effect of that is weakened by the unexpectedness of the main clause syntax. In stanza 3 the second sentence has an air of conclusion because the last item in the list (line 33) is twice as long as the others. In the final sentence there is a distinct tailing off, as another list concludes with a very brief item, 'in us', formed of apparently humdrum little words.

The power of the poetic form in this case is not delivered through the syntax.

## 11.6 Grammetrics

Having picked out points in both syntax and metrics, it is helpful to consider them together, to see how the syntax is distributed in line and stanza. We shall plot the state of syntax at line ends only, using the following analysis:

1 *arrest*   there is a clear prediction of more to come;
2 *continue* the structure appears to be complete but continues with optional syntactic choices;
3 *complete* the structure appears to be complete;
4 *list*   the structure continues with further paradigmatic choices;
5 *stretch* an already arrested structure is subject to further arrest.

This analysis is applied twice at each line end:

1 to the state of the line at its end, without looking ahead;

2  to the relationship between this line and the way the syntax
develops in the next. (This is blank if line-end and sentence-
end coincide).

The analysis is shown in Table 11.5. A number of points can be
made, building on previous observations. The only sentences
without initial arrest are the two short ones, with three lines
apiece. Stanza 1 is dominated by *list*, stanza 2 by *continue*, and stanza
3 by *continue* in the first half and *list* in the second half.

As noted above (11.5.4), lines 15, 26 and 31 end with a verb of
indecisive transitivity and ergative quality.

## 11.7 Lexis

Unusual collocation can be grouped as follows.

### 11.7.1

'sudden plain'
'persistent star'
'rim of the world'
'yearning flute'

This is an assortment of lively juxtapositions, each of which can be
interpreted fairly easily: a low-flying aircraft encounters sudden
plains after the peaks and hills but the stars are constant above.
'Rim' is an interesting substitution for 'edge' or 'end': 'yearning' is a
transferred epithet.

### 11.7.2

'consequential sun'
'computations of every rising moon'

As well as unusual collocations, these examples each contain a long
word which is usual in lyric verse and draws attention to the
expressions; 'multiplying his love' is possibly a third example, and
'destinations' in a list with 'love' and 'dreams' draws some attention
to itself. All these patterns are in the second stanza. Elsewhere only
'unparalleled' has more than three syllables, but it is sufficiently
poetic to blend in well.

### 11.7.3

(Along) Each sudden plain, persistent star

|  | line | End-line state | Next line development |
|---|---|---|---|
| Stanza 1 | 1 | arrest | stretch |
|  | 2 | arrest | complete |
|  | 3 | complete | continue |
|  | 4 | list | list |
|  | 5 | list | list |
|  | 6 | list | list |
|  | 7 | list | list |
|  | 8 | list | list |
|  | 9 | list | complete |
|  | 10 | complete | continue |
|  | 11 | list | complete |
|  | 12 | complete |  |
| Stanza 2 | 13 | arrest | list |
|  | 14 | stretch | complete |
|  | 15 | list | list |
|  | 16 | list | continue |
|  | 17 | continue |  |
|  | 18 | complete | continue |
|  | 19 | continue | continue |
|  | 20 | continue |  |
|  | 21 | arrest | continue |
|  | 22 | continue | continue |
|  | 23 | continue | complete |
|  | 24 | complete |  |
| Stanza 3 | 25 | arrest | complete |
|  | 26 | complete | continue |
|  | 27 | continue | continue |
|  | 28 | continue |  |
|  | 29 | arrest | arrest |
|  | 30 | stretch | complete |
|  | 31 | list | list |
|  | 32 | list | list |
|  | 33 | list |  |
|  | 34 | continue | list |
|  | 35 | continue | list |
|  | 36 | list |  |

Table 11.5 Grammetric structures of the poem

The columns of his thought,
Down deeply anxious limbs
and great inclines of the heart

Perched upon a chord of time,
His yearning flute unfolds
The lovely burden of her eyes
To feed his nimble fingers.

in stone
in ivory, in us.

These extracts show metaphorical usage. The middle one does not contrast with literal expression, and indeed there are traces of metaphor throughout the first nine lines of stanza 3. It can be considered purely lyric despite the pun on 'chord'.

In the other two examples, a list switches abruptly from literal to metaphorical. The searching in stanza 1 is topographical at first – 'along the peaks', etc., and then without change of preposition switches to metaphor 'along the columns of his thought', and maintains this for three lines, before returning to topography in line 9.

At the end of the poem there is a small-scale pattern that is similar. A literal use of 'in' meaning 'made of' starts a list, but the third and final use of it is quite different, 'they sit in us'. The closest literal meaning is *'within'*, and that has to be interpreted metaphorically just as is necessary in line 20.

### 11.8 *Information structure*

Table 11.6 shows one of the main patterns of information structuring in the poem. The subjects of main clauses are a grammatical reflection of 'topic'; so for example, the fact that Krishna is prominent as a main clause subject means that a number of statements are made concerning Krishna. From the table we can take the following points.

### 11.8.1

All the items which are subjects of main clauses are introduced before they occupy this position. There are two types of introduction:

1  pronoun reference forwards, anticipating the occurrence of the item (line 1, with a secondary pattern in line 13);

| Subject | Line | Reference | Syntactic position |
|---|---|---|---|
| | 1 | *he* → Krishna | subject of subordinate clause |
| | 2 | *the world* → world | object of subordinate |
| | 3 | | clause |
| *Krishna* | 6 | *his* ← Krishna | modifier of prepositional object |
| | 12 | *a face* → face | object |
| | 13 | *her* ← face | modifier of prepositional object |
| *that face* | 15 | | |
| | 16 | *his* ← Krishna | modifier of object |
| *she* ← face | 18 | *him* ← Krishna | modifier of prepositional object |
| *each* ← Krishna/face | 20 | *the other* ← Krishna/face | prepositional object |
| *the blue god* ← Krishna | 21 | *his* ← Krishna | modifier of subordinate clause subject |
| | 21 | *his votive flute* → flute | subordinate clause subject |
| | 22 | *his* ← Krishna | modifier of object |
| | 22 | *love* ← face | object of subordinate clause |
| | 22 | *the gopis* ← face | apposition to main clause object |
| | 23 | *them* ← face | modifier of prepositional object |
| | 24 | *one* ← face | modifier of prepositional object |
| *his yearning flute* | 26 | *his* ← Krishna | modifier of main clause subject |
| ← his votive flute | 27 | *her* ← face | modifier of prepositional object |
| | 28 | *his* ← Krishna | modifier of object |
| | 30 | *her* ← face | modifier of prepositional object |
| *the world* | 31 | | |
| | 32 | *itself* ← world | object |
| | 33 | *their* ← Krishna/face | object |
| *they* ← Krishna/face | 34 | | |

→ forward } } Indication of the location of the co-referential main clause
← backward } } subject

Table 11.6 Information structure of the poem

2  first occurrence of the item as another structural element
  (lines 2, 12, 26).

## 11.8.2

'Krishna' is the only main clause subject of the first stanza. In the
second, Krishna (as 'the blue god') and the face (as 'that face', 'she')
share subject position and are combined in 'each' (line 20). In the
third stanza, 'His yearning flute' and 'the world' are new subjects,
and the final one, 'they', is a reference to Krishna and the face.

## 11.8.3

Reference to 'Krishna' occurs frequently in non-subject position
(lines 1, 6, 16, 18, 21, 22, 28) and so does reference to the face (lines
12, 13, 22, 22, 23, 24, 27, 30). 'World' has two other references (2,
32) and 'flute' one (21). The combination of 'Krishna' and 'the face'
has a referent in lines 20 and 33.

## 11.8.4

I have used 'face' for one of the two dominating main clause
subjects, because that is its first form. However it is a complex
meaning which can be singular ('that face', 'she', 'one', 'her') or
plural ('the gopis', 'them'), and means more than we normally mean
by 'face'. It seems to mean something closer to 'partner(s)'; the
ambiguity of number suggests that any partner represents them
all. This point is important in interpreting lines 23-4, which might
otherwise suggest that Krishna feigned even-handedness with his
affections, but secretly preferred one girl and was constant to her.

## 11.8.5

Clauses which include references to both 'Krishna' and 'face' are
interesting, because they relate them to each other. In lines 3, 10
and 12 ('Krishna ... searched ... a face') there is the first example;
then a block of them in 18, 20, 23 and 24. These occurrences are all
in the second stanza, on either side of the remarkable line 20:

**Till each stood within the other**

In other examples (lines 15-16, 21-2, 26-7) the reference is at a less
important syntactic place, in the modifier of the noun group.

## 11.9 Discourse structure

The abstract, underlying pattern of human discourse has a three-part structure which we shall label

| | |
|---|---|
| **Posit** | **(P)** |
| **React** | **(R)** |
| **Determine** | **(D)** |

The structure may not be physically realized in every instance at every stratum, but it is hypothesized that we interpret discourse with reference to such a model. However large or small are the units being described, they should:

1  be analysable in terms of a P-R-D underlying structure;
2  be derived from P-R-D analysis of a superior structure in a hierarchy of the type shown schematically in Figure 11.3.

To explain Posit-React-Determine, let us assume that at any point in a discourse there are two, and only two, *participants* (one participant may be several people or may be a writer's construct like 'It is commonly held that ...'). The *posit* element is something put forward by one participant which is substantially different from what has gone before. The *react* element is understood as a reaction to the posit from another viewpoint. The third element is produced by one of the participants on behalf of both of them, clarifying, concluding, evaluating, naming, etc., what has been achieved in the previous two contributions. If that is not challenged, then it stands as a determination of the unit of discourse.

The largest unit of discourse is the *artefact*, or complete text or discourse, and the smallest is approximately the *clause complex* (one main clause with its attendant subordinate clauses).

Let us work downwards in seeking P-R-D structures in this text. It is convenient that it has three stanzas, though that is not necessarily a clue to its discourse structure. However the main

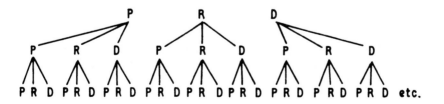

Figure 11.3

clause subjects strongly support a division by stanza. The first concerns Krishna, the second concerns his relations with the gopis, and the third provides a further relationship between the lovers and the world. The identification of stanza 3 as *determining* is confirmed by the change in finite verb tense from past (lines 1 and 2) to present (line 3).

Things cannot be done in the past, or in the future, or in a hypothetical world. They can only be done at the moment we call 'the present', and so verbal actions are normally expressed in the tense which expresses the moment of their utterance. However, the present tense in English can refer to a moment, or to a habitual or permanent state of affairs. Perhaps an initial reading of lines 26–33 will suggest a momentary event (though line 25 is a strong hint that it is not); the paradox in lines 34–5 keeps us guessing, but the 'stone' and 'ivory' of lines 35–6 refers to typical statues of Krishna and his lover, and asserts permanence.

We can expect each stanza to suggest a P-R-D structure internally, and we are not disappointed. In stanza 1, lines 1–3 introduce Krishna's search and time it; lines 4–9 place it, and lines 10–12 express its conclusion. Lines 4–9 do not have the surface structure of a clause complex, and surface grammar may well be over-ridden by interpretation of the discourse. This is an important technical matter, but one which would divert the main argument if pursued here.

Stanza 2 divides into three sentences, one about her in relation to him, one about her and him in relation to each other, and one about him in relation to the more complex notion of her/them. The third sentence begins with the word 'so', which marks it as a conclusion, explicating the previous pair of sentences.

The third stanza also obligingly contains three sentences, differentiated by main clause subject. The final sentence begins 'and so', signalling a determining unit. (Note that the other occurrence of 'so' in line 30 is a degree adverb and quite different). Furthermore, the last word of the poem alters the whole discourse structure, which has been entirely in the third person. The pronouns for direct verbal interaction are first and second, marking the status of the two participants at any moment of the discourse. It would be fair to say that 'us' is the least expected or predicted word in the poem. Suddenly, the author involves his readers directly.

We conclude that the poem fits well into a P-R-D model, as shown in Figure 11.4.

Figure 11.4

## 11.10 Final comments

The neatness of the previous section makes it important to stress that the text was not chosen by me. Elsewhere, the analytic points which are made have been selected from a fairly comprehensive study. Care has been taken to distinguish internal evidence from external, and to bring out secondary meanings which, although rejected on the grounds of the coherence of the text as it unfolds, may play a part in the overall experience of the poem. The presentation cannot avoid some repetition of observation, but it has been kept to a minimum.

If one assumes that everything in the text is there for a purpose, one finds ready confirmation either in one or other of the following.

1  In the unfolding of the poem – in mimetic effect. The search takes a long time, and it takes a long time proportionately to tell it. The reciprocal development of the lovers is reflected in the syntax of the second stanza; the contrast between time moving and standing still creeps up on us in the last stanza and is put clearly in a paradox at the end. The last, totally unexpected word drives the whole poem into a fleeting moment of direct interaction with the reader, reversing the general tendency for sentences and stanzas to end on a quiet note.

2  In the structure of the poem seen all at once; the balances, contrasts, predictions, resolutions of obscurity, etc. In particular the poem seen as a learning experience for the last sentence suggests great care in composition.

# BIBLIOGRAPHY

Sinclair, J. McH. (1982), 'Lines about lines' in R. Carter (ed.), *Language and Literature*, London, Allen & Unwin, pp. 163-75.

# 12

# What is a poem?

*James Thorne*

*The interaction of form and interpretation is further elaborated in this chapter by James Thorne. His purpose is twofold. Firstly, the relationship between stylistic analysis (largely concentrated on the study of* form*) and literary criticism (generally concerned with matters of* interpretation*) is addressed. On the basis of two positions taken by a representative of either discipline vis-à-vis Robert Frost's poem 'Stopping by woods', Thorne demonstrates which possibilities for interpretation the poem offers. The question then becomes which of these interpretations is to be judged as more adequate.*

*The answer to this question must be based (so Thorne's second argument runs) on a detailed stylistic analysis of the processing of the text. Such an analysis reveals two basically different types of reading, i.e. an 'obvious' and a 'non-obvious' one. It is shown that the latter allows for a more coherent interpretation of all textual elements.*

*This analysis of the specific way in which readers tend to interpret a poem is then taken further in order to reveal the nature of poetic texts. Thorne's argument in this respect revives the position of Empson, assigning ambiguity a central position in a definition of poetic texts. Poetry, in other words, typically generates multiple meanings. Hence, when confronted with a poem, readers (at least in our culture) employ reading strategies that allow for such ambiguity. This implies that both 'obvious' and 'non-obvious' meanings must merge into a coherent interpretation. Textual analysis then is fruitful only in so far as it bears upon the strategies readers employ in coping with such ambiguous texts.*

The debate between Henry Widdowson (1972) and Sydney Bolt (1972), started in *The Use of English* and continued by Widdowson (1975) in his book *Stylistics and the Teaching of Literature*, raises important questions about the nature of stylistic analysis and its relationship to literary criticism. The debate centres around Widdowson's analysis of Robert Frost's poem 'Stopping by woods'.

> Whose woods these are I think I know.
> His house is in the village though;
> He will not see me stopping here
> To watch his woods fill up with snow.
>
> My little horse must think it queer
> To stop without a farmhouse near
> Between the woods and frozen lake
> The darkest evening of the year.
>
> He gives his harness bells a shake
> To ask if there is some mistake.
> The only other sound's the sweep
> Of easy wind and downy flake.
>
> The woods are lovely, dark and deep.
> But I have promises to keep,
> And miles to go before I sleep,
> And miles to go before I sleep.

Widdowson (1972, p. 247) describes his analysis as exemplifying 'an approach ... which focuses on the way language is patterned to create a message which characterizes the poem as a unique act of communication'. 'Patterns' are the product of repeated occurrences of linguistic forms, each pattern realizing a theme.

The pattern Widdowson discerns in the first stanza of the poem is manifested by the 'preponderance of pronominal forms'. He sees particular significance in the fact that the possessive pronoun 'his' occurs twice and 'whose' once, leading him 'to surmise that the theme of the poem as a whole has something to do with possession as well as something to do with woods' (Widdowson, 1975, p. 118). The possessive pronouns in the second and third stanzas ('my little horse', 'his harness bells') also signal the theme of possession, but here Widdowson also detects the introduction of another and contrasting theme. 'Easy' in the phrase 'easy wind' and 'downy' in 'downy flake' refer to 'intrinsic' properties. 'We might say, then, that, in the second and third verses, the woods, the wind and the falling snow are seen as symbolizing a natural freedom from constraint, a world apart from that which is circumscribed by a human system of rights and obligations' (Widdowson, 1975, pp. 119–20). Both themes reappear in the last stanza:

> just as the wind is naturally easy, so the woods are naturally lovely, dark and deep. These qualities are contrasted with human values as the theme of possession is restated. Whereas, however, possession in the first verse is associated with rights, in the last verse it is associated with obligation. The use of the verb 'have' is interesting here ... One might say that what is suggested here is that the first person in the poem has woods, but the possession of promises does not bestow rights, it imposes obligations. (Widdowson, 1975, p. 120)

The 'meaning' of the final stanza is:

> The woods are lovely, dark and deep (and represent as such a reality of elemental freedom) but (my reality must be that of social constraints and this is represented by the fact that) I have promises to keep. Only in sleep is there freedom from responsibility. (Widdowson, 1972, p. 120)

Bolt's general comment on Widdowson's (1972) analysis is one I think many people would want to make; if this is a stylistic analysis of 'Stopping by woods', who needs stylistic analysis? Who needs to have it demonstrated to him that the poem can be read as a first-person description of a man pausing on a journey in winter to look at some beautiful woods which belong to someone else, and concluding with a statement which implies that in some sense this kind of behaviour is incompatible with his everyday social responsibilities? Surely no one who is a native speaker of English. And if someone learning English (a kind of reader Widdowson has particularly in mind) was unable to interpret these lines in this way then the only conclusion to be drawn is that he has not learnt sufficient English. Moreover, as Bolt rightly points out, in talking only about this reading Widdowson is missing the most important point about the poem, what, in fact, makes it a poem. This is that at the same time as it can be read in this way (what from here on I shall call 'the more obvious reading') it can be read in another and quite different way. Bolt says:

> When the reader thinks twice about what the last line means, he realises there must be a latent meaning beneath the manifest one. This reveals itself as a metaphor – 'a long way to go before I die'. On re-reading, one now registers the attractive woods as the Forest of Death, and additional meaning attaches to every line. The poem as a whole rejects death without denying its appeal. Death's House is, of course, the graveyard. (1972, p. 245)

Since Bolt does not make the point it is important to add that it is not just he and his students who have read the poem in this way. Almost without exception, the literary critics who have written about 'Stopping by woods' have come to the conclusion that it is the expression of a death wish.[1] The most striking feature of Widdowson's commentary is his failure to recognize even the possibility of this reading.

In response to Bolt's criticism Widdowson says: 'My own feeling is that this is altogether too weighty a construction to place on this simple repetition, and I see no warrant in the text for his interpretation' (1972, p. 24b). And yet previously he has said that 'the inherent ambiguity of poetry is unresolvable ... and this means that no matter how exhaustive an analysis is made it can never exhaust all possible meanings' (Widdowson, 1972, p. 246). And he goes on to say:

> I do not wish to question the value of Mr. Bolt's intuitive sense of what the poem is about, and there seems to me to be no point at all in arguing about the essentially aesthetic issue of the relative validity of alternative interpretations based upon intuition. What one can argue about is the methodological issue of how one might guide students towards some kind of strategy for interpretation. (Widdowson, 1972, p. 246)

Here Widdowson is returning to one of the main themes of his book; the relationship between stylistics and literary criticism. Earlier he has said that stylistic analysis is not intended to take the place of traditional literary criticism but to 'prepare the way for it to operate more effectively ... to serve as a base from which literary criticism ... can conduct its operations' (Widdowson, 1972, p. 116). However, at the same time he adheres to the view that:

> the meanings which literature conveys are of their nature
> elusive of precise description. There must be a point, therefore,
> where a consideration of the linguistic features of a piece of
> literary discourse shades off into an intuitive sense of
> significance. (Widdowson, 1972, p. 116)

But the way Widdowson develops this second point effectively subverts the first. On nearly every other occasion on which he discusses the roles of the stylistician and the literary critic it is the divergence rather than the convergence of their aims that he stresses. Stylistics, we are told, is concerned with 'painstaking linguistic exactitude' (Widdowson, 1975, p. 116), with interpretations which are the result of a 'careful consideration of supporting linguistic evidence' (1975, p. 117). Literary criticism, on the other hand, involves 'the exercise of intuition and ... the appreciation of the artistic value of the message which the literary work conveys' (Widdowson, 1975, p. 116), 'imaginative responses' and 'the appreciation and evaluation of the broader aesthetic significance of literary works' (p. 117). Expressed in these terms, it is difficult to see how there could be any point of contact between stylistics and literary criticism. Far more seriously, as far as Widdowson's own claims for stylistics are concerned, it makes it difficult to see how stylistic analysis could make any contribution to our understanding of what poems are and how they work. By making the claim that the readings that literary critics impose upon poems – non-obvious, interesting readings, such as Bolt's reading of 'Stopping by woods' – cannot be grounded in a linguistic analysis of the text, he lays himself open to the counterclaim that the only readings that can be so grounded are readings which are obvious and uninteresting; a claim which his own reading of 'Stopping by woods' would seem to bear out.

It is, of course, not uncommon to find similar views being expressed by literary critics. Lynen, in the course of expounding a reading of 'Stopping by woods' which he describes as neither 'new nor surprising', says:

> The poem is not just a record of something that once happened
> to the poet, it points outward from the moment described
> toward far broader areas of experience. It expresses the conflict
> which everyone has felt between the demands of practical life,
> with its obligations to others and the poignant desire to escape
> into a land of reverie, where conscience is dimmed and the
> senses made independent of necessity. There is no overt

symbolism in 'Stopping by woods', and yet the reader finds his vision directed in such a way that he sees the poet's purely personal experience as an image of experience common to all. The wide scope of the meaning becomes obvious in the final lines. These state the conflict in a simple, realistic way: the poet will have to fulfil certain duties, perhaps just chores about the farm before he can go to bed, but the 'promises', the 'sleep', and 'the miles to go' widen to include more important aspects of his life and further elements of everyman's life. 'Sleep' here is, of course, the well-earned reward at the end of a day's work; but reaching out beyond this, as indeed the whole poem transcends its rural setting, the idea of sleep merges with the final sleep, death itself. It stands in contrast to the snowy woods, whose temptation is to irresponsible indulgence ending in loss of consciousness: it is normal death, the release at the end of a life in which man has kept his promises and travelled the whole journey through human experience. (Lynen, 1960, pp. 2-3)

But he goes on to say: 'Yet when one examines it, one is at a loss to say just how Frost's images direct the reader's mind to his broader area of meaning' (1960, p. 4).

It is this point of view, whether it is put forward by a stylistician or a literary critic, that I feel must be contested. Put simply, my own view is that if a considerable number of people interpret a text in a certain way then it should be possible to show what it is about the language of the text that causes them to do so.

In the case of 'Stopping by woods', to show why readers interpret it as a death wish it is necessary first to make two simple grammatical points. The first concerns the word 'but' in the second line of the last stanza. 'But' here is used (as it is most frequently used) to indicate to the reader that certain inferences he is likely to have drawn as a result of reading the previous clause are, in fact, wrong. (This is why, while it sounds quite normal to say 'We went to the swimming pool but did not swim', it sounds distinctly odd to say 'We went to the swimming pool but swam'. On being told that someone went to a swimming pool it is natural to assume that he swam.) Thus part of the information gained from one reading (what I am calling 'the more obvious reading') is that it is assumed that the reader will assume that the fact the woods are 'lovely, dark and deep' would make the first person of the poem want to stay contemplating them. However, this would be a false assumption because he has social obligations, the fulfilment of which will take him far away from the spot by the end of the day. But, notice, there is something about this 'obvious' reading that is not entirely obvious. The fact that the woods are described as lovely provides sufficient grounds for assuming that the first person of the poem might want to stand looking at them. (There is no need to speculate about whether they are 'symbolic freedom' as Widdowson suggests or 'images of perilous enchantment' as Lynen (1960, p. 5) suggests.) But what has the fact that they are also described as 'dark and deep' got to do with this? For most people it is openness and light that makes woods attractive.

The second point concerns the clause 'before I sleep'. Clauses of this type are always ambiguous. They can be what traditional grammar books call 'time clauses', and this is how 'before I sleep' is taken in the more obvious reading. As such it can be paraphrased as before nightfall, before the end of the working day, before the time at which one retires to rest, the time after which occupational and social duties can, and must, be ignored. But clauses like this can also be of a different type and open to a different interpretation. One can see this quite clearly if the clause 'before I sleep' is placed in a different context; for example, 'I always need to take two sleeping pills before I sleep'. Of course, here too it is still possible to take 'before I sleep' as a time clause, but (presumably because reading it in this way makes the fact that sleeping pills induce sleep seem irrelevant) it is not this but another reading that is salient; one in which it is taken as a type of result clause, paraphrasable as 'before I am able to sleep'. It is in this way that the clause is taken in the second, the less obvious, reading. But then how are we to make sense of the implication that the fact that the woods are described as 'lovely, dark and deep' should cause us to assume that the first person of the poem cannot sleep there, an assumption that carries with it the further assumption that he should want to sleep there? The answer is that we make sense of it by taking the words 'dark', 'deep' and 'sleep' not in their literal but in certain of their metaphorical meanings, thereby reading the poem as the expression of a death wish.

To know the literal meaning of a word is to know a stereotype.[2] Thus to know the literal meaning of 'sleep' is to know that typically sleeping involves undressing, getting into a bed, closing one's eyes, and allowing oneself to lapse into unconsciousness for a certain length of time, after which one wakes. Understanding the word 'sleep' when it is used in an utterance in its literal sense involves drawing the probable inferences that someone gets undressed, gets into bed, closes his eyes, etc. Understanding a word metaphorically involves drawing some inferences and rejecting or suppressing others.[3] In constructing the less obvious reading of 'Stopping by woods' one rejects all the possible inferences except one; the inference that the first person of the poem wants to lapse into a state of unconsciousness.

Both 'dark' and 'deep' are examples of words that are used so frequently in their metaphorical senses that most dictionaries enter them under separate headings. Among those that the OED gives for 'dark' are: 'Characterized by absence of moral or spiritual light. Obscure in meaning, hard to understand. Obscure to 'the mind's eye', or to memory; indistinct, indiscernible. Hidden from view or knowledge; concealed, secret. Of whom or which nothing is generally known. Void of intellectual light.' Among the figurative meanings given for 'deep' are: 'Hard to fathom or 'get to the bottom of'; penetrating far into a subject, profound. Lying below the surface; not superficial; profound. Solemn; grave. Deep-rooted in the breast; that comes from or enters into one's inmost nature or feelings; that affects one profoundly. Said of actions, processes etc. in which the mind is profoundly absorbed or occupied'.

Typically, the dictionary uses one metaphor to explicate the meaning of another, in the case of 'light' one forming part of an extensive network of metaphors. Because sight is the most important of our senses, 'to see' comes to mean 'to understand'. Because for one 'to see' there must be light, 'light' comes to be used for the capacity to understand, and hence for human capacities in general. To lack 'moral light' is to lack the capacity to take moral decisions, to distinguish between good and bad courses of action. To lack 'spiritual light' is to lack the capacity to distinguish between experiences that are significant and insignificant. To be 'void of intellectual light' is not to be guided by the 'light of reason', by that which is 'illuminating', to be 'totally in the dark', not 'to see'. To be without these capacities is to be without the capacities which are constitutive of consciousness itself, in the absence of which we are reluctant to ascribe to an individual not only consciousness but life. ('The people that walked in darkness have seen a great light: they that dwell in the land of the shadow of death, upon them hath the light shined' (Isaiah ix. 2); 'Put out the light, and then put out the light' (Othello, V. ii. 7).) It is to be in the state the thought of which most profoundly affects us but which is most profoundly unknown to us because nobody ever experiences it. The woods, then, because of characteristics that they do not have, have the characteristics of death. And yet at the same time they are 'lovely'; that is, they are attractive, pleasing, gratifying, even, possibly, erotic. Which is why we assume that someone who describes them in this way should want to identify with them, surrender himself (his self), lapse into unconsciousness, die.

The above is intended not as a commentary on how one should read 'Stopping by woods', but as a commentary on how everyone (or at least everyone who knows what a poem is - a point to which I shall return) does, in fact, read it. I believe this is so even though in most cases the reader remains almost entirely unaware of having constructed this reading, usually only registering a vague feeling that there is something more to the poem than the obvious reading, and even though those who are conscious of having constructed this reading are unable to explain how they have done so. I believe that we read these lines in this way because we cannot help reading them in this way. We make sense of the lines because we cannot help making sense. It is a manifestation of an essential characteristic of all cognitive processes, what the psychologist Sir Frederick Bartlett called 'the effort after meaning' (1932, pp. 44-5). The same impetus that makes us interpret a few lines on a piece of paper as a face (and which makes it very difficult for us to see them as just a few lines on a piece of paper) makes us attach meanings in this way, because it is only by attaching meanings in this way that we can construct a reading into which every word fits. Taking, say, 'dark' in its literal meaning, or any of these words in any other of their metaphorical meanings, will not do it. These other possible meanings are, as it were, filtered out. Only taking the words 'dark', 'deep' and 'sleep' in the way I have described produces a reading that is fully coherent, and only at this point does the effort after meaning cease.[4]

But why should we need to construct this reading in addition to the obvious reading? For two reasons, one of which I have already touched upon. The obvious reading is not fully coherent. The description of the woods as 'dark' and 'deep' cannot be fitted into it properly. To make sense of the implication that the first person of the poem should want to stay gazing at them we have to concentrate on the fact that they are described as 'lovely' and virtually ignore the fact that they are also described as 'dark' and 'deep'.

Nor is this the only inconsistent element. In the context of this reading, 'whose' in the phrase 'whose woods' is taken as a possessive genitive. But the fact that these are the first words in the poem, plus the fact that they owe their position to the inverted word order, gives them a particular emphasis that the rest of the reading fails to sustain. Why should the sight of the woods on a winter's evening make the first person of the poem think about their owner? Why should he worry about whether or not the owner can see him? The obvious reading prompts these questions without providing answers to them. On the other hand, in the case of the less obvious reading, where 'whose' is taken not as a possessive genitive but as a descriptive genitive (cf. 'Greenland's icy mountains', 'Noah's flood'), the reason for the emphasis placed upon the phrase 'whose woods' is obvious. The question of 'whose woods' (in this sense) they are is, of course, central to the whole reading. Notice also the different force that attaches to the expression 'I think I know' in the two readings. In the first 'I think' is not a main clause but a 'parenthetical clause'; that is, it is used as a way of making an assertion sound less assertive. (This is the only way in which it could be taken in 'Whose woods these are I know, I think'.) In the second 'I think' is a main clause, and the expression 'I think I know' is the reluctant admission of certain knowledge. It is the contrast between these two readings that generates the irony associated with these lines.

The second reason why we construct a second reading for the poem brings us back to the question of knowing what a poem is, by which I mean knowing how to read a poem. This is, of course, a very large question and I have space here only for a few oversimplified generalizations. However, it is obvious that forty years after the publication of Empson's *Seven Types of Ambiguity* (1947) it is still necessary to point out that many poems are texts which are intended to be read in more than one way. Most of what Widdowson has to say about ambiguity is beside the point. What matters is not that 'Stopping by woods' can be read either in what I have been calling the more obvious or the less obvious way, but that it can be read in both. Frost has found a form of words that describes looking at nature in a way that accords with the view that this is a normal, innocent, even praiseworthy, activity, and at the same time describes it as dangerous and morbid. We value the poem (or should) for this reason, and for this reason only. (Not, to cite some well-worn apologies for poetry, because it is morally edifying, or shows us the world in a new way.) We read poems (or should) in a way which is quite different from the way in which we read other texts, because in the case of other texts it is the imposition of one, and only one, meaning that is important.

Learning to read a poem is not a matter of learning to pay attention to the repetition of linguistic forms, phonological, lexical, or syntactic. It is a matter of learning to hear what normally we must be deaf to; the inexhaustible ambiguity of utterances.

# NOTES

1  For example Wellek and Warren (1949), pp. 194–5; Lynen (1960), pp. 3–6; Thompson (1961), pp. 25–7.
2  Cf. Putnam (1975), pp. 139ff.
3  Cf. Cohen and Margalit (1972), pp. 722ff.
4  Discussing the two-line Chinese poem:

> Swiftly the years beyond recall
> Solemn the stillness of this Spring Morning

Empson writes:

> Lacking rhyme, metre, and any overt device such as comparison, these lines are what we should normally call poetry only by virtue of their compactness; two statements are made as if they were connected, and the reader is forced to consider their relations for himself. The reason why these facts should have been selected for a poem is left for him to invent; he will invent a variety of reasons and order them in his own mind. This I think is the essential fact about the poetical use of language. (1947, p. 25)

# BIBLIOGRAPHY

Bartlett, F. (1932), *Remembering. A Study in Experimental and Social Psychology*, Cambridge, Cambridge University Press.
Bolt, S. (1972), 'Stylistic analysis', *The Use of English*, vol. 24, pp. 245–6.
Cohen, L. J. and Margalit, A. (1972), 'The role of inductive reasoning in the interpretation of metaphor', in D. Davidson and G. Harman (eds), *Semantics of Natural Language*, Dordrecht, D. Reidel, pp. 722–40.
Empson, W. (1947), *Seven Types of Ambiguity*, London, Chatto & Windus.
Lynen, J. F. (1960), *The Pastoral Art of Robert Frost*, New Haven, Yale University Press.
Putnam, H. (1975), 'Is semantics possible?', in *Philosophical Papers. Vol. 2, Mind, Language and Reality*, Cambridge, Cambridge University Press, pp. 139–52.
Thompson, L. (1961), *Fire and Ice: The Art and Thought of Robert Frost*, New York, Russell & Russell.

Wellek, R. and Warren, A. (1949), *Theory of Literature*, New York, Harcourt Brace & Co.

Widdowson, H. G. (1972), 'Stylistic analysis and literary interpretation', *The Use of English*, vol. 24, pp. 28–33.

Widdowson, H. G. (1975), *Stylistics and the Teaching of Literature*, London, Longman.

# 13

# The reader's need for conventions

When is a mushroom not a mushroom?[1]

---

*Irene R. Fairley*

*As shown in Thorne's essay in the previous chapter, the same poem apparently allows for both an 'obvious' and a 'non-obvious' reading. In an experiment probing the nature of reader strategies empirically, Irene Fairley demonstrates how readers divided roughly between these two alternatives. Responses to Sylvia Plath's poem 'Mushrooms' were collected and subsequently analysed. On the basis of these data, Irene Fairley describes the way in which readers arrive at their interpretations. Comparing these to the responses of a more skilled reader reveals the latter to employ strategies from both groups of readers.*

*Simultaneously, the chapter documents particular difficulties in interpretation readers are faced with when presented with modern poetry. This allows for a delineation of a programme for the acquisition of literary knowledge and understanding. What emerges is that trained readers do tend to strive for pluralism in their interpretations, allowing for a range of potential readings within a given framework, hence seemingly corroborating Thorne's position.*

*This raises the issue of literary education. In what way can interpretative abilities of students be improved? Reading literary criticism will not do, as is shown by an analysis of critics' responses to Plath's poem. As Fairley demonstrates, such critical texts are mainly geared towards more experienced readers. Hence the group of less-skilled readers may not (fully) profit from such a reading. Consequently, more general* principles *and* strategies *for teaching literature need to be set forth.*

## 13.1

Stylistics has proved to be an important tool for the description and classification of texts and has provided literary studies with perceptive analyses of the function of language in literature. Now with the advent of a reader-oriented criticism, stylistics can be propitiously applied to the study of transactions between reader and text.[2] A multitude of new questions clamour for attention. For instance, do textual language-patterns direct reader attention? What cues are picked up by readers and why? Literary education assumes that student readers can improve, but as researchers we need to determine more precisely the nature of the skills we wish to promote.

Anyone who is engaged in the teaching of literature is aware of the great diversity of response possible for any given text, no matter how 'simple' the text may be – or seem to be. There is also a range of response that we may expect, and, indeed, strive for in classroom discussion when we teach literature. The phenomenon of diversity and similarity is intriguing, complex. We tend to think of the response range as in some way 'controlled' by the text, and stylistics has – sometimes rather rigidly – tended to emphasize this aspect. Diversity seems more closely linked to the reader and such factors as individual personality, age, sex, education and cultural background, context for reading, and so forth. Nevertheless, we expect to find areas of consensus for any given text and to be able to identify adequate or preferred readings. As Armstrong (1983, p. 364) contends, there are 'standards and restrictions' that permit us to test for the validity of a reading and to set limits for plural meanings.

Inadequate readings may arise from a faulty interaction of reader and text, in that readers may overlook textual language patterns or be unaware of reading goals. Experienced readers develop a script for reading. They know what to expect when confronting a literary text and how to proceed. They read selectively and actively, asking questions, anticipating structures and drawing inferences. An experienced reader has 'a rich internal set of expectations about successful comprehension' (Kintgen, 1983, p. 25). Language influences reading and interpretation only when readers are already sensitive to the types of structures that 'operate' in literary texts; that is, know what to look for. Agreement about these structures, strategies for discovering them, and interpretive goals are conventions for reading in that they are culturally determined and need to be learned.

Much of the recent discussion of interpretive conventions has been focused on experienced readers or on ideal readers who may be little more than a semiotic function – 'the repository of the codes which account for the intelligibility of the text' (Culler, 1981, p. 38). Such research provides valuable understanding of the conventions of our culture. Yet there has been a bias, perhaps even abhorrence, which has stifled serious consideration of inexperienced readers. Such a bias is unfortunate, for if we wish to understand fully the process of reading and interpreting, studying novice readers can help us to observe how textual strategies are being acquired and applied – or not being acquired and applied. The difficulties that relatively inexperienced readers have with texts may clarify for us the kinds of interpretive moves that require more formal training. Culler assures us that

> the whole institution of literary education depends upon the
> assumption that ... one can learn to become a more competent
> reader and that therefore there is something (a series of
> techniques and procedures) to be learned. We do not judge
> students simply on what they know about a given work; we
> presume to evaluate their skill and progress as readers, and
> that presumption ought to indicate our confidence in the
> existence of public and generalizable operations of reading
> (Culler (1981), p. 125)

## 13.2  Undergraduate reader responses

In the following pages I will review a study of undergraduate responses to a poem in order to discuss their reading strategies.[3] The study provides some interesting divergences of interpretation and evidence of how they were arrived at. One hundred and nine students, enrolled in sections of a Freshman English course that included an introduction to literature, responded to a question-naire. They were given two pages, one containing the poem, and another the questions. The poem, 'Mushrooms' by Sylvia Plath, was reproduced as below with stanza numbers included for reference purposes.[4]

**Mushrooms**

Overnight, very
1 Whitely, discreetly,
Very quietly

Our toes, our noses
2 Take hold on the loam,
Acquire the air.

Nobody sees us,
3 Stops us, betrays us;
The small grains make room.

Soft fists insist on
4 Heaving the needles,
The leafy bedding.

Even the paving.
5 Our hammers, our rams,
Earless and eyeless,

Perfectly voiceless,
6 Widen the crannies,
Shoulder through holes. We

Diet on water,
7 On crumbs of shadow,
Bland-mannered, asking

Little or nothing.
8 So many of us!
So many of us!

We are shelves, we are
9 Tables, we are meek,
We are edible,

Nudgers and shovers
10 In spite of ourselves.
Our kind multiplies:

We shall by morning
11 Inherit the earth.
Our foot's in the door.

Readers were asked to respond to four questions.

1 Underline the words or phrases that you believe most clearly express the meaning of the poem.
2 Which stanza was most difficult for you to understand, and

why? If you need additional space please continue your reply on the back of this page.

3  Were there any individual words which gave you difficulty? If yes, which ones? Try to explain why they are difficult.

4  On the reverse of this page, or the page containing the poem, please provide your interpretation of the poem, and support it with quotations from the poem.

In reviewing results, I will focus on the responses to question 4 and will discuss responses to other questions as they shed light on the process of interpretation. Results are also presented in Tables 13.1, 13.2 and 13.3 and Figure 13.1.

Once the more idiosyncratic readings, such as the poem is about 'born again Christians' (no. 26) or 'people who ride the T [public transport system]' (no. 46), which were given without support or explanation, are set aside, interpretations divide into major groups and subgroupings. A large set of forty-eight readers, whom I will call Group I, reads this as a nature poem, a poem about how mushrooms grow. They read referentially, making such comments as 'The poem is telling about mushrooms and how they grow at night. *Overnight*. How they multiply and what are their uses' (no. 4). Some readers are more specific.

This is basically the life span of the mushroom. From the time it cracks the soil 'Acquire the air' to the final eating stage – 'we are tables' ... They hit the shelves in cans 'we are shelves' then

| Stanza | Frequency | Rank |
|--------|-----------|------|
| 5 | 27 | 1 |
| 4 | 22 | 2 |
| 9 | 18 | 3 |
| 2 | 12 | 4 |
| 10 | 10 | 5 |
| 1 | 7 | 6 |
| 8 | 5 | 7 |
| 7 | 4 | 8.5 |
| 11 | 4 | 8.5 |
| 3 | 3 | 10 |
| 6 | 2 | 11 |

Table 13.1  Most difficult stanza:  Question (2) results

| Inherit | 1 | Nobody | 13.3 |
|---|---|---|---|
| earth | 2 | sees | 13.3 |
| the (stanza 11, line 2) | 3 | us (stanza 3, line 1) | 13.3 |
| We (stanza 11) | 4.3 | edible | 16 |
| shall | 4.3 | multiplies | 17 |
| foot's | 4.3 | So (stanza 8, line 2) | 18.25 |
| by | 7.3 | many (stanza 8, line 2) | 18.25 |
| morning | 7.3 | of (stanza 8, line 2) | 18.25 |
| Our (stanza 11) | 7.3 | us (stanza 8, line 2) | 18.25 |
| in | 10.3 | We (stanza 9, line 3) | 22.5 |
| the (stanza 11, line 3) | 10.3 | are (stanza 9, line 3) | 22.5 |
| door | 10.3 | Our (stanza 10) | 24.5 |
|  |  | kind | 24.5 |

Table 13.2 Words in rank order* (1–25)

*Words of the last stanza occupy ranks 1–12 in a ranking of frequency results for question 1.

|  | Frequency | Rank |
|---|---|---|
| loam | 30 | 1 |
| rams | 10 | 2 |
| hammers | 8 | 3 |
| nudgers | 7 | 4.5 |
| shovers | 7 | 4.5 |
| whitely | 6 | 6 |
| crannies | 4 | 7.5 |
| bland-mannered | 4 | 7.5 |
| paving | 3 | 9.3 |
| shelves | 3 | 9.3 |
| tables | 3 | 9.3 |

Table 13.3 Most difficult words*

*Only words with a frequency of 3 or more are included for question 3 results.

eventually the table 'we are tables'. (no. 50)

This poem is celebrating the continuance of nature. That silently vegetative life and therefore all life is perpetuating. Man can not destroy this serenity because the poem states 'nobody sees us, stops us, betrays us'. This implies the helplessness of man against nature. (no. 71)

16        10
Overnight, very
19        24
Whitely, discreetly,
24    26
Very quietly

7    8    5    6
Our toes, our noses
16  17  15  15    17
Take hold on the loam,
11    11    12
Acquire the air.

42        42    42
Nobody sees us,
30  30    30      30
Stops us, betrays us;
16    18      19      18      18
The small grains make room.

14    14    10    10
Soft fists insist on
10      8      9
Heaving the needles,
9    11    11
The leafy bedding,

2      2      3
Even the paving.
9        11      9    9
Our hammers, our rams,
23    19    23
Earless and eyeless,

26        31
Perfectly voiceless,
10    10      11
Widen the crannies
9          9        9    14
Shoulder through holes. We

28  26    26
Diet on water,
21    23    22    22
On crumbs of shadow,
16        15        23
Bland-mannered, asking

30    29    30
Little or nothing.
35    35    35 35
So many of us!
25    25    25 25
So many of us!

22    22    25      22 22
We are shelves, we are
24    28 28  32
Tables, we are meek,
34    34    40
We are edible,

26        22    26
Nudgers and shovers
19 19  19      19
In spite of ourselves.
33    33      36
Our kind multiplies:

46  46 45      45
We shall by morning
64  62  63
Inherit the earth.
45  46  44 44    44
Our foot's in the door.

Figure 13.1 Underlining frequencies.

Another representative response moves sequentially through the poem:

> I believe that it's what the title says it is. The poem deals with mushrooms and how they grow. 'Overnight very whitely' symbolizes the mushroom that thrives in cool dark places, mushrooms grow best at night. They most often grow wild in the woods: 'Nobody sees us, stops us or betrays us'. They grow at a fast rate and all they need is water and shade and this is brought out in the line 'We Diet on water, on crumbs of a [sic] shadow' and mushrooms grow in bunches often pushing each other aside and should they start growing unwatched they will continue to grow in great numbers. (no. 44)

A second set, whom I will call Group II, reads mushrooms as losers: the meek, oppressed people who take over the world, the silent majority seeking upward mobility, or children and the threat of overpopulation. Or they may read mushrooms as some evil force slowly conquering. A number of readers in this group connect the mushroom image to atomic destruction. In general, the two groups provide literal readings (I) and figurative readings (II).

Both the individual reader responses and the responses of the readers as groups enable us to trace some sources of plural meanings in the reading conventions that are followed. Of particular interest is the motivation of Group II readers to go beyond a referential reading. The move to read 'Mushrooms' as other than descriptive poetry appears to stem from an awareness of an attempt to apply particular reading conventions. The strategies are plural and do not appear to function hierarchically, but rather as a shifting or flexible constellation of options. Some may be dependent on or suggested by others. Among the interpretive conventions that I will refer to in discussing responses will be intertextuality, reading for human significance, reading for coherence or unity, accounting for endings, for metaphor, for deictics, resolving language contradictions, or anomalies.

### 13.2.1 Group I readers

Group I readers, while interpreting literally, will frequently express dissatisfaction with their reading or with specific elements in the poem that remain outside their account. Only one reader who found lines he could not relate seemed content to let them remain unrelated – but even he as an *afterthought* to his interpretation suggests that the poem is really a 'mushroom trip' and that this 'often happens when people trip': that is, their thoughts may seem unrelated (no. 33). Although his comment may be meant simply to be amusing, his move to seek another level of explanation suggests that he has internalized the convention of reading for unity. Expecting to be able to account for all elements, he moves to a model that permits inferences about the speaker's state of mind. What at first seems to be a merely flippant remark provides evidence of how presupposing reading for unity as a goal of interpretation leads the reader to another level of mimesis and a reading beyond descriptive poetry.

Most readers in Group I follow the conventions for descriptive poetry in which 'the conversion of first-order mimesis to second-order mimesis need not take place' (Culler (1981), p. 96). They read the title as a 'sign of the author's intention' (Riffaterre (1978), p. 72) and may simply question items that they cannot readily fit into their literal interpretation. For example, one reader insists:

> 'Mushrooms' is all about how the mushrooms break through
> the surface. While they supposedly do this 'quietly' and
> 'discreetly' they also 'heave' and 'ram' upwards towards the
> surface. The mushrooms are, in fact, 'earless, eyeless and
> perfectly voiceless' yet burst forth with life. They ask 'little or
> nothing' of the earth, but to be able to live. They are
> everywhere and no matter how small a part of the earth they
> are, 'their foot's in the door'. (no. 19)

Nevertheless he goes on to question stanza 10. Another reader, no. 6, remarks on, but does not worry about, the fact that words in stanza 10, like 'nudgers and shovers', lead to unrelated thoughts.

Most often literal readers found stanzas 4 and 5 troublesome. Their remarks identify the problems they have with these stanzas: finding the referent for 'soft fists', relating semantic contents to the description of mushrooms, accounting for contradictions of tone. A great many cite stanza 5 as the most difficult: 'I can't associate those words with a mushroom' (no. 9); 'What was meant by that?' (no. 11); 'there are different meanings for these words [paving, hammers, rams], and I don't know which way your usage wants them to mean' (no. 41). One reader trying to cope with stanza 4 says,

In most other stanzas I can understand and find even far-fetched relations to mushrooms. Yet in this stanza there seems to be no connection ... There is one remote connection ... 'the leafy bedding' which refers to the leaves and grass which are around it as it grows. (no. 56)

Another reader complains about 'Soft fists': 'Why do they put this in? When I think of fists I always think of a hard, dirty, atmosphere' (no. 94).

Even readers who do not articulate problems with stanzas 4 and 5 may indicate inability to deal with them. For instance, some persons neglect discussing them altogether. Respondent no. 60, providing a paraphrased meaning beside each stanza, neglects to comment at all on 4 and 5:

stanza 1    mushrooms are bright white in color, also very quiet
stanza 2    they grow from the ground and up into the air
stanza 3    they are unnoticed by anybody
stanza 4
stanza 5
stanza 6    they grow almost anywhere without much of a problem
stanza 7    they survive on water and need nothing special
stanza 8    there are so many mushrooms and yet they require very little for survival
stanza 9    mushrooms come in various shapes and sizes and all are edible
stanza 10   other forms of plant life are trying to grow and the mushrooms keep on multiplying
stanza 11   in a very short time they will appear all over the earth, and in our homes

The responses to question 2 regarding the most difficult stanza showed overwhelming selection of stanzas four and five (refer to Table 13.1). Thus the frequency data for question 2 supports observations about reading difficulties based on the interpretive responses (question 4). Similarly, Figure 13.1, which presents question 1 underlining results as frequencies above words, corroborates readers' avoidance of words and stanzas that are difficult or puzzling. These are less frequently selected as expressing the meaning of the poem.[5]

Still other readers have problems accounting for the last stanza.

A reader puzzles:

> The mushrooms seem to be talking about themselves. They call themselves meek and Bland-mannered then they turn around and say that they are going to inherit the world: become dominant – like that is their only goal in life. The tone of voice seems to change abruptly from soft to loud and overpowering. (no. 63)

Thus, many readers perceive language contradictions in the poem and express a desire to resolve them. But literal readers do not necessarily have the script that would help them to achieve such resolutions.

Some readers struggle with Plath's use of personification: 'Why toes, noses?' (no. 14); 'Why the personification?' (no. 70). One reader complains: 'The poem is told from a mushroom's point of view and we see that it is trying to say that they are harmless. They do not bother anyone, they grow overnight and they are gone by morning ... I could not tell who's soft fists they were or what needles they were heaving. It was confusing' (no. 22). The presence of language signalling human features puzzles literal readers. Referring to stanza 5, a reader queries: 'What does that have to do with a mushroom; except that you know it's not a person' and also cites stanza 10: 'nudgers and shovers ... what are they?' (no. 43). Many readers deal with the personification by treating it as incidental to the description of mushrooms: they *look* like toes and noses, and they *are* earless, eyeless and voiceless.

Group I readers select a subset of lexical items from the poem and base their intepretation on it. They tend to ignore vocabulary items they do not know or understand, as well as lines which they cannot integrate into their reading. Many fail to get beyond an initial, referential reading of the poem, although such a move is clearly necessary for an inclusive reading of 'Mushrooms'. Some of these readers, however, become disturbed by items that they cannot fit into their interpretation. Their expression of frustration and unhappiness is significant as it reveals an expectation of unity. These readers are at least familiar with the convention that interpretation should account for all aspects of the poem. They expect to be able 'to bring under some general heading the particulars that the poem lists and describes' (Culler (1981), p. 69), but they may not have learned the strategies that would enable them to provide a coherent and consistent reading.

## 13.2.2  Group II Readers

Readers who move to a second level, often directly after acknowledging a literal one, make use of a variety of strategies and provide a range of interpretations in which mushrooms are a threatening force. They give indications of assuming that 'a poem says one thing and means another' (Riffaterre (1978), p. 1). For instance, mushrooms may be a vegetable form of life that takes over, or 'aliens' (no. 53), 'martians or outer space invaders' (no. 46), in a 'science fiction type theme' (no. 7). Such readers appear to follow a convention that allows for the reversibility of figures; they read the propositions of the poem as literally true in a metaphorical world. They bring a number of descriptive codes into play as they search for generalized meanings. Their comments link 'quietly' and 'discreetly' with the idea of multiplication and with the phrases 'inherit the earth' and 'our foot's in the door'. They refer to the aliens as 'they' but the victims sometimes become 'we': 'we will be overrun' (no. 29); 'they are ... moving into our realm without the consciousness or awareness of any person or thing' (no. 53). Readers do this despite the use of the first-person pronoun for the threatening force within the poem. Their tendency to become the recipient of the threat suggests another very general reading strategy; looking for themes of human significance, of universal interest or applicability. They *expect* Mushrooms to be more than mushrooms.

In a particularly interesting instance, one reader first provides a literal interpretation but then experiences difficulty with both stanzas 4 and 5 'because they [mushrooms] are being described as meek, quiet, discreet which seems to be the mood of the poem when in these 2 stanzas words like fists and heaving seem to interrupt the poem' (no. 55). This reader goes on to interpret Plath's poem as

> describing a situation that may never come true yet still gives
> the reader much to think about. The fact that mushrooms
> might inherit the earth could only be possible if the human race
> was entirely wiped out. In this respect it [the poem] gives the
> reader a sense of awareness that he had better take heed to the
> silent things which may be a hazard to his very existence.

By using a strategy of accounting for contradictions of language and mood, this reader came up with a more inclusive, figurative reading.

A large set of the figurative readings identifies the threatening force as human, so that humans (as mushrooms) are pitted against humans. Most often these readings cite lines from the last stanza, a strategy we may refer to as attention to endings, or closure. One reader concludes that: 'The repressed people of the world will rebel. This interpretation is reinforced by the last stanza' (no. 18). Another decides that: 'Up until then we were looking at the growth of mushrooms imaginatively through the eyes of the mushrooms. Yet in the last stanza they take on a human quality that had up until then not been seen. That was reasoning ability ... intellectual actions ... the power to think and reason about world domination' (no. 75).

Readers provide evidence of the convention of reading for intertextuality – that is, reading the poem with reference 'to other texts and to the clichés and descriptive systems of a culture that result from the repetition of connections and associations in texts' (Culler (1981), p. 105). Several readers cite the clichés: 'The author uses the paradox of mushrooms, although quiet and humble, slowly growing and "inheriting the earth", possibly to indicate his feelings about the type of person that gets ahead in life, or the means by which most people accomplish anything ("our foot's in the door")' (no. 31 is quoted, but responses 3 and 95 were quite similar). The importance of the last stanza for readers is confirmed by the results for question 1. As Table 13.2 and Figure 13.1 show, the entire last stanza accounts for the twelve highest frequencies assigned by readers in the underlining task. (Closure prominence is also recorded in Fairley (1979), (1982)).

Readings of the last stanza reflect both expectations of closure and attention to the convention of intertextuality. From a stylistic point of view, this overlapping of conventions corresponds to overdetermination (Riffaterre (1978), pp. 21–2). A peculiar juxtaposition of references in the final stanza permits readers to bring into play cultural codes not usually associated with mushrooms or a vegetable form of life. It may even be the case that reading for intertextuality leads some individuals to the possibility of figural reading. After a quite literal account, 'It conveys the silent but quick rise of mushrooms after the summer thunderstorm', one reader suddenly concludes with 'they seem to be Christian mushrooms: "We are meek ... we shall by morning Inherit the earth"' (no. 27). Another responder explains, '"the meek shall inherit earth" is the theme here', and adds, 'It is interesting to note that mushrooms grow underground; where the meek would be during a nuclear war' (no. 2). Although the line in stanza 9 is 'we are meek', readers overwhelmingly make connections between stanzas 9 and 11 and paraphrase the text as '*the* meek shall inherit'. There is ample indication of reading for intertextuality. It is not clear, though, whether intertextuality prompts the move to relate parts of the poem, or whether the reverse sequence of strategies may occur.

There is evidence that another strategy, reading for oppositions, comes into play here as well. Some readers point to an inherent contradiction in the language, which can be perceived as present in the Christian intertext. One reader, no. 17, explains that the quiet language of the poem gives way to a boldness that increases at stanza 10. Readers may even identify the dichotomy they perceive in terms of specific lexical items: 'It is about mushrooms but I think it is also about mankind (mushrooms = mankind). Basically, I think it says both how insignificant and yet how powerful we are. Words like "acquire" (stanza 2), "insist" (stanza 4), "paving", "hammers" (stanza 5), "Inherit" (stanza 11), show our strength' (no. 57).

We can see, then, that many Group II readers follow the interpretive strategy of taking the poem as metaphorically true in a literal world. The landscape of the poem becomes reflective of some larger human concern that occupies the poet. These readers find human references in two intertexts, one the Christian allusion and the other the salesman's cliché. Overwhelmingly, readers identify a personification of the mushrooms as human 'have nots'. Is such a move a response to the poem's closure or to the first introduction of human features in lexical items? Or is it prompted by particular words or phrases that may be contradictory? Perhaps such aspects of protocol are individually determined. Only occasionally do readers make explicit comments: 'As the poem goes on about stanza 6 it starts to talk about people' (no. 49).

Responses in this study suggested that some readers may begin with a preferred orientation, either literal or figurative. Those who tend to read literally have difficulty with words that are marked for human features or intentionality. They tend to question words like 'toes', 'fists', 'noses', 'hammers', 'rams', 'shoulder', concentrating on what can be referentially explained and visualized. On the other hand, those who read figurally question the words 'tables' and 'shelves': 'I've heard of mushroom clouds, phallic mushrooms, magic mushrooms, but not shelves and tables' (no. 27). Such readers may show a tendency away from visualization, moving more directly to a figural level.

Group II readers seem to be on the alert for human significance and sensitive to the presence of personification. They may note the 'physical humanization of mushrooms' (no. 75) and cite, for example, 'toes', or 'noses', or make interpretive comments like: 'Humans push and shove in crowded streets trying to move, grow like mushrooms growing in multitudes' (no. 95). Several readers identify human features as they move sequentially through the poem:

> The poem isn't really talking about mushrooms but rather uses some of the qualities that a mushroom possesses and applies them to human qualities. Nobody pays attention to something or somebody who is very small and 'meek' so it is possible for that small group to 'very quietly ... take hold of the loam'. And because of their small size nobody sees them or stops them or betrays them because they are of no immediate threat. The same is true with an inferior group of people. They can build up without anybody noticing, 'widen the crannies shoulder through holes'. The holes or gaps left by an unsuspecting society. Stanza 10 tells that this group is inferior or at least believes themselves at the moment to be inferior with the line 'nudgers and shovers in spite of ourselves'. The ending is almost like a warning and it has a hopeful tone to it also. 'We shall by morning inherit the earth. Our foot's in the door' tells the reader that this group has a lot of confidence in themselves. Many times through history all that was needed in order to attain victory was confidence and perseverance. (no. 59).

A second reader who interpreted similarly includes:

> The mushrooms being described as discreet, and quiet, could be people. The poem goes on to elaborate how they take hold of the loam and acquire air. This could represent beginning of life by getting a firm grasp and good foothold. The line nobody sees us supports the idea of discreet and quiet, as if it were people. Why don't others see them? Perhaps it is an underpriviledged group, the handicapped fits in. Voiceless, earless, and eyeless support this idea. Widen the crannies and shoulder through holes shows a difficult path as a handicapped person would have. (no. 48).

In their responses both of these readers, like no. 27 cited above, identify stanza 9 as difficult. The first reader simply questions: 'How are they shelves and tables?' (no. 59). The second works toward a resolution: 'Stanza 9 is difficult to explain but by being tables, shelves and meek and edible shows how they are looked upon as something of little meaning', and comments additionally, 'One has to realize the shape of a mushroom to picture it as a table or shelf' (no. 48). It is interesting to note that stanza 9 ranks third, following 5 and 4, as the most difficult stanza selected by readers (see Table 13.1). While literal readers find stanzas 4 and 5 troublesome, figural readers are puzzled by stanza 9.

Group II of the undergraduates demonstrates the acquisition of conventions necessary for figural reading. These readers seem to understand that 'a rhetorical figure is a situation in which language means something other than what it says' (Culler, (1981), p. 41). In arriving at their interpretations they make use of several strategies – moving from a literal to a figurative level, paying attention to oppositions, and reading for intertextuality, for closure, for human significance. They seek a unified, inclusive reading in which they can account for elements that may not at first have appeared to be related. They have learned to look beyond what is given in the text, if necessary, to construct a system of interrelationships.

### 13.2.3 General observations

Considering the entire set of undergraduate readers, we may draw from their refreshingly candid responses some general observations. For one, they are far from being 'innocent' readers. They have expectations about texts and specifically about poetic texts. Students follow strategies that they have learned, presumably from previous reading experience and instruction in literature. They certainly show signs of having been initiated into the community of readers in our culture, but they display an uneven acquisition of its conventions. For instance, in this study nearly half of the students did not go beyond a literal reading.[6]

The study also documented some problems students have with poetic language. Results for question 3 show that thirty students selected the word 'loam' as difficult, pointing perhaps to a largely urban group of readers or to the word's increasing rarity. Other words identified as difficult are, in order of their frequency rank: rams, hammers, nudgers, shovers, whitely, crannies, bland-mannered, paving, shelves, tables (see Table 13.3). Most students are troubled, 'not so much that there are difficult words but trying to relate their meaning and understanding to the poem' (no. 51). Uncommon words like 'loam', deviant forms like 'whitely', and metaphorical extensions like 'hammers' and 'rams', trip up students who have not fully developed a script for reading poems.

### 13.3 More experienced readers

How would the approaches of more experienced readers, such as graduate students or literary critics, differ from the undergraduate responses?

An extensive reading by a graduate student is available for the Plath poem. Sharon Silkey and Alan Purves (1973) have published a study in which Purves presents and reproduces, with very little commentary, his student's notes. Silkey's reading reflects an English graduate student's familiarity with reading conventions. It provides an instructive comparison with the undergraduate readings, even though the studies are not matched with respect to response time (roughly two hours versus one) and context (home versus classroom). It is, nevertheless, useful to consider similarities and differences in the approaches.

Silkey makes use of the same strategies that are evident in the undergraduate responses. She includes both literal and figurative readings, looks for human significance, and pays attention to dichotomy, to personification, to closure, and to intertextuality. Her response runs to six pages; thus, rather than quote at length I will focus on points of comparison.

Silkey's very first response signals her figural inclination. She focuses on items with human associations, and reconstructs a biblical allusion in much the same way that the undergraduates do, by making connections between stanzas 9 and 11.

tozes, nozes
baby fists
'crannies,' grannies
'diet on water.'    'crumbs'    hermit

Next to last stanza

                crowds

The meek? shall inherit the earth.

                *The Bible* by God
                    (ostensibly)

salesmen    'foot's in the door'    meek?
                (Silkey and Purves (1973), p. 64)

She immediately attends to the search for human significance, which remains a guiding principle much in evidence in her responses. In her sixth reading (a lengthy response) she looks for specific analogies: 'Are the small grains weak, nice people who don't make it in the survival of the fittest game?' And further on, 'An unthinking mass multiplies and by morning we inherit the earth. Yich' (p. 66). In her last reading, the fifteenth, she states, 'These mushrooms could be fallout, or sinister Hollow Men. Frightening to think that Hollow Men multiply and inherit the earth' (p. 71).

Like some of the Group II readers, Silkey shows a strong predilection for reading figurally, rather than literally. Not until her tenth reading does she comment on visual images, recalling how 'the *mushrooms* in my sister's backyard pop up overnight', but visual associations lead her to a figural reading: 'THE BIG BOMB' (p. 67). Not until her twelfth response does she acknowledge a literal reading, and then she does so only briefly: 'Like the roots of trees that crack cement as they grow, these mushrooms widen the crannies. This poem could be a charming little verse that is really about mushrooms. But the last stanza frightens me. The implied "meek" from "inherit the earth" doesn't merge very well with that "foot's in the door"' (p. 70). A similar sequence of thoughts opens her last response: 'This poem fits together very well if you read it merely on a literal level. Still the poem disturbs me, especially the last stanza. I think some of the things I've drawn from the poem are a bit far-fetched, yet I am still unwilling to read it on a literal level' (p. 70-1). Thus, she is not *really* convinced that the poem 'fits together very well' when read literally. Elements in the poem, particularly in the last stanza, frustrate her efforts to read for unity and cause her to shift back and forth from literal and figural perspectives. Again, like some of the Group II readers, she is not able to do much with the words 'tables' and 'shelves'. All she offers is, 'in fairytales, fairies use mushrooms as tables and chairs' (p. 70).

Throughout her readings Silkey employs the convention of intertextuality; her use of this device shows more sophistication and awareness than the undergraduates of cultural codes and possible intertexts. Her second reading introduces another biblical allusion: 'Go forth & multiply' (p. 65). In her third reading she associates 'rams' with the golden calf. Then the word 'betray' leads her to think of Christ. She mentions the bomb and Hiroshima. Beginning with her eighth response she makes references to poetic tradition, bringing into her comments Hopkins, Coleridge, Sartre, Joyce and T. S. Eliot.

Silkey demonstrates well another strategy that is much less evident in the undergraduate readings: the convention of reading ungrammaticalities or oddities as signs (Riffaterre (1978), p. 2). Undergraduates tend to ignore or at best question such items. Silkey concentrates on them and reads them for significance: '"Acquire the air" is a funny phrase. It's like taking a possession instead of the usual things you do with air like inhale or breathe or sniff' (p. 65). Among phrases she contends with, she tries several times to account for 'bland-mannered'. Finally, she looks up 'bland' in *Webster's New World Dictionary of the American Language* (an option not available to the undergraduates). Her deliberations include: '"bland-mannered" smooth-mannered, soothing manners, indifferent manners, straighten out the syntax; it might help' (p. 68); 'bland-mannered – asking little or nothing. These darling little mushrooms are polite, perfectly innocuous, of course' (p. 70).

She worries more about deictics, time references (which do not, however, lead her to any interpretive insights). She also worries about pronouns. For instance, she tries to clarify groupings: '*We* are one group. The small group is the only other group. 2 groups Small grains make room; therefore we are not stopped. They pretend they don't see & are afraid to betray. To whom could they betray us if there are only 2 groups?' (p. 66). Later, she again questions, 'Who is the "we"? the mushrooms, the mushroom shaped clouds, the messed-up people? You, when you first read the poem, should have assumed that "we" was the mushrooms. That would have been a more literal reading, but you seem to have a tremendous inability to grasp the obvious' (p. 69).

Silkey takes a problem-solving approach from the very beginning, assuming that meaning will not be obvious, and that the actual language of the poem is indeed only the iceberg tip. Her readings show familiarity with the kinds of operations that are called for to fill out what the poem conceals. She has learned a set of questions to ask and a set of strategies to help her find answers. From her very first responses she seems aware of what an adequate reading would achieve. Of course, she also brings into play a greater store of historical, literary and cultural knowledge. She does not hesitate to express her feelings or to evaluate her own responses.

What seems of particular interest is the way Silkey's fifteen separate responses to the poem incorporate the range of meanings created by the undergraduates. Her deliberations seem almost a tribute to plural meanings. While undergraduates tend to offer one or perhaps two readings, Silkey seems to understand that there is a range of interpretations possible within the conventions. She also shows the more experienced reader's ability to synthesize and evaluate; her overriding concern is to construct the most plausible reading. Sometimes she comments on her interpretation, rejects her own remarks as trivial or digressive, or reminds herself to return her attention to the text.

### 13.4 How to increase competence?

Is such literary awareness to be the province of specialists, or do we wish to make competence more general? Most educators would, I believe, endorse the objective of making literary competence accessible, but our methods of initiating readers are not always very effective. How to educate undergraduates better, like many of the Group I readers discussed above, is a pressing issue.

Can less experienced readers be helped to increase their competence by reading literary criticism? Although it is a common practice in university classes, it may not be a practical approach to improving scripts for reading. For one thing, critics often 'explain away discrepancies that are meant to confound the reader' (Culler, 1981), p. 67); they tend to minimize textual problems as reading problems. Their concern is usually with evaluating a poet's work, or with arguing for a particular reading, rather than overtly demonstrating interpretive goals and reading strategies. This difference of objectives can be seen in critical references to 'Mushrooms'.

Reviews of *The Colossus* sometimes include remarks about the poem. William Dickey (1962), comparing Plath and Hollander, explains his *preference* for Plath's work 'because her subjects are more accessible', and goes on to remark that, 'Miss Plath is narrower in tone than Hollander; she often deals with landscape and the figures in it, and her voice, while gracefully varied, is persistently serious. Sometimes she makes excursions into mythology, sometimes she considers, with forceful imagination, the consciousness of crabs, mushrooms, snake-charmers' (p. 762). Another reviewer, Guy Owen (1963), *evaluates* Plath as 'a rare talent and a consummate craftsman'. Owen continues, 'She cannot, like most young poets, be labelled "promising", for she has already written a handful of perfect poems ("Aftermath", "Mushrooms", and "Spinster", among others) and developed a voice all her own' (p. 209).

In a longer review, A. E. Dyson (1961, p. 182) focuses on the poem as *illustrative* of a particular quality in Plath's work:

> In *Mushrooms*, the quality of menace is even more chillingly
> detected in the sinister, almost cancerous proliferation of
> fungus. This macabrely ironic vision of a form of life infinitely
> lower than man simply waiting in endless patience to 'Inherit
> the earth' has the vividness of science fiction at its best,
> without being in the least sensational. (The associations which
> the word 'mushroom' have for us since Hiroshima may
> enhance the effectiveness, which is not, however, dependent
> upon them.)

For later critical references the poem becomes a reflection of Plath's
*psychological state* and is evaluated in relation to the rest of her work,
as well as the work of other poets. For example, Edward Butscher
(1976, pp. 244–5) explains:

> Only in 'Mushrooms', an odd and attractive little poem written
> later at Yaddo, would she reduce the extraneous matters to a
> core truth, shove her consciousness directly into the eye of
> nature itself. Though strongly influenced by Emily Dickinson,
> 'Mushrooms' is closest in spirit to Theodore Roethke in that it
> assumes a vegetable identity in the murky realm of
> preconscious infancy. In form, a lean and whimsical form Emily
> would have appreciated, the poem never misses a beat, sounds
> simulating sense in a felicitous merger of eye and ear: 'Our
> toes, our noses/Take hold on the loam,/Acquire the air'.
> Anthropomorphic mushrooms have freed Sylvia's lines of
> clutter, suggesting the success of 'resolve', perhaps because the
> concept had a simplicity of design that required no convoluted
> parentheses of layered reflections and cross references ... The
> play upon the prediction of Jesus that the meek would inherit
> the earth is ironic without being brilliantly so, yoking Sylvia's
> real distance from the rest of ordinary humanity with her
> prevalent consciousness of a threatening nature and man.

More recently, Jon Rosenblatt (1979) takes up the poem in a
chapter about Plath's *Beginnings*. He introduces it as 'a fine example
of Plath's treatment of the theme of death in *The Colossus*' (p. 57),
and as 'representative of the poems that deal with animals and
nature' (p. 58). Before moving to a critical evaluation of the poem as
too limited – because 'Plath caricatures human reality by projecting
only aggressiveness onto the natural object' (p. 60) – Rosenblatt
provides two pages of analysis with considerable attention to sound

and diction. One paragraph, in particular, deals with language in the poem:

> The difference between 'Mushrooms' and the earlier apprentice work lies in the specific attention Plath has paid, first, to the visual details of the fantasized animallike mushrooms and, second, to the aural qualities of her language. Visually, the poem gives us a race of mobile mushrooms: animal or human forms are projected onto these small natural shapes. The mushroom's roots become toes; their stems, noses; their caps, fists. These creatures quietly and 'whitely' push through the forest floor like an army of soldiers. Here Plath's visual imagination anticipates the later brilliant images of *Ariel*: 'bedding' and 'paving' are 'heaved' up; the 'shelves' and 'tables' of the caps cover the once-pastoral forest area. With an ironic nod to Tennyson's 'flower in the crannied wall'. Plath finds sinister 'crannies' through which the mushrooms 'shoulder' their way into the light. As in the later poem 'Elm', Plath makes nature speak in its own voice out of a consciousness that is animate through and through. (p. 59)

While these critical treatments of the poem, especially the last, may enhance our understanding of 'Mushrooms' and help us to see it in relation to the larger body of Plath's work, they could hardly suffice as texts from which to learn strategies for literary interpretation. Indeed, they are not *intended* as such. Essays focused on critical commentary are directed to experienced readers who are familiar with the styles and goals of critical discourse. However, public interpretations may serve to provide textual models from which a semiotics of reading can be derived.

## 13.5 Future directions

Traditionally, instruction has focused on historical, biographical, or new-critical approaches, for example, and interpretations of texts have been handed down. But not all readers can successfully intuit from demonstrations the principles they need to become better readers. While inexperienced readers have much to gain from studying individual literary works, they also need to be taught more directly the presuppositions of interpretation. Literary education assumes that student readers can improve; as researchers we need to determine more precisely the nature of the skills we wish to promote. If we can make more explicit the principles involved in interpretation – and more precise the description of reading strategies – then we might improve our methods of teaching. The new reader-centred classroom approach that is developing is certainly a move in the right direction. I do not believe it is sufficient unless accompanied by presentation and discussion of goals, principles and strategies.

*Principles* need to be set forth, such as: look for human significance; expect parts of a text to be cohesive according to some overall composite plan; expect to arrive at a meaning that is more than simply the literal meaning of each textual part; and expect the final section to provide an appropriate conclusion. (These principles are, of course, culturally determined and subject to change. For instance, deconstructionists would make different assumptions.) So, too, can we set up other, genre-specific strategies which account for different ways to read poems, stories, plays, comedy, tragedy, romance, science fiction and so forth. Finally, it is not enough to tell students to read for human significance, or to read for unity, or to organize the narrative into mysteries and solutions.[7] Students need, as well, to learn the appropriate *strategies* that will enable them to recognize cues that point to possible human significance, models that will help them to organize specific details under a generalization, or the specific questions and answers they are likely to need for various genres. Such formulations must be explicitly set forth. Indeed, they would make worthy projects for researchers in stylistics and semiotics.

# NOTES

1   This article appeared in *Style*, vol. 20, no. 1, Spring, 1986, pp. 1–18. Earlier versions of this work were presented at the Annual Meeting of the Modern Language Association, December 1983, and at the Rhode Island College English Colloquium Series, October 1984.
2   For a review of theoretical approaches to reader-response criticism see Suleiman and Crosman (1980). Cooper (1985) presents more empirical and pedagogical approaches.
3   Support for this study, conducted in the spring of 1980, by a grant from Northeastern University's Research and Scholarship Development Fund is gratefully acknowledged. I want to thank teaching assistants in the Department of English for their cooperation and the undergraduates who provided responses. The students, from five sections of Freshman English II, represent diverse major fields. Their unedited responses are identified by number when quoted.

4 'Mushrooms', by Sylvia Plath, was first published in *Harper's* (July 1960, p. 25), and later included in *The Colossus* (1962, pp. 37–8). According to Ted Hughes (1971, p. 191), Plath composed the poem in the autumn of 1959 during a stay at Yaddo where they took long walks and 'devised exercises of meditation and invocation'.

5 It seems generally to be the case that in underlining, readers avoid words and stanzas that they have independently selected as difficult. The pattern is also observed in an earlier study (Fairley, 1979) where a similar questionnaire was used with students responding to a poem by E. E. Cummings. In the present study, as well as in two earlier response studies, readers show a purposeful selection in underlining. Although the number of words selected varies in each of the poems read, the number of words underlined per person does not increase in proportion to the length of the text. Readers in two groups responded to the Cummings poem of sixty-two words with mean underlinings of 18.3 and 16.3 (Fairley (1979), p. 339). For a poem by William Carlos Williams having fifty-six words, readers had a mean of 19.5 underlinings (Fairley (1982), p. 89). In this study the Plath poem has 113 words, twice the number of the previous poems, yet the underlining mean score is 24.5. Perhaps this pattern reflects a general reading strategy, an expectation of finding a limited core of salient words.

6 Petrosky (1985, pp. 75–6) presents a more grim picture. He cites conclusions of the 1981 third National Assessment of Educational Progress for reading and literature that, 'American schools have been reasonably successful in teaching students to recall textual information and make inferences in the multiple choice format, but have failed to teach more than 5 per cent or 10 per cent of all students to move beyond initial readings of texts'. Petrosky is concerned that 'students have not learned the response skills that would allow them to make written interpretations and look for evidence to support their interpretations by referring to the reading selections of their own ideas and values'.

7 Kintgen (1983) takes the position that 'In their present form Culler's (1981) conventions are not much help to somebody who does not already know how to use them: they lack the explicitness that is a prime requisite of linguistic theories' (p. 179). He argues that the various conventions Culler presents are, rather, 'constituents of successful interpretations, of the answer the reader seeks' (p. 181).

# BIBLIOGRAPHY

Armstrong, P. B. (1983), 'The conflict of interpretations and the limits of pluralism', *PMLA*, vol. 98, pp. 341–52.

Butscher, E. (1976), *Sylvia Plath: Method and Madness*, New York, Seabury.

Cooper, C. R. (ed.) (1985), *Researching Response to Literature and the Teaching of Literature: Points of Departure*, Norwood, Ablex.

Culler, J. (1981), *The Pursuit of Signs*, Ithaca, Cornell University Press.

Dickey, W. (1962), 'Responsibilities', *Kenyon Review*, vol. 24, pp. 756–64.

Dyson, A. E. (1961), 'Review of Sylvia Plath: *The Colossus and Other Poems*', *Critical Quarterly*, vol. 3, pp. 181–5.

Fairley, I. R. (1979), 'Experimental approaches to language in literature: reader responses to poems', *Style*, vol. 13, pp. 335–64.

Fairley, I. R. (1982), 'On reading poems: visual and verbal icons in Williams Carlos Williams' "Landscape with the fall of Icarus"', *Studies in Twentieth Century Literature*, vol. 6, no. 2, pp. 67–97.

Hughes, T. (1971), 'The chronological order of Sylvia Plath's poems', in C. Newman (ed.), *The Art of Sylvia Plath: A Symposium*, Bloomington, Indiana University Press.

Kintgen, E. (1983), *The Perception of Poetry*, Bloomington, Indiana University Press.

Owen, G. (1963), 'Review of Sylvia Plath: *The Colossus and Other Poems*', *Books Abroad*, vol. 37, p. 209.

Petrosky, A. R. (1985), 'Response: a way of knowing', in Cooper (1985), pp. 70–83.

Plath, S. (1962), *The Colossus and Other Poems*, New York, Knopf.

Riffaterre, M. (1978), *Semiotics of Poetry*, Bloomington, Indiana University Press.

Rosenblatt, J. (1979), *Sylvia Plath: The Poetry of Initiation*, Chapel Hill, North Carolina University Press.

Silkey, S. and Purves, A. (1973), 'What happens when we read a poem', *Journal of Aesthetic Education*, vol. 7, no. 3, pp. 63–72.

Suleiman, S. R. and Crosman, I. (eds) (1980), *The Reader in the Text: Essays on Audience and Interpretation*, Princeton, Princeton University Press.

# 14

# What happens
# in 'Whatever happened?'?

*Graham Trengove*

*The principles and strategies pointed to in Irene Fairley's essay in the previous chapter are discussed in more detail in this chapter by Graham Trengove. In view of the importance of establishing links between a text's formal structure and its interpretation, the question arises as to whether or not this should be taught formally. In other words: How do you teach the relationship between form and interpretation? The position taken by Graham Trengove is that the technicalities of formal structure required for this purpose should be kept to a minimum. Informal terminology, grammatical concepts and the integration of everyday knowledge of the world may go a long way in classroom instruction.*

*Instead of proposing this* in abstracto, *a poem by Philip Larkin is discussed as an illustration of this position. Even the text's more complicated semantic aspects can be made clear, so Trengove demonstrates, without the help of much specialized language or of other technicalities; an appeal to linguistic and literary intuitions will do. What is needed, though, is some sense of the overall relation of form and function of the text. In particular the oscillation between particularity and generality of meaning is taken to be a central issue in this respect.*

Perhaps most of those who read this book will have a foot in three camps, or, if that is too Mandevillean an image, will share an allegiance to the study of language, to the study of literature, and to demonstrating to students the worth of conducting the two in tandem.

However, whatever might be the climate of opinion elsewhere, in Britain undergraduates are not usually enthusiastic about the idea of marrying the two. They have for the most part been left by their secondary education with less knowledge of the formal description and analysis of language than were earlier generations, or than are many of their overseas contemporaries. Nevertheless, at least in their own view, they have got on pretty well in their reading of novels, plays and, with less certainty, poetry. Bringing them to see the advantages of paying systematic attention to the language of literature, to see that their understanding and even enjoyment of what they read can be enhanced by our approach, requires care. They can easily be overwhelmed by a descriptive and analytical apparatus for which the payoff is too long coming.

This danger is largely avoided in the introductory collection *Language and Literature* (Carter, 1982), in which A. Rodger (1982), writing on Auden's poem 'O where are you going?', charts an interesting pedagogic path past it. Intended as an exhaustive accounting for the literary effect of every last word, it is by far the longest chapter. It takes time to read, and his editor was right not to send him in to open the batting. But, in addition to offering many acute insights, it has the great attraction of showing how much can be done with the minimum of linguistic apparatus presented in advance. As he says,

> there is very little in this interpretation of Auden's poem which cannot be acquired through familiarity with a good modern grammar of English which links form to meaning, a good citation dictionary of contemporary English, and a little disciplined thinking about how people really do talk to each other and what they are trying to do by means of the things they say and the way in which they say them. (p. 160)

The 'good modern grammar' which he draws on is Quirk and Greenbaum's *A University Grammar of English*. It has to be acknowledged that no-one is going to acquire familiarity with that overnight, but it is accessible to reference and to use it profitably for our purposes does not need prolonged exposure to linguistic theory. Possibly more useful in this context is its fellow derivative from *A Grammar of Contemporary English* (Quirk *et al.*, 1972), that is,

Leech and Svartvik's (1975) *Communicative Grammar of English*, which is arranged according to function rather than structure. That this grammar was conceived with the interests of non-native learners in mind in no way disqualifies it for first-language users – rather the reverse. But whichever grammar is employed, few students whose interests are primarily literary will regard it as bedside reading, or settle down to systematic study of it at any other moment. However, they can be encouraged to develop a useful familiarity with it over time if we show them that it is possible to draw on it selectively as part of a Spitzerian circle.

I intend now to attempt a demonstration that a little linguistics can go a long way in the illumination of a literary text. I hope it will be accepted that the aspects of grammar I touch on are not too abstruse or too difficult for the neophyte. Though some terms are perhaps unfamiliar to the beginner, I shall not stray far from the surface structure of language. The text which gives occasion for their use is a poem by Philip Larkin.[1]

> **Whatever happened?**
>
> **At once whatever happened starts receding.**
> **Panting, and back on board, we line the rail**
> **With trousers ripped, light wallets, and lips bleeding.**
>
> **Yes, gone, thank God! Remembering each detail**
> **We toss for half the night, but find next day**
> **All's Kodak-distant. Easily, then (though pale),**
>
> **'Perspective brings significance,' we say,**
> **Unhooding our photometers, and, snap!**
> **What can't be printed can be thrown away.**
>
> **Later, it's just a latitude: the map**
> **Points out how unavoidable it was:**
> **'Such coastal bedding always means mishap.'**
>
> **Curses? The dark? Struggling? Where's the source**
> **Of these yarns now (except in nightmares, of course)?**

I choose to discuss this poem with students firstly because it continues to give me pleasure (possibly a naive reason from the point of view of some stylisticians, but one for which I do not apologize), and secondly because I believe that the reason it does this has to do with Winifred Nowottny's (1962, p. 9) observation that 'syntax is important to poet and to critic alike because it produces strong effects by stealth'.

I want to reveal the sources of my pleasure to those whom I am teaching, and thereby develop their ability to respond independently to similar stimuli encountered elsewhere. In the terms that Jonathan Culler (1975) has given currency to, I hope thereby to refine their 'literary competence'. It is not difficult to argue that this requires a carefully constructed scheme of teaching extending over several years. Such programmes do exist in some institutions. However, where they do not, it is not necessary to wait until they are established before beginning. Insight and appreciation can be developed by appealing to very limited, selected linguistic terminology.

The satisfactions that the poem offers are many. Not least of these is the opportunity to see Larkin working within the constraints of a rather uncommon form, that of the *terza rima* sonnet. But what specially pleases and interests me is the delicate shifting or shading between particularity and generality in the reference of the poem. I like its combination of elliptical dramatic narrative and universal statement, and I like the uncertainty experienced, as the poem is being read, about which mode is dominant at any point. This is the perception I seek to transmit, not in order to impose a unique reading, but as a rationale for the exploration of the linguistic features which trigger it, at least for me.

My starting point with students is to ask whether they think that the poem is concerned with a single event or with some general aspect of human experience. Most incline to the latter view. I then ask whether this arises from the conditioned expectations of poetry as an institution which should make statements or observations of general applicability, or from the presence in the poem of linguistic markers of the generic, or from both. Consideration of these questions requires examination of the language.

In the absence of other suggestions from students, I propose areas for investigation, and suggest that they might look first at verb forms, and especially tense markings. While their terminology may not be that of modern grammarians, there are few who have no labels for these features. They are thus in a position to recognize quickly that most verb forms marked for tense are simple present; the three exceptions occur either in the title, 'happened', or in subordinate clauses, 'happened' (line 1) and 'was' (line 11). This suggests a first, tentative location of the poem in present time. Support for such a reading is found in the second tercet. 'Yes, gone, thank God!' presupposes a question which is not included in the poem, and its elliptical dependence on this is consonant with direct speech, and thus with a dramatic representation of events underway. On the other hand, the set of time adverbials used is associated with the narrative of past events; 'at once', 'then', 'next day' and 'later'. This prompts a different view of the function of the present tense forms; it may be more helpful to recognize them as a feature appropriate to popular colloquial narrative, as for example in the telling of jokes.

At this point I find it useful to question the traditional label 'present tense' and tell them of other terms proposed, that is, 'past and non-past'. Asking why these should be on offer, I remind them of sentences such as 'Gentlemen prefer blondes' and 'Omo washes whiter', and elicit without difficulty the observation that these sentences enunciate what are, or are held to be, constant truths. Set to find a parallel sentence in the poem they point readily enough to 'Perspective brings significance'. Once having thus been brought to recognize that present tense verbs may have a generic function, they can be directed to consider the fact that 'perspective' has no accompanying article. This means that it refers not to a particular view, perhaps of the topography within which the events occurred, but rather to an abstraction, the ability to see one set of events against the background of wider experience. This generic reading based on syntax is given support by the foregrounding of the nouns, which are polysyllabic and Latinate in their morphology, and which students are likely to see as belonging to educated, abstract discourse. Here we may also note a lexical instance of the central procedure of the poem; in that the co-text calls up the notion of photography ('Kodak-distant', 'photometers', 'snap!', and 'printed'), we probably first interpret 'perspective' as referring to our visual apprehension of the specific physical setting. The collocation with 'significance' then encourages us to shift to a more abstract reading in which 'perspective' is more nearly synonymous with 'detachment', a generalization about our processing of experience.

At this point, it is profitable to direct attention to personal pronouns. In our experience of the poem so far we are unlikely to understand the first person pronouns as including us, the addressees of the poem. The 'we's of the first two tercets are taken to be exclusive rather than inclusive, referring only to the persona and his companions. However, given that the quoted clause in line 7 is best read as a generalization, it is a natural step to read the quoting clause, the super-ordinate 'we say', as also a generalization. 'We' is then inclusive, of all addressees, and thus generic. 'Say', in turn, is then perceived as a simple present expressing a general truth.

This exposure of different possible interpretations of words commonly disregarded in so-called 'close readings', words which might elsewhere be called polyvalent grammatical items, is crucial to the emergence of the reading of the whole poem which I favour. I take it that Larkin is exploring the temporal and psychological relationship between specific events and human memory of them. Early in the poem he gives us, in tantalizingly oblique and incomplete detail, information about a particular and local incident. Thereafter he represents our human propensity to edit our experience, to remember of our past only what we choose, and to erect baffles and filters against total recall, in the form of generalizations and truisms, which can be bypassed only in dreams, or rather nightmares.

There are other linguistic reflections of this governing theme to be discussed, but before continuing in that direction, I acknowledge that this formalist approach does not provide a framework for everything that one would hope to hear in the course of a discussion of the poem. Stylistics must have pragmatics as a component. It is the reading skill corresponding to this that is called into play when we move from 'the tantalizingly oblique and incomplete detail' of the text to a more satisfyingly complete understanding of the fictional situation it relates to. The latter we might verbalize thus. A group of unidentified people return to their ship from an excursion ashore where they met with physical violence and spent or lost their money. At first disturbed by vivid recollections of these events, they find that, with the passage of time, these immediate impressions are replaced by partial, perhaps edited, memories which are reconstructed in conformity with received wisdom about the world. It is only when they are ruled by their unconscious that they ever genuinely recover the original experience. In all this they are representative of humanity at large.

Larkin himself held that 'poets write for people with the same background and experience as themselves'.[2] He would have agreed that a successful encounter with his work depends not at all on access to a 'myth-kitty' but very much on everyday knowledge; for example, that ships but not aeroplanes have rails. It is by having this knowledge that we can construct the appropriate implicature from the phrase 'back on board' (line 2); that is, that the participants are re-boarding a ship rather than an aeroplane. Knowledge of the world and aspects of discourse such as implicature are inescapably called into play here and elsewhere in the poem. Let us consider the phrase 'coastal bedding'. This is a label for a geological phenomenon often causally associated with shipwreck, and this students need to be told if they do not already know it. Secondly, they need to recognize that it is a term more appropriate to technical writing than to casual conversation. Thirdly, they need to be able to see that the generalization 'Such coastal bedding always means mishap' (that is, shipwreck) does not sit quite squarely with the situation alluded to in line 3. 'Torn trousers' and so on are not perhaps the most probable and salient consequences of shipwreck, and anyway the notion of shipwreck is itself apparently cancelled by their safe return on board. There is then a gap between the event and its later description such that the reference to coastal bedding might be seen as an instance of the editing process under discussion. Why should Larkin choose this technical phrase in particular? I cannot believe that he was unaware that 'bedding' is a familiar colloquialism for sexual intercourse. If this sense is admitted to our reading, it will allow us to reconstruct more convincingly a scene of shore-leave, loose women and brawling, one which its participants might well wish to remember only selectively. In all these ways and others, a pragmatic approach is clearly helpful. However, I return to noting the linguistic markers of generalization in this sentence – the present tense form 'means', the use of 'such', and of the adverb 'always' – and to underlining what I find to be the operational convenience of this focus, limited and partial as it may be.

I now resume my former line of argument, in the belief that engagement with the text on this level is as much a social act as calling on pragmatic skills. Although it may not be immediately recognized as such, the relationship between the title and the first line is an adumbration of Larkin's message. As so often in his work, the title is an integral part of the whole, not a convenience for compilers of contents pages, or merely an afterthought. Exposing this requires first that students be invited to consider what paraphrases they might offer for the question which forms the title. This need not offend those who object to resorting to paraphrase as a general critical procedure.[3] What is asked for is a set of utterances which might replace this one in non-literary discourse. This does not call on literary judgment, but rather on knowledge of the language at large. The response is likely to include alternatives such as 'What in heaven's name happened?',

'What on earth happened?', 'What the hell happened?', and others less socially acceptable.

The next stage is to draw attention to the repetition of the clause in the first line of the poem. The close succession of the two at first suggests an identity of meaning, but it does not take long before someone points out that the second instance can hardly be read as a question, and that the same paradigm of paraphrases cannot be called on here. Invited now to find others which will fit, they will offer without much hesitation both 'everything which happened' and 'anything which happened'; that is to say, though they will not perhaps say it, the original clause can be paraphrased by a noun phrase which includes a qualifying (otherwise, a post-modifying) relative clause. They have now applied the criterion which allows Quirk et al. (1972, p. 737) to identify 'whatever happened' as a 'nominal relative clause'. It may be useful at this stage to refer students to the appropriate section of the grammar. More to the point is that, by this means or another, they should be brought to raise from their unconscious into their formal knowledge of English the recurrent use of the compound pronouns 'whoever' and 'whatever' to express universal meaning.

They are now in a position to recognize that our entry point to the poem, its title, is one where a question is posed in such a way as to suggest surprising, interesting and particular events, which we are thus encouraged to expect more information about. In the first line, however, we are redirected to a generalization about how those events, and others in our own experience, are psychologically processed by those who undergo them.

The question which the title suggests is to be the focus of the poem is thereafter answered only in the most elliptical and allusive fashion. 'Curses? The dark? Struggling?'; the fragmentary noun phrases, marked graphically to be read with a question intonation, indicate the persona recalling features of the particular incident. But his final question refers to 'these yarns'. A first reading of the demonstrative might assign it an anaphoric, cohesive function; see it as referring to the specific narrative which we infer from the evidence of these fragments. But they would seem to belong to one narrative, one yarn, whereas we confront a plural noun phrase. On reflection, recalling from our experience of language at large that 'these' may be the equivalent of 'such' or the post-posed phrase 'of this type', we may prefer to recognize here another realization of the universalizing process detected elsewhere (Quirk et al. (1972), p. 703). The persona, and ultimately Larkin, is querying the source of all yarns of this kind.

In another contribution to *Language and Literature* John Sinclair (1982, p. 163) declares that as a stylistician he is sensitive to avoid the charge of 'ad-hocery'. He seeks to evade it by identifying what he calls 'focats', focusing categories which relate 'latent linguistic patterning to meaning' (1982, p. 174). Having investigated examples of these, which he calls 'arrest' and 'extension', he concludes: 'If further work suggests, and it does, that a great proportion of stylistic analysis can be effected through a small and finite set of focats, then the groundwork of a theory of literary communication emerges' (1982, p. 175). I suggest that it makes sense to include in that 'small and finite set' the constellation of linguistic features which allows the slipping between the universal and the particular in the Larkin poem just discussed. Such a procedure is by no means peculiar to it; the manipulation of generic markers is rather a widespread poetic practice. It is one more focusing category to which students' attention can usefully be drawn when they are considering a particular piece of writing. By such means they can be led to the progressive accumulation of what has variously been called 'a theory of literature' and 'literary competence', and to a more complete and effective engagement in the social practice of interpretive reading.

# NOTES

1  Philip Larkin (1955), *The Less Deceived*, London, Marvell Press.
2  Philip Larkin (1983), *Required Writing*, London, Faber & Faber, p. 69.
3  Those with inhibitions about applying paraphrase to the elucidation of poetry should see Walter Nash, 'The possibilities of paraphrase', in Brumfit and Carter (1986), pp. 70–88.

# BIBLIOGRAPHY

Brumfit, C. J. and Carter, R. A. (eds) (1986), *Literature and Language Teaching*, Oxford, Oxford University Press.

Carter, R. (ed.) (1982), *Language and Literature*, London, Allen & Unwin.

Culler, J. (1975), *Structuralist Poetics*, London, Routledge & Kegan Paul.

Leech, G. N. and Svartvik, J. (1975), *A Communicative Grammar of English*, London, Longman.

Nowottny, W. (1962), *The Language Poets Use*, London, Athlone Press.

Quirk, R., Greenbaum, S., Leech, G. and Svartvik, J. (1972), *A Grammar of Contemporary English*, London, Longman.

Quirk, R. and Greenbaum, S. (1973), *A University Grammar of English*, London, Longman.

Rodger, A. (1982), '"O where are you going?"; a suggested experiment in classroom stylistics', in Carter (1982), pp. 123–61.

Sinclair, J. (1982), 'Lines about "Lines"', in Carter (1982), pp. 163–76.

'One only knows the things one tames,' said the fox. 'People have no more time to know anything. They buy things already made from the shopkeepers. But, as there are no shops where one can buy friends, people have no more friends. If you want a friend, tame me!'

'What must one do?' said the little prince.

'One must be very patient,' the fox replied. 'First, you will sit down here, a little distance away from me, like that, in the grass. I will look at you from the corner of my eye and you will say nothing. Language is the source of misunderstanding. But every day, you can sit a little closer to me ...'

A. de Saint-Exupéry,
*Le Petit Prince*

# Name Index

# Subject Index